STUDIES IN INTERNATIONAL TRADE POLICY

Studies in International Trade Policy includes works dealing with the theory, empirical analysis, political, economic, legal relations, and evaluations of international trade policies and institutions.

General Editor: Robert M. Stern

John H. Jackson and Edwin Vermulst, Editors. *Antidumping Law and Practice: A Comparative Study*

John Whalley, Editor. *Developing Countries and the Global Trading System.* Volumes 1 and 2

John Whalley, Coordinator. *The Uruguay Round and Beyond: The Final Report from the Ford Foundation Project on Developing Countries and the Global Trading System.*

John S. Odell and Thomas D. Willett, Editors. *International Trade Policies: Gains from Exchange between Economics and Political Science*

Alan V. Deardorff and Robert M. Stern. *Computational Analysis of Global Trading Arrangements*

Jagdish Bhagwati and Hugh T. Patrick, Editors. *Aggressive Unilateralism: America's 301 Trade Policy and the World Trading System*

Ulrich Kohli. *Technology, Duality, and Foreign Trade: The GNP Function Approach to Modeling Imports and Exports*

Robert M. Stern, Editor. *The Multilateral Trading System: Analysis and Options for Change*

J. Michael Finger, Editor. *Antidumping: How It Works and Who Gets Hurt*

Stephen V. Marks and Keith E. Maskus, Editors. *The Economics and Politics of World Sugar Prices*

Horst Herberg and Ngo Van Long, Editors. *Trade, Welfare, and Economic Policies: Essays in Honor of Murray C. Kemp*

David Schwartzman. *The Japanese Television Cartel: A Study Based on* Matsushita v. Zenith

Barry Eichengreen. *Reconstructing Europe's Trade and Payments: The European Payments Union*

Alan V. Deardorff and Robert M. Stern, Editors. *Analytical and Negotiating Issues in the Global Trading System*

Edwin Vermulst, Paul Waer, and Jacques Bourgeois, Editors. *Rules of Origin in International Trade: A Comparative Study*

Alan V. Deardorff and Robert M. Stern, Editors. *The Stolper-Samuelson Theorem: A Golden Jubilee*

The Stolper-Samuelson Theorem

The Stolper-Samuelson Theorem: A Golden Jubilee

Edited by
Alan V. Deardorff and Robert M. Stern

with the assistance of
Sundari R. Baru

Ann Arbor

THE UNIVERSITY OF MICHIGAN PRESS

Copyright © by the University of Michigan 1994
All rights reserved
Published in the United States of America by
The University of Michigan Press
Manufactured in the United States of America
⊗ Printed on acid-free paper

1997   1996   1995   1994   4   3   2   1

A CIP catalogue record for this book is available from the British Library.

Library of Congress Cataloging-in-Publication Data

The Stolper-Samuelson theorum : a golden jubilee / edited by Alan
    V. Deardorff and Robert M. Stern, with the assistance of Sundari R.
    Baru.
        p.   cm. — (Studies in international trade policy)
    Includes bibliographical references and index.
    ISBN 0-472-10533-7 (acid-free paper)
    1. International trade. 2. Protectionism. 3. Free trade.
4. Production (Economic theory) I. Deardorff, Alan V.   II. Stern,
Robert Mitchell, 1927–   .   III. Baru, Sundari R.   IV. Series.
HF1379.S76   1994   94-31944
382—dc20   CIP

Contents

Chapter

Part I. Introduction and Overview

Part II. The Original Statement

III. Refinements, Extensions, and Verification

THE REVIEW OF ECONOMIC STUDIES.

LL COMMUNICATIONS TO:
THE SECRETARY,
REVIEW OF ECONOMIC STUDIES.
HOUGHTON STREET, W.C.2.

Fairfield,
Prestbury, _____ 193
Cheshire.
18th Oct. 1941

Dear Mr. Stolper,

We are putting the article which you
and Mr Samuelson have written on Protection and Real Wages into the forthcoming
number of the Review. Under the new arran
gement it is due to come out next month,
so I should be very glad if I might have
notice of any correction or ammendments.
by return of Clipper. I am having the
diagrams traced from the pencil drawings
Paul Sweezy sent with the article. I
don't think any question will arise about
them, as they seem perfectly clear.

When you write would you let me know if
you want more than the customary 25 free
offprints. Additional copies 6d.

I do congratulate you on having found a
new point in the theery of international
trade.

Yours sincerely,

Ursula K. Hicks

EDITORS:
H. S. ELLIS
H. M. GROVES
E. A. KINCAID
B. W. LEWIS
FRITZ MACHLUP
R. E. MONTGOMERY

P. T. HOMAN, MANAGING EDITOR

American Economic Review

(Published by the American Economic Association)

104 McGraw Hall, Cornell University, Ithaca, New York

May 2, 1941

Rec'd

Professor Paul A. Samuelson
Department of Economics
Massachusetts Institute of Technology
Cambridge, Massachusetts

Dear Professor Samuelson:

Professor Ellis and I have both read with care
the article submitted by you and Mr. Stolper. It
raises a problem of editorial judgment which I very
much dislike to face. We both agree that the article
is a brilliant theoretical performance, and since we
wish to have from time to time good and substantial
theoretical articles in the Review, we very much
dislike to reject it. On the other hand, we agree
that it is a very narrow study in formal theory, which
adds practically nothing to the literature of the
subject with which it is nominally concerned. Indeed,
by your own admission in the last pages, it is practically
a complete "sell-out". It does not, in other words,
have anything to say about any of the real situations
with which the theory of international trade has to
concern itself.

Because it is so good of its sort, I am very much
torn in my mind. My final decision, however, is to
return it to you. I should, however, like to add this
suggestion, that starting from the first paragraph on
page 2, referring to Ohlin, you attempt to write something
relevant that really will have some bearing upon the
practical problem that you introduce at the beginning and
end of the article. Certainly there must be some things
to be said on this subject, even though they cannot be
reduced to the neat theoretical treatment used in your
present article.

Sincerely yours,

Paul T. Homan

PTH:B
Ms. enc.

Part I

Introduction and Overview

CHAPTER 1

INTRODUCTION

Alan V. Deardorff and Robert M. Stern

The year 1991 was very special in the intellectual history of international trade theory for it marked the golden jubilee of the publication of Wolfgang Stolper and Paul Samuelson's pathbreaking article, "Protection and Real Wages," in the *Review of Economic Studies*.[1] Prior to the publication of the Stolper-Samuelson article, the effect of trade or protection on real wages had not been clearly established, since the conditions governing the associated changes in prices and wages had not been rigorously worked out. The reason that the Stolper-Samuelson article was pathbreaking was that they showed for the first time, using general equilibrium analysis, how and why the wage of workers--if labor were the relatively scarce factor--could rise by more than the price of the imported good when a tariff was imposed. This relation between trade/protection and real wages later became known as the Stolper-Samuelson theorem, and it has served as one of the central results of the Heckscher-Ohlin model of trade and returns to factors that has been at the core of trade theory for the past half century.

It is interesting, looking back, that the significance of the Stolper-Samuelson paper was not fully appreciated at the time. Indeed, the paper was rejected by the *American Economic Review*, although with some apologies by the Managing Editor, Paul T. Homan, as expressed in his letter of May 2, 1941 that is reproduced below. We also have reproduced the October 14, 1941 letter of acceptance from the *Review of Economic Studies* in which Ursula K. Hicks congratulates Stolper and

---

[1] The initial idea for celebrating the Stolper-Samuelson golden jubilee grew out of a conversation with Ronald W. Jones in connection with his paper, "Reflections on the Stolper-Samuelson Theorem," which was prepared for a festschrift honoring Murray C. Kemp.

Samuelson somewhat reservedly for "having found a new point in the theory of international trade."

Evidently it was not foreseen fully at the time what was so remarkable about the original Stolper-Samuelson theorem and how great an inspiration it would provide for subsequent theoretical and empirical research in international trade. In retrospect, it seemed fitting therefore to celebrate the golden jubilee of the publication of the Stolper-Samuelson article as an important event in its own right. It also seemed fitting to honor its originators, one of whom, Wolfgang Stolper, has been our colleague and friend at the University of Michigan for many years, and the other of whom, Paul Samuelson, has had a long and distinguished career at MIT.

Accordingly, we set aside the afternoon and evening of November 15, 1991, to celebrate the occasion.[2] Over the years, a number of distinguished economists and political scientists had contributed importantly to the theoretical refinement and extension of the theorem, as well as to its empirical application. We invited ten of these contributors to come to Ann Arbor to participate in an afternoon symposium, in particular to reflect upon their own work and the work of others pertaining to the theorem. Those invited included: Jagdish Bhagwati; Ronald W. Jones; Wilfred J. Ethier; John S. Chipman; Paul R. Krugman; Edward E. Leamer; Robert E. Baldwin; Stephen Magee; Ulrich Kohli; and Ronald Rogowski. Wolfgang Stolper and Paul Samuelson were also present at the symposium, and it was attended by

---

[2] We wish to acknowledge the financial assistance for the symposium that was made available by the Office of the Provost, University Council of International Academic Affairs, and Rackham Graduate School of the University of Michigan.

a large number of Michigan faculty and graduate students and other invited guests. Following a dinner in the evening, Stolper and Samuelson used the occasion to provide further reflections on their collaboration and the significance of their work.

We also wanted to provide a permanent record of this golden jubilee celebration, which is what occasions this book.[3] We thought that it would be useful in particular to reprint the original Stolper-Samuelson article as well as a number of the most influential articles that were published subsequently as extensions and refinements of the Stolper-Samuelson theorem.[4] The original Stolper-Samuelson article thus appears as Chapter 3 below, and it is followed in Chapters 4-13 by the later seminal contributions to the Stolper-Samuelson literature of: Lloyd Metzler (1949); Jagdish Bhagwati (1959); Ronald W. Jones (1965,1985); John S. Chipman (1969); Murray Kemp and Leon Wegge (1969); Wilfred J. Ethier (1974,1982); Ronald W. Jones and Jose A. Scheinkman (1977); and Stephen P. Magee (1980). The symposium contributions by the invited participants appear as Chapters 14-23.[5] It will be noted in this connection that all of these symposium contributions, including the longer chapters by John S. Chipman and by Edward E. Leamer, are papers written especially for the symposium and published here for the first time. The further reflections by Stolper and Samuelson on their collaborative effort appear as Chapters 24-25.

To help readers find their way through the book, Chapter 2 immediately following provides an overview of the Stolper-Samuelson

---

[3] We wish especially to thank Tonia Short and Judith Jackson of the Institute of Public Policy Studies of the University of Michigan for their assistance in the typing and editing of the manuscript materials and Lorrie Lejeune of the University of Michigan Press for helping to design and complete the camera-ready copy for publication.

[4] We are grateful to Ronald W. Jones for helping us to choose the articles to be reprinted.

[5] Jagdish Bhagwati was unable to attend the symposium, but he prepared some comments that appear in Chapter 14.

theorem written by Alan Deardorff. Then, at the end of the book in Chapter 26, an annotated bibliography and a subject index of the Stolper-Samuelson theorem are presented. This annotated bibliography was compiled and edited with the assistance of Sundari R. Baru.

The preparation of this book has been a great pleasure for us, both intellectually and personally. We offer it as a fitting tribute to the truly remarkable contribution that Wolfgang Stolper and Paul Samuelson have made to the theory of international trade.

CHAPTER 2

OVERVIEW OF THE STOLPER-SAMUELSON THEOREM

Alan V. Deardorff

The Stolper-Samuelson Theorem is remarkable for a number of reasons, not least of which is that it states what might appear obvious to many outside of economics. In its simple form with two factors of production, two goods, and two countries, it says that protection helps the scarce factor or, equivalently, that free trade hurts the scarce factor. Viewed from the perspective of a labor-scarce country like the United States, where the scarcity of labor is evidenced by the height of the wage relative to less developed countries, this result seems self evident to many politicians and others in the public at large. They say that of course free trade lowers wages in the United States, since it makes American labor compete with foreign labor that may be paid only a fraction as much.

But economists knew, before Stolper and Samuelson, that it was not this simple. There were reasons to expect labor to gain from trade, along with the rest of the economy. And at worst, even if trade were to lower wages relative to the prices of some goods, it was expected to raise them relative to others. The effect on the real wage would then be an "index number problem" that could not be resolved unambiguously with theory alone. It was the contribution of Stolper and Samuelson to show that theory could resolve this ambiguity, and that the "obvious" result was after all true.

They showed this so compellingly that subsequent literature has been devoted to showing that it is either more true, or less true, than they thought. The contributions in this volume--starting from the Stolper-Samuelson article itself and then including many of the subsequent classic contributions to this literature as well as the remarks of the Symposium panelists--illustrate this same give and take between the truth and falsity of the basic proposition. On the one hand, many have tried with some success to extend the Theorem beyond the assumptions on which it was originally based. Others have stressed the limitations of the result. Together, all of these contributions have greatly expanded our understanding of the effects of tariffs on factor prices. But in doing this, these contributions have left us with perhaps more uncertainty about the true effect than ever. As will be discussed below, what we now know with some confidence is that protection, or indeed anything that raises the relative price of imports, will benefit *some* factor of production and harm some other, and that the intensities with which goods use factors do play a role in general in determining which factors gain and which lose. But outside the confines of the two-factor, two-good model in which Stolper and Samuelson worked, it appears to be impossible to say what will happen to any particular factor except in special cases.

I. Background of the Stolper-Samuelson Theorem

It is worth reviewing why a Theorem that stated "the obvious" was greeted with surprise, and then why the obvious turned out to be, after all, correct.

While the public might have felt it self evident that high-wage workers could only lose from competition with their low-wage counterparts abroad, one of the earliest messages of economics and especially of the theory of international trade had been that this fear was misplaced. In Ricardian trade theory, workers had high wages because they were more productive than workers abroad, and in that one-factor world the gains from trade were certain to translate into increased real wages for workers in both countries.

Even in a more general world where comparative advantage might be based on things other than technological differences, standard supply and demand analysis typically predicted that prices would respond only partially to shocks, and therefore that a wage change would be only a fraction of the size of a price change that caused it. If free trade lowered the price of some import goods, therefore, the wage might fall, but it would fall by less than import prices had fallen. It would therefore leave workers better off to the extent that they chose to consume the cheaper imports.

This is a typical result in partial equilibrium analysis, as well as in some general equilibrium models that most closely mimic partial equilibrium, such as the specific factors model. With a price or wage determined by conventionally shaped supply and demand curves, an upward shift of one of them, say, will lead to a rise in the equilibrium price or wage that is smaller than the initial upward shift of the curve. Thus if the demand for labor is determined by the prices of the goods that it helps to produce, and if the prices of these rise due to a tariff, then the demand curve for labor will shift up and raise the equilibrium wage. But one would expect that the upward shift would be no larger than the price change caused by the tariff. And if so, this conventional analysis will yield a wage increase that is even smaller.

This is correct if there is sufficient immobility of factors across industries to justify the use of partial equilibrium analysis or something similar.[1] But if all factors are mobile, then, as we learned from Stolper and Samuelson, partial equilibrium analysis is misleading. With mobility, wages are determined in a country-wide labor market and that market interacts with the markets for all goods and all other factors. It is incorrect to analyze the problem in terms of only one of them. If there are two or more factors, then at a minimum, since trade requires at least a second industry to produce goods in exchange for the imported good, one must look at two industries together and ask how they interact with each other and with factor markets. Thus the problem is one of general equilibrium.

Before Stolper and Samuelson, general equilibrium models had become the subject of a quite sophisticated branch of economic theory. But this general equilibrium theory had so far succeeded primarily in setting out rather large general equilibrium systems and exploring their properties. It had not been particularly fruitful in terms of generating useful predictions about the market effects of economic behavior and

---

[1] In the specific factors model the specificity of all factors but labor permits the wage to be determined in a simple supply and demand framework.

policy. These problems had remained in the province of partial equilibrium analysis.

General equilibrium models had, however, begun to appear in international trade theory. The writings of Heckscher and Ohlin on the determination of patterns of trade included many insights that were explicitly general equilibrium in nature. To see that a country will export the goods that use intensively its abundant factor, for example, requires simultaneous consideration of all goods markets and factor markets. That these authors had not obtained the Stolper-Samuelson Theorem themselves, and thus confounded our problem of naming it, is probably due to the fact that they had not yet developed or applied the mathematical tools that would make the problem tractable for Stolper and Samuelson.[2]

In any case, our heros did use general equilibrium analysis. They formulated a simple two-sector general equilibrium model in mathematical terms, then used it to examine various properties of the system. The one that they found most interesting and surprising became their theorem. They were able to show that, when a tariff in a labor-scarce country raises the price of an import good relative to exports, it raises the wage of labor by even more. Thus the wage rises relative to all goods, including the one whose price has gone up most due to the tariff. Because of this there is no index number problem. The buying power of the wage is increased, no matter what workers choose to consume, and even without their being given a share of the tariff revenue.

---

[2] Heckscher (1919), in a three-factor model with labor, capital, and land, came close to the Stolper-Samuelson Theorem in several statements. However, he dealt only in terms of factor prices relative to each other or relative to a numeraire. He did not explicitly examine them relative to prices of goods, as would be needed for evaluating them in real terms. Likewise, Ohlin (1933, p. 25) understood that trade would reduce the relative price of the scarce factor, but he was explicit in stating, contrary to the Stolper-Samuelson Theorem, that "In terms of goods, its price may rise." Benham (1935), examining a two-by-two model of the effects of taxes on factor prices, actually came quite close to the Stolper-Samuelson Theorem without quite getting it.

In short, Stolper and Samuelson showed not just that a tariff on labor-intensive imports would raise the wage relative to the prices of other factors. That is true, but it was already well-known, and it was not conclusive as far as the welfare of workers was concerned. What they showed instead was the stronger result that the wage would rise relative to the prices of all goods as well, and therefore that it would make workers unambiguously better off.

II. Versions of the Stolper-Samuelson Theorem

There are several ways of stating the Stolper-Samuelson Theorem. Some of these are equivalent to one another; others are distinct and require different sets of assumptions for their validity. Some versions cannot be stated at all without first setting up the context in which they are valid in some detail, and we will not attempt to do that here. Others, however, are quite simple, and it is worthwhile collecting them in one place.

We have already, in our opening paragraph, stated simple forms of two of them:

- **Protection helps the scarce factor.**
- **Free trade hurts the scarce factor.**

These two, with "hurts" and "helps" interpreted in terms of effects on the real wage, come closest to capturing what Stolper and Samuelson themselves apparently had in mind with the title of their paper. From the symmetry with which their model handles the two factors of production, both statements should be expanded to include effects on the abundant factor as well. Further, if "protection" means any increase in tariffs and "free trade" means any reduction, then the two statements are equivalent. However, by interpreting "free trade" more strictly as a comparison only to autarky, then the first statement becomes what Bhagwati (1959) [Chapter 5 below] labeled the General version, while the second becomes his more limited Restrictive version:

1. General Version

An increase in protection raises the real wage of the scarce factor of production and lowers the real wage of the abundant factor of production.

2. Restrictive Version

Free trade lowers the real wage of the scarce factor and raises that of the abundant factor compared to autarky.

At the heart of both versions however, as Bhagwati showed, is a simple and strong relationship between goods prices and factor prices that has nothing to do with factor scarcity or abundance and is independent of whether prices change because of protection or for any other reason. Bhagwati gave this version no name, but we will call it the Essential Version, since it embodies the essence of Stolper and Samuelson's insight and has also taken its place in the literature as the version most frequently cited:

---

3. Essential Version

An increase in the relative price of a good increases the real wage of the factor used intensively in producing that good, and lowers the real wage of the other factor.

This is the version that Jones (1965b) [Chapter 6 below] subsequently proved most elegantly with his algebraic approach to general equilibrium systems. His proof will be provided below.

The connections among these three versions of the Theorem are straightforward. The Essential version requires the fewest assumptions for its validity, as we will note further below. The Essential Version then implies the Restrictive Version if additional assumptions are made so as to guarantee the validity of the Heckscher-Ohlin Theorem as well. And the Restrictive Version in turn implies the General version if one more assumption is made to rule out what has come to be called the Metzler Paradox.

To explain things further, we may note that, unlike the General and Restrictive Versions, the Essential Version has nothing directly to do with trade, or even with more than one country. It merely states the effects within a country of a change in prices there. But if the Heckscher-Ohlin (H-O) Theorem also holds, then there is a simple relationship between the change in prices from autarky to free trade and the scarcities and intensities of factors. That is, since the move from autarky to free trade always raises the relative price of the export good, and the H-O Theorem says that the export good must use the abundant factor intensively, the Essential Version and the H-O Theorem together imply that a move from autarky to free trade will raise the real wage of the abundant factor and lower the real wage of the scarce factor. Thus whatever may be the assumptions needed for the Essential Version, the Restrictive Version requires those assumptions as well, plus enough additional assumptions to generate the H-O Theorem. These are primarily that technologies be identical across countries and that they not display relevant factor intensity reversals.

To go the next step to the General Version, one needs only to assure that an increase in non-prohibitive protection will have the same qualitative effect on domestic prices as a move from free trade all the way to autarky. In what was the first major contribution to the Stolper-Samuelson literature, Metzler (1949b) [Chapter 4 below] pointed out that this will not happen automatically--an additional assumption is needed. He showed that if the revenue from a tariff is spent heavily on the export good (or if the revenue is distributed to consumers and their marginal propensity to spend on the export good is high enough), and if foreign demand for that good is inelastic, then the tariff can raise the relative price of the export good on the world market so much that the domestic price actually rises rather than falls. In that case, protection will change factor prices in directions opposite to the Stolper-Samuelson predictions. Thus the General Version requires all of the assumptions of the Essential Version, plus all of the assumptions of the H-O Theorem, plus a condition on the propensity to spend the tariff revenues in relation to the elasticity of demand for the export good.

The General Version, then, is the least generally valid of the three, since it requires the most assumptions, but it makes the broadest statement about the effects of protection on real wages. The Essential Version, in contrast, is the most generally valid, but it does not directly address the effects of protection *per se*, unless one equates protection with a change in prices. It is perhaps ironic, therefore, that the Essential Version has been the closest we have to a standard form for the Stolper-Samuelson Theorem, considering what those authors set out to write about.

All three of these versions of the Theorem are most clearly valid only in a model of two goods and two factors. With more than two of either, there are numerous problems, including that of defining what one means by factor scarcity and factor intensity. Indeed, the Essential Version, as stated, explicitly assumes that there are only two factors when it speaks of the "other" factor, though this could be avoided by speaking instead of the factor used least intensively.

In addition, if the number of goods does not equal the number of factors, then it turns out that the mapping from goods prices to factor prices that is needed for the Essential Version is either not unique or not well defined. This has led some writers to look only at the case of "even technologies," where the number of factors equals the number of goods, even though this might be regarded as too special a case.

In any event, it was quickly discovered that, even if the definitions of abundance and intensity could be extended to higher dimensions, proofs of the resulting versions of the theorem often could not. Much of the early literature on the Theorem struggled with this problem, usually without much success.

Chipman (1969) [Chapter 7 below], for example, sought what he called both a "weak version" and a "strong version" of the Theorem with even technologies. The weak version would include only the factor that gains from a price increase, while the strong version would also include the losses to all other factors. A statement of the strong version would be as follows:

**4. Strong Version with
Even Technology**

A rise in the price of any good, all other prices remaining constant, causes an increase in the real return to the factor used intensively in producing that good and a fall in the real returns to all other factors.

This version requires, at a minimum, a restriction on technology that permits an unambiguous definition of intensively used factors, and even then it turns out to be difficult to obtain this result. The Strong Version reduces tautologically to the condition that the matrix logarithmically relating goods prices to factor prices (see Θ^{-1} below) be a "strong irreducible Minkowski Matrix." This just says that it has all diagonal elements greater than one and all off-diagonal elements negative. Chipman was able to obtain sufficient conditions for only the first of these properties, and only in the 3x3 case. Thus he proved only the weak version of the Stolper-Samuelson Theorem alluded to above. Kemp and Wegge (1969) [Chapter 8 below] followed with somewhat stronger results, including a particular factor intensity relationship that is a necessary, though not sufficient, condition for the Strong version. Finally, Uekawa, Kemp and Wegge (1973) did a more complete job of delineating the matrix properties that would yield the Strong version, though the economic interpretation of these properties, which they provided, is difficult.

It was Ethier (1974) [Chapter 9 below] who first published the key to generalizing the Theorem to higher dimensions. For even technologies he stated and proved a version of the theorem that Jones and Scheinkman (1977) [Chapter 10 below] later restated in terms of goods and factors being "friends" and "enemies." A good is "friend" to a factor if a rise in the price of the good, all other goods prices constant, leads to an unambiguous rise in the real return to that factor; it is "enemy" to a factor if the same price change leads to an unambiguous fall in the real return.

---

5. Friends and Enemies Version

Every good is a friend to some factor and an enemy to some other factor.

This had been known before. Kemp and Wan (1976) printed an unpublished memorandum from Meade (1968) that stated and proved the result, apparently for even technologies. Kemp and Wan also showed this result to be valid for uneven technologies. It is therefore largely independent of numbers of goods and factors. It rests instead most critically on the assumption of non-joint production, as noted by Jones and Scheinkman. This Friends and Enemies Version has proven to be the simplest and most intuitive version of the Theorem available for more than two goods and factors, and it is widely cited.

This result is remarkably robust, as we will see below when we discuss the proof. The reason is partly that it does not, as the Strong Version would have done, attempt to say something about all factor prices. But it also benefits from saying nothing about *which* factors will be the friends and enemies. That is, it does not attempt to define intensively and non-intensively used factors or to use such definitions to specify which factors will gain and lose from a price change. This is part of the beauty of this version, since it makes the proof extraordinarily simple. But it is also a weakness: it tells us less about the world than the other versions attempt to do.[3]

Jones and Scheinkman also examined the converse to the Friends and Enemies Version stated above--that every factor has both a friend and an enemy. They found that this does not hold in general, as for example in the two-good, three-factor, specific factors model, where mobile labor is affected ambiguously by any price change. For even technologies, they were able to show that every factor has at least one enemy, but even then they could not assure the existence of a friend.

This could be important from a political economy perspective, since it means that some factors may not have any good for which they would unambiguously benefit from a price increase, and for which they would therefore want to lobby for changes in trade policy. In a more recent follow up on this discussion, however, Jones (1985) [Chapter 13 below] has proven a slightly weaker version of the converse proposition that

---

[3] In fact, however, beyond two dimensions the Strong Version's prediction of which factors gain and lose is also not very useful, since one must really solve the entire system of equations in order to identify them.

serves this purpose: with even technologies every factor has a *group* of goods that, if all of their prices rise together relative to goods not in the group, then the real return to the factor will rise. Thus with even technologies, every factor has at least one enemy and at least one group-friend, in this sense.

The final version of the Theorem that we will mention here is due to Ethier (1982a) [Chapter 12 below]. Following on higher dimensional extensions of other results in trade theory that established correlations among economic variables, Ethier sought a correlation version of the Stolper-Samuelson Theorem.   What he found was a three-way relationship involving a vector of changes in factor prices, a vector of changes in goods prices, and a particular matrix of factor requirements. He showed that the product of the first vector, the matrix, and the second vector must be non-negative. The interpretation of this result was not as clear as one might like, but it seems to say something like the following:

---

6. Correlation Version

For any vector of goods price changes, the accompanying vector of factor price changes will be positively correlated with the factor-intensity-weighted averages of the goods price changes.

A formal statement and proof of this version will be provided below.

This version is in a sense complementary to the Friends and Enemies version. The Friends and Enemies version makes a statement about only two factors for each good, and if there are many factors, this means that there are many about which it has nothing to say.   The Correlation Version, on the other hand, is a statement about all factor prices together. On the other hand, the statement that the Friends and Enemies Version makes is a strong one: that particular factors unambiguously gain and lose. The correlation version does not even address whether gains and losses are real, and even then makes only an average statement about all relative factor price changes. Thus the Correlation Version is a weak statement about all factor prices, while the Friends and Enemies Version is a strong statement about only an unspecified few.

Together, however, the two versions give us quite a bit of information about how prices of factors respond to prices of goods in general equilibrium with many goods and factors. Together they confirm two of the basic insights of the original Stolper-Samuelson Theorem: (1) that some factors stand unambiguously to gain and to lose from the price changes caused by protection; and (2) that the general pattern of gains and losses is related to the intensities with which factors are used in production of the goods. At the end of the day (or half century), and despite the difficulties early writers had in generalizing the Stolper-Samuelson result, it seems that their insights have held up remarkably well.

III. The Logic of the Stolper-Samuelson Theorem

Under the usual assumptions of the Heckscher-Ohlin model, including two factors and two goods, the Stolper-Samuelson story can be told simply. Considering the General Version stated above, the logic is as follows. Suppose that a country increases a tariff on its import good. A number of logical implications follow, each of which is stated below.

1. In a small country, the tariff will raise the price of the imported good--relative to the export good, which we take as numeraire--by the amount of the tariff.

2. With homogeneous goods, the rise in price of the import good will be matched by an equal rise in price of the import-competing good.

3. This rise in the relative price of the import-competing good will cause the economy's resources to shift towards it and away from the export good.[4]

4. This shift of resources will raise demand for, and hence the relative price of, the factor used intensively in the import-competing industry, relative to the factor used less intensively.

5. From the Heckscher-Ohlin Theorem, import competing goods will make intensive use of the country's scarce factor. Therefore, the factor whose relative price has risen must be the scarce factor.

6. With free entry into the import-competing sector, zero profit requires that the *average* prices of all factors employed there rise (relative to the price of the numeraire export good) by the same amount as the rise in price of the import-competing good.

7. If the scarce factor is not the only factor employed in the import competing sector, the rise in its relative factor price means that its price must also rise relative to this average, and hence relative to the price of the import competing good.

8. Since the prices of imports and import-competing goods are equal and have both risen relative to all other prices, this rise in the scarce factor price is therefore an increase relative to *all* goods, and therefore is also an increase in real terms.

Depending on which version of the Theorem is being considered, most or all of these logical steps are present in the numerous proofs of the Stolper-Samuelson Theorem to which we now turn.

---

[4] Actually, this shift of resources is not crucial to the theorem, though it does aid the intuition. If there were fixed-coefficient technologies in both industries, there would be no shift in resources. The change in relative factor prices in step 4 would still have to occur, however, in order to maintain zero profits in both industries.

IV. Proofs of the Stolper-Samuelson Theorem

Many different approaches have been taken to proving the Stolper-Samuelson Theorem in its various forms. We will indicate only a few of these here, selecting those that have, in our view, proven to be the most simple, durable, and/or illuminating. Not surprisingly, the proof that Stolper and Samuelson themselves provided is not on our list. They were exploring new territory, and the tools at their disposal from previous research were limited. Therefore their proof was more cumbersome than is now necessary.

We will consider here only the Essential Version of the Theorem stated above, plus its higher dimensional extensions. This relieves us of the need to handle the details also of the Heckscher-Ohlin Theorem, as well as the details of international demand and the specification of how tariff revenue is disposed of. Instead, we will need to consider only goods prices, factor prices, and the technology and behavior that relate the two.

Notation:

Largely following Jones (1965b) [Chapter 6 below], a more or less standard notation has developed for discussions of the Stolper-Samuelson Theorem. Let

m = the number of factors.
n = the number of goods.
w = m-vector (row) of factor prices.
p = n-vector (row) of goods prices.
A = $\{a_{ij}\}$ = mxn matrix of unit factor requirements.
  a_{ij} = quantity of factor i used to produce one unit of good j.
  $A = A(w)$ indicates that A is chosen from the available techniques of production so as to minimize unit production costs, wA.
Θ = $\{\theta_{ij}\}$ = mxn matrix of factor shares.
  $\theta_{ij} = w_i\, a_{ij} / p_j$

Finally, for any variable, x, we use the "hat algebra" of Jones (1965b), whereby

$$\hat{x} = d \ln x = dx/x$$

The Jones (1965b) Proof of the Essential Version

At the core of any version of the Stolper-Samuelson Theorem is the zero-profit condition that must hold in any perfectly competitive sector that is actively producing. In this notation, and interpreting the vectors of goods and goods prices as including only those goods that are being produced, this condition is

$$p = wA \quad .$$

(1)

Totally differentiating equation (1) and noting from cost minimization that any feasible marginal changes in factor requirements must leave costs unchanged, i.e.,

$$w \; dA = 0 \; ,$$

(2)

it follows that

$$\hat{p} = \hat{w} \, \Theta \quad .$$

(3)

If Θ is square, as in the two-good, two-factor case of the Essential Version above, and if Θ is also non-singular, then (3) can be solved for $\hat{w}$ in terms of $\hat{p}$:

$$\hat{w} = \hat{p} \, \Theta^{-1}$$

(4)

Suppose that goods and factors are numbered such that good i uses factor i relatively intensively. Then the Essential Version is equivalent to having the diagonal elements of Θ^{-1} be greater than one, and the off-diagonal elements be negative. For in that case, a rise in one good's price, the other held constant, will raise the corresponding factor price by even more, while reducing the other factor price.[5]

In the 2x2 case, as Jones showed, this is easily established. Note that the θ_{ij} are factor shares and that they sum to one across factors in a given industry:

$$\sum_{i=1}^{2} \theta_{ij} = \sum_{i=1}^{2} \left(\frac{w_i a_{ij}}{P_j}\right) = 1 \quad , \quad j=1,2 \tag{5}$$

Calculating Θ^{-1} one finds

$$\Theta^{-1} = \begin{pmatrix} \dfrac{\theta_{22}}{\theta_{22}-\theta_{21}} & \dfrac{-\theta_{12}}{\theta_{11}-\theta_{12}} \\[2em] \dfrac{-\theta_{21}}{\theta_{22}-\theta_{21}} & \dfrac{\theta_{11}}{\theta_{11}-\theta_{12}} \end{pmatrix} \tag{6}$$

With good 1 intensive in factor 1, so that $\theta_{11}-\theta_{12}=\theta_{22}-\theta_{21}>0$, it follows immediately that the diagonal elements of Θ^{-1} are indeed greater than one and the off-diagonal elements negative.

Jones used this pattern to derive the following relationships between changes in good and factor prices for the two-good case:

$$\hat{P}_1 \mathrel{\overset{>}{\underset{<}{=}}} \hat{P}_2 \;\Rightarrow\; \hat{w}_1 \mathrel{\overset{>}{\underset{<}{=}}} \hat{P}_1 \mathrel{\overset{>}{\underset{<}{=}}} \hat{P}_2 \mathrel{\overset{>}{\underset{<}{=}}} \hat{w}_2 \tag{7}$$

---

[5] Clearly, with $n=m>2$ this same condition implies the Strong Version with Even Technologies that was also mentioned above, though we will not deal here with any of the proofs of that version because of their limited generality.

He described this as the "magnification effect" for prices, since it says that any change in relative goods prices will lead to a magnified pair of changes in relative factor prices.[6]

The Lerner-Pearce Geometry of Stolper-Samuelson

Stolper and Samuelson themselves used a geometric argument to establish the Theorem, combining the use of a production possibility frontier with what was apparently the first adaptation of the Edgeworth box diagram to production. This was used to illustrate the complete competitive allocation of two factors to two industries, but also, and especially, the surprising possibility for, say, capital-labor ratios to rise in both industries at the same time that aggregate factor endowments are constant. More recent geometric treatments of the entire Heckscher-Ohlin model have tended to favor use of the Lerner-Pearce diagram, however, where the factor prices consistent with producing two goods are inferred from the unit isocost line that is tangent to both of two unit-value isoquants. A change in goods prices causes the curves to shift in a simple and determinate way that easily displays the resulting changes in factor prices.

Thus in Figure 1, we start with the (solid) unit value isoquants for goods X and Y in the space of factors capital K and labor L. For initial prices p_x^0 and p_y^0, these are the isoquants for outputs $X = 1/p_x^0$ and $Y = 1/p_y^0$, each worth one unit of the numeraire. If both goods are produced with perfect competition, they must also cost one unit, and therefore the unit isocost line must be a straight line that is tangent to both of these isoquants. This is the solid straight line shown, the intercepts of which are therefore $1/w^0$ and $1/r^0$, indicating the only fac-

---

[6] He also showed a similar magnification effect for quantities, implying the Rybczynski Theorem.

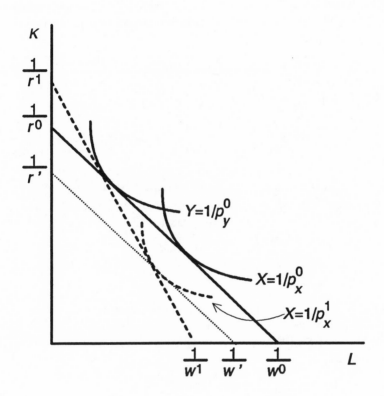

Figure 1
The Lerner-Pearce Diagram for
Showing the Stolper-Samuelson Theorem

tor prices consistent with incomplete specialization at the initial goods prices.[7]

To see the Stolper-Samuelson Theorem, now let relative prices change. Holding the price of Y fixed, let the price of the labor-intensive good X go up, thus pulling the x-unit-value isoquant proportionally inward toward the origin, to the dashed isoquant for $X=1/p_x^1$ shown in the figure. Constructing the new common tangent to the old y-isoquant and the new x-isoquant, the increased slope of the dashed straight line indicates immediately that the ratio of labor's wage to the rental on capital has increased. For the Stolper-Samuelson Theorem, however, we also need to know that the wage has risen more than the price of X, and that the rental has fallen. The latter is clear from the increase in the $1/r$ intercept. The size of the wage increase can be seen by comparing w^1 to w', which is constructed as a wage increase that is proportional to the price of X by drawing the dotted isocost line parallel to the initial one, but tangent to the new unit-value isoquant for X. Evidently the wage has increased by more than the price of X and we get the result.

The Geometric Dual of Mussa

Mussa (1979) provided another geometric exposition of the Heckscher-Ohlin Model in terms of its dual that was particularly simple in its treatment of the Stolper-Samuelson Theorem. This is shown in Figure 2.

---

[7] These are unique only if the common tangent is unique, which in turn can be assured by assuming the absence of factor intensity reversals (FIRs). This of course is the point made by the Factor Price Equalization Theorem of Samuelson (1948). If factor prices are not unique, however, because of the presence of one or more FIRs, then only one set will still be consistent with equilibrium for a given country's factor endowments. Therefore it is not necessary to rule out FIRs for the validity of the Essential Version of the Stolper-Samuelson Theorem. One only requires that a FIR not be located at exactly the factor ratio equal to the country's endowments, since that would make the factor share matrix Θ singular, and would make the construction below, when we change prices, indeterminate.

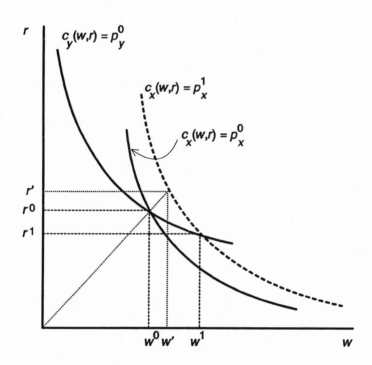

Figure 2
The Geometry of the Dual
and the Stolper-Samuelson Theorem

Given initial prices of the two goods, p_x^0 and p_y^0, the two solid curves show the minimum factor prices consistent with zero profits in each industry. With X the labor intensive good, the factor price frontier for the X industry is closer to the wage axis than is the frontier for the Y-industry. Zero profits in both industries require being on both curves at the same time, and thus at their intersection, w^0 and r^0.

An increase in the price of good X to p_x^1 shifts the factor price frontier for the X industry proportionally outward, and would support, in that industry only, equal proportional increases in both factor prices, to w' and r'. However, as is clear from the figure, the intersection of the two curves moves instead down and to the right, showing a drop in the rental to r^1 together with a rise in the wage to w^1 that is greater than the price increase.

The Friends and Enemies Version

Recall that the Friends and Enemies Version of Stolper-Samuelson says only that a rise in a single goods price will raise the real return to *some* factor and lower the real return to *some* other. It does not say anything about effects on other factors, when there are more than two. Nor does it say *which* factors will be affected in these ways. With such limited objectives, it is perhaps not surprising that the proof of this version is quite simple. Nonetheless it took several decades of others searching for more complicated relationships before Ethier (1974) published this. And it required the further insight of Kemp and Wan (1976) and Jones and Scheinkman (1977) to indicate the full generality and simplicity of this result.

Suppose that any good, say good 1, rises in price, so that $\hat{p}_1 > 0$, all other prices remaining constant. Equation (3), written out for good 1, then says that some weighted average of the factor price changes must be positive:

$$\sum_{i=1}^{m} \theta_{i1} \hat{w}_i = \hat{p}_1 > 0 \tag{8}$$

It also says that for any other good, say good 2, another weighted average of the factor price changes must be zero:

$$\sum_{i=1}^{m} \theta_{i2} \hat{w}_i = \hat{p}_2 = 0 \tag{9}$$

These two equations imply immediately that some factor's price rises by at least as much as $\hat{p}_1$ and that some other factor's price does not rise at all. If the owners of these factors consume positive amounts of good 1 and some other good, then their real returns rise and fall respectively.

More in the spirit of Stolper-Samuelson, however, would be real changes that do not depend on even these minimal assumptions about consumption. Such real changes can be guaranteed if industries 1 and 2 (recalling that any industry could have served as good 2) both use positive amounts of the same list of factors. These need not be all of the factors in the economy; a common subset will do. For then the strictly increasing factor price implied by (8) implies a strictly decreasing factor price in (9). And the latter in turn implies that some factor price in (8) rises by strictly more than $\hat{p}_1$. Thus, regardless of the factor owners' consumption patterns, one factor--the "friend" of good 1--gains in real terms from the increase in price of good 1, while another factor--the "enemy"--loses in real terms.

Ethier's Correlation Result

It was also Ethier, this time in 1984, who showed that goods price changes and factor price changes must be in some sense correlated. Consider any vector of factor price changes, $\hat{w}$, and the associated vector of goods price changes, $\hat{p}$, satisfying (3). As long as the latter are non-zero, we have

$$\hat{w} \, \Theta \, \hat{p}^T = \hat{p} \, \hat{p}^T > 0 \tag{10}$$

since $\hat{p} \; \hat{p}^{\;T}$ is the sum of squares of the price changes. Thus, there is a positive inner product between either the proportional wage changes $\hat{w}$ and an intensity-weighted vector of proportional price changes $\Theta \hat{p}^{\;T}$, or between the proportional price changes $\hat{p}^{\;T}$ and an intensity-weighted vector of proportional wage changes $\hat{w} \Theta$. Ethier interprets this result, or something similar, as showing correlations.[8] However, as discussed in Deardorff (1981), the sign of an inner product implies a correlation only under certain additional conditions, such as that one of the vectors has a zero mean.[9]

To get this result as a true correlation, then, assume that prices of goods are normalized on, say, the unit hyperbola, so that $\prod_{j=1}^{n} p_j = 1$.[10]

It then follows that $\sum_{j=1}^{n} \ln p_j = 0$, that $\sum_{j=1}^{n} \hat{p}_j = 0$, and

hence that

$$\sum_{i=1}^{m} [\sum_{j=1}^{n} \theta_{ij} \, \hat{p}_j] = \sum_{j=1}^{n} \hat{p}_j \sum_{i=1}^{m} \theta_{ij} = \sum_{j=1}^{n} \hat{p}_j = 0 \tag{11}$$

---

[8] Actually, Ethier derives such a relationship for absolute, rather than proportional, price and wage changes, and by using the Mean Value Theorem he obtains it for discreet rather than infinitesimal changes.

[9] For any two n-vectors x and y, the sign of the correlation is the same as the sign of their covariance: $\text{Cov}(x,y) = \sum (x_i - \bar{x})(y_i - \bar{y}) = x \, y^T - n \bar{x} \, \bar{y}$, where bars indicate vector means. Thus if either mean is zero, the sign of the correlation is the same as that of the inner product.

[10] This normalization is possible only if all prices are positive, as they must be in any case for $\hat{p}$ to be well defined.

It is therefore the case that the m-vector $\Theta\hat{p}$ sums to zero, and the inner product in (10) does after all imply a correlation. That is,

$$Cor(\hat{w},\Theta\hat{p}^{\,T}) > 0$$

$$(12)$$

Note that $\Theta\hat{p}^{\,T}$ is a vector of factor-share-weighted, or factor-intensity-weighted, averages of the goods price changes. Thus it will have positive elements for those factors that are most intensively used in production of goods whose relative prices have risen, and negative elements for those factors most intensively used in falling price sectors. The positive correlation says that, on average, factors used intensively in rising-price sectors will themselves rise in price, while factors used intensively in falling-price sectors will fall in price. As usual with correlation results of this sort, it says nothing about the behavior of any individual price or wage, any one of which may therefore rise or fall.

V. Comparison of the Stolper-Samuelson Theorem with Implications of the Specific Factors Model

Perhaps the most problematic aspect of the Stolper-Samuelson Theorem, at least in its original versions that apply to the 2x2 model, is its assumption that factors are mobile between industries and therefore are paid a common factor price wherever they are employed. This assumption drives the strong implication of the Theorem that all factors either gain or lose in real terms from a price change, and also that it is the identity of the factor, and not the industry in which it is employed, that determines whether it gains or loses. Dissatisfaction with this aspect of the Heckscher-Ohlin Model led, in the early 1970s, to the re-emergence of the Ricardo-Viner model of trade, in which at least some factors are specific to industries. This model, which has come most commonly to be called the Specific Factors Model, was revived by Samuelson (1971) and Jones (1971), and then further developed by such authors as Mussa (1974), Mayer (1974), and Neary (1978). The implications of this model appear at first to contradict the Stolper-Samuelson Theorem, in that specific factors have their real returns determined by their industry of employment, not their country-wide factor market, while real prices of non-specific factors tend to be affected in indeterminate ways by price changes.

It is easy, therefore, to view the factor-price implications of the specific factors model as an alternative to the Stolper-Samuelson Theorem, and to regard them as superior to the latter, at least in the short run, for explaining the interests of factor owners in the real world. This view gained empirical support with the study of Magee (1980) [Chapter 11 below], who examined the lobbying positions of representatives of capital and labor with respect to free trade. He found that capital and labor tend *not* to take opposite sides in the debate over trade liberalization, as one would predict from the 2x2 Stolper-Samuelson Theorem, but rather that capital and labor in a given industry tend to take the same side. Instead, it is the industry of employment that determines whether both factors lobby for trade or against it. This is exactly what one would expect from an extreme specific factors model, in which both labor and capital are immobile across industries, and it has therefore been taken as evidence against the Stolper-Samuelson Theorem.[11]

As we have seen by now, however, it is only the strong versions of the Theorem--those that derive from a two-factor, two-good model--that are contradicted by this evidence. The weaker Friends and Enemies and Correlation versions are quite consistent with it, and with the specific factors model in general. For example, in a two-sector model with mobile labor, and capital that is specific to each sector, each good is friend precisely to its own specific capital and enemy to the other specific capital. And since specific factors, by definition, have zero factor shares in other sectors than their own, their intensity-weighted price changes will give exclusive weight to their own sector's price, which leads easily to the kind of correlation result that we presented last.

Thus, while the specific factors model is often viewed as an alternative to the simple two-sector Heckscher-Ohlin model with

---

[11] See Baldwin (1984) for further enunciation of this view. Grossman and Levinsohn (1989) also find empirical evidence that the response of stock market returns to import prices favors the specific factors model.

implications that contrast starkly with the Stolper-Samuelson Theorem, it can as well be viewed as a particular specification of a more general Heckscher-Ohlin framework in which the weakest but most general versions of Stolper-Samuelson hold perfectly well.

VI. Conclusion

The Stolper-Samuelson Theorem was a truly seminal contribution, in that it stimulated a tremendous amount of other literature. In this overview chapter we have cited only a few of these contributions, concentrating on some of the most important ones that have refined both the statement of the Theorem and its proof. Many of these extensions have sought to take the Theorem beyond the original confines of the two-factor, two-good model in which it was first proved, and we have seen that these efforts have ultimately been quite successful. There have been many other extensions as well, which have looked for the result in other models, allowing for such complications as intermediate inputs, nontraded goods, external economies of scale, international factor mobility, endogenous factor supply and factor heterogeneity, and on and on. Rather than review this huge literature here, we instead refer the reader to the Annotated Bibliography later in this volume, together with the Subject Index that accompanies it. It is hard to imagine another result, at least in international trade theory, that might have stimulated such an outpouring of additional research.

While most of these extensions and applications have been predictably within the bounds of international trade theory, some have not. In perusing this literature, we were particularly intrigued to find applications of Stolper-Samuelson to problems removed from trade, and sometimes even from economics. Willis (1991), for example, applied the Theorem to a problem in the economic demography of the household: the linkage between a wife's shadow price of time and the shadow price of children, in a model of child quality and fertility behavior. And further removed by discipline, though closer in topic, political scientist Ronald Rogowski (1990) used a version of the Stolper-Samuelson Theorem to explain why some countries are characterized by urban-rural conflict and others by class conflict. Finally, and less surprisingly, the Stolper-Samuelson Theorem has been central to a number of studies in economic history, such as Pope (1972), Martin (1989), and Inkster (1990). Because we are less likely to come across such contributions outside of our own field, the fact that we even know about these few suggests that there may well be many more.

In this volume we present the original Stolper-Samuelson contribution, as it first appeared, together with several of the more important articles discussed above as extending and refining their insights. We also present commentaries on the Theorem and its subsequent role in economics by several of those who are in the best position to evaluate it: those who have themselves worked on extending the theorem, as well as others who have applied it or gone beyond it in their own work. We hope that this collection will provide a fitting tribute to one of the most significant intellectual achievements in economics, while at the same time being a useful tool for those who will continue to teach and use the Stolper-Samuelson Theorem in their work.

References (Not Included in the Annotated Bibliography)

Deardorff, A.V.   1981.   "The General Validity of the Law of Comparative Advantage," *Journal of Political Economy* 88: 941-57.

Mayer, W.   1974   "Short-Run and Long-Run Equilibrium for a Small Open Economy," *Journal of Political Economy* 82: 955-967.

Neary, J.P.   1978   "Short-Run Capital Specificity and the Pure Theory of International Trade," *Economic Journal* 88: 488-510.

Ohlin, Bertil. 1967. *Interregional and International Trade*, Revised Edition, Cambridge, MA: Harvard University Press.

Samuelson, P.A.   1948.   "International Trade and the Equalisation of Factor Prices," *Economic Journal* 58: 163-184.

Part II

The Original Statement

15

PROTECTION AND REAL WAGES*

By Wolfgang F. Stolper‖ and Paul A. Samuelson‡

Introduction§

Second only in political appeal to the argument that tariffs increase employment is the popular notion that the standard of living of the American worker must be protected against the ruinous competition of cheap foreign labour. Equally prevalent abroad is its counterpart that European industry cannot compete with the technically superior American system of production. Again and again economists have tried to show the falaciousness of this argument. Professor Taussig, for example, stated that "perhaps most familiar and most unfounded of all is the belief that complete freedom of trade would bring about an equalisation of money wages the world over. . . . There is no such tendency to equalisation."[1] And Professor Haberler classifies the argument that wages

---

* *The Review of Economic Studies*, Volume IX (November, 1941), pages 58–73. Reprinted by the courtesy of the *Review of Economic Studies* and the authors.

‖ Swarthmore College.

‡ Massachusetts Institute of Technology.

§ The following article is reprinted without significant change from the original text.

[1] F. W. Taussig, *International Trade*, p. 38. The statement might have been made equally well with respect to real wages, since in the classical formulation the prices of internationally traded goods cannot diverge in different countries by more than the cost of transfer. In his *Principles* there is a passage which might be interpreted in the opposite direction. "Under certain contingencies, it is conceivable that protective duties will affect the process of sharing and so will influence wages otherwise than through their effect on the total product." 4th ed., p. 517. But the phrasing is not quite clear and refers probably to the share in national income rather than to the absolute size. We have not found any similar

might suffer from international trade among those "that do not merit serious discussion. . . . An equalisation of wages comes about only if labour is mobile [between countries]."[2]

More recently, however, the writings of Ohlin seem to suggest that a re-examination of this accepted doctrine might be fruitful. It is the intention of the present paper to show that definitive statements are possible concerning the effects of international trade upon the relative remunerations of productive agencies, and more important, upon their absolute real incomes. That this is possible is surprising since the voluminous literature appears to contain only statements of possibilities and presumptions rather than of necessities. Indeed, in the beginning we expected to do no more than delineate factors which would indicate a likelihood in one direction or another, and only in the course of the investigation did we discover that unambiguous inferences were possible. It may be illuminating, therefore, to follow in the exposition our original sequence of thought rather than attempt the most direct derivation of theorems.

THE EFFECT OF TRADE UPON RELATIVE FACTOR PRICES

According to the train of thought associated with the name of Ohlin, differences in the proportions of the various productive factors between countries are important elements in explaining the course of international trade. A country will export those commodities which are produced with its relatively abundant factors of production, and will import those in the production of which its relatively scarce factors are important.[3] And as a result of the

---

passage either in *The Tariff History of the United States, in International Trade,* or in *Free Trade, the Tariff, and Reciprocity.*

[2] G. Haberler, *The Theory of International Trade,* pp. 250–251, bracketed expression ours. See also the preceding sentence on p. 251 where Haberler expressly denies that movement of goods will lead to an equalisation of factor prices. However, as will be discussed below, he does in another place introduce important qualifications to this denial.

[3] Professor Viner has shown that this line of reasoning was not unknown to the classical economists. See his *Studies in the Theory of International Trade,* pp. 500–507.

shift towards increased production of those goods in which the abundant factors predominate, there will be a tendency—necessarily incomplete—towards an equalisation of factor prices between the two or more trading countries.[4] Although partial, the movement in the direction of equalisation is nevertheless real and can be substantial.

Assuming, as we shall throughout, that the total amounts of the factors of production remain fixed, it is clear from the Heckscher-Ohlin theorem that the introduction of trade must lower the relative share in the real or money national income going to the scarce factor of production. For the total return to a factor equals its price times the amount employed, and since we assume full employment before and after trade, the total returns to the factors are proportional to the rates per unit. This argument seems to have relevance to the American discussion of protection versus free trade. If, as is generally thought, labour is the relatively scarce factor in the American economy, it would appear that trade would necessarily lower the relative position of the labouring class as compared to owners of other factors of production.

So far we have dealt only with the relative shares of the various factors and have not gone into the effect upon absolute shares. Before entering upon this latter problem, it is of considerable interest to mention the most important currently held viewpoints.

SOME EXISTING VIEWS

Nobody, of course, ever denied that the workers employed in the particular industry that loses a tariff could be hurt in the short-

---

[4] B. Ohlin, *Interregional and International Trade*, Chapter II and elsewhere. This appears to be a novel theorem largely unknown to the classical economists, or at least completely unmentioned in Viner's masterful review of doctrine. Perhaps the earliest clear enunciation of this doctrine is that of E. Heckscher in a 1919 article in the *Ekonomisk Tidskrift*, cited by Ohlin. [This paper appears as Chap. 13 in the present *Readings* volume under the title of "The Effect of Foreign Trade on the Distribution of Income."] Heckscher apparently gives no prior references. Unfortunately, this important contribution is in Swedish, and we are indebted to Mr. Svend Laursen for a paraphrasing of its contents. Because of its extensive development at the hands of Ohlin, we shall refer to it as the Heckscher-Ohlin theorem.

run, but according to the classical theory, in the long-run there
would be an increased demand for those commodities in which the
country had a comparative advantage, i.e. where labour is more
productive.[5] Although money wages might fall, the removal of a
tariff would result in a still larger reduction in price levels so that
the real wage must rise.   In the words of Taussig, "The question of
wages is at bottom one of productivity.   The greater the productivity of industry at large, the higher will be the general level of
wages."[6]

How can this argument be reconciled with the Ohlin type of
discussion?   If there were only one commodity produced, then
indeed the marginal productivity of labour would depend simply
on the relative quantities of labour and capital as a whole.   And
the same would be the case with more than one commodity if
labour and capital were combined in the same proportions in the
production of each.   A balanced movement of the factors of production from one employment to another would then leave the
marginal productivities of labour and capital unchanged.

Now, it is true that under the assumptions of pure competition—
homogeneity, and perfect mobility of labour—the value of the
marginal product of labour (expressed in terms of any commodity)
must be the same in each occupation; it nevertheless does not follow
that this will depend simply on the proportion of labour and capital
as a whole.   For in so far as capital and labour are combined in
different proportions in each occupation, any change from one
production to another will change the "value marginal productivity" of labour (however expressed), even though it will, of course,
still be equal in all occupations.   In this sense the value marginal
productivity of labour as a whole may be considered to depend
upon a kind of weighted average of the effective demands for the
various producible commodities.   It is the essence of the argument

---

[5] "The free-trader argues that if the duties were given up and the protected
industries pushed out of the field by foreign competitors, the workmen engaged in
them would find no less well-paid employment elsewhere." F. W. Taussig,
Principles of Economics, 4th ed., Vol. 1, p. 516.

[6] Ibid., p. 517.

of the previous section that international trade in accordance with the principle of comparative advantage so shifts production and the relative effective derived demands as to produce the Heckscher-Ohlin effect.

It is not surprising that the classical argument should not have touched upon the problem of relative and absolute shares since for most purposes the older economists implicitly assumed a one factor economy or an economy in which different factors of production were applied in a dose whose proportions never varied. It is to their credit as realists that again and again they relaxed these assumptions, but they were not always able to weld into a synthesis these excluded effects.[7]

Among more modern writers, who are nevertheless in the classical tradition, it has long been recognised that a small factor of production specialised for the production of a protected commodity might be harmed by the removal of tariffs.[8] This has received particular attention in connection with the problem of non-competing groups in the labour market. Certain sub-groups of the labouring class, e.g. highly skilled labourers, may benefit while others are harmed. Thus, Ohlin holds that it is quite possible under certain circumstances for free trade to reduce the standard of living of the manufacturing labouring class. "If manufacturing and agricultural labourers form two non-competing groups, high protection of manufacturing industries may raise the real wages of the workers in these industries at the expense of the other factors."[9] Similarly, Haberler remarks that " . . . in the short-run, special-

---

[7] A good case can be made out that even Ricardo did not adhere narrowly to a labour theory of value, but this is not the place to enter into controversy on this subject. See, however, John Cassels, "A Re-intepretation of Ricardo on Value," *Quarterly Journal of Economics*, Vol. 49, pp. 518 ff.

[8] "It is perfectly clear that the imposition of a prohibitive tariff on the import of raw silk into the United States would increase the rents of the owners of land suitable for the growth of mulberry trees and the earnings of workers, if there be such, completely specialised in caring for silkworms." M. C. Samuelson, "The Australian Case for Protection Re-examined," *Quarterly Journal of Economics*, November, 1939, p. 149.

[9] Ohlin, op. cit., p. 306.

338   TARIFFS AND THE GAINS FROM TRADE

ised and immobile groups of workers, like the owners of specific
material factors, may suffer heavy reductions in income when for
one reason or another they are faced with more intense foreign
competition."[10]   Once the principle that no factor can benefit from
a tariff has been broken, one is tempted to ask whether similar
results are not possible for a large factor of production even if only
two factors are assumed.   For the logic of the case seems the same
whether two classes of labour are considered to be non-competing
or whether the "non-competing" factors are labelled "capital"
and "labour" respectively.

In treating this problem Haberler expresses doubt that a large
and mobile factor such as labour can be harmed by unrestricted
international trade.   "We may conclude that in the long run the
working-class as a whole has nothing to fear from international
trade, since, in the long run, labour is the least specific of all factors.
It will gain by the general increase in productivity due to the international division of labour, and is not likely to lose at all seriously
by a change in the functional distribution of the national income."[11]
This is not a dogmatic necessity, but rather regarded as the most
probable situation.   For lower on the same page Haberler recog-
nises explicitly a possible qualification.   If labour enters more importantly in the protected industry, it might possibly be harmed by
free trade.[12]

Viner criticises Haberler's conclusion, maintaining that there
appears to be "no a priori or empirical grounds for holding this to be
an improbable case."[13]   In this connection Viner is concerned
primarily with the relative share of labour in the national money
income.   In his discussion he introduces as an element in the
problem the prices which consumers must pay for commodities,
particularly imports and exports with and without protection.
Thus, he says, "But even if labour on the average had low occu-
pational mobility and were employed relatively heavily in the

---

[10] Haberler, op. cit., p. 195.
[11] Haberler, ibid., p. 195.
[12] Similar views are attributed to Wicksell, Carver, Nicholson, and others.
[13] Viner, op. cit., p. 533.

PROTECTION AND REAL WAGES   339

protected industries, its real income might still rise with the removal of tariff protection . . . if it was an important consumer of the hitherto protected commodities, and if the price of these commodities fell sufficiently as a result to offset the reduction in money wages in the new situation."[14]

Ohlin and other modern writers raise this problem, but it can also be found in the older literature. Bastable, for example, in good classical fashion points out that free trade may force a food exporting country "to bring worse soils into cultivation, and to raise the value of food, thus permitting of an increase in the amount of agricultural rent. In this instance, the labourers, and possibly the capitalists, may suffer while the landlords gain."[15]

We may sum up as follows: (1) In the narrowest classical version the problem of the effect of trade upon the relative and absolute shares of various productive factors could hardly arise since only one factor is assumed. (2) Outside the confines of this rigid system it has long been recognised that the relative and possibly even the absolute share of a small specific factor of production *might* be increased by protection. This received particular attention in connection with the problem of non-competing groups. (3) With reference to large categories, opinion is more divided. Almost all admit the possibility of a decline in the relative share of a large factor of production such as labour as a result of free trade. Many even admit the possibility of a decline in the real income of a large factor of production. But all writers consider highly improbable a decline in the absolute shares, and many believe the same with respect to the relative shares. Some take the position that no *a priori* presumption is possible in connection with the last problem. (4) The vast majority of writers take it as axiomatic that a calculation of effects upon real income must take into consideration the behaviour of prices of commodities entering into the consumer's budget. Thus, if the owners of a factor of production consume only

---

[14] Viner, ibid., p. 533.
[15] C. F. Bastable, *The Theory of International Trade*, 4th ed., p. 105.

the exported good (in Professor Pigou's terminology this is the wage good), a different result will be reached than if the wage good were imported. And since in the real world consumption is diversified so that the concept of a wage good is an oversimplification, a difficult index number problem would appear to be involved.

It is the purpose of the present investigation to show that under rather general assumptions definite conclusions can be derived concerning the absolute share of a factor (a) even when there is perfect domestic mobility of factors of production and a complete absence of specificity, (b) even if we are dealing with as few as two large factors of production, and (c) without any recourse to the index number problem or to the concept of a wage good.

Assumptions of the Analysis

For purposes of the analysis we shall start out with rather simplified assumptions, considering subsequently the effect of more realistic modifications. In order to keep the number of variables down to manageable proportions we assume only two countries. This involves no loss of generality since the "rest of the world" may always be lumped together as Country II. For the sake of exposition and diagrammatic convenience, only two commodities are considered, labelled respectively "wheat," A, and "watches," B. To accord with the Ohlin assumptions the production functions of each commodity are made the same in both countries and involve only two factors of production identified for convenience as labour (L) and capital (C).[16]

Moreover, by means of a simple device it is possible to avoid detailed consideration of the second country since all of its effects upon the first operate via changes in the price ratio of the two traded commodities.[17] We shall call this price ratio of wheat to watches

---

[16] It might possibly give rise to less confusion if instead of capital the second factor were called land because of the ambiguities involved in the definition of capital. The reader who is bothered by this fact is invited to substitute mentally land for capital in all that follows.

[17] For an example of the use of this device see P. A. Samuelson, "The Gains from International Trade," *Canadian Journal of Economics and Political Science*, May, 1939.

P_a/P_b. It is irrelevant for our argument just why the exchange ratio of the two commodities is different after international trade is established; it is sufficient that it does change.[18]

The effect of international trade upon the shares of the productive factors can now be analysed by varying P_a/P_b as a parameter from its value as determined in the absence of trade, or with a given amount of protection, to its new value after free trade is opened up. Throughout we follow the conventional method of comparative statics, disregarding the process of transition from the old to the new equilibrium. Full employment of both factors is assumed to be realised before and after the change, and each factor is assumed to have perfectly complete physical mobility.[19] Throughout pure competition is assumed. The following symbols are used:

The amount of labour used in producing A............... L_a
The amount of labour used in producing B.............. L_b
The amount of capital used in producing A.............. C_a
The amount of capital used in producing B.............. C_b
The total amount of labour used in producing both A and B L
The total amount of capital used in producing both A and B C
The marginal physical wheat productivity of labor........ MP_{L_a}
The marginal physical wheat productivity of capital....... MP_{C_a}
The marginal physical watch productivity of labor........ MP_{L_b}
The marginal physical watch productivity of capital....... MP_{C_b}

It is assumed that regardless of trade the total amounts of each factor of production remain unchanged. Therefore, we have the following obvious identities:

-----

[18] In the limiting case P_a/P_b would be unchanged. Also, in the classical constant cost case of a large country facing a smaller one, trade may take place, but to an extent insufficient to result in complete specialisation on the part of the large country, and hence P_a/P_b may be unchanged. This exception is touched upon later.

[19] We should like to emphasize that in our argument there is no dependence upon imperfections in the labour market such as form the basis for the Manoilesco type for defense of a tariff. See M. Manoilesco, *The Theory of Protection and International Trade* (1931).

$$L_a + L_b = L \dots \dots \dots \dots \dots \dots (1)$$
$$C_a + C_b = C \dots \dots \dots \dots \dots \dots (2)$$

The production functions relating each good to the inputs of the factors allocated to its production can be written respectively as:

$$A = A \ (L_a, \ C_a) \dots \dots \dots \dots \dots (3)$$
$$B = B \ (L_b, \ C_b) \dots \dots \dots \dots \dots (4)$$

Because we are concerned with proportions and not with the scale of the process, these functions are assumed to be homogeneous of the first order.

It is a well-known condition of equilibrium that the ratio of the marginal productivities of the two factors must be the same in each occupation, because otherwise there would be a transfer from lower to higher levels. Symbolically this can be expressed as follows:[20]

$$\frac{MP_{L_a}}{MP_{C_a}} = \frac{MP_{L_b}}{MP_{C_b}} \dots \dots \dots \dots \dots (5)$$

We are still lacking one condition to make our equilibrium complete. If we add as a known parameter the value of P_a/P_b, that is, the price ratio between the two goods, wheat and watches, all our unknowns will be completely determined: the amounts of each factor of production allocated to the various commodities (L_a, L_b, C_a, C_b), the amounts produced of each good (A, B) and most important for the present investigation, the marginal physical productivities of each factor in terms of each good (MP_{L_a}, MP_{C_a}, MP_{L_b}, MP_{C_b}).

But what is the meaning in terms of all of the above magnitudes of labour's real wage? This is not an easy question to answer if, as is usually true, labour consumes something of both commodities. In principle it is of course possible to determine whether a given individual's real income has gone up or down if one has detailed knowledge of his (ordinal) preference field. But we cannot gather

---

[20] Of course, this holds only if something of both commodities is produced, that is, if trade does not result in complete specialisation. The effect of this qualification is treated below.

such knowledge simply from observation of the price changes which take place. Possibly an index number comparison of the type associated with the names of Pigou, Haberler, Könus, Staehle, Leontief, and others could serve to identify changes in real income. But we shall later show that this is unnecessary. At this point, purely for reasons of exposition, we shall consider the highly restrictive case where labour consumes only one of the commodities, that is, where there is a single wage good. In this case the real wage in terms of that good is an unambiguous indicator of real income[21] because of the proportionality between occupations indicated in condition (5). It is the marginal physical productivity of labour in the production of the wage good.

The effect of international trade upon the real wage (thus defined) could now be determined mathematically by varying P_a/P_b, the price ratio of the two goods, and observing how the marginal physical productivity of labour in the wage good industry is affected. One could perform this purely mathematical computation by differentiating our equilibrium equations with respect to P_a/P_b, treating as variables all the unknowns listed above. The result of this procedure, not shown here because of its purely technical character, would be found to involve a sum of terms of necessarily different sign, and without introducing further economic content into the problem, we would not be able to achieve a definite result, but would be forced, like the older writers, simply to indicate that all things are possible. However, by introducing further economic content of no less generality than theirs, we shall find that definite results can be derived.

THE ELIMINATION OF THE INDEX NUMBER PROBLEM

With the assumptions made so far it is hardly surprising that no more definite results have been reached. For no assumption has as yet been made as to which country is relatively well supplied with

---

[21] It is true that we have been talking about the real wage rate and not about the total amount of real wages, but as we have assumed full employment before and after any change and unvarying total amounts of the factors of production, it follows that the real wage sum will always be proportional to the real wage rate.

capital or with labour. To begin with we make two assumptions. The first is that the country in question is relatively small and has no influence on the terms of trade. Thus, any gain to the country through monopolistic or monopsonistic behaviour is excluded. Secondly, it is assumed that the removal of the duty will not destroy the formerly protected industry, but only force it to contract.

Now in equilibrium the value marginal productivity (expressed in terms of any *numéraire*) must be the same in all occupations, and so must be the wage. Therefore, whatever wage labour receives in the wage good industry it must also receive in any other employment. Moreover, any change in the value marginal productivity and, therefore, the wage rate of labour in the wage good industry must mean a corresponding change in the wage rate in all other employments. It follows that we can tell what will happen to real wages (rates as well as sums) of labour as a whole by investigating what will happen to wages in the wage good industry. Since the relevant value marginal productivity, and hence the wage of labour in the wage good industry, is in terms of the wage good, and since labour gets the same wage in all occupations, a decline of the marginal productivity of labour in the wage good industry means a fall in the real wage rate and the real wage sum of labour as a whole.

In other words, whatever will happen to wages in the wage good industry will happen to labour as a whole. And this answer is independent of whether the wage good will be imported or exported, and can be reached without any discussion of what will happen to prices of the commodities as a consequence of international trade.[22]

Assume, for example, (a) that the country in question is relatively well supplied with capital, and (b) that the proportion of labour to capital is lower in the production of wheat than in the production of watches. There is nothing restrictive about these assumptions because in terms of our previous assumptions one of the countries must be relatively well supplied with a given factor, and through our postponement of the constant cost case for later

---

[22] In connection with a slightly different problem the same point is made by F. Benham, "Taxation and the Relative Prices of Factors of Production," *Economica*, N. S. Vol. 2, 1935, pp. 198–203.

discussion the importance of labour must be greater in the production of one of the commodities. And since the names "wheat" and "watches" are arbitrary, by re-naming the variables all possible cases could be expressed in the formulation given above.

Two alternative cases must now be considered. (1) The good in whose production capital is relatively important (wheat) is also the wage good. (2) The good in whose production labour is relatively important (watches) is the wage good. Each of these possibilities must be considered in turn.

(1) The introduction of trade will shift production in the direction of the good with "comparative advantage." According to the Ohlin analysis—even though he would not employ the previous term—this will be wheat which uses much of the abundant factor. Its production will expand, and part of it will be exported, while watch production will contract, and part of the watch consumption will be satisfied by imports. This shift in production will be accompanied by a transfer of *both* labour and capital from the watch industry to the wheat industry. But by a reduction in the production of watches more labour will be set free than can be re-employed at the same rates in the production of wheat. This is because the amount of capital released, while sufficient to employ a worker in watch production, is insufficient to employ him in wheat growing at the old wage rate. Hence wage rates have to go down in wheat growing, and it follows from the changed factor proportions that the real wage must also decline. It would be clearly incorrect to argue—as one familiar with the orthodox theory of international trade would be tempted to do—that in addition to this decline in productivity due solely to changed factor proportions, there must be added a further loss to the worker *qua* consumer resulting from the inevitable price rise of the exported wage good.

(2) We turn now to the case where watches are the wage good. On the face of it this case would seem to admit only of an ambiguous answer, since any definite conclusion in the productivity sphere would have to confront a necessary fall in the (relative) price of the wage good. Fortunately, that is not so. This case admits of no less definite an answer than the previous one.

The introduction of trade will increase the production of wheat and decrease that of watches. As shown in the previous case, this will entail a movement of both labour and capital. But just as labour has less capital to work with in wheat production than formerly, so does labour now have less capital to work with in the production of watches. This is brought about by the change in relative remunerations of the factors necessary to result in the reabsorption of the otherwise redundant labour supply. Therefore, regardless of the behaviour of consumer's goods prices, the lowering of the proportion of capital to labour in the production of watches must adversely affect the marginal physical productivity of labour there, and hence, along now familiar lines, the real wage.

We see, therefore, that the seemingly opposite cases lead to exactly the same result. *International trade necessarily lowers the real wage of the scarce factor expressed in terms of any good.* It follows that we are now in a position to drop the assumption of a single wage good. For if the real wage declines in terms of every good, real income must suffer regardless of the tastes and expenditure patterns of the labourers as consumers. Not only can we avoid making index number comparisons, but it is also unnecessary to make the assumption of uniform tastes of all workers which such comparisons implicitly presuppose.

DIAGRAMMATICAL TREATMENT

It may be useful to illustrate the above arguments graphically. In Fig. 1 we plot the familiar substitution curve (production possibility or transformation curve) between the two commodities in the given country. Before trade, equilibrium will have taken place at M with a price ratio corresponding to the slope of the tangent there. International trade will change the price ratio of the two goods, and a new equilibrium point may be taken as N with more wheat production, less watch production, and a higher price ratio between wheat and watches. This diagram represents the result of a fairly complicated economic process by which the given fixed amounts of productive factors are optimally allocated between the two commodities in accordance with marginal productivity con-

PROTECTION AND REAL WAGES 347

ditions that guarantee a maximum amount of one commodity for preassigned given amounts of the other. For many international trade problems this "short-circuiting" is an advantage; but it omits the essential features of the present problem, and so we must go back of the substitution curve to the underlying production relations.

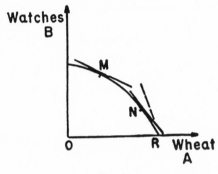

Fig. 1

This is done in Fig. 2 which consists of a modified box diagram long utilised by Edgeworth and Bowley in the study of consumers' behaviour. This rather remarkable diagram enables us to represent the relations between six variables on a two dimensional figure. On the lower horizontal axis is indicated the amount of capital used in the production of wheat. On the left-hand vertical axis is indicated the amount of labour used in the production of wheat. Because the amount of each factor which is not used in the production of wheat must be employed in the production of watches, the upper horizontal axis gives us, reading from right to left, the amount of capital used in the production of watches. Similarly, the right-hand vertical axis, reading downwards, gives us the amount of labour used in the production of watches. The dimensions of the box are, of course, simply those of the unchanging given total amounts of the two productive factors. Any point in the box represents four things: measuring from the lower left-hand corner the amounts of labour and capital used to produce wheat, and measuring from the upper right-hand corner the amounts of labour and capital used in the production of watches.

348   TARIFFS AND THE GAINS FROM TRADE

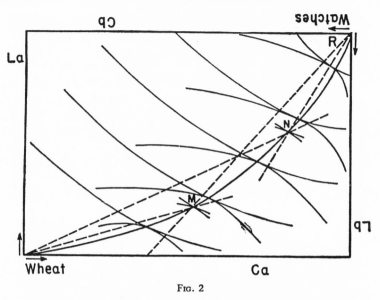

Fɪɢ. 2

Disregarding for the moment the other commodity, watches, it is clear that every point in the box corresponds to a given production of wheat, and hence lies on a uniquely determinable "isoquant" or "equal-product" contour line of the production surface.   There is a one-parameter family of such curves with the shape as indicated by the lines, convex to the lower left-hand corner. Turning now to the production of watches, there also exists a one-parameter family of equal-product curves convex to the upper right-hand corner, and indicated in the diagram by a second family of curves.

We are now in a position to derive the substitution curve.   Any point in the box taken at random corresponds to given amounts of watch and wheat production, but not necessarily to a point on the substitution curve.   Only those points which reflect an optimal allocation of resources according to the marginal ₍ productivity relations stated earlier correspond to points on the substitution or opportunity cost curve.   The locus of points representing optimal positions is clearly given by joining all the points of tangency of the two sets of contour lines. It corresponds geometrically to Edgeworth's *contract curve*, and although the present study does not deal with bargains between contracting parties, we shall retain this descriptive title. If we hold the production of one good constant and thus move along a given isoquant, we will only stop when there is the maximum possible amount of the other good, or when we have reached the highest possible isoquant of the other family. This will be so only at a position of tangency where the ratios of the marginal productivities of the two factors are the same in each line of production.

Under the assumption of "linear and homogeneous" production functions in two inputs, the contract curve must have the shape indicated in our figure. On the contract curve we have indicated points M and N corresponding to the situation before and after trade. It can now be shown graphically how the following somewhat paradoxical statement can be true: even though the proportion of total capital to total labour remains the same in both lines together, nevertheless the introduction of trade lowers the proportion of capital to labour in each line; and the prohibition of trade, as by a tariff, necessarily raises the proportion of capital to labour in each industry. Although it seems intuitively anomalous, it is graphically clear from the diagram that a movement from N to M raises the proportion of capital to labour in watches, the total proportions remaining unchanged as indicated by the box. The proportion of labour to capital in the production of wheat with trade is indicated by the slope of the angle of the dotted line going between N and the wheat origin. A similar dotted line between the same origin and M shows the proportion of labour to capital in the production of wheat after trade. Its being less steep than the other makes it clear that the ratio of capital to labour has increased. Utilising similar dotted lines between the watch origin and the points M and N, it is likewise seen that the abolition of trade increases the proportion of capital to labour in the production of watches.

How can we reconcile the graphical result with our numerical intuition which tells us that when each of two quantities goes up, an average of them cannot remain constant? An examination of the exact relationship between the proportions of capital to labour in each line and the proportions in both at once dispels the paradox. The proportion in both is found to be not a simple average but a weighted arithmetic mean of the proportions in each as indicated by the following identity:

$$\frac{L_a}{L}\frac{C_a}{L_a} + \frac{L_b}{L}\frac{C_b}{L_b} = \frac{C}{L} \dots\dots\dots\dots\dots\dots\dots\dots\dots\dots (6)$$

The weights are simply the proportions of the total labour supply used in the respective industries. The abolition of trade raises the proportion of capital to labour in each line, but at the same time through the reverse operation of the principle of comparative advantage automatically gives more weight to the industry which uses the lesser amount of capital to labour.

Thus, we have shown conclusively that a restriction of trade will increase the proportion of capital to labour in both lines. It follows necessarily that the real wage in terms of each commodity must increase regardless of any movements of prices of the consumer's goods. For within each industry, increasing the capital which co-operates with labour raises the marginal productivity of labour expressed in physical units of that good. Not only are the labourers of that industry better off with respect to that good, but by the equivalence of real wages everywhere (expressed in terms of any good) labour in general is better off in terms of that good. If the real wage in terms of every good increases, we can definitely state that real income has increased. This is one of the few cases in economic analysis where a given change moves all relevant magnitudes in the same direction and obviates the necessity of a difficult, and often indefinite, index number comparison.

Under the assumed conditions—(a) two commodities, (b) produced by two factors of production, and (c) where trade leaves something of both commodities produced but at a new margin— it has been unequivocally demonstrated that the scarce factor must be harmed absolutely. This is in contrast to the accepted doctrine which may be fairly represented as saying that trade *might* conceivably affect adversely the relative share of a factor, but cannot be expected to harm absolutely an important factor of production. Not only is the latter possible, but under the posited conditions it follows necessarily.

THREE OR MORE COMMODITIES

If the above conclusion held only for two commodities, its interest even for theory would be limited. It is of interest to show, therefore, that the introduction of any number of commodities in no way detracts from the validity of our conclusions. Of course, no simple graphical device can be used to portray this because of the increased number of variables.

One method of approaching the problem might be to arrange the commodities in a sequence according to the relative importance of labour in each. This is not unlike the ordering of commodities long used by Mangoldt,[23] Edgeworth, and others to explain which commodities will be imported and which exported when more than two commodities are introduced into the classical theory of comparative advantage. In our case, however, costs are not constant and are not expressible in a single homogeneous unit of a factor or in a given composite factor.

For the present purpose one need not rely upon such a construction, but need only realise that the introduction of trade will increase the production of those commodities which use relatively much of the abundant factor, and will lower the production of the commodities using relatively little of the abundant factor. Accompanying this, there will be the familiar Heckscher-Ohlin tendency towards partial equalisation of factor prices in the two countries, the price of the scarce factor falling in relationship to the price of the abundant factor. By itself this tells us nothing concerning the absolute burden or benefit from trade, but deals only with the effect upon relative shares. We cannot simply infer from this anything concerning the behaviour of absolute shares. For it is not as if international trade leaves the total amount of real national

---

[23] J. Viner, op. cit., p. 458; G. Haberler, op. cit., pp. 136–140.

income unchanged so that the more one factor receives, the less there will be left for the other. On the contrary, it has been shown elsewhere that trade must increase the national income under the conditions here postulated.

It is nevertheless true that the introduction of trade will harm absolutely the scarce factor of production. To demonstrate this we must recall the fact that at the new higher relative price of capital to labour there will inevitably be a *relative* substitution of labour for capital *in each line* of production. In exactly the same way a restriction upon trade will raise the price of the scarce factor, labour, relative to the abundant factor, capital. There is nothing paradoxical in the fact that the ratio of capital to labour can increase in every line, while the ratio of total capital to total labour remains constant. The explanation given in the two commodity case whereby the weights in the arithmetic mean change in an appropriate fashion holds without modification when there are any number of commodities.

It is now a simple matter to show that the physical marginal productivity of labour in each line must increase, and because of the equalisation of wages in all lines, expressed in terms of any commodity, it immediately follows that restriction of trade increases the real wage of workers expressed in terms of each and every commodity. This obviates the necessity for any index number comparison or for any consideration of the worsening of the terms of trade.

THE CASE OF COMPLETE SPECIALISATION

The reader of the above argument will have realised that its remarkable simplicity springs from the fact that we may infer the real wage of workers in terms of a given good from the real marginal physical productivity of those workers who produce that good. This requires that before and after trade some finite amount, however small, be produced of every good. In a world where technological conditions are conducive towards the maintenance of the state of pure competition implicit in all our previous argument, and where regional factor endowments are not too dissimilar this is perhaps not too unrealistic an assumption. However, it is still desirable to see what remains of the argument when this assumption is dropped. This is even more so because in the course of the argument it will be shown that the classical theory was not so much incorrect as limited in scope.

Provided that costs are not constant, and that something of both goods was previously consumed, price changes brought about by international trade will at first shift the margin of production, but will still leave some production of both commodities. At one crucial price ratio corresponding to the slope of the tangent at *R* in Fig. 1 the production of one of the commodities will cease completely, and further changes will not alter the specialisation. Up until the critical price ratio is reached, the introduction of trade worsens the position of labour according to the previous arguments. But what happens after this critical price ratio?

There is no essential loss of generality in considering the two commodity case. For the commodity which is still produced, the real wage is determined as before by the physical productivity of the workers in that line. Up until the critical price ratio at which complete specialisation takes place, the scarce labour factors have been shown to lose. Beyond this critical price ratio their physical productivities remain unchanged. It is clear, therefore, that the real wage in terms of the export good using little labour is necessarily harmed by the introduction of trade.

With respect to the imported commodity the matter is more complicated, and the final result is indeterminate. Up to the critical price ratio we know that the real wage in terms of this commodity must fall. But after specialisation, the level of real wages can no longer be determined by the productivity of workers in this line since there are no such workers. One cannot avoid bringing into the analysis the price ratio between the two consumers' goods, that is, the terms of trade. Given this price ratio, it is possible to convert real wages in terms of one commodity into real wages in terms of the other. It becomes apparent that beyond the critical point the real wage in terms of the non-produced, imported good must begin to increase. This is to be balanced against the earlier loss of real wages in terms of this same good taking place before the critical point was reached. Whether the result will be on balance favourable or unfavourable cannot possibly be determined on *a priori* grounds, but rests upon the technological and economic features of the countries in question. Even if in a limited number of cases we could determine that the real wage in terms of the imported good would increase, there would still be involved a problem of weighing against this the demonstrated loss in real wages expressed in terms of the good in which the country has a comparative advantage. Here again the final result would be indeterminate, although in favourable cases an index number comparison might be decisive.

Applying this same line of reasoning to the constant cost case of the classical theory of international trade, it is seen that theirs is one of the special unambiguous cases. Either a single factor of production or a never varying composite dose of factors is assumed. Because of constant costs the slightest change in the price ratio of the goods will lead instantaneously to complete specialisation. There results no shifting of the proportions of the factors, and hence no deterioration of wages in terms of either good. On the contrary, in terms of the imported good there must be an improvement in real wages with a consequent increase in real income. This is made intuitively obvious from the consideration that trade necessarily increases the real income of a country, and in the classical case the proportion of income going to the respective factors cannot be changed by trade. It is the latter feature of the classical theory which constitutes one of its important short-comings.

MORE THAN TWO FACTORS

One by one we have been able to drop our various restrictive assumptions with only slight modifications of results. Still there remains the problem of introducing into the analysis more than two productive factors. Unfortunately, this entails more serious consequences.

In the first place, the definiteness of the Heckscher-Ohlin theorem begins to fade. With three or more factors of production it is certainly not necessary that the result of trade is to make the ratios of factor prices in the respective countries more closely approach unity. Some may do so, but others may diverge depending upon complicated patterns of complementarity and competitiveness.[24] Whether on balance the movement towards equalisation exceeds the tendency towards diversification is not a meaningful question until a non-arbitrary method of weighting these changes is specified. Furthermore, even the concepts of scarce and abundant factors lose their sharpness of definition.

The fact that the Heckscher-Ohlin theorem breaks down when many factors of production are involved affords an explanation of its failure to account for the facts *if the production functions in the two countries differ, or if the factors of production of different countries are not identical.* By appropriate terminological conventions it is always possible to attribute differences in the production functions to differences in amounts of some factors of production (knowledge, available free factors, etc.). Similarly, if the factors of production of different countries are regarded as non-comparable and incommensurable,[25] this can be classified as an extreme case of factor disproportionality, but there must be more than two factors. We conclude, therefore, that the Heckscher-Ohlin theorem does not necessarily hold in the case of constant costs or multiple factors of production.

It does not follow that our results stand and fall with the Hecksher-Ohlin theorem. Our analysis neglected the other country completely. If factors of production are not comparable between countries, or if production functions differ, nevertheless, so long as

---

[24] See Ohlin, op. cit., pp. 96–105 and passim. [In 1946 the junior author, P. A. S., changed his mind on this point, coming to believe that *so long as something of each good is produced in every region, the Ohlin analysis asserts complete equalization of all factor prices, regardless of the number of commodities, regions, or factors.*]

[25] If the extreme classical assumption of immobility of labour between countries were valid, then over time the working populations of the various countries would become differentiated culturally, genetically, and in the limit cease to be of the same species. But those in the narrower classical tradition are least in a position to bring this up as an argument against the Heckscher-Ohlin theory, for in expositing the comparative cost doctrine they repeatedly (and sometimes unnecessarily) compare labour (costs, productivities, hierarchies, etc.) in various countries.

356   TARIFFS AND THE GAINS FROM TRADE

the country has only two factors, international trade would necessarily affect the real wage of a factor in the same direction as its relative remuneration.[26] The only loss to our analysis would be the possibility of labelling the factor which is harmed as the "scarce" (relative to the other country) one.

However, we must admit that three or more factors of production within a single country do seriously modify the inevitability of our conclusions. It is not only that the relatively scarce factor can be defined only circularly as the one whose price falls most after trade, but even if we do know the behaviour of relative factor prices, i.e. relative shares in the national income, it seems that we cannot infer unambiguously that the physical marginal productivities move in the same direction. Even though these continue to depend only upon the proportions of the factors in the respective industry, diverse patterns of complementarity and competitiveness emerge as possibilities. It is outside the scope of the present paper to attempt a catalogue of the various conceivable permutations and combinations.

This lack of definiteness in the more complex case is typical of attempts to go beyond the level of abstraction current in economic theory. We have resisted the temptation to lump together diverse factors into two composite factors and thereby achieve the appearance of versimilitude, although others may care to do so for some purpose.

CONCLUSION

We have shown that there is a grain of truth in the pauper labour type of argument for protection. Thus, in Australia, where land may perhaps be said to be abundant relative to labour, protection might possibly raise the real income of labour.[27] The same

---

[26] This is in contrast to the problem of the effect of a technological innovation to which Professor Haberler (op. cit., p. 195) has compared the effects of trade: Technological change shifts the production function, and no inferences concerning the new marginal productivity relationships are possible. As we have shown, trade leads to definite effects.

[27] See D. B. Copland, "A Neglected Phase of Tariff Controversy," *Quarterly Journal of Economics*, 1931, pp. 289–308; K. L. Anderson, "Protection and the

may have been true in colonial America. It does not follow that the American working man to-day would be better off if trade with, say, the tropics were cut off, because land suitable for growing coffee, rubber, and bananas is even scarcer in America than is labour. The bearing of the many factor case will be obvious.

We are anxious to point out that even in the two factor case our argument provides no political ammunition for the 'protectionist. For if effects on the terms of trade can be disregarded, it has been shown that the harm which free trade inflicts upon one factor of production is necessarily less than the gain to the other. Hence, it is always possible to bribe the suffering factor by subsidy or other redistributive devices so as to leave all factors better off as a result of trade.[28]

Historical Situation: Australia," *Quarterly Journal of Economics*, November, 1938, pp. 86–104; M. C. Samuelson, op. cit., pp. 143–149.

[28] Viner, op. cit., p. 534; P. A. Samuelson, op. cit., p. 204.

Part III

Refinements, Extensions, and Verifications

THE JOURNAL OF
POLITICAL ECONOMY

Volume LVII	FEBRUARY 1949	*Number 1*

TARIFFS, THE TERMS OF TRADE, AND THE DISTRIBU-
TION OF NATIONAL INCOME

LLOYD A. METZLER

I

THE classical concept of the gains from international trade was essentially a concept of increased productivity. The gains from trade, in the classical view, consisted of an increased output of all goods and services, made possible through specialization and exchange. In other words, the classical "law of comparative advantage" demonstrated that, with a given amount of productive resources in every country, it was possible, by an interchange of goods, for all countries to consume more of all commodities. In addition to its description of the potential gains from trade, the classical theory, from the time of John Stuart Mill, also gave an excellent account of how these gains are actually divided among different countries. Stated more broadly, the theory of reciprocal demand, which was added to the classical doctrine by Mill, indicated how international exchange affects the distribution of world income among countries.[1] With its strong emphasis upon productivity and upon

the division of the gains from trade between different countries, however, the classical doctrine, as well as the subsequent theoretical work of neoclassical economists, seriously neglected the closely related problem of how international trade affects the division of income within each country among the various factors of production.[2] The classical theory and its neoclassical refinements could show well enough how a country, considered as a unit, tends to benefit from specialization and trade; but these doctrines had very little to say about how the gains of real income within each country are divided among labor, capital, and land.[3]

[2] In view of the fact that the marginal-productivity theory of distribution did not appear until late in the nineteenth century and in view, further, of the generally recognized opinion that even the present theory of distribution has many deficiencies, it is perhaps not surprising that the influence of international trade upon the distribution of income was inadequately discussed by the classical economists. But, even with due allowances for the backward state of distribution theory, the lag in the development of this aspect of international trade was surprisingly long.

[1] J. S. Mill, *Essays on Some Unsettled Questions of Political Economy* (1844), Essay I.

[3] Although the question of income distribution arose early in the nineteenth century in the English

The division of the gains from trade among the different factors of production or, what amounts to substantially the same thing, the influence of international trade upon the distribution of national income is a subject which has received an adequate theoretical treatment only in comparatively recent times. The pioneer works in this branch of international economics were, of course, the studies which E. F. Heckscher[4] and B. Ohlin[5] made during the years between the two world wars. It is a curious fact that, just as the classical discussion of the terms of trade had neglected or left unsolved the related problem of the distribution of income, so the more recent contributions to the study of income distribution have neglected the complications arising out of changes in the terms of trade. Indeed, at the very beginning of his article Heckscher asserted that a discussion of the gains from trade has no relevance to the problem of income distribution. "No attention is paid," he said, "to the advantages one particular country may achieve, by means of protection, in altering the relation between supply and demand of a certain commodity and thereby wholly or partly letting the 'foreigner pay the duty'; since this problem has been discussed so widely, and since it is

not relevant in the present connection, it seems unnecessary to discuss it here."[6] In the historical development of the theory of international trade, questions of income distribution have thus been rather sharply separated from questions of productivity and of gains or losses to a country as a whole.

In view of this distinct cleavage in the purely theoretical aspects of international trade, it is not surprising that the practical application of economic theory to the particular problem of tariffs has suffered from a similar lack of integration. On the one hand, the concept of reciprocal demand has been employed to demonstrate how tariffs may improve a country's terms of trade—i.e., reduce the prices it pays for its imports relative to the prices it receives for its exports—but little attempt has been made to employ this same concept in showing how the resulting increase of real income is divided among the different factors of production. Indeed, there has at times been a tendency in the classical theory to deny that tariffs exert any influence at all upon the distribution of national income.[7] On the other hand, when a theory of the influence of international trade upon the distribution of income was finally developed, this theory was based in part, as the preceding quotation from Heckscher

---

controversy over the Corn Laws, the results of the controversy in this respect were inconclusive and had no permanent influence on the theory of international trade. Cf., however, C. F. Bastable, *The Theory of International Trade* (London: Macmillan & Co., Ltd., 1903), chap. vi.

[4] "Utrikhandelns verkan på inkomstfördelningen" ["The Influence of Foreign Trade on the Distribution of Income"], *Ekonomisk Tidskrift*, (1919), Part II, 1–32. Subsequent references to this paper have been taken from a translation into English prepared by Professor and Mrs. Svend Laursen and to be published shortly in the American Economic Association's "Readings in International Trade and Finance."

[5] *Interregional and International Trade* (Cambridge, Mass., 1933), chap. ii and *passim*.

[6] Heckscher, *op. cit.*, p. 2.

[7] The following statement by Taussig illustrates the point: "The general proposition that a high rate of wages is a result of high productiveness of industry is simple and undeniable. . . . Beyond doubt there remain questions which are more difficult. Just how and through what channel or mechanism does high productivity lead to the high wages? And what determines the share of the total product, be that great or small, which shall go to the laborer, the employer, the owner of capital, the owner of land? But these questions, the most important and perhaps the most complex in the field of economics, *lie quite outside the tariff controversy* . . . "(quoted from *Free Trade, the Tariff, and Reciprocity* [New York, 1920], p. 54). Italics added.

demonstrates, upon the assumption that the influence of tariffs upon the terms of trade can be neglected. But, despite this historical separation of two important aspects of tariff theory, it is easily shown that changes in a country's terms of trade are closely related in a number of ways to changes in the distribution of its national income. It is the purpose of the present paper to show some of the relations between these two distinct and heretofore largely independent branches of tariff theory. Since Heckscher's work is basic to the later studies of tariffs and income distribution, it seems advisable to present a brief summary of his principal conclusions.

Heckscher began his discussion, as did the classical economists, with the assertion that trade between countries depends upon the law of comparative advantage, i.e., upon the fact that the ratio of the cost of production of two commodities is different in one country from the corresponding cost ratio in another. Unlike the classical economists, however, Heckscher placed great emphasis upon the way in which the supplies of various factors of production affect comparative costs. He argued, in particular, that comparative costs in one country differ from those in another primarily because the relative degree of scarcity of some factors of production differs between countries and because different commodities require varying proportions of the factors of production.[8] Suppose, for example, that one country, Alpha, has a large amount of land per worker as compared with another country, Beta. The ratio of rent to wage rates will then be lower in Alpha than in Beta, since land in the former country will be used to the point where its marginal product is relatively small. Consider, now, the

[8] Heckscher, *op. cit.*, p. 6.

comparative costs in the two countries of producing two products, wheat and textiles. Since wheat requires a larger amount of land per worker than textiles do, the money cost of producing a unit of wheat, relative to the cost of producing a unit of textiles, will be lower in Alpha than in Beta. In other words, Alpha will have a comparative advantage in wheat, the product requiring relatively large amounts of its abundant factor, while Beta will have a comparative advantage in textiles.

It is a simple step from these basic propositions concerning comparative advantage to the final conclusions of Heckscher with respect to the distribution of income. Suppose that Alpha and Beta are initially isolated and self-sufficient but that trade is finally opened up between the two countries. Alpha, the low-rent country, will then export wheat and Beta, where rents are comparatively high and wages low, will export textiles. This exchange of goods has a definite and predictable influence upon the demand for land and labor in the two countries. In each country the demand for factors of production is increased in the export industry and reduced in the industry competing with imports; but, as Heckscher pointed out, the proportions in which the factors of production are required in the export industry are not exactly the same as the proportions in which they are released by the industry competing with imports. In the present illustration the expansion of the wheat industry in Alpha requires, at prevailing wages and rents, a small number of workers per acre of land, while the contraction of the textile industry, under the pressure of competition from abroad, releases a relatively large number of workers and only a small amount of land. The shift of resources from textiles to wheat thus increases the relative scarcity of land in Alpha, the country which initially had a comparatively large supply of that factor. Wages per unit of labor accordingly fall in Alpha, relative to rent per unit of land. In other words, the shift in production which was brought about by international trade has given land, the relatively abundant factor in Alpha, a larger share of the total product. An analogous argument could easily be presented—and, indeed, has been presented both by Heckscher and, later, by Ohlin—to show that in Beta, where land is relatively scarce and labor abundant, international trade increases wage rates relative to rents. The central feature of the Heckscher-Ohlin analysis is thus the proposition that international trade, by increasing the demand for each country's abundant factors, tends to equalize the relative returns to the factors of production in different countries.[9]

[9] Whether international trade achieves a *complete* or only a *partial* equalization of relative and absolute factor returns in different countries has been a controversial issue. Heckscher, working with a simple model in which the coefficients of production were fixed, argued that the equalization would be complete in both an absolute and a relative sense. Thus, on p. 15 of the article previously cited, he said: "With fixed supplies of the factors of production and the same technique of production in all countries, we have seen that the final effect of international trade, with unimportant reservations, is the equalization of the *relative* prices of the factors of production. We must next inquire whether the equalization will be *absolute* as well as *relative*, i.e., whether rent, wages and interest for the same qualities of the factors of production will amount to the same real return in all countries. This proposition has not thus far been demonstrated, but it is an inescapable consequence of trade." If the coefficients of production were variable, on the other hand, Heckscher believed that substitutions of one factor for another would lead to different techniques of production and hence to differences in relative and absolute factor returns between countries (*ibid.*, p. 16). It was this latter conclusion, rather than the former one, which was subsequently adopted and elaborated by Ohlin and which became more or less the generally accepted view (*op. cit.*, pp. 37–39). Samuelson, however, in a recent study prepared independently of Heckscher's

With this brief introduction, we may now examine the relation of the Heckscher-Ohlin theory to the tariff problem. In view of the tendency of international trade to equalize relative factor returns among different countries, it might seem that the owners of a factor of production which is relatively scarce in a given country would have a strong interest in restricting international trade; for by so doing they could preserve the relative scarcity which might otherwise be threatened by competition from abroad. In a country with an abundant supply of land and a limited supply of labor, for example, the working class might well benefit by tariffs on manufactured goods. Superficially at least, the Heckscher-Ohlin analysis lends support to the pauper-labor argument for tariffs.

Against this view, it may be objected that the conclusions with regard to the influence of trade upon the distribution of national income take account only of the *relative* position of a particular factor of production and make no allowance for the fact that the *absolute* return of the scarce factor may deteriorate even when its relative position improves. Tariffs interfere with the allocation of resources, and, if the real income of an entire nation is thus reduced by protective duties, it may be small compensation to the scarce factor that it now obtains a larger share of the reduced total. Fifty per cent of a

work, has shown that the equalization of relative and absolute returns may be complete even when account is taken of factor substitutions. In other words, Heckscher's first conclusion—i.e., the conclusion that equalization is *complete*—is applicable even to the case of variable coefficients of production (P. A. Samuelson, "International Trade and the Equalization of Factor Prices," *Economic Journal*, LVIII [June, 1948], 163–84). This suggests that the theory of international trade might have been advanced considerably, in the English-speaking world at any rate, by an earlier translation of Heckscher's pioneer article.

national income of 75 is clearly worse than 40 per cent of a national income of 100.[10] But this possibility of a divergence in the movements of *real* and *relative* returns need not detain us further; for Stolper and Samuelson, in a study which forms a sequel to the works of Heckscher and Ohlin, have shown that the real return and the relative return of a particular factor of production are likely to move in the same direction.[11] In other words, if a tariff increases the share of the national income accruing to the working class, it will also improve the workers' standard of living, and conversely. According to the Stolper-Samuelson argument, a country with a comparatively small labor supply could thus increase its real wage rate by means of protection, even though national income as a whole were thereby diminished. To use a common expression, the workers would get not merely a larger share of a smaller pie but a share which was larger, in absolute magnitude, than their previous smaller share of a larger pie. The detrimental effects of the tariff would be shifted entirely upon the country's "abundant" factors of production.

These results follow directly from two assumptions. The first is that a tariff causes factors of production to be shifted from export industries to industries competing with imports. If labor, as before, is taken to be the country's relatively scarce and high-cost factor of production, it follows from the Heckscher-Ohlin conclusions that the export industries will be those requiring a comparatively small amount of labor in relation to other factors, while the industries

[10] Unless conspicuous consumption and social standing are more important than the absolute standard of living.

[11] W. F. Stolper and P. A. Samuelson, "Protection and Real Wages," *Review of Economic Studies*, IX (1941), 58–73.

competing with imports will require a large proportion of labor to other factors. In the absence of changes in factor prices, the shift of resources brought about by a tariff accordingly leads to a scarcity of labor and an excess supply of land and other factors. Wage rates rise relative to rents, and in all industries a substitution of land for labor occurs. This brings us to the second fundamental assumption, namely, that the marginal physical productivity of a given factor in any industry depends exclusively upon the proportion of that factor to the other factors of production. More explicitly, it is assumed that the marginal product of a factor declines as the ratio of that factor to others in a particular industry is increased. Stolper and Samuelson show that, when wages rise relative to rents, the resulting substitution of land for labor causes the ratio of labor to land to decline in all industries. To put the matter another way, the surplus of land and scarcity of labor arising from the shift of resources from exports to industries competing with imports can be eliminated only if there is a reduction, in all industries, in the ratio of labor to land. But if this occurs, then, according to our second assumption, the marginal product of labor must have increased in all industries, compared with the former position of equilibrium. If competitive conditions prevail or if the degree of monopoly is about the same in one industry as in another, it follows that the real wage rate must have increased, regardless of whether this real return is measured in export goods or in the commodities of the industries competing with imports.

Although this conclusion concerning the influence of tariffs upon real wages represented a definite improvement in the theory of tariffs, a number of ques-

6 LLOYD A. METZLER

tions still remained unanswered. Like the earlier works on the subject, the later study by Stolper and Samuelson made no allowance for changes in the terms of trade. The rigid separation between the classical theory of the gains from trade and the modern theory of the distribution of income has thus continued to exist even in the most recent contribution to the subject. This naturally raises the question of whether modifications in the existing theory of tariffs are required if changes in the terms of trade and in the distribution of income are considered simultaneously. The classical theory of the gains from trade demonstrated that, under certain conditions of international demand, a country could increase the external purchasing power of its exports by means of tariffs on imports and that, if this favorable movement in its terms of trade were sufficiently large, the real income of the country imposing the tariff might be increased despite the unfavorable effects of the tariff upon the allocation of resources. Now, since Stolper and Samuelson assumed that a country's external terms of trade were unaffected by a tariff, they were actually considering the least favorable case possible with respect to the real income of the country imposing the duty; the tariff, in the Stolper-Samuelson argument, interfered with the allocation of resources without bringing about any offsetting favorable movement in the terms of trade. Real income of the country as a whole was therefore unambiguously reduced by the import duty.

Let us consider, for a moment, a more favorable case. Suppose that a particular country's exports and imports are important influences on world markets and that a tariff reduces the external prices of imports, relative to the prices of exports, to such an extent that real income

for the country as a whole is clearly increased. How does this alter the conclusions summarized above concerning real and relative wage rates? Assuming, as before, that the country has a scarcity of labor and therefore imports commodities requiring a large amount of labor, it might appear at first glance that the tariff would increase real wages, perhaps to a considerable extent; for, if the real as well as the relative returns of labor are increased by a tariff even when the duty reduces real income of the country as a whole (the Stolper-Samuelson case), it might seem that the rise in real wages would be even greater if real income as a whole were increased. To return to our previous analogy, it would surely seem better for labor to receive a larger share of an increasing pie than to receive a larger share of a diminishing pie. Although this argument seems plausible, it is actually misleading, for the improvement in terms of trade affects not only real income as a whole but also the degree of scarcity of the so-called "scarce" factors. Paradoxical as it may seem, when changes in the terms of trade are taken into consideration, tariffs or other impediments to imports do not always preserve or increase the scarcity of the scarce factors of production. Under some conditions of international demand the industries competing with imports and the scarce factors of production, which are usually required in large amounts in such industries, may benefit from free trade and suffer from protection.

The precise conditions of international demand required to bring about such an unexpected result are described in Section II. The argument is presented by means of the familiar Mill-Marshall schedules of reciprocal demand.[12]

[12] The reader will recognize that in adopting this method I have not added anything essentially new

II

Whether a tariff injures or benefits a country's scarce factors of production depends largely upon how it affects the output of exports and of commodities competing with imports. If output expands in the industries competing with imports and contracts in the export industries, the increased demand for scarce factors of production in the expanding industries will normally exceed the supplies made available in the contracting export industries; and, as Stolper and Samuelson have shown, the real returns as well as the relative shares of the scarce factors in the national income will thus be increased. In a large part of the nontechnical literature dealing with tariffs, and even in some of the technical literature, a shift of this sort is normally taken for granted; indeed, it is frequently regarded almost as a truism that tariffs injure export industries and benefit industries competing with imports. Nevertheless, when both primary and secondary price changes are taken into consideration, this is by no means a self-evident proposition. To be sure, the tariff itself is the cause of a direct increase in the domestic prices of imports over and above world prices, and this constitutes an immediate benefit to the industries competing with imports. But, on the other hand, the tariff is also the cause of a series of events which tend to reduce the world prices of the country's imports relative to the prices of its exports—i.e., to improve the terms of trade—and this secondary reduction of world prices of

to the well-known classical technique. My purpose, rather, is to apply this technique to a problem which was seldom discussed and never strongly emphasized in the classical literature. In doing this, I have made particular use of the classical theory in the form in which it was expounded by A. P. Lerner ("The Symmetry between Import and Export Taxes," *Economica*, III [new ser., 1936], 308–13).

imports relative to exports may more than offset the initial primary increase.

Now it is reasonable to suppose that resources will not be permanently shifted from the export industries to the industries competing with imports unless the net effect of all primary and secondary price changes is an increase in the domestic prices of imports (including tariffs) relative to the domestic prices of exports. Whether a tariff increases or reduces the real and relative returns of the scarce factors, therefore, depends upon the magnitude of the favorable movement in the terms of trade, compared with the size of the tariff. If the former is greater than the latter, the final effect of the tariff will be a reduction of the domestic prices of imports relative to the prices of exports, and resources will accordingly be shifted from industries competing with imports to the export industries. In other words, the industries producing commodities for export will expand, after tariffs are imposed, while industries competing with imports will contract, an outcome diametrically opposite to the usual expectation. Suppose, for example, that the ratio of the world prices of a country's imports to the world prices of its exports is initially taken to be $1:1$. Suppose, now, that a tariff of 50 per cent ad valorem is placed upon all imports and that, as a result of the ensuing reduced demand for imports, the ratio, in world prices exclusive of tariffs, of import prices to export prices falls to $1:2$. The domestic price ratio, which differs from the world price ratio by the amount of the tariff, will then be $1.5:2$, compared with $1:1$ before the tariff was imposed. The tariff has thus reduced the domestic prices of imports relative to the prices of exports, and a transfer of resources from the "protected" industries to the export indus-

8   LLOYD A. METZLER

tries may accordingly be anticipated. Under these circumstances the effects of the tariff upon the distribution of income are exactly opposite to the conclusions reached by Stolper and Samuelson; the scarce factor of production, i.e., the factor relatively most important in the industries competing with imports, suffers both a relative decline in its share of the national income and an absolute decline in its real return. The most important factor of production in the export industries, on the other hand, enjoys both a

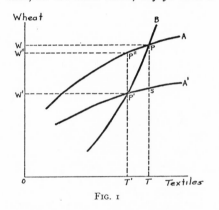

FIG. 1

relative and an absolute increase of income.

The magnitude of the favorable movement of the terms of trade which occurs when tariffs are imposed obviously depends upon conditions of international demand in a way that has been familiar to all economists at least since the time of Mill. It is therefore appropriate to state the argument in terms of the Mill-Marshall equations of reciprocal demand. As before, I shall assume that there are two countries—Alpha and Beta—producing two commodities—wheat and textiles—and that, for the reasons discussed above, Alpha has a comparative advantage in the production of wheat, while Beta has an advantage in textiles. In

Figure 1, the curves A and B represent the reciprocal demand schedules of the two countries, Alpha and Beta, for imported textiles and wheat, respectively, under conditions of free trade.[13] Equilibrium is established at the point P, which implies that Alpha imports an amount OT of textiles in exchange for OW of wheat. Suppose, now, that Alpha imposes an ad valorem duty of 50 per cent upon imported textiles. If we neglect for a moment the effects of the spending of the proceeds of the tariff by the government of Alpha, it is clear that the initial effect of the tariff is to reduce the demand schedule facing the exporters of textiles in Beta from A to A'. In other words, textile importers in Alpha will now be willing to give to the exporters in Beta only TS units of wheat for OT of textiles; a money value equal to the additional amount, SP, which citizens of Alpha formerly gave to Beta, now goes to the Alpha government as a duty. This means that SP is 50 per cent of TS or that TS is two-thirds of TP, and similarly for any other point, such as P', on the new demand schedule.

After the tariff has been imposed, the new equilibrium in terms of quantities actually traded is at P', at which point OW' units of wheat are exported by Alpha and OT' units of textiles are imported. Unless B is a straight line from the origin, which implies that the demand in Beta for the exports of Alpha is infinitely elastic, it is obvious from Figure 1 that the tariff will improve the

[13] In all the figures the reciprocal demand schedules are assumed to depend not only upon conditions of demand but also upon conditions of production. The elasticity of a given reciprocal demand schedule is thus a combined result of substitutions on the part of consumers and shifts of resources on the part of producers (see W. W. Leontief, "The Use of Indifference Curves in the Analysis of Foreign Trade," *Quarterly Journal of Economics*, XLVII [1933], 493–503).

terms of trade of Alpha. The fraction OT'/OW' is clearly larger than OT/OW, which means that Alpha obtains more units of textiles for a given amount of wheat than was true under free trade. Or, to put the matter another way, the world price of textiles, exclusive of the tariff, has fallen, relative to the world price of wheat. The bargaining position of Alpha, the country imposing the tariff, is thus improved. Such an improvement in Alpha's terms of trade is, of course, completely explained by the classical theory of international trade and would not need to be considered further except for its influence upon the distribution of income. In order to see how the tariff has affected the distribution of income in Alpha, we must look at domestic prices rather than at world prices. This means that the tariff must be added to the world price of textiles. Measured in terms of their export commodity, the total outlay of the residents of Alpha for imported textiles, including their outlay for the tariff, is not OW', in Figure 1, but OW''', an amount 50 per cent greater than OW'. In other words, in terms of value actually expended, the residents of Alpha are giving up the equivalent of OW''' units of wheat for OT' units of textiles; the domestic ratio of exchange is therefore given by the fraction OT'/OW'''. Now, since OT'/OW''' is less than OT/OW in Figure 1, it is obvious that, with the schedules of reciprocal demand there assumed, the tariff has caused the domestic price of textiles in Alpha to rise, relative to the price of wheat; land and labor are therefore shifted from wheat to textile production; and the relative share of labor in the national income, as well as the real wage rate, is increased.

It is easily shown that this conclusion is valid for reciprocal demand schedules other than those depicted in Figure 1, as

long as the demand of Beta for the products of Alpha is elastic. The foregoing argument may therefore be generalized as follows: If the world demand for a country's exports is elastic and if we neglect the effects of government expenditures on the demand for imports, (1) a tariff always increases the domestic prices of imports relative to the prices of exports; (2) the improvement in the terms of trade is not sufficient, in this case, to offset the tariff itself; (3) the protected industries become more profit-

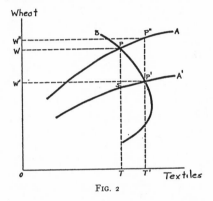

FIG. 2

able, relative to the export industries; (4) resources are shifted from the latter to the former; and (5) the real returns to the country's scarce factors of production, as well as these factors' share in the national income, are increased. The Stolper-Samuelson conclusion is thus valid, even when changes in the terms of trade are taken into account, as long as the demand for exports is elastic.

When the demand for exports is inelastic, the conclusions of the last paragraph must be reversed. This situation is depicted in Figure 2, where the demand of Beta for the product of Alpha is assumed to be inelastic at the equilibrium point, P. In other words, in the neighborhood of P the residents of Beta are willing to give up decreasing amounts of textiles in exchange for an increasing amount of wheat. The notation is the same as in Figure 1. The original equilibrium is at P; but, after the tariff is imposed, the point of balanced trade moves to P', at which point Alpha gives up OW' units of wheat in exchange for OT' units of textiles. As before, the terms of trade move in favor of Alpha. Indeed, in the present example a greater amount of textiles is obtained for a smaller amount of wheat, and the favorable movement in the terms of trade of Alpha is now so great that the domestic price of textiles, including the tariff, is lower, relative to the price of wheat, than it was before the tariff was imposed. This is shown in Figure 2 by the fact that OT'/OW'' is greater than OT/OW.

When the demand for a country's exports is inelastic, the foregoing argument shows that a tariff, far from protecting the industries competing with imports, may actually make these industries worse off than under free trade. In Figure 2, for example, the tariff on textile imports into Alpha reduces the domestic price of textiles, relative to the price of wheat, and leads to a shift of resources in Alpha from the textile industry to the wheat industry. This result is, of course, well known from the classical and neoclassical theories of international trade; but, so far as I am aware, its implications for the distribution of income have never been fully discussed. Figure 2 implies that, when the demand for a country's exports is inelastic, the scarce factors of production—those required in comparatively large amounts in the import industries—actually suffer both a relative and an absolute decline in income when tariffs are increased. Although it seems paradoxical, the scarce factors of production and the industries competing

with imports, under the conditions of Figure 2, actually achieve economic gains from free trade and suffer losses from protection. In other words, if labor is the scarce factor of production and the standard of living is therefore high, a country is not likely to be able, by means of tariffs, to protect its workers from the competition of "cheap foreign labor" unless the demand for its exports is elastic. Some of the implications of this conclusion for producers of primary products who are attempting to industrialize by means of tariffs are discussed in Section III.

Nothing has been said, as yet, about how the government which imposes import duties disposes of the resultant revenue. In this respect the preceding discussion of Figures 1 and 2 is deficient, for the manner in which the government revenues are spent will obviously influence the reciprocal demand schedule of the country introducing the tariffs. If the customs revenues are used in part to purchase imported goods, for example, the reciprocal demand schedule of Alpha will not fall from A to A' but will lie somewhere between these two curves. In the classical discussion of this question two limiting examples were usually considered: the customs revenues were assumed to be spent either entirely upon the export goods of the taxing country or entirely upon imports.[14] The reader will no doubt have recognized that Figures 1 and 2 belong to the first of these alternatives. No part of the tariff proceeds, in these two illustrations, is spent on imported goods; for, if it were, the reciprocal demand schedule would not fall, as assumed in the figures, by the full amount of the tariff. Moreover, it is easy to see

[14] See, e.g., A. Marshall, *Money, Credit, and Commerce* (London, Macmillan & Co., Ltd., 1929), pp. 344-48.

that both diagrams implicitly assume the full proceeds of the tariffs to be spent on goods formerly exported from Alpha. Thus at the new equilibrium point, P', Alpha exports OW' of wheat to T. The equilibrium point, P', however, is stated in world prices, and this equilibrium corresponds to a domestic ratio of exchange in Alpha, including tariffs, of OT' units of textiles for OW''' units of wheat. In other words, at the new domestic price ratio, exporters in Alpha offer OW''' units of wheat, an amount which exceeds the purchases of wheat in Beta by $W'W'''$. The supply of wheat is thus not equal to the demand unless this excess supply is purchased by the government of Alpha. But the excess supply of wheat, $W'W'''$, is simply the amount of duties collected by the government of Alpha, measured in the export product of that country. Figures 1 and 2 are thus implicitly based upon the assumption that the tariff-imposing country uses the entire proceeds of the tariff to purchase goods from its own exporters.

Such an assumption is clearly unrealistic. It would be more reasonable to suppose that the purchasing power acquired through customs duties is divided in some manner between the purchase of domestic goods and the purchase of imports. Before considering this intermediate case, however, it may be useful, following the Marshallian tradition, to go from the one extreme, at which customs revenues are used entirely in the purchase of the tariff-imposing country's export product, to the other extreme, at which the customs revenues are devoted entirely to the purchase of imports. This second extreme case is represented by Figure 3. As in the earlier diagrams, equilibrium is initially at P, with Alpha giving up OW units of wheat in exchange for OT units of textiles. A tariff of 50 per

cent is imposed upon textile imports into Alpha, but, unlike the earlier examples, the government collecting the duties is now assumed to spend the entire proceeds upon imported textiles. The additional demand for imports by the government accordingly prevents the demand schedule of Alpha for the products of Beta from falling as far as it otherwise would have fallen. In Figure 3 the new demand schedule, including government demand for imports, is given by the line A'', whereas the private demand alone has fallen, as before, to the line A'.

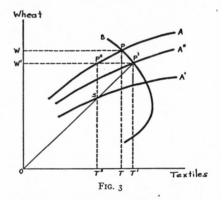

FIG. 3

The relations between the three demand schedules—A, A', and A''—may be illustrated by considering the point P'' on the old schedule, A. This point indicates that, before the tariff was imposed, the traders in Alpha would have been willing to give up OW' units of wheat for OT'' units of textiles. When the new tariff becomes effective, the private traders' demand schedule drops, as before, from A to A'. The vertical distance between A and A' thus indicates the amount of the tariff, measured in wheat, corresponding to any given level of textile imports. In Figure 3, for example, the distance SP'' is 50 per cent of $T''S$. Suppose, for purposes of illustration, that the world rate of exchange between wheat and textiles, exclusive of any tariffs, were given by the slope of the line OSP' drawn through the origin of Figure 3. Consumers and traders in Alpha would then purchase OT'' units of textiles, for which they would pay $T''S$ units of wheat to B and an additional SP'' units of wheat to their own customs officials. But the government of Alpha is assumed, in the present example, to spend the entire tariff revenues on imported commodities, and this means that the amount SP'' must be exchanged for textiles at the world price ratio. At this given ratio, the government collecting the duties would accordingly acquire an amount of textiles equal to $P''P'$ in exchange for customs revenues which, measured in wheat, amount to SP''. The final effect of the tariff on the demand schedule of Alpha, including the government demand for imports as well as the private demand, is thus found to be a horizontal shift in the entire schedule, the relative extent of the shift being exactly equal to the rate of the tariff. The distance $P''P'$, in Figure 3, for example, is 50 per cent of the distance $W'P''$. The new demand schedule, A'', might have been derived by more direct methods, but the preceding argument, I believe, shows more clearly than most others why A'' must lie between A and A'.[15]

With these preliminary remarks we may now return to the effects of the tariff on prices at home and abroad. As in the earlier examples, the tariff improves the terms of trade of the country imposing it, which means that the price of Alpha's imports, exclusive of the tariff, declines relative to the price of that country's exports. This is shown in Figure 3 by the

fact that Alpha now imports a larger amount of textiles (OT') in exchange for a smaller amount of wheat (OW'). These terms of trade, however, are measured in foreign prices, and, as before, it is the domestic price ratio rather than the foreign price ratio which governs the distribution of income in the taxing country. The domestic price of textiles in Alpha is higher than the foreign price by exactly the amount of the tariff; and when this is taken into account, it is clear from Figure 3 that the final effect of the tariff, including both primary and secondary effects, is to raise the domestic price of textiles relative to the price of wheat. In other words, under the conditions assumed in Figure 3, the direct influence of the tariff in raising the price of textiles in Alpha is more important than is its indirect influence in improving that country's terms of trade. As far as private traders and consumers are concerned, the domestic rate of exchange is given, as in the earlier examples, by the point P''. The private traders obtain OT'' units of textiles in exchange for OW' units of wheat. The remaining $T''T'$ units of textiles are, in effect, paid to the government of Alpha as customs duties. Now, since the demand schedule A'' was derived from the schedule A by a horizontal shift, it is apparent from the diagram that the point P'' on the old schedule must lie to the left of the original equilibrium point P. And, as in Figure 1, unless the demand schedule of Alpha has an infinite elasticity, the point P'' represents for that country a higher domestic price of textiles relative to the price of wheat than does the point P.

When the proceeds of a tariff are spent entirely on imports, as in Figure 3, it is evident that the domestic price of imports rises, in the country imposing the tariff, relative to the domestic price of

---

[15] If the demand of Alpha for the product of Beta is inelastic, A' will actually lie *above* the curve A; i.e., under these circumstances a tariff will *increase* the demand of Alpha for the products of Beta.

TARIFFS, TERMS OF TRADE, AND NATIONAL INCOME 13

exports, even though the foreign demand for the exported commodity is inelastic. The tariff accordingly leads, as in the earlier example depicted by Figure 1, to a shift of resources from the export industry, wheat, to textiles, the industry competing with imports. Both the real income and the relative share in the national income of the scarce factor, labor, are thereby increased in the manner envisaged by Stolper and Samuelson. In other words, when customs duties are employed entirely in the purchase of imports, no modifications are required in the Stolper-Samuelson conclusion that tariffs benefit the factors of production which are required in relatively large amounts in the industries competing with imports. And this is true regardless of the size of the elasticity of demand for a country's exports. If the foreign demand is extremely inelastic, the improvement in terms of trade will, of course, prevent import prices in the high-tariff country from rising by a large amount and will thereby mitigate to some extent the influence of the tariff on the distribution of income. But in any event the direction, if not the size, of the change in income distribution will be substantially as envisaged in the earlier work on the subject.

We have now illustrated the effects of a tariff with two extreme examples. In the first, the customs duties were assumed to be spent entirely upon the export goods of the taxing country, while in the second the duties were spent entirely in the purchase of imports. It remains only to consider the intermediate and more realistic case in which expenditure of the tariff revenues is divided in some manner between export goods and imports. Before presenting a geometric illustration of this intermediate case, however, a few general statements are needed concerning the relations between tax revenues and governmental expenditures.

The fiscal systems of most modern states are so complex that it is virtually impossible to associate any particular expenditure with a given type of revenue. What sense does it make, under such conditions, to assert that the proceeds of a tariff are spent in a certain manner on home goods and imports? How can any particular expenditure or group of expenditures be identified as a direct consequence of tariff revenues? Some economists have gone so far as to say that the problem is an impossible one and that the circular flow of income through the government accounts cannot be traced in such an exact manner. Although there is considerable substance to this argument, it seems to me that the conclusion to which it leads is nevertheless unduly pessimistic. Even without attempting to find a direct link between every individual expenditure and every item of revenue, it may yet be possible to say that expenditures as a whole, including private expenditures as well as public, have been affected in a certain way by an increase or a decrease of tariffs. For most purposes, including the present one, it is probably best to regard government expenditures as fixed and largely independent of the particular type of taxation employed to collect revenues. If the over-all budgetary deficit or surplus is likewise the result of an independent decision, tariffs can then be envisaged as replacing or supplementing other forms of taxation. In other words, an increase in government revenues from customs duties can be associated directly with a decrease in some other form of taxation or can be considered as making unnecessary an increase in some other form of taxation. When viewed in this way, the problem of

14   LLOYD A. METZLER

tracing the effects of tariffs on the circular flow of income is largely shifted from the governmental to the private sphere of the economy. The question now is not how the tariff affects *government* expenditures on export and import goods but how the change in taxation affects *private* expenditures. The increase in customs revenues means that other forms of taxation, such as income taxes, for example, can be correspondingly reduced; and the added income thereby made available to the private sector of the economy will normally be spent in a cer-

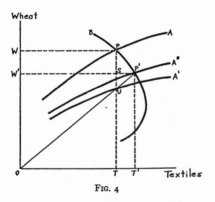

FIG. 4

tain way on imports and domestic goods. Suppose, for example, that income-earners, on the average, spend about 20 per cent of their incomes on imported goods, including raw materials and semifinished goods as well as finished goods. A reduction of income taxes, made possible by increased customs duties, will then lead to an increase in expenditures on imports equal to roughly two-tenths of the customs duties. Although there is no immediate connection between the customs revenues themselves and the added expenditures on imports, we can nevertheless say that the latter were indirectly the result of the former. More generally, if the marginal propensity to import of the

private sector of the economy is k, we can carry out our examination of the effects of the tariff *as though* a fraction k of all customs revenue was actually spent on imported goods; the remaining part of the remitted taxes, or a fraction $1 - k$ of customs duties, can then be regarded as spent, directly or indirectly, on the purchase of export goods.[16] The size of k will, of course, vary with the nature of the taxation system, but this is a refinement which cannot be discussed here.

With these ideas in mind, consider, now, the situation in Figure 4. As in the earlier diagrams, foreign trade is initially in equilibrium at the point P, with Alpha exporting OW units of wheat and importing OT units of textiles; and once again this equilibrium is disturbed by a 50 per cent tariff on textile imports. Unlike the previous illustration, however, the proceeds of the tariff are now assumed to be divided in the proportions k and $1 - k$ between the purchase of imports and exports, respectively. It makes no fundamental difference in the geometric argument whether these proportions are determined directly by government purchases or indirectly through the reduction of other taxes.[17] Figure 4 has been

[16] The argument at this point is distinctly classical in that added income is assumed to be entirely spent, directly or indirectly, in the purchase either of home goods or of imports. There is, of course, no logical reason why a propensity to save could not be introduced along with the two propensities to spend; but this would raise a number of vexatious questions concerning the effects of tariffs upon employment which could not possibly be given adequate treatment within the limits of the present study.

[17] This statement is an approximation which is strictly accurate only when the size of the tariff is small. If the tariff is substantial, the shift in demand will not be the same when the government spends the customs revenues as when they are spent by private traders. The difference is attributable to the fact that private traders pay duties on their added purchases from abroad, whereas the government does not. But this is a matter of detail which does not affect the substance of the argument, and it may accordingly be left over to a later paper.

drawn with such values for k, the marginal propensity of Alpha to import, and η, the price elasticity of demand for Alpha's exports that the favorable movement in that country's terms of trade exactly offsets the direct effect of the tariff itself, leaving the domestic price ratio of the two commodities unchanged. But, before discussing the relation between the marginal propensity to import and the price elasticity which is necessary to bring about this result, a word should be said about the three reciprocal demand schedules A, A' and A''. The line A', as in Figure 3, represents the private demand for imports after the tariff is imposed, without making any allowance for the expenditure, direct or indirect, of the customs revenues. Thus the distance UP is 50 per cent of TU, etc. Now consider a world rate of exchange of the two commodities, exclusive of the tariff, represented by the slope of the diagonal OP'. Neglecting the effects of spending the duties, private traders and consumers in Alpha, at this rate of exchange, would import OT of textiles and would export TU of wheat. The tariff received by the government, expressed in the exports of the taxing country, would then be UP. This amount would be returned to the residents of Alpha in the form of reduced taxes, and part of the income so received would be used to augment the demand for imports. In the diagram the assumption is made that a proportion equal to US/UP of this added income is spent on imports; in other words, $k = US/UP$. At the given foreign price ratio, importers in Alpha would thus obtain an additional amount of textiles equal to SP', or TT', which means that expenditure of the tariff revenues would have the effect of shifting the point U on the line A' over to the point P' on line A''.[18] A similar construction

could be developed for any other point on A'.

After the tariff becomes effective, the new demand schedule of Alpha facing the exporters of Beta, including indirect as well as direct effects on the tariff, is, of course, the line A''. The demand schedule of Beta for the products of Alpha has not been altered, and the point of equilibrium between the two countries, in terms of quantities actually imported and exported, accordingly shifts from P to P' in Figure 4. Where Alpha formerly exported OW units of wheat and imported OT of textiles, she now exports a smaller quantity of wheat (OW') in exchange for a larger quantity of textiles (OT'). The gain to the taxing country, regarded as a unit, is obvious; the foreign price of textiles has fallen, relative to the foreign price of wheat, and this favorable movement in Alpha's terms of trade is so great that the country obtains more textiles than before in exchange for a smaller amount of wheat. And yet, if we look at the domestic price ratio in Alpha, including the tariff, we find that this ratio is exactly the same as before the tariff became effective. To put the matter another way, the direct effect of the customs duty in raising the price of textiles in Alpha, relative to the price of wheat, is exactly offset by its indirect effect through the change in world prices. The new foreign price ratio—i.e., the ratio exclusive of the tariff—is shown in Figure 4 by the line OP'. The domestic price ratio in Alpha, which differs from the foreign ratio only by the tariff, will therefore be given by the slope of a line through the origin (not shown in the diagram) whose vertical distance from the OT

[18] This statement again ignores the fact that the private traders pay duties on their added imports as well as on their original imports. If the tariff is small, however, these "duties on duties" will be insignificant compared with the duties on total imports.

axis is 50 per cent above the vertical distance of a corresponding point on OP'. Since OP' cuts the schedule, A', at U, a point which is directly below P, and since the original shedule A is 50 per cent above A', it follows that the new domestic price ratio in Alpha is represented by the original equilibrium point, P. In other words, the relative prices actually paid and received by consumers and producers of the two goods in Alpha are unaltered by the tariff.

Under these circumstances it may, at first, seem paradoxical that the country imposing the tariff should alter the physical quantity of its exports and imports at all. Relative domestic prices remaining unchanged, producers of both textiles and wheat in Alpha presumably continue to produce the same quantities of the two commodities as before. No shift in resources between the two industries takes place, and the distribution of income earned in production is therefore the same as before the tariff was imposed. How does it happen, then, that Alpha exports a smaller amount of wheat than in the original equilibrium and imports a larger amount of textiles? The answer to this question is to be found in the effects of the customs duties upon the circular flow of income. Since the revenues received from the tariff enable the government of Alpha to reduce other taxes without disturbing its expenditures upon goods and services, income available to the factors of production increases, even though total output remains unchanged. And, according to our original assumption, a fraction k of this increased income is devoted to imports, while $1 - k$ is spent on goods produced by the export trades. Thus both the rise in imports (TT') and the fall in exports $(W'W)$ are indirect consequences of added purchases

in Alpha from the proceeds of the customs duties themselves. Indirectly, the customs proceeds are used both to purchase goods which would otherwise have been available for export and to increase the volume of imports. Here is perhaps the clearest case imaginable in which, to use a familiar expression from innumerable tariff controversies, "the foreigner pays the tax."

In Figure 4 the reciprocal demand schedules of both countries and the marginal propensity of Alpha to import have been drawn in such a way that a tariff on imports leaves all domestic price ratios in the taxing country unaltered. We must now see whether this result can be generalized. In other words, instead of considering a given tariff rate of 50 per cent, we shall consider a general rate, τ, and, instead of assuming a particular set of reciprocal demand schedules and a given marginal propensity to import, we shall assume a general set of demand schedules and a general propensity to import. We may then inquire what relations must exist between all these functions in order that a tariff shall leave the taxing country's domestic price ratios unchanged. It turns out that the answer to this question depends upon only two functions, the price elasticity of demand for imports abroad, i.e., the price elasticity in Beta, and the marginal propensity of the taxing country, Alpha, to import. The symbol, η, will be used to indicate the elasticity of demand for imports in Beta, while k, as before, will be used to indicate the marginal propensity of Alpha to import. The precise relation between η and k which is required to bring about the situation depicted in Figure 4 was first derived more than a decade ago by Lerner; but, since Lerner's work was presented in a somewhat different context, it seems desirable to give a slightly modified version here.[19]

If relative prices in the taxing country are unaffected by the tariff, this means, as noted before, that the primary influence of the duty in raising the domestic price of imports in Alpha is exactly offset by its secondary influence upon world prices or upon the terms of trade. Suppose that this is actually true. In other words, suppose that the decline in the world price of textiles, relative to the world price of wheat, is just sufficient to offset the tariff in Alpha. We now wish to know what conditions of demand and supply must prevail in order that this new world price ratio shall be an equilibrium ratio. In view of the fact that the reciprocal demand schedules represent both a demand for one commodity and a supply of another, it will be sufficient to consider either the supply and demand for textiles or the supply and demand for wheat. Equilibrium in the one market implies equilibrium in the other, and it is therefore unnecessary to consider both. As a practical matter it is perhaps easiest to consider the supply and demand for textiles.

Since the domestic price ratio in Alpha remains unchanged, that country's demand for textile imports is influenced only by the expenditure of the tariff proceeds. With a tariff rate of τ, customs duties as a percentage of the value of private imports will likewise be τ. By assumption, a proportion, k, of these duties is spent on imports. The relative increase in the demand for imports in Alpha will therefore be $k\tau$. The question now is whether and under what circumstances this increased demand in Alpha will be matched by an equivalent increase in supply from Beta. The demand in Beta

[19] Lerner, *op. cit.*, pp. 310–11.

for the exports of Alpha is assumed to be inelastic; and, when the world price of textiles declines, as it does when the tariff is imposed, Beta therefore offers an increased amount of textiles in exchange for a reduced quantity of wheat. Using the notation of Figure 4, the relative increase in the supply of textile exports from Beta is TT'/OT. This, in turn, is approximately equal to $-\beta(W'W/OW)$, where β is the elasticity of the reciprocal demand schedule, B. But $W'W/OW$ represents the additional wheat consumption in Alpha, relative to the previous level of exports, and this additional expenditure arises entirely from the proceeds of the tariff. An amount $k\tau$ was spent on imports, and the remainder, or $(1 - k)\tau$, is accordingly spent on wheat formerly exported. The quantity $W'W/OW$ is thus equal to $(1 - k)\tau$, and the additional supply of textile exports from Beta may be expressed thus: $-\beta(1 - k)\tau$. If this additional supply is to equal the additional demand, we must have[20]

$$k\tau = -(1 - k)\tau\beta, \qquad (1)$$

or, dividing both sides by τ,

$$k = -(1 - k)\beta. \qquad (2)$$

This is one way of expressing the condition that must be met if a tariff is to leave the taxing country's internal prices unaltered. The term β, however, represents the elasticity of the reciprocal demand schedule B, and it is frequently more useful to express the results, as Lerner has done, in terms of the elasticity of the ordinary money demand schedule. If η represents this latter elasticity, it is well known that, subject to certain sup-

[20] The expression $(1 - k)\tau\beta$ is positive because, with an inelastic demand for imports in Beta, β is negative.

ply limitations, $\beta = 1 - 1/\eta$.[21] Substituting this value of β in equation (2), we have

$$k = -(1-k)\left(1 - \frac{1}{\eta}\right), \qquad (3)$$

and, after simplifying, this becomes

$$\eta = 1 - k . \qquad (4)$$

In words, this says that, if a tariff is to leave domestic price ratios and the distribution of income within the taxing country unaltered, the foreign elasticity of demand for that country's exports must be equal to the difference between unity and the marginal propensity to import of the country imposing the tariff. If a country has a marginal propensity to import of 0.25, for example, a tariff imposed by that country will not leave domestic price ratios unchanged unless the foreign elasticity of demand for its exports is 0.75. If the foreign elasticity is smaller than this, the tariff will cause the domestic prices of imports to fall relative to the domestic prices of exports. On the other hand, if the foreign elasticity is larger than 0.75, the tariff will increase domestic import prices relative to export prices.

The practical consequences of these results will be discussed in Section III; but before proceeding further it seems desirable to summarize the main argument of the present section. The conclusions are intimately related to the proposition developed by Stolper and Samuelson that

[21] Let t equal the quantity of textiles that Beta is willing to export, and let w represent that country's demand for imported wheat. The elasticity, β, of the reciprocal demand schedule is then $dt/dw \cdot w/t$. But the quantity t, from one point of view, is simply the total outlay of Beta for imports, w. In money terms, in other words, $t = pw$, where p is the import price of wheat. β may therefore be written $\beta = d(pw)/dw \cdot w/pw$. Upon simplifying and carrying out the indicated differentiation, this becomes $\beta = 1 + dp/dw \, (w/p) = 1 - 1/\eta$, the elasticity, η, being defined now in the Marshallian sense.

any event, other than a change in technology, which leads to a shift in resources from one industry to another will increase both the real income and the relative share in total income of the factor required in relatively large amounts in the expanding industry. A corollary of this, of course, is the proposition that the factor of production required in relatively large amounts in the contracting industry will find both its real return and its relative share of the total income reduced. The problem of how a tariff influences the distribution of income is, therefore, largely resolved into a discussion of the effects of the tariff in shifting resources from one industry to another. The shift in resources, in turn, depends upon how the tariff affects domestic prices; for it may be taken for granted that, if resources shift at all, they will move into industries the products of which have enjoyed relative price increases. The present section has therefore been devoted largely to a discussion of the influence of customs duties on domestic prices of both exports and imports.

We have found that a tariff has two effects, which influence relative domestic prices in opposite directions. On the one hand, the tariff itself represents a direct increase in import prices, and, on the other hand, the resulting reduction in the demand for imports depresses the foreign prices of these goods relative to corresponding prices for export goods. The net effect upon relative prices at home thus depends upon which of these forces is the stronger. By following a technique originally expounded by Lerner, we have shown that a tariff will not increase the relative domestic price of imports unless η, the foreign elasticity of demand for the country's exports, is greater than $1 - k$, where k is the marginal propensity to import.

Although the final conclusions with respect to prices have been presented in four diagrams, the first three are really special cases of the fourth. In Figures 1 and 2, the proceeds of the tariff were assumed to be spent entirely on export goods, and the marginal propensity to import was thus implicitly set at zero. Since the expression $1 - k$ then had a value of unity, it was found that the tariff would not increase the relative domestic price of imports unless the foreign elasticity of demand for the country's exports was greater than unity. In Figure 3, on the other hand, the proceeds of the tariff were assumed to be spent entirely upon imports, and this was equivalent to assuming a marginal propensity to import of unity. The value of $1 - k$ for the special case represented by Figure 3 was thus zero; and we found that a tariff always increased the relative domestic price of imports, no matter how small the foreign elasticity of demand for the country's exports. Now, since $1 - k$ is in all circumstances less than unity, it is clear that, if the foreign demand for a country's exports is elastic with respect to prices, a tariff will always increase domestic import prices relative to export prices. In all such cases the shift of resources will be toward industries competing with imports and away from the export industries. The factors of production used in relatively large amount in the protected industries will consequently gain, both absolutely and relatively, while the factors used in large amounts in the export trades will lose. All this is completely in accord with the Heckscher-Ohlin conclusions as well as with the work of Stopler and Samuelson. It is only when the foreign demand for a country's exports is inelastic that the earlier works on the subject require modification. When the foreign demand is sufficiently inelastic, a tariff, far from protecting industries competing with imports at the expense of the export trades, may actually benefit the latter at the expense of the former. If this happens, resources tend to be shifted from the "protected" industries to the export industries, and the factors of production which are used in relatively large amounts in the export industries enjoy both a relative and an absolute increase in real income.

III

The aspect of tariff theory which the preceding discussion outlines most sharply is the potential or actual conflict of interests that may arise between a country's relatively scarce factors of production and the remainder of the economy. The classical dictum that real wages and the returns to other factors of production depend upon productivity remains true in a general way, of course; but that this dictum cannot be applied to the particular problem of tariffs without numerous reservations and exceptions. It cannot be asserted, for instance, that tariffs necessarily reduce productivity and thereby lower the real incomes of all factors of production. In the first place—and this is an argument of which the classical economists were fully aware—tariffs, under favorable circumstances, may improve a country's terms of trade so much that real income for the country as a whole is thereby increased. But this is a familiar argument to which the present paper has made no particular contribution. The point to be emphasized is a second reservation, namely, that the returns to each of the factors of production do not necessarily move in the same direction as general productivity or real income of the economy as a whole. In other words, regardless of whether a high-tariff policy increases or diminishes real income for a country as a whole, such a policy is likely to affect some factors of production favorably and others adversely. This point of view, in fact, might be stated even more strongly: the real income of a country's scarce factors of production is not likely to be increased by a tariff unless world demand is such that the tariff clearly diminishes the country's total income; and, conversely, the scarce factors are not likely to be injured by a tariff unless the tariff benefits the rest of the economy.

To clarify these propositions, consider a country having a comparative scarcity of labor and importing commodities with a high labor content. Stolper and Samuelson have shown that, *if the terms of trade are not affected,* a tariff in such a country will probably increase both the real wage rate and the proportion of the national income accruing to the working class. Now, if the terms of trade remain unchanged, this means that the tariff, while disrupting the allocation of resources and thereby tending to reduce real income for the country as a whole, has not succeeded in bringing to the economy the benefits of a more favorable bargaining position in world markets. In other words, when the terms of trade remain unaltered, a tariff causes an unambiguous reduction in a country's real income as a whole. But this is precisely the condition, according to the Stolper-Samuelson argument, when a tariff increases the absolute and relative return to labor, the country's scarce factor of production. If I may return to an earlier metaphor, the scarce factor of production receives a larger piece of a smaller pie. But what if the size of the pie is increased by the tariff? How does labor fare under these circumstances? An increase in real income for the economy as a whole is, of

course, possible, provided that the tariff causes a sufficient improvement in the terms of trade to offset its interference with the allocation of resources. A substantial improvement in the terms of trade could take place, however, only if the foreign demand for the country's exports was inelastic; and in this event, as we have seen, there is a strong probability that the tariff, far from protecting the industries competing with imports, would actually injure these industries and lead to a transfer of resources from them to the export industries. This shift in resources would reduce the degree of scarcity of labor and thereby lead to a reduction in both its relative and its absolute return.

The conflict of interests which the preceding summary emphasizes is in sharp contrast to the doctrine of a harmony of interests which occupied such a prominent place in the work of many nineteenth-century liberal economists. The preceding argument has shown that, with respect to problems of commercial policy, the economic interests of such broad groups as manual workers, landlords, and capitalists are not likely to coincide. A policy of reducing tariffs may therefore be the source of widespread political cleavages, quite apart from the pressure which is inevitably exerted by the industries immediately affected. This, of course, is no argument against reducing trade barriers. Rather, it is simply an indication that the political conflicts inherent in tariff reduction may have a much broader base than would be supposed from concentrating one's attention upon the protected industries alone.

The fact that the influence of tariffs on the distribution of income can be a matter of considerable economic and political significance is demonstrated, I believe, by a well-known report on the tariff in

TARIFFS, TERMS OF TRADE, AND NATIONAL INCOME   21

Australia, which was published in 1929.[22] This report, prepared by a committee of Australian economists at the request of the Australian prime minister, presented both the terms-of-trade argument and the distribution-of-income argument in favor of the Australian tariffs. The Australian economy is characterized by an abundant supply of land, relative to the supply of labor and capital; and Australia, therefore, has a comparative advantage in agriculture, particularly in wheat and wool. The committee argued that if tariffs were reduced, Australian manufacturing would be retarded and resources would be diverted from manufacturing to agriculture. But, since the world demand for agricultural products, especially the demand for wheat, is decidedly inelastic, it was felt that an increase in Australian wheat exports would lead to a substantial reduction in world wheat prices. In short, the eventual effect of the tariff reduction would be a considerable deterioration in the Australian terms of trade.[23] Much more important than the deterioration in terms of trade, however, was the effect which the committee expected a tariff reduction to have upon the distribution of income. In general, the labor component of most manufactured products is considerably greater than the labor component of agriculture. A shift of resources from manufacturing to agriculture would therefore lessen the relative scarcity of labor, thus reducing real wages and increasing rents. It was this adverse effect upon the distribution of income which the committee of Australian economists regarded as the principal deterrent to a general tariff reduction.[24]

[22] *The Australian Tariff: An Economic Enquiry* (Melbourne, Australia, 1929).

[23] *Ibid.*, p. 80.

[24] *Ibid.*, Part VII.

What can be said about the Australian point of view in the light of the discusison in Section II? In the abstract a good case can be made both for the terms-of-trade argument and for the distribution-of-income argument in favor of tariffs. *But this is true only when each argument is considered separately.* When the two are presented together, the validity of one of the two arguments becomes doubtful. It may well be true that the world demand for Australian wheat is inelastic, as the committee implies, and that a tariff reduction might therefore lead to serious deterioration of Australia's terms of trade. But if this is actually the case, then it is unlikely, as we have seen in Section II, that a tariff reduction would lead to a shift of resources from manufacturing to agriculture. When the Australian economy finally became adjusted to the tariff reduction, domestic prices of manufactured goods might actually be higher relative to agricultural prices than before the tariff was reduced. And, if this should happen, the reduction of tariffs would be the cause of a shift of resources *into* the protected industries, with a concomitant increase in the proportion of the national income accruing to workers. Paradoxical as it seems, the Australian manufacturing industries might be better "protected" and receive more encouragement under free trade than under a system of protective tariffs.[25]

[25] This statement, as well as subsequent remarks concerning the foreign trade of the Latin-American countries and the United States, requires one modification. The theoretical treatment in Sec. II was based upon the assumption that the protective duty was a general duty applicable to all or virtually all types of import. If this is not true, the final results will obviously differ somewhat from those presented in Sec. II. It is intuitively evident, for example, that a tariff on a particular commodity constituting a small part of total imports will increase the domestic price of that commodity relative to the prices of exports, even though the foreign demand for the country's exports is quite inelastic; for in this case

This idea is not new, Quite the contrary, it is implicit in much of the nineteenth-century work on the theory of reciprocal demand. Nevertheless, it is an idea which would no doubt be received with great incredulity, not to say outright disbelief, by the average Australian businessman. How, he might ask, could he possibly benefit from a reduction of the tariff on his own manufactures? To some extent his disbelief is probably a result of an instinctive and well-founded distrust of what the economist calls the "process of adjustment"; for, if Australia should attempt, after a substantial unilateral reduction of tariffs, to maintain her exchange at the old rates relative to other currencies, a new equilibrium in her balance of payments could be achieved only by a reduction in real income or by a general deflation of prices and costs. The businessman is rightfully suspicious of both of these "processes of adjustment." If Australia were willing to alter the foreign value of her currency, on the other hand, the adjustment to the new situation might be achieved in a less painful manner. Even in this event, however, it seems doubtful whether producers in the protected industries would concede that a reduction in tariffs would benefit them; for most of them would probably be unwilling to carry through the argument to its logical conclusion. Of course, if a typical producer were asked whether he would prefer a 50 per cent tariff with the pound sterling selling for 1.25 Australian pounds or no tariff with the pound sterling selling for 2.50 Australian pounds, he would probably immediately see the advantage to himself of the latter arrangement. And, if the demand for Australia's exports is really inelastic, this is precisely the sort of choice with which the producer is confronted; for, as we have seen, when the foreign demand is inelastic, there is a strong probability that the indirect effects of the tariff on the terms of trade will more than offset the direct effects on domestic prices. Nevertheless, if tariffs were actually reduced in Australia and if the Australian pound began to depreciate as a consequence, it seems highly probable that many businessmen would complain of their losses from the tariff reduction without associating the tariff in any direct way with their gains from the depreciation of their currency.

This tendency to look only at immediate effects and to ignore secondary consequences is well illustrated by Australia's tariff experience after the first World War, recounted by A. H. Tocker in the *Economic Journal*.[26] Under the pressure of a balance-of-payments deficit, Australian tariffs were substantially increased in 1921. The higher customs duties, together with Australian borrowing in London and a generally improved world economic situation, brought about a marked improvement in the balance of payments; and the Australian banks began to accumulate sterling balances in London. At that time Australia was on a sort of informal sterling-exchange standard, but with no legal commitment to maintain a fixed rate of exchange between the Australian pound and the pound sterling. The accumulation of sterling balances by the Australian banks in 1922 finally induced the banks to sell these balances at a discount, whereas in

the adjustment of the terms of trade will occur largely through price changes among the duty-free imports. Whether the presence of nontaxed imports requires a substantial revision of the conclusions of Sec. II depends upon the ratio of duty-free imports to total imports. But this is a question which I shall discuss in a later paper.

[26] "The Monetary Standards of New Zealand and Australia," *Economic Journal*, XXXIV (1924), 556–75.

1921 a slight premium on pounds sterling had prevailed. The decline in the Australian price of sterling was clearly a result, to some extent at least, of the higher tariffs; but, despite this obvious connection, there were complaints, according to Tocker, that the banks were deliberately pursuing an independent foreign-exchange policy that was detrimental to Australian business interests. "The Australian," said Tocker, "who recently complained that the banks were using their big balances in London to nullify the effects of the tariff, and to attack the protected Australian industries, voiced an economic truth more profound than he knew, and one quite beyond the power of bankers to control."[27]

Although it was a comparatively small incident, the Australian experience illustrates a rather widespread tendency on the part of businessmen to take account only of the immediate or direct effects of tariffs and to ignore their secondary or indirect repercussions upon exchange rates and relative costs. This attitude largely explains, in my opinion, why protective tariffs frequently are strongly supported by the industries directly affected, even though it is widely recognized, at the same time, that the demand for a country's exports is quite unresponsive to changes in price. With their constant and unremitting attention required in the solution of immediate and pressing problems of production and sales, few businessmen have either the time or the

inclination to trace the final consequences of tariffs through all their various ramifications; and the price that is paid for this "direct" approach is an exaggerated idea of the effectiveness of tariffs in protecting home industries.

The tendency to exaggerate the effectiveness of tariffs in raising or maintaining the incomes of a country's scarce factors of production is by no means limited to Australia. Quite the contrary, it is a tendency which is perhaps even more pronounced in other countries, particularly in Latin America. Like Australia, the Latin-American countries have a comparative advantage in the production of foodstuffs and raw materials. Their leading exports include such products of agriculture and the extractive industries as coffee, crude petroleum, copper, sugar, cotton, nitrates, wheat, and meat.[28] Most of these exports are commodities for which the world demand is decidedly inelastic; and, since the Latin-American countries in many instances provide a substantial proportion of the world's supply of such goods, it seems likely that the external demand for their exports as a whole may be quite inelastic even over considerable periods of time. The Latin-American foreign trade, which consists largely of exporting primary products, for which the world demand is inelastic, in exchange for manufactured goods, thus has marked similarities to the Australian foreign trade. And, like the Australians, the Latin-Americans are dissatisfied with the distribution of national income which this type of trade engenders. Indeed, the problem of income distribution is probably a much more pressing one in many parts of Latin America

[27] *Ibid.*, p. 571. In citing these Australian experiences, I have no intention of casting a reflection upon the intelligence of any particular group. The so-called "direct" approach to international economics and the neglect of secondary repercussions are perhaps even more common in the United States. A typical example is the belief that in normal times export surpluses are desirable, while foreign loans are undesirable. This point of view is encountered with regrettable frequency in the halls of Congress as well as among Americans of other walks of life.

[28] For an excellent summary of the pattern of Latin-American trade see R. F. Behrendt, *Inter-American Economic Relations* (New York: Committee on International Policy, 1948), pp. 1–33.

than it is in Australia, for the Latin-American people as a whole have not benefited, as have the Australians, from the scarcity of labor in relation to natural resources. In other words, the Latin-American problem is not simply a problem of maintaining the standard of living in the face of a growing population but rather a problem of raising the standard of living as a whole.

Although Latin America's comparative advantage up to the present time has clearly been in the agricultural and extractive industries, the region as a whole has nevertheless had many areas of subsistence farming, in which the productivity of workers was extremely low; and one of the important economic purposes of the present move toward industrial development is to provide alternative and more useful employment for these low-productivity workers. Whether the current programs of industrialization will attain the various economic, political, and social goals which have been set for them is a question which cannot be discussed here. My purpose in mentioning the Latin-American programs is simply to indicate their relation to the tariff problems analyzed in this paper. To a very considerable extent the governments of South and Central America have sought to encourage domestic manufacturing by means of tariffs upon the importation of competing products; and, in view of what has been said above, it seems probable that this particular part of the program may contain a basic inconsistency.[29] If the demand for Latin America's exports as a whole is actually inelastic—and there is little reason to

doubt this—the preceding discussion suggests strongly that tariffs may accomplish little either in protecting Latin-American manufacturing or in increasing the share of the workers in national income.

This does not mean, of course, that the tariffs entail no economic benefits to the countries imposing them, but the benefits may be quite different from those originally contemplated. With the low price elasticity of demand for their products, the countries of Latin America are in a particularly good position to employ tariffs as a means of achieving more favorable terms of trade. A favorable movement in the Latin-American terms of trade, however, means an increase in the prices received for exports relative to the prices paid for imports; and, to the extent that such a shift occurs, part or all of the protection intended for domestic manufacturing is wiped out. In other words, since tariffs do not alter the basic techniques of production, any benefits which they confer upon one industry or one segment of the population are likely to be at the expense of another industry or another segment of the population. The Latin-American tariffs cannot, at the same time, benefit industry at the expense of agriculture and benefit agriculture at the expense of industry; and, although these tariffs are imposed upon manufactured goods, it is possible that, in the end, world conditions of demand may be such that the tariffs actually injure the industries which they are intended to protect. In the language of the foregoing discussion, the favorable movement in the terms of trade may more than offset the initial effects of the tariff in raising domestic prices of manufactured goods. And, even if the conditions of demand are not so extreme, it remains true, in any event, that the degree of

[29] The extent to which the Latin-American programs of industrial development depend upon tariff protection is indicated by a survey made by the United Nations (see United Nations, Department of Economic Affairs, *Economic Development in Selected Countries* [Lake Success, 1947], pp. 1-150).

protection afforded by Latin-American tariffs is much smaller than appears at first glance to be the case.

It should perhaps be emphasized that these remarks are by no means intended to imply that industrialization is a bad policy for Latin America. This broader problem, involving as it does sociological and political as well as extremely complex economic questions, is entirely beyond the scope of the present paper. My purpose here is simply to indicate one of the limitations to a policy of industrialization by means of protective tariffs.

The foregoing remarks concerning the influence of tariffs on the industrial development of agricultural countries bear a close resemblance to a proposition stated more than a century ago by Friedrich List. Although List thought that protective duties on manufactures are a useful means of promoting industrial growth, it was by no means his view that such duties are appropriate under all circumstances and at all stages of economic development. He divided the economic growth of a country into four periods, and it was in only two of these periods that he regarded protective duties as beneficial to manufactures. "In the first period, agriculture is encouraged by the importation of manufactured articles; in the second, manufactures begin to increase at home, whilst the importation of foreign manufactures to some extent continues; in the third, home manufactures mainly supply domestic consumption and the internal markets; finally, in the fourth, we see the exportation upon a large scale of manufactured products, and the importation of raw materials and agricultural products."[30] It was in the second and third of these periods that List thought protective duties would be

effective in raising the level of industrial activity. With regard to countries in the first and fourth stages of development, free trade was preferred to protection. In other words, free trade was thought to be better than protection both for an undeveloped country specializing in agriculture and raw materials, and for a highly developed industrial nation. For the latter, tariffs on manufactures were considered unnecessary, since the industrial country had already achieved a strong competitive position in the world's markets for manufactured goods.[31] For the former, i.e., for the completely undeveloped country, List thought that tariffs were likely to defeat their purpose.[32] It is in this respect that his conclusions are similar to those given in the present paper, for it has been argued above that, in countries whose exports consist largely of primary products, tariffs will probably afford little, if any, encouragement to manufacturing.

The comparison must not be carried too far. Although List concluded, as I have above, that a policy of protection is a questionable method of increasing manufacturing output in an undeveloped country, his reasons for holding this view were not exactly the same as my own. According to List, a prosperous and powerful industrial nation must possess a well-developed commercial system in addition to its factories. And in the early stages of economic development List believed that free trade rather than protec-

[30] Friedrich List, *National System of Political Economy*, trans. G. A. Matile (Philadelphia, 1846).

[31] *Ibid.*, chap. iv.

[32] "The economical education of a country of inferior intelligence and culture, of one thinly populated, relatively to the extent and fertility of its territory, is effected most certainly by free trade, with more advanced, richer, and more industrious nations. Every commercial restriction in such a country aiming at the increase of manufactures, is premature, and will prove detrimental, not only to civilization in general, but the progress of the nation in particular . . ." (*ibid.*, pp. 78–79).

tion would promote this prerequisite to industrialization. Commercial enterprises would be encouraged because free trade would increase the volume of commercial transactions. In this manner an undeveloped country, according to List, would achieve a certain degree of economic and cultural sophistication more quickly under free trade than under protection. But, once this position was reached and the country was ready to begin the development of manufacturing, List believed that further economic progress would be promoted by protective tariffs.[33]

It is somewhat ironical that, by employing the classical method of comparative statics, I have reached a conclusion which, in one respect at least, is in agreement with one of the most anticlassical economists of the nineteenth century. List's approach to the problem was highly dependent upon a dynamic theory of economic development and involved, in addition, a liberal admixture of political considerations. My own approach, by contrast, has been static in character and limited exclusively to economic arguments. But both the dynamic and the static approaches have led, in one respect, to the same conclusion. It is a moot question whether List, in advocating free trade for backward countries, could have had in mind some of the arguments advanced in the present paper concerning the elasticity of demand for raw materials and agricultural commodities. In view of his aversion to classical economics, however, such a possibility seems rather remote.

The arguments in favor of free trade for undeveloped countries, whether stated in List's terms or in the terms of the present paper, might be called "infant-country" arguments for free trade, just

as the arguments for protection of undeveloped industries have generally been called "infant-industry" arguments for protection. And just as the latter, in practical application, frequently raise difficult questions concerning exactly what constitutes an infant industry, so the former also raise questions as to what constitutes an infant country. In discussing the tariff history of the United States, for example, List assumed that by the early decades of the nineteenth century the United States had passed beyond the primitive and undeveloped stage in which free trade would have been beneficial. He believed, in other words, that tariffs were helpful in promoting manufacturing in the United States throughout the early part of the nineteenth century.[34] In order to substantiate or refute this assertion from List's point of view, it would be necessary to make a detailed factual study of the state of American agriculture and commerce at the time. But if the question is approached from the point of view of the present paper, there is at least one circumstance which suggests that the actual degree of protection to American manufacturing may have been considerably less than intended and considerably less important in American economic development than List supposed. Throughout the first half of the nineteenth century the United States was in a position, as far as foreign trade was concerned, quite like the position of Australia and the Latin-American countries today. She was predominantly an exporter of raw materials and agricultural products and an importer of manufactured goods. Thus, in the period from 1820 until the outbreak of the Civil War, American exports of raw materials and unprocessed foodstuffs accounted for

[33] *Ibid.*, pp. 181–82.   [34] *Ibid.*, chap. ix.

TARIFFS, TERMS OF TRADE, AND NATIONAL INCOME 27

more than two-thirds of the total value of exports.[35] Moreover—and this is perhaps even more important—approximately three-fourths of these exports of primary products consisted of raw cotton, of which the United States at the time was by far the most important source of world supply. In view of the dominant position of the United States in the world cotton market and in view, further, of the dominance of cotton and other primary products in American exports as a whole, there is a strong probability that the demand for American exports during the first half of the nineteenth century was inelastic with respect to price. If this conjecture is correct, it follows from the analysis above that, considering both the primary and the secondary effects of the tariffs on domestic prices, the policy of protection to manufactures must have had a relatively small effect upon the rate of industrial growth in the period before the Civil War. Indeed, the net effect of protection during this period may even have been slightly adverse to manufacturing as a whole.[36]

The conjecture that early American tariff policy probably exerted a comparatively minor influence upon the growth of domestic manufactures is in substantial agreement with the well-known conclusion which Taussig reached by a somewhat different method. After a detailed study of a number of protected industries, including the textile and iron and steel industries, Taussig concluded that

their rate of expansion had not been substantially affected by the ebb and flow of protective measures. Thus, in discussing the period before 1860, he said in his *Tariff History of the United States:*

... In the main, the changes in duties have had much less effect upon the protected industries than is generally supposed. Their growth has been steady and continuous, and seems to have been little stimulated by the high duties of 1842, and little checked by the more moderate duties of 1846 and 1857.[37]

In his *International Trade*, published thirty years later, Taussig recognized the special nature of United States exports during the first half of the nineteenth century—i.e., the high proportion of raw materials and agricultural products for which the world's demand was comparatively rigid—but there is no evidence that this feature of American trade had anything to do with his original conclusion concerning the effects of protective duties.[38] His views regarding the early tariffs were largely derived from empirical observation, and, when he later studied the history of protected industries during the years 1860–1930, he modified his earlier opinions somewhat.[39] In particular, he cautiously advanced the view that the protective system may have contributed to the development of American manufactures.

At first glance, this later conclusion of Taussig's seems to contradict the argument of the present paper that exporters of raw materials and other primary products are not likely to find a general tariff system, short of completely prohibitive duties, an effective means of promoting

[35] These and subsequent figures on United States foreign trade have been computed from data in United States Department of Commerce, *Statistical Abstract of the United States.*

[36] This statement, like others in the present section, must be interpreted in a long-run sense. There is no intention to deny that during the period of adjustment a tariff on a particular product may afford the protected industry a substantial measure of protection.

[37] F. W. Taussig, *The Tariff History of the United States* (4th ed.; New York, 1898), p. 152.

[38] F. W. Taussig, *International Trade* (New York, 1928), p. 148.

[39] See F. W. Taussig, *Some Aspects of the Tariff Question* (3d enl. ed.; Cambridge, Mass., 1931), *passim.*

industrial development. A further examination of the statistics of United States
exports, however, resolves at least a part
of this apparent conflict. Although foodstuffs and raw materials, particularly
raw cotton, continued throughout the
nineteenth century to be important
United States exports, these products,
with the passing of the years, nevertheless became considerably less significant,
relative to total exports. At the close of
the nineteenth century, for example, exports of primary products accounted for
less than half of total exports, compared
with a proportion of two-thirds in 1830.
The decline in the relative importance of
primary exports was, of course, accompanied by a corresponding increase in the
importance of manufactured exports.
Thus, during the second half of the nineteenth century, American exports were
not dominated by primary products to
the extent that had been true earlier. Increasingly the United States was becom-
ing an exporter of a wide variety of manufactures as well as the staple raw materials and foodstuffs. It follows that, with
regard to the second half of the nineteenth century at any rate, there is no
conflict between the results of this paper
and Taussig's conclusion that the tariff
system provided a limited stimulus to
manufactures; for the United States
after the Civil War was rapidly developing beyond the simple stage of an agricultural exporter.[40] The character of
American exports was changing sufficiently to reduce some of the earlier
rigidity of foreign demand and, accordingly, to make tariffs more effective in
increasing the domestic prices of the protected products.

[40] A further factor in the increasing effectiveness
of tariffs in protecting domestic industries was the
lower proportion of dutiable imports to total imports.

IV

In concluding this paper, a word
should be said about the relation of the
arguments presented here to the earlier
work of Heckscher and Ohlin. As noted
in Section I, the well-known view of both
Heckscher and Ohlin is that international trade tends to equalize the relative returns to different factors of production
among the trading countries. In other
words, it is their view that trade increases the relative demand, and therefore the relative return, of the factor of
production which is comparatively most
abundant and comparatively cheapest
in a particular country. In this manner
wages tend to be raised relative to the returns to other factors of production, in
countries which have a large population
in relation to their other resources.
Superficially it might seem that any
measure, such as a tariff reduction, which
reduces the impediments to international
trade, would have these same effects. In a
country with a large supply of land, for
example, it might be expected, following
the Heckscher-Ohlin argument, that a
tariff reduction would increase rents and
lower wages. But we have found in Section II that, if the demand for a country's
exports is inelastic, this result does not
necessarily follow. Under some conditions with respect to international demand a reduction of tariffs may *increase* the demand for a country's
scarce factors and *reduce* the demand for
its abundant factors. How can this conclusion be reconciled with the view of
Heckscher and Ohlin that international
trade always increases the demand for a
country's abundant factors?

Despite superficial differences, the
conclusions reached in this paper are essentially consistent with those of Heckscher and Ohlin. The contradictory ap-

pearance of the conclusions is attributable entirely to a difference in the point of comparison. When Heckscher and Ohlin say that international trade increases the demand for a country's scarce factors, they mean that the demand is increased *compared with the demand in a state of complete isolation.* In other words, they are comparing free trade or restricted trade with a state of affairs in which there is no trade at all; and this is by no means the same as comparing trade under one tariff system with trade under smaller tariffs. The argument presented in Section II, that an increase in customs duties may reduce the demand for a country's scarce factors of production, was limited in its application to tariff changes within a range for which the foreign demand for the country's exports had a certain degree of inelasticity. In other words, the argument was valid only for movements along a limited part of the foreign reciprocal demand schedule. Now, in order to make the present analysis comparable to that of Heckscher and Ohlin, we should have to consider an

increase in tariffs so large that all imports were eliminated. In short, all tariffs on all commodities would have to be completely prohibitive. From the nature of the reciprocal demand schedules, however, it is apparent that if tariffs were gradually increased to a level where they threatened to cut off all trade, the point of equilibrium would sooner or later move to a position where the foreign demand for the tariff-imposing country's exports was elastic. Thereafter, any further increases in tariffs would increase the demand for the country's scarce factors and reduce the demand for its abundant factors, in the manner envisaged by Heckscher and Ohlin. When the present technique is applied to changes in foreign trade as great as those envisaged by Heckscher and Ohlin, my conclusions are thus in agreement with theirs. An appearance of conflict arises only when one attempts to apply to the entire reciprocal demand schedule an argument which is applicable only to a segment of that schedule.

UNIVERSITY OF CHICAGO

PROTECTION, REAL WAGES AND REAL INCOMES [1]

1. IN a recent article in this JOURNAL [2] on " Protection and Real Wages: A Restatement," Mr. Lancaster has re-examined the famous Stolper–Samuelson theorem and concluded:

" This paper does not deny that protection will raise the real wage of one of the factors, but shows that no general statement about which of the factors this will be can be deduced from the relative ' scarcity ' of the factors in the Stolper–Samuelson sense.

" Although the Stolper–Samuelson theorem ' Protection raises the real wage of the scarce factor ' is shown to be an incorrect generalisation, a restatement in the form ' Protection raises the real wage of the factor in which the imported good is relatively more intensive ' has general validity."

It is proposed in Section I of this paper to review systematically the original Stolper–Samuelson contribution, therewith to advance a critique (distinct from Mr. Lancaster's criticism, which is not accepted), of the Stolper–Samuelson formulation of the theorem and then to restate the theorem: this restatement being considered to be the only true and general statement about the effect of protection (prohibitive or otherwise) on real wages of factors in the context of the basic Stolper–Samuelson model. The logical truth of the restated theorem is briefly analysed then in the context of alternative models. Section II proceeds to extend the scope of the discussion with the argument that, with a non-prohibitive tariff, a sharp distinction must be drawn between the impact on the real wage of a factor and the effect on its real income; some implications of this distinction are then analysed.

I. PROTECTION AND REAL WAGES

2. In the following analysis, we shall take the *basic* Stolper–Samuelson model to mean that the protecting country has two factors, two commodities enjoying different factor intensities, linear and homogeneous production functions subject to diminishing returns (along isoquants) and incomplete specialisation in production. Full employment of factors, pure competition and perfect mobility of factors are also assumed.

Founded on this model, we have three alternative formulations of the theorem concerning the impact of protection on the real wages of factors:

(1) *Restrictive Stolper–Samuelson Theorem.* " International trade necessarily lowers the real wage of the scarce factor expressed in terms of

---

[1] This paper was read to the Nuffield Economics Society. My thanks are due to Professor Hicks and J. Black for substantial help with the exposition of the paper. I am also happy to record my heavy indebtedness to Professor Harry Johnson, who has been generous with suggestions that have led to numerous improvements in the paper.

[2] ECONOMIC JOURNAL, June 1957, pp. 199–210. The following quotation is from p. 199.

any good." [1]   This formulation restricts itself to the comparison of the free-trade real wage with the self-sufficiency real wage of the scarce factor. The comparison is confined to the case of a prohibitive tariff and excludes non-prohibitive protection. The theorem can be rewritten as follows: prohibitive protection necessarily raises the real wage of the scarce factor.

(2) *General Stolper–Samuelson Theorem.* Protection raises the real wage of the scarce factor.[2] This formulation is clearly intended to be more general and includes non-prohibitive tariffs as well. To emphasise this, we may rewrite it thus: protection (prohibitive or otherwise) necessarily raises the real wage of the scarce factor.

(3) *Stolper–Samuelson–Metzler–Lancaster Theorem.* " Protection [prohibitive or otherwise] raises the real wage of the factor in which the imported good is relatively more intensive." [3]

In the ensuing analysis any reference to " the Stolper–Samuelson theorems " should be taken to relate to the initial two formulations alone; reference to the last formulation will always be by its full title.

3. We can begin by setting out the basic elements in the argument leading to the twin formulations of the Stolper–Samuelson theorem:

(1) protection increases the internal relative price of the importable good:

(2) an increase in the relative price of a good increases the real wage of the factor used intensively in its production;

(3) the importable good is intensive in the use of the scarce factor. Therefore,

(4) protection raises the real wage of the scarce factor.

These arguments must each be closely examined.

4. Concerning argument (1), we must distinguish between prohibitive and non-prohibitive protection:

(i) Protection will necessarily raise the relative price of the im-

---

[1] Stolper and Samuelson, " Protection and Real Wages," *Readings in the Theory of International Trade* (A.E.A., Blakiston Co., 1949), p. 346.

[2] The actual formulation of the general Stolper–Samuelson theorem is from Lancaster, *op. cit.,* p. 199.   While the bulk of their analysis relates explicitly to the restrictive formulation, there are several indications that Stolper and Samuelson had in mind the general formulation as well: (1) a large number of quotations they cite from other authors to outline the problem refer to tariffs in general rather than to tariffs of a prohibitive nature alone; (2) they feel it necessary to assume that " the country in question is relatively small and has no influence on the terms of trade. Thus any gain to the country through monopolistic or monopsonistic behaviour is excluded " (*op. cit.,* p. 344); this assumption is quite superfluous, as we shall later see, if we wish to sustain only the restrictive formulation of the theorem; and (3) the title chosen for the article is not " International Trade and Real Wages " but " Protection and Real Wages." Lancaster, *op. cit.,* p. 201, also construes the Stolper–Samuelson theorem in its general form; thus witness his argument that " Protection will cause a movement in the *general direction* $Q'Q$, away from the free-trade point towards the self-sufficiency point " (my italics).

[3] Lancaster, *op. cit.,* p. 199. This theorem has been given its stated name on grounds which are made explicit later.

portable good when the tariff is prohibitive; the free-trade relative price of the importable good is lower than under self-sufficiency.[1]

(ii) Non-prohibitive protection may either raise, leave unchanged or lower the internal relative price of the importable good. Metzler has demonstrated that this last " perverse " possibility will occur, in the context of our present model, when the elasticity of foreign demand for imports (η_x) is less than the domestic marginal propensity to consume exportable goods (c).[2] It follows, then, that if imports are not inferior goods in the protecting country's consumption this case requires inelastic foreign demand; and we can ensure that the internal relative price of the importable good always rises with the imposition of a tariff by assuming *either* elastic foreign demand (sometimes done in the form of assuming a small country) *or* a big enough tariff (in the limit, a prohibitive tariff) for demand to be elastic.

5. Argument (2) follows necessarily from the basic Stolper–Samuelson model. To show this simply, we should recall the technological features of the model employed by Samuelson some years later in this JOURNAL [3] to demonstrate factor-price equalisation: these features are identical with those of the Stolper–Samuelson model in all respects. We propose thus to avoid altogether the use of the box-diagram and work instead with the unique relationships that Samuelson derived in these later articles between commodity price-ratios, factor price-ratios and factor proportions in the two industries in a country, from the given assumptions concerning technology alone. These are summarised in Fig. 1, which is reproduced, with slight changes, from Samuelson's 1949 article.[4]

Let L_C and L_F represent the labour employed in producing clothing and food respectively; T_C and T_F being the quantities of land so employed.

[1] This is true except in a *limiting* case where the terms of trade will not change with trade. This case, however, can be ruled out, in the context of the model used here, by assuming that the community indifference curves (used here without any welfare connotation) are strictly convex. This limiting case will henceforward be ignored.

[2] Metzler, " Tariffs, the Terms of Trade and the Distribution of National Income," *Journal of Political Economy*, February 1949, pp. 1–29. It should be emphasised that the Metzler formula for determining the impact of protection on the internal commodity price-ratio relates to the case where the initial situation is that of free-trade. Where, however, the initial situation itself has a tariff and the impact of *increased* protection is the subject of analysis, the " perverse " possibility mentioned in the text will occur, as argued in Section II, when a slightly altered condition is fulfilled. The discussion in Section I, however, is confined to initial situations of free trade, as with Stolper and Samuelson, Metzler and Lancaster.

[3] " International Trade and the Equalisation of Factor Prices," ECONOMIC JOURNAL, June 1948, pp. 163–84; and " International Factor-Price Equalisation Once Again," ECONOMIC JOURNAL, June 1949, pp. 181–97.

[4] This diagram is to be found on p. 188 of Samuelson's 1949 ECONOMIC JOURNAL article, *op. cit.* Full exploration of this diagram is to be found in an excellent article by Professor Johnson, " Factor Endowments, International Trade and Factor Prices," *Manchester School*, September 1957, pp. 270–83. Professor Johnson, however, works with a slightly adapted diagram, to be found in Harrod, " Factor-price Relations Under Free Trade," ECONOMIC JOURNAL, June 1958, pp. 245–55. On grounds of economy, the discussion of this well-known diagram has been kept brief in this paper.

736   THE ECONOMIC JOURNAL   [DEC.

W/R represents the ratio of wages to rents; L/T the factor endowment ratio of the country; and P_F/P_C the price of food over the price of clothing. Clothing is the labour-intensive industry, food the land-intensive industry, at all relevant factor price-ratios. $(L_C/T_C > L_F/T_F$ at all relevant W/R.)[1] As wages fall relatively to rents, the price of food is shown to rise relatively to that of clothing in a monotonic fashion. The factor endowment ratio of the country (L/T) fixes the range of the diagram which is relevant. This is a purely technology-determined diagram, and demand conditions are totally absent from it.

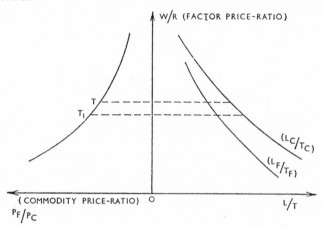

FIG. 1

T being any given commodity price-ratio (P_F/P_C), change it to T_1 such that the relative price of food rises. With it, the labour-to-land ratios in both food and clothing will rise. The marginal physical product of land in both products will thus rise and of labour fall, so that the real wage of land will be unambiguously increased and of labour decreased. Increase in the relative price of food thus increases the real wage of land, the factor intensively employed in its production; and reduces the real wage of labour, the factor intensively used in producing clothing (whose relative price has fallen).

This argument, it should be noted, rests on the assumption, part of the basic Stolper–Samuelson model, that the rise of the relative price of food does not go so far as to make the country specialise completely on food, in so far as the fall in the real wage of labour is concerned; for, once the country is specialised completely, further increases in the relative price of food will raise the real wage of *both* labour and land, which is destructive of the full validity of argument (2).

Given the basic Stolper–Samuelson model, therefore, an increase (de-

---

[1] Although the factor-intensities of the commodities may be reversible, they *cannot* reverse for a country with a *given* factor endowment. At the present stage of our argument, therefore, we do not need to make the strong assumption that factor-intensities are non-reversible at *all* factor price-ratios.

crease) in the relative price of a good will necessarily increase (decrease) the real wage of the factor intensively used in its production.

6. Argument (3) that the importable good is intensive in the use of the scarce factor is really the well-known Heckscher–Ohlin theorem. The crucial question that it raises is: does the Heckscher–Ohlin theorem follow from the basic Stolper–Samuelson model? To answer this question, we should first have to define " factor scarcity." We may choose from three alternative definitions of factor scarcity:

A. Lancaster Definition. A country's scarce factor is that which is used more intensively in the production of the importable good. This definition may be described as tautological, since it turns the Heckscher–Ohlin theorem into a valid proposition by *definition*. It may also be described as an internal definition, since it excludes any comparison with the foreign country. It has been suggested by Lancaster.[1]

B. Heckscher–Ohlin Definition. A country's scarce factor is that whose relative price is higher than abroad under self-sufficiency. This may also be described as a price definition, since the country's scarce factor is that factor which is more expensive prior to trade than abroad. This definition has been used by Heckscher and Ohlin.[2]

C. Leontief Definition. A country's scarce factor is that of which there are fewer physical units per unit of the other factor than abroad. This may also be described as a physical definition, since it defines scarcity with reference to the relative physical quantities of factors.[3]

Using each of these definitions in turn, let us analyse the Heckscher–Ohlin theorem.

A: If the Lancaster definition of factor scarcity is used, then the Heckscher–Ohlin theorem holds by definition.

B: If the Heckscher–Ohlin definition of factor scarcity is used then the further assumptions of international identity of production functions and non-reversibility of factor-intensities of commodites between the

---

[1] Lancaster, *op. cit.*, p. 208, argues that " the only acceptable definition " of a scarce factor is that which defines it as the factor " which is used more intensively in the good of which more is produced in isolation than in trade." It is of some interest to note that tariffs designed to influence distribution are probably set with reference to such internal criteria: to raise the real wage of labour, for instance, tariffs are imposed on labour-intensive industries rather than on products of industries using a factor which is scarcer at home than abroad; with the possible exception of the pauper-labour argument for such tariffs.

[2] For a convincing attribution of the authorship of this definition of factor scarcity to Heckscher and Ohlin, see a masterly article by R. Jones, " Factor Proportions and the Heckscher–Ohlin Theorem," *Review of Economic Studies*, 1956–57, pp. 1–10. The definition may be also illustrated in terms of Fig. 1: country *A* is labour-abundant and country *B* land-abundant if, under self-sufficiency, $(W/R)_A < (W/R)_B$.

[3] W. Leontief, " Domestic Production and Foreign Trade: The American Capital Position Re-examined," *Proceedings of the American Philosophical Society*, September 28, 1953; reprinted in *Economia Internazionale*, February 1954. Again, country *A* is labour-abundant and country *B* land-abundant if, under self-sufficiency, $(L/T)_A > (L/T)_B$.

two countries will suffice to ensure the full validity of the Heckscher–Ohlin theorem.[1]

C: If the Leontief definition of factor scarcity is used, then the three-fold assumptions of non-reversibilities of factor-intensities of commodities between the trading countries and the international identity of both production functions and tastes will ensure the validity of the Heckscher–Ohlin theorem.[2]

7. We can now sum up on the Stolper–Samuelson formulations as follows: [3]

A. (1) The restrictive Stolper–Samuelson theorem is logically true if we use: (a) the basic Stolper–Samuelson model, and (b) the Lancaster definition of factor scarcity.

(2) The general Stolper–Samuelson theorem is logically true if we use the further assumption that the elasticity of foreign demand is greater than the marginal propensity to consume exportable goods ($n_x > c$).

B. (1) The restrictive Stolper–Samuelson theorem is logically true if we use: (a) the basic Stolper–Samuelson model, (b) the Heckscher–Ohlin definition of factor scarcity, (c) the assumption of international identity of production functions, and (d) the assumption of non-reversibility of factor-intensities of commodities between the countries.

(2) The general Stolper–Samuelson theorem is logically true if we use the further assumption that $n_x > c$.

C. (1) The restrictive Stolper–Samuelson theorem is logically true if we use: (a) the basic Stolper–Samuelson model, (b) the Leontief definition of factor scarcity, (c) the assumption of international identity of production functions, (d) the assumption of non-reversibility of factor-

[1] This can be seen readily from Fig. 1. If $(W/R)_A < (W/R)_B$ and production functions with non-reversible factor-intensities are common between the countries, then we can see that $(P_F/P_C)_A > (P_F/P_C)_B$ under self-sufficiency and the labour-abundant country A will necessarily export the labour-intensive commodity, clothing. We could, of course, specify what appears to be a less restrictive condition than that set out in the text: for instance, we could sustain the Heckscher–Ohlin theorem by assuming merely that, instead of identical production functions between countries, the differences in the production functions are not large enough to outweigh the effect of differences in factor scarcity on the pre-trade commodity price-ratios. We have preferred to use the strong condition (identity of tastes) instead of the weak one on the ground that the use of the latter seems to be bad methodology, amounting to the argument that the Heckscher–Ohlin definition of factor scarcity will suffice to sustain the Heckscher–Ohlin theorem if other factors do not work to invalidate it.

[2] The Heckscher–Ohlin theorem would not hold as a logically true proposition in this case unless we also postulate now international identity of tastes (or the weak postulate that differences in tastes between countries do not affect the issue). This follows from the fact that while, with identical production functions, country A will show a bias towards the production of the labour-intensive commodity, clothing, by virtue of her physical abundance in labour, this bias in production may be more than offset by a bias in A towards the *consumption* of clothing: such that, in self-sufficiency, we find that $(P_F/P_C)_A < (P_F/P_C)_B$ and country A, although physically abundant in labour, would export the land-intensive commodity, food.

[3] The phrase " logically true " in the following statements is used in the strict mathematical sense: " A statement that is true in every logically possible case is said to be *logically true* " (Kemeny, Snell and Thompson, *Introduction to Finite Mathematics* (Prentice-Hall, 1957), p. 19.

intensities of commodities between countries, and (*e*) the assumption of international identity of tastes.

(2) The general Stolper–Samuelson theorem is logically true if we use the further assumption that $n_x > c$.

A tree-diagram, based on this analysis, is presented in Table I.

8. We are now in a position to decide whether Stolper and Samuelson derived their theorems logically. Aside from their basic model:

(1) they adopt, though without complete clarity, the Heckscher–Ohlin definition of factor scarcity and the postulate concerning the non-reversibility of factor-intensities; and, quite explicitly, the assumption of international identity of production functions: [1] this establishes the restrictive Stolper–Samuelson theorem as logically true (B(1));

(2) they further assume that " the country in question is relatively small and has no influence on the terms of trade "; [2] this establishes the general Stolper–Samuelson theorem as logically true (B(2)).

9. No critique of the Stolper–Samuelson formulations can thus be founded on the argument that they are not logically true, given the premises. What we could say, however, is that the theorem should be founded as closely as possible on the *basic* Stolper–Samuelson model alone; and

(1) that, if we use the Heckscher–Ohlin definition of factor scarcity, the assumptions that we find ourselves making about the international identity of production functions and the non-reversibility of factor-intensities to sustain the twin formulations of the Stolper–Samuelson theorem are, on this criterion, *restrictive*; and

(2) that, if we use the Leontief definition of factor scarcity (as we should probably want to since it is, in a sense, the most " objective " definition we could adopt in this context), we discover ourselves adopting the threefold restrictive assumptions (C(1)) of international identity of production functions and tastes plus the non-reversibility of factor-intensities of commodities, to sustain the Stolper–Samuelson formulations.[3]

10. It will be remembered, however, that these restrictive assumptions were made only because we wished to use argument (3) concerning the validity of the Heckscher–Ohlin theorem.[4] This may also be seen indirectly from

---

[1] Stolper and Samuelson, *op. cit.*, pp. 335–40. Some of the argument is, of course, obscure in view of the pioneering nature of the article: a sympathetic interpretation, therefore, is called for. Metzler, *op. cit.*, p. 5, also adopts the Heckscher–Ohlin definition of factor scarcity in discussing the Stolper–Samuelson theorem.

[2] Stolper and Samuelson, *op. cit.*, p. 346.

[3] The additional restrictive assumption that $\eta_x > c$ has not been listed here because we wish at this stage to concentrate on only those restrictive assumptions which are made to sustain argument (3).

[4] It is important to remember that these assumptions are restrictive only in so far as we wish to found our theorem exclusively on the basic Stolper–Samuelson model.

TABLE I

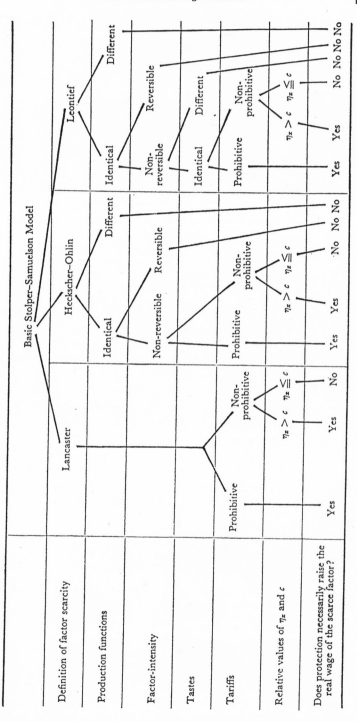

the fact that, if we use the Lancaster definition of factor scarcity, no such restrictive assumptions are necessary (A(1)): for the Heckscher–Ohlin theorem has been rendered valid by definition!

The suggestion follows readily from these considerations that we should reformulate our theorem in terms of arguments (1) and (2) alone, while eliminating the use of the troublesome argument (3). This can be done readily: protection (prohibitive or otherwise) raises the real wage of the factor intensively employed in the production of the importable good. This theorem is logically true if we use: (*a*) the basic Stolper–Samuelson model, and (*b*) the assumption that $n_x > c$.

This theorem has been described as the Stolper–Samuelson–Metzler–Lancaster theorem on the following grounds:

(1) It is *implicit* in the Stolper–Samuelson argument, towards the end of their paper: " It does not follow that our results stand and fall with the Heckscher–Ohlin theorem. Our analysis neglected the other country completely. If factors of production are not comparable between countries, or if production functions differ, nevertheless, so long as the country has only two factors, international trade would necessarily affect the real wage of a factor in the same direction as its relative remuneration." [1]

(2) Metzler *explicitly* states it as " the Stolper–Samuelson conclusion that tariffs benefit the factors of production which are required in relatively large amounts in the industries competing with imports." [2]

(3) Lancaster advances this formulation directly as an *alternative* to the Stolper–Samuelson formulations considered above on the ground that it is more general than the latter.

11. Whereas, however, Lancaster's observation that the Stolper–Samuelson formulations are "non-universal" (restrictive) is well taken, the argument by which he supports it is erroneous and different from that set out in this paper. Lancaster proceeds by establishing, with the aid of a highly ingenious model, the proposition that, in the context of the basic Stolper–Samuelson model combined with the assumption of a small country facing fixed terms of trade, differences in demand conditions (" which good is the wage-good ") will affect the composition of a country's foreign trade. On this proposition he founds the following critique:

" The non-universality of the [Stolper–Samuelson] theorem is due to incorrect formulation: if the scarce factor is defined as that which is used more intensively in the good of which more is produced in isolation

---

[1] Stolper and Samuelson, *op. cit.*, pp. 355–6. Homogeneity of factors between countries has not been listed separately as an assumption in this paper because it is believed that this is implicit in both the Heckscher–Ohlin and the Leontief definitions of factor scarcity.

[2] Metzler, *op. cit.*, p. 13. Metzler, of course, does not state it as a rival formulation, but it is abundantly clear that he is aware that this formulation is implicit in the general Stolper–Samuelson theorem.

than in trade (the only acceptable definition), then the previous analysi
has shown that different wage-goods may make for different facto₁
scarcities. In this sense, the Stolper–Samuelson formulation is meaningless, since the phrases ' real wages . . . in terms of any good ' and
' scarce factor ' represent incompatible concepts." [1]

The following comments on Lancaster's critique seem warranted here, in
view of our preceding analysis.

To begin with, it is difficult to understand what Lancaster means by the
statement that " the previous analysis has shown that different wage-goods
may make for different factor scarcities. In this sense, the Stolper–
Samuelson formulation is meaningless, since the phrases ' real wages . . .
in terms of any good ' and ' scarce factor ' represent incompatible concepts." Which good will be imported into a country will depend in our model
on the pre-trade commodity price-ratios in the trading countries; these
price-ratios are determined by domestic supply and demand; and domestic
demand is affected by " which good is the wage-good." If the scarce factor
is defined tautologously as that which is used intensively in the importable
good it follows then, from elementary considerations, that " different wage-
goods may make for different factor scarcities." But surely, how can this
render the Stolper–Samuelson formulations *meaningless* or make ' real wages
. . . in terms of any good ' and ' scarce factor ' *incompatible* concepts? And,
more pertinently, why should this make the Stolper–Samuelson formulation
" non-universal " ?

Indeed, if the tautologous definition of factor scarcity is adopted, as Lancaster suggests, then the general Stolper–Samuelson theorem and the Stolper–
Samuelson–Metzler–Lancaster theorem are *identical*: the phrases " scarce
factor " and " factor intensively employed in the importable good " can be
used interchangeably. Lancaster cannot, therefore, claim one formulation
to be " non-universal " and the other to be " universally true ": on his own
definition of factor scarcity, the two formulations come to the same thing!

To be sure, Lancaster's critique would be valid (though, as we have
shown, incomplete) only if the physical, Leontief definition of factor scarcity
were proven to have been adopted by Stolper and Samuelson, and were
adopted by Lancaster as well; as formulated, however, the criticism is
merely erroneous.[2] In failing to investigate precisely what Stolper and
Samuelson assumed by way of their definition of factor scarcity, Lancaster
has further by-passed the only legitimate critique that can be sustained
against the actual formulation of the theorem by Stolper and Samuelson:
namely, that advanced in this paper.

---

[1] Lancaster, *op. cit.*, p. 208.

[2] Lancaster has pointed out to me, in private communication, that he really had in mind the
physical definition of factor scarcity, despite the printed commitment to the tautologous definition:
the tenor of the argument on p. 209, *op. cit.*, seems to suggest this, although it follows upon the
formulation of the tautologous definition. None of the criticism advanced here should obscure
that fact that Lancaster has handled his model with admirable expertise.

12. Our task is yet incomplete. Even the Stolper–Samuelson–Metzler–Lancaster formulation does not found the theorem completely and solely on the basic model. We must still make the restrictive assumption that $\eta_x > c$. We should, however, clearly want to go the whole way and remove all restrictive assumptions and restate the theorem to include the entire matrix of possibilities: such that the theorem is logically true, given only the basic Stolper–Samuelson model. This formulation is: [1]

> *Protection (prohibitive or otherwise) will raise, reduce or leave unchanged the real wage of the factor intensively employed in the production of a good according as protection raises, lowers or leaves unchanged the internal relative price of that good.*

This is really the fundamental theorem that Stolper and Samuelson contributed to our knowedge of the properties of the basic model they were using. Given the basic model, our formulation is logically true for all possible cases.

13. It should perhaps be emphasised that the preceding analysis has been centred entirely on the problem of analysing the impact of protection on real wages of factors in the context of the basic model employed by Stolper and Samuelson. It should be possible, of course, to analyse the problem afresh in terms of models employing alternative assumptions. This, however, would be mostly destructive of the full validity of our theorem.

If we allow for complete specialisation with trade, for instance, we can claim only that protection will raise, lower or leave unchanged the real wage of the factor in which the *exportable* good is postulated to be intensive according as protection raises, lowers or leaves unchanged the internal relative price of the exportable good. But we cannot extend the theorem to the factor postulated to be used intensively in the production, if any, of the importable good because any increase in the internal relative price of the exportable good after complete specialisation must raise the real wage of *both* factors.

However, if we allow the optimum factor-proportions within industries, at given factor price-ratios, to change with scale, our theorem will continue to be logically true and the real wage of the factor intensively employed in a good will rise, fall or be unchanged according as the internal relative price of that good rises, falls or is unchanged with the imposition of protection. [2]

---

[1] This formulation stems directly from argument (2), which is founded exclusively, as the reader will remember, on the basic Stolper–Samuelson model.

[2] An apparent exception to this proposition may be investigated. Where the optimum factor-ratio changes with scale, at given factor price-ratios, it may happen, for instance, that if the production of labour-intensive importables expands, a higher proportion of labour is released than is needed in import-substitution, even though importables are *on average* more labour-intensive. In this case, increase in the production of importables will lead to a *rise* in the labour-to-land ratios, and hence *reduce* the real wage of labour. This case, however, does not constitute an exception to our theorem, because such technology involves a concave production frontier, so that increase in the production of importables occurs when the price of importables *falls* (and not rises). Hence the logical truth of our proposition, even when we allow for changing optimum factor-ratios with scale.

On the other hand, if we allow for changing returns to scale in either o both of the two activities, clearly it becomes impossible to maintain that ou theorem will be logically true.

II. PROTECTION AND REAL INCOMES

14. Our analysis has so far been concerned with the original Stolper-Samuelson problem of discovering the impact of protection on the *real wage* earned by factors in employment. It seems useful, however, to emphasise that if we are interested in finding out the net change in the *real income* of the factors it is only in the case of a prohibitive tariff that a complete identity obtains between change in real wage and change in the real income of a factor. Where the tariff is non-prohibitive, the complication arises from the revenue earned by the Government. If this revenue is assumed to be redistributed to the owners of factors according to some formula, factors will derive incomes *both* from the real wage in employment and from the redistributed proceeds of the tariff-revenue.

Hence arises the interesting possibility that the factor whose real wage has been damaged by protection may still find its real income improved if the formula for the redistribution of the tariff-revenue is heavily biased in its favour. Since this possibility constitutes a qualification to the generally accepted implication of the Stolper–Samuelson analysis, it should be of some interest to delimit the conditions under which it may occur.

To begin with, this possibility of over-compensating the damaged factor *from the tariff-revenue* clearly cannot arise unless the real income of the country as a whole is improved by protection. We know from the preceding analysis that where the real wage of one factor is reduced, that of the other necessarily rises; hence, if protection did not bring some gain to the country as a whole, it should be impossible to overcompensate the factor with the damaged real wage (from tariff-revenues). To rephrase the proposition, then, accrual of gain to the protecting country from the imposition of protection is a necessary, though not sufficient, condition for the possibility of over-compensating the factor with the damaged real wage.[1]

In the following brief analysis we seek to relate this proposition to Metzler's formula for determining the impact of protection on the internal commodity price-ratio: partly to establish link with Metzler's pioneering analysis in this field and largely because it enables us to define, and distinguish between, situations in which the factor with the damaged real wage will be export-intensive (intensively used in exportables) and those where it will be import-intensive. The discussion is then briefly extended to the

---

[1] That is to say, whereas the country must have gained from protection before the damaged factor can be overcompensated from the tariff-revenues (necessary condition), this gain must be large enough to permit overcompensation (sufficient condition).

1959]   PROTECTION, REAL WAGES AND REAL INCOMES   745

case where the initial situation is that of a tariff instead of free-trade and the effect of an *increase* in protection is the subject of inquiry.

15. In Fig. 2 let O_b be the foreign reciprocal demand curve facing country A. F is the free-trade point, OF yielding the corresponding terms of trade. I_a' is the trade-indifference curve of A passing through F at a tangent to OF and intersecting O_b at U. Its postulated curvature derives from

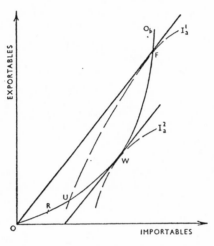

FIG. 2

the assumption of strict convexity of the production frontier and community indifference curves.

(1) Assume that the tariff-added offer curve of country A intersects O_b at U. The internal relative price of the importable good is then given by the slope of the trade-indifference curve I_a' at U, which is clearly, by virtue of the postulated curvature of I_a', greater than at F. We can deduce, therefore, that protection can leave the real income of the country unchanged only if the internal relative price of the importable good rises from the free-trade level with the imposition of protection (in turn, only if $\eta_x > c$).

(2) Similarly, by considering points on O_b to the left of U such as R, we can argue that protection can reduce the real income of the country only if the internal relative price of the importable good rises with protection (in turn, only if $\eta_x > c$).

(3) However, protection can increase the real income of the country whether the internal relative price of the importable good rises, is unchanged (W) or falls with the imposition of protection (in turn, whether $\eta_x \gtreqless c$).

Thus, where $\eta_x \leq c$, the real income of the country will necessarily improve with the imposition of a tariff; whereas if $\eta_x > c$, the real income may rise, fall or be unchanged.

16. Where the comparison is confined to the real income and real wage of the factors in an initial free-trade position and after the imposition of a tariff, we can then conclude as follows:

(1) the export-intensive factor will necessarily become better off and it may be possible to overcompensate the import-intensive factor if $\eta_x < c$; [1]

(2) neither factor will become worse off and at least one better off if $\eta_x = c$; [2] and

(3) the import-intensive factor will necessarily become better off and it may be possible to overcompensate the export-intensive factor if two conditions obtain: (i) $\eta_x > c$, and (ii) the tariff is small enough to yield some gain to the country.

If we assume that importables are not inferior goods in the protecting country, it is clear, then, that inelastic foreign demand ($\eta_x < 1$) is a necessary, though not a sufficient, condition for the emergence of the possibility of overcompensating the import-intensive factor. Where, however, foreign demand is elastic and importables are not inferior goods, the export-intensive factor will necessarily find its real wage reduced by protection; and, for the possibility of overcompensating it to arise, it will be necessary, though not sufficient, that the tariff be small enough to make the country better off than under free-trade.

17. If, however, we wish to compare the real incomes and wages of factors in an initial situation of a tariff and after *increase* in the tariff, the analysis must be somewhat modified.

To begin with, the Metzler formula must be altered so as to read: the internal relative price of the importable good will rise, be unchanged or fall according as $\eta_x \gtrless \dfrac{1 - c'(1 + t)}{1 - c't}$ where t is the initial tariff-rate and $c' = (1 - c)$ is the domestic marginal propensity to consume importables. [3]

---

[1] When $\eta_x < c$ we know now that: (1) the internal relative price of the importable good falls, thus increasing the real wage of the export-intensive factor and reducing that of the import-intensive factor; and (2) the country must have become better off. Hence the proposition in the text.

[2] Where $\eta_x = c$, we know that: (1) the internal relative price of the importable good is unchanged, thus leaving unchanged the real wages of both factors; and (2) the real income of the country must increase. Hence the proposition in the text.

[3] This formula is derived from the following analysis, furnished by Professor Johnson and replacing my earlier, unsatisfactory attempt.

Symbols: Let p be the *external* terms of trade, measured as the price of the importable good over the price of the exportable good, t the initial tariff rate and $\pi = p(1 + t)$ the *internal* terms of trade. c' is the marginal propensity to consume importables, at the initial terms of trade. C is the initial

It will be seen that where the initial situation is that of free-trade, t will be zero and the formula will reduce to the well-known Metzler formula.

Secondly, the impact on the real income of the country will not bear the same relationship to the shifts in the internal commodity price-ratio as in the previous analysis with the free-trade initial situation. It can be demonstrated, by a geometrical argument analogous to that used earlier, that although the internal relative price of the importable good must still rise for the country to be as well off as prior to the increased tariff, both reduction and increase in the real income of the country are now consistent with any shift in this price.

Thirdly, arguing from the optimum tariff theory, we can claim that the real income of the country will improve with increased protection if two conditions obtain: (i) the pre-increase tariff rate is less than the optimum tariff rate $t < \dfrac{1}{\eta_x - 1}$; and (ii) *either* the post-increase tariff rate is also less than the optimum tariff rate *or*, if it exceeds the optimum tariff rate, it is small enough to leave some gain in real income to the country from the increase in tariff.

---

domestic consumption of importables, Y their production and $M \equiv C - Y$ the initial quantity of imports. $r_m = (\eta_x - 1) = \dfrac{p}{M} \cdot \dfrac{\delta Sm}{\delta p}$ ($Sm \equiv M$) is the elasticity of foreign supply of importables; and $R = tpM$ is the tariff revenue.

Analysis: The simplest approach to the problem is to assume the internal terms of trade to be constant and to investigate the excess demand for importables when t changes. If the excess demand is positive, the internal terms of trade will rise to restore equilibrium; if negative, they will fall: assuming, of course, that we have " well-behaved " substitution elasticities in production and consumption.

Now, $R = tpM = \dfrac{t}{1 + t}\pi \cdot M$. With π constant, we have $\dfrac{dp}{dt} = -\dfrac{p}{(1 + t)}$. The shift in the demand for imports due to the change in the tariff is then given by:

$$\frac{dC}{dt} = c'\frac{dR}{dt} = c'\pi \left\{ \frac{1}{(1 + t)^2}M + \frac{t}{(1 + t)} \cdot \frac{dM}{dt} \right\}$$

The shift in the supply of imports is given by:

$$\frac{dM}{dp} \cdot \frac{dp}{dt} = \frac{M}{p} \cdot r_m \cdot \frac{dp}{dt} = -\frac{M}{(1 + t)} \cdot r_m$$

The excess demand for importables is then given by:

$$\left(\frac{dC}{dt} - \frac{dM}{dt} \right)$$

$$= \frac{c'\pi}{(1 + t)^2} \cdot M + \left\{ \frac{c'\pi t}{(1 + t)} - 1 \right\} \left\{ \frac{-M}{(1 + t)} \right\} r_m$$

$$= \frac{M}{(1 + t)} \{ c'p + (1 - c'pt)r_m \}$$

Substituting $r_m = \eta_x - 1$, assuming p to be unity initially by choice of units and simplifying, we arrive at the formula that the excess demand for importables will be positive, zero or negative according as:

$$\eta_x \gtreqless \frac{1 - c'(1 + t)}{1 - c't}$$

It will be seen that this formula reduces to the Metzler formula when t is zero.

These considerations lead to the following conclusions: [1]

(1) The export-intensive factor will necessarily become better off and it may be possible to overcompensate the import-intensive factor from *increased* tariff-revenues when three conditions obtain:

(i) $\eta_x < \dfrac{1 - c'(1 + t)}{1 - c't}$; (ii) $t < \dfrac{1}{\eta_x - 1}$; and (iii) *either* the post-increase tariff rate is also less than the optimum tariff rate *or*, if it exceeds the optimum tariff, it is still small enough to leave some gain in real income to the country from the increase in the tariff.

(2) The import-intensive factor will necessarily become better off and it may be possible to overcompensate the export-intensive factor from *increased* tariff-revenues when three conditions obtain:

(i) $\eta_x > \dfrac{1 - c'(1 + t)}{1 - c't}$; (ii) $t < \dfrac{1}{\eta_x - 1}$; and (iii) *either* the post-increase tariff rate is also less than the optimum tariff *or*, if it exceeds the optimum tariff, it is still small enough to leave some gain in real income to the country from the increase in protection.

(3) Where, however, $\eta_x = \dfrac{1 - c'(1 + t)}{1 - c't}$, the real wage of neither factor changes with the increase in protection. It follows, therefore, that the real income of both factors will increase, decrease or remain unchanged according as the increase in tariff raises, lowers or leaves unchanged the real income of the country: assuming, of course, that the tariff-revenues are divided among the factors in a given proportion.

18. In conclusion, it should be re-emphasised that the brief discussion presented here has been concerned only with the limited task of exploring some of the implications of the proposition that accrual of gain to the protecting country from the imposition of protection is a necessary, though not sufficient, condition for the emergence of the possibility of overcompensating, from tariff-revenues, the factor with the damaged real wage. It is planned to present a rigorous analysis of the sufficient conditions for the emergence of this possibility in a subsequent article.[2]

                                                        JAGDISH BHAGWATI
Nuffield College,
  Oxford.

[1] The first two propositions that follow assume that the factor stated to become necessarily better off continues to receive *at least* the same revenue as in the initial situation; this assumption being made explicit by the use of the phrase " from *increased* tariff-revenues." This assumption is needed because otherwise improvement merely in the real wage of a factor due to increased protection could be offset by an accompanying unfavourable distribution of tariff-revenues to the factor after the increase in the tariff.

[2] This calls for a rigorous analysis of distribution and demand, so that factor earnings and income subsidies from tariff-revenues could be related to real incomes of factors. Such analysis would preclude us from taking as given, as we have done here, the set of community indifference curves: this practice has been adopted in the present paper for strictly pedagogic reasons.

3

The Structure of
Simple General
Equilibrium Models

Ronald W. Jones

1. Introduction

It is difficult to find any major branch of applied economics that has not made some use of the simple general equilibrium model of production. For years this model has served as the work-horse for most of the developments in the pure theory of international trade. It has been used to study the effects of taxation on the distribution of income and the impact of technological change on the composition of outputs and the structure of prices. Perhaps the most prominent of its recent uses is to be found in the neoclassical theory of economic growth.

Such intensive use of the simple two-sector model of production suggests that a few properties are being retranslated in such diverse areas as public finance, international trade, and economic growth. The unity provided by a common theoretical structure is further emphasized by the dual relationship that exists between sets of variables in the model itself. Traditional formulations of the model tend to obscure this feature. My purpose in this chapter is to analyze the structure of the simple competitive model of production in a manner designed to highlight both the dual relationship and the similarity that exists among a number of traditional problems in comparative statics and economic growth.

The model is described in sections 2 and 3. In section 4 I discuss the dual nature of two theorems in the theory of international trade associated with the names of Stolper and Samuelson on the one hand and Rybczynski on the other. A simple demand relationship is added in section 5, and a problem in public finance is analyzed—the effect of excise subsidies or taxes on relative commodity and factor prices. The static model of production is then reinterpreted as a neo-classical model of economic

This paper was originally published in *Journal of Political Economy* 73 (December 1965): 557–572.

growth by letting one of the outputs serve as the capital good. The dual of the "incidence" problem in public finance in the static model is shown to have direct relevance to the problem of the stability of the balanced growth path in the neoclassical growth model. In the concluding section of the chapter I show how these results can be applied to the analysis of technological progress. Any improvement in technology or in the quality of factors of production can be simply viewed as a composite of two effects, which I shall term the "differential industry" effect and the "differential factor" effect. Each effect has its counterpart in the dual problems discussed in the earlier part of the paper.

2. The Model

Assume a perfectly competitive economy in which firms (indefinite in number) maximize profits, which are driven to the zero level in equilibrium. Consistent with this, technology in each of two sectors exhibits constant returns to scale. Two primary factors, labor (L) and land (T), are used in producing two distinct commodities, manufactured goods (M) and food (F). Wages (w) and rents (r) denote the returns earned by the factors for use of services, whereas p_M and p_F denote the competitive market prices of the two commodities.

If technology is given and factor endowments and commodity prices are treated as parameters, the model serves to determine eight unknowns: the level of commodity outputs (two), the factor allocations to each industry (four), and factor prices (two). The equations of the model could be given by the production functions (two), the requirement that each factor receive the value of its marginal product (four), and that each factor be fully employed (two). This is the format most frequently used in the theory of international trade and the neoclassical theory of growth.[1] I consider, instead, the formulation of the model suggested by activity analysis.

The technology is described by the columns of the A matrix,

$$A = \begin{pmatrix} a_{LM} & a_{LF} \\ a_{TM} & a_{TF} \end{pmatrix},$$

where a_{ij} denotes the quantity of factor i required to produce a unit of commodity j. With constant returns to scale total factor demands are given by the product of the a's and the levels of output. The requirement that both factors be fully employed is thus given by equations (1) and (2). Similarly, unit costs of production in each industry are given by the

Ronald W. Jones   32

columns of A multiplied by the factor prices. In a competitive equilibrium with both goods being produced, these unit costs must reflect market prices, as in equations (3) and (4).[2]

$$a_{LM}M + a_{LF}F = L, \tag{1}$$

$$a_{TM}M + a_{TF}F = T, \tag{2}$$

$$a_{LM}w + a_{TM}r = p_M, \tag{3}$$

$$a_{LF}w + a_{TF}r = p_F. \tag{4}$$

This formulation serves to emphasize the dual relationship between factor endowments and commodity outputs on the one hand (equations (1) and (2)) and commodity prices and factor prices on the other (equations (3) and (4)).

In the general case of variable coefficients the relationships shown in equations (1)–(4) must be supplemented by four additional relationships determining the input coefficients. These are provided by the requirement that in a competitive equilibrium each a_{ij} depends solely upon the ratio of factor prices.

3. The Equations of Change

The comparative statics properties of the model described in section 2 are developed by considering the effect of a change in the parameters on the unknowns of the problem. With unchanged technology the parameters are the factor endowments (L and T) and the commodity prices (p_M and p_F), the right-hand side of equations (1)–(4).

Let a hat ($\hat{\ }$) indicate the relative change in a variable or parameter. Thus, $\hat{p}_F$ denotes dp_F/p_F and $\hat{L}$ denotes dL/L.[3] The four equations in the rates of change are shown in (1a)–(4a):

$$\lambda_{LM}\hat{M} + \lambda_{LF}\hat{F} = \hat{L} - [\lambda_{LM}\hat{a}_{LM} + \lambda_{LF}\hat{a}_{LF}]. \tag{1a}$$

$$\lambda_{TM}\hat{M} + \lambda_{TF}\hat{F} = \hat{T} - [\lambda_{TM}\hat{a}_{TM} + \lambda_{TF}\hat{a}_{TF}], \tag{2a}$$

$$\theta_{LM}\hat{w} + \theta_{TM}\hat{r} = \hat{p}_M - [\theta_{LM}\hat{a}_{LM} + \theta_{TM}\hat{a}_{TM}], \tag{3a}$$

$$\theta_{LF}\hat{w} + \theta_{TF}\hat{r} = \hat{p}_F - [\theta_{LF}\hat{a}_{LF} + \theta_{TF}\hat{a}_{TF}]. \tag{4a}$$

The λ's and θ's are the transforms of the a's that appear when relative changes are shown. A fraction of the labor force is used in manufacturing (λ_{LM}), and this plus the fraction of the labor force used in food production (λ_{LF}) must add to unity by the full-employment assumption (shown by equation (1)). Similarly for λ_{TM} and λ_{TF}. The θ's, by contrast, refer to the factor shares in each industry. Thus, θ_{LM}, labor's share in manufacturing, is given by $a_{LM}w/p_M$. By the zero profit conditions, θ_{Lj} and θ_{Tj} must add to unity.

In this section I assume that manufacturing is labor-intensive. It follows that labor's share in manufacturing must be greater than labor's share in food, and that the percentage of the labor force used in manufacturing must exceed the percentage of total land that is used in manufacturing. Let λ and θ be the notations for the matrices of coefficients shown in (1a), (2a) and (3a), (4a):

$$\lambda = \begin{pmatrix} \lambda_{LM} & \lambda_{LF} \\ \lambda_{TM} & \lambda_{TF} \end{pmatrix} ; \quad \theta = \begin{pmatrix} \theta_{LM} & \theta_{TM} \\ \theta_{LF} & \theta_{TF} \end{pmatrix}.$$

Since each row sum in λ and θ is unity, the determinants $|\lambda|$ and $|\theta|$ are given by

$$|\lambda| = \lambda_{LM} - \lambda_{TM} \quad \text{and} \quad |\theta| = \theta_{LM} - \theta_{LF},$$

and both $|\lambda|$ and $|\theta|$ are positive by the factor-intensity assumption.[4]

If coefficients of production are fixed, equations (1a)–(4a) are greatly simplified as every $\hat{a}_{ij}$ and, therefore, the λ and θ weighted sums of the $\hat{a}_{ij}$ reduce to zero. In the case of variable coefficients, sufficient extra conditions to determine the $\hat{a}$'s are easily derived. Consider, first, the maximizing role of the typical competitive entrepreneur. For any given level of output he attempts to minimize costs; that is, he minimizes unit costs. In the manufacturing industry these are given by $(a_{LM}w + a_{TM}r)$. The entrepreneur treats factor prices as fixed, and varies the a's so as to set the derivative of costs equal to zero. Dividing by p_M and expressing changes in relative terms leads to equation (6). Equation (7) shows the corresponding relationship for the food industry:

$$\theta_{LM}\hat{a}_{LM} + \theta_{TM}\hat{a}_{TM} = 0, \tag{6}$$

$$\theta_{LF}\hat{a}_{LF} + \theta_{TF}\hat{a}_{TF} = 0. \tag{7}$$

With no technological change, alterations in factor proportions must balance out such that the θ-weighted average of the changes in input coefficients in each industry is zero.

This implies directly that the relationship between changes in factor prices and changes in commodity prices is *identical* in the variable and fixed coefficients cases, an example of the Wong-Viner envelope theorem. With costs per unit of output being minimized, the change in costs resulting from a small change in factor prices is the same whether or not factor proportions are altered. The saving in cost from such alterations is a second-order small.[5]

A similar kind of argument definitely does *not* apply to the λ-weighted average of the $\hat{a}$'s for each factor that appears in the factor market-clearing relationships. For example $(\lambda_{LM}\hat{a}_{LM} + \lambda_{LF}\hat{a}_{LF})$ shows the percentage change in the total quantity of labor required by the economy as a result of changing factor proportions in each industry at unchanged outputs. The crucial feature here is that if factor prices change, factor proportions alter in the same direction in both industries. The extent of this change obviously depends upon the elasticities of substitution between factors in each industry. In a competitive equilibrium (and with the internal tangencies implicit in earlier assumptions), the slope of the isoquant in each industry is equal to the ratio of factor prices. Therefore the elasticities of substitution can be defined as in (8) and (9):

$$\sigma_M = \frac{\hat{a}_{TM} - \hat{a}_{LM}}{\hat{w} - \hat{r}}, \tag{8}$$

$$\sigma_F = \frac{\hat{a}_{TF} - \hat{a}_{LF}}{\hat{w} - \hat{r}}. \tag{9}$$

Together with (6) and (7) a subset of four equations relating the $\hat{a}$'s to the change in the relative factor prices is obtained. They can be solved in pairs; for example (6) and (8) yield solutions for the $\hat{a}$'s of the M industry. In general,

$$\hat{a}_{Lj} = -\theta_{Tj}\sigma_j(\hat{w} - \hat{r}), \qquad j = M, F;$$

$$\hat{a}_{Tj} = \theta_{Lj}\sigma_j(\hat{w} - \hat{r}), \qquad j = M, F.$$

These solutions for the $\hat{a}$'s can then be substituted into equations (1a)–(4a) to obtain:

$$\lambda_{LM}\hat{M} + \lambda_{LF}\hat{F} = \hat{L} + \delta_L(\hat{w} - \hat{r}), \tag{1b}$$

$$\lambda_{TM}\hat{M} + \lambda_{TF}\hat{F} = \hat{T} - \delta_T(\hat{w} - \hat{r}), \tag{2b}$$

$$\theta_{LM}\hat{w} + \theta_{TM}\hat{r} = \hat{p}_M, \tag{3b}$$

$$\theta_{LF}\hat{w} + \theta_{TF}\hat{r} = \hat{p}_F, \tag{4b}$$

where

$$\delta_L = \lambda_{LM}\theta_{TM}\sigma_M + \lambda_{LF}\theta_{TF}\sigma_F,$$

$$\delta_T = \lambda_{TM}\theta_{LM}\sigma_M + \lambda_{TF}\theta_{LF}\sigma_F.$$

In the fixed-coefficients case, δ_L and δ_T are zero. In general, δ_L is the aggregate percentage saving in labor inputs at unchanged outputs associated with a 1% rise in the relative wage rate, the saving resulting from the adjustment to less labor-intensive techniques in both industries as relative wages rise.

The structure of the production model with variable coefficients is exhibited in equations (1b)–(4b). The latter pair states that factor prices are dependent only upon commodity prices, which is the factor-price equalization theorem.[6] If commodity prices are unchanged, factor prices are constant and equations (1b) and (2b) state that changes in commodity outputs are linked to changes in factor endowments via the λ matrix in precisely the same way as θ links factor price changes. This is the basic duality feature of the production model.[7]

4. The Magnification Effect

The nature of the link provided by λ or θ is revealed by examining the solution for $\hat{M}$ and $\hat{F}$ at constant commodity prices in (1b) and (2b) and for $\hat{w}$ and $\hat{r}$ in equations (3b) and (4b).[8] If both endowments expand at the same rate, both commodity outputs expand at identical rates. But if factor endowments expand at different rates, the commodity intensive in the use of the fastest growing factor expands at a greater rate than either factor, and the other commodity grows (if at all) at a slower rate than either factor. For example, suppose labor expands more rapidly than land. With M labor-intensive,

$$\hat{M} > \hat{L} > \hat{T} > \hat{F}.$$

This *magnification effect* of factor endowments on commodity outputs at unchanged commodity prices is also a feature of the dual link between commodity and factor prices. In the absence of technological change or excise taxes or subsidies, if the price of M grows more rapidly than the price of F,

$$\hat{w} > \hat{p}_M > \hat{p}_F > \hat{r}.$$

Turned the other way around, the source of magnification effect is easy to detect. For example, since the relative change in the price of either commodity is a positive weighted average of factor-price changes, it must be bounded by these changes. Similarly, if input coefficients are fixed (as a consequence of assuming constant factor and commodity prices), any disparity in the growth of outputs is reduced when considering the consequent changes in the economy's demand for factors. The reason, of course, is that each good requires both factors of production.

Two special cases have been especially significant in the theory of international trade. Suppose the endowment of only one factor (say labor) rises. With $\hat{L}$ positive and $\hat{T}$ zero, $\hat{M}$ exceeds $\hat{L}$ and $\hat{F}$ is negative. This is the Rybczynzki theorem in the theory of international trade: at unchanged commodity prices an expansion in one factor results in an absolute decline in the commodity intensive in the use of the other factor. (See Rybczynski [17] and also Jones [13a], chapter 1.) Its dual underlies the Stolper-Samuelson [21] tariff theorem.[9] Suppose $\hat{p}_F$ is zero (for example, F could be taken as numeraire). Then an increase in the price of M (brought about, say, by a tariff on imports of M) raises the return to the factor used intensively in M by an even greater relative amount (and lowers the return to the other factor). In the case illustrated, the *real* return to labor has unambiguously risen.

For some purposes it is convenient to consider a slight variation of the Stolper-Samuelson theorem. Let p_j stand for the *market* price of j as before, but introduce a set of domestic excise taxes or subsidies so that $s_j p_j$ represents the price received by producers in industry j; s_j is one plus the *ad valorem* rate of subsidy to the industry.[10] The effect on factor prices of an imposition of subsidies on commodities is derived from equations (3c) and (4c):

$$\theta_{LM}\hat{w} + \theta_{TM}\hat{r} = \hat{p}_M + \hat{s}_M, \tag{3c}$$

$$\theta_{LF}\hat{w} + \theta_{TF}\hat{r} = \hat{p}_F + \hat{s}_F. \tag{4c}$$

At fixed commodity prices, what impact does a set of subsidies have on factor prices? The answer is that all the subsidies are "shifted backward" to affect returns to factors in a *magnified* fashion. Thus, if M is labor-intensive and if the M industry should be especially favored by the subsidy,

$$\hat{w} > \hat{s}_M > \hat{s}_F > \hat{r}.$$

The *magnification* effect in this problem and its dual reflects the basic structure of the model with fixed commodity prices. However, if a demand relationship is introduced, prices are determined within the model and can be expected to adjust to a change in factor endowments or, in the dual problem, to a change in excise subsidies (or taxes). In the next section I discuss the feedback effect of these induced price changes on the composition of output and relative factor prices. The crucial question to be considered concerns the extent to which commodity price changes can dampen the initial magnification effects that are produced at constant prices.

5. The Extended Model: Demand Endogenous

To close the production model I assume that community taste patterns are homothetic and ignore any differences between the taste patterns of laborers and landlords. Thus, the ratio of the quantities consumed of M and F depends only upon the relative commodity price ratio, as in equation (5):

$$\frac{M}{F} = f\left(\frac{p_M}{p_F}\right). \tag{5}$$

In terms of the rates of change, (5a) serves to define the elasticity of substitution between the two commodities on the demand side, σ_D:

$$(\hat{M} - \hat{F}) = -\sigma_D(\hat{p}_M - \hat{p}_F). \tag{5a}$$

The effect of a change in factor endowments at constant commodity prices was considered in the previous section. With the model closed by the demand relationship, commodity prices adjust so as to clear the commodity markets. Equation (5a) shows directly the change in the ratio of outputs consumed. Subtracting (2b) from (1b) yields the change in the ratio of outputs produced:

$$(\hat{M} - \hat{F}) = \frac{1}{|\lambda|}(\hat{L} - \hat{T}) + \frac{\delta_L + \delta_T}{|\lambda|}(\hat{w} - \hat{r}).$$

The change in the factor-price ratio (with no subsidies or taxes) is given by

$$(\hat{w} - \hat{r}) = \frac{1}{|\theta|}(\hat{p}_M - \hat{p}_F),$$

so that, by substitution,

$$(\hat{M} - \hat{F}) = \frac{1}{|\lambda|}(\hat{L} - \hat{T}) + \sigma_S(\hat{p}_M - \hat{p}_F),$$

where

$$\sigma_S \equiv \frac{1}{|\lambda||\theta|}(\delta_L + \delta_T).$$

σ_S represents the elasticity of substitution between commodities on the *supply* side (along the transformation schedule).[11] The change in the commodity-price ratio is then given by the mutual interaction of demand and supply:

$$(\hat{p}_M - \hat{p}_F) = -\frac{1}{|\lambda|\,(\sigma_S + \sigma_D)}(\hat{L} - \hat{T}). \tag{10}$$

Therefore the resulting change in the ratio of commodities produced is

$$(\hat{M} - \hat{F}) = \frac{1}{|\lambda|}\frac{\sigma_D}{\sigma_S + \sigma_D}(\hat{L} - \hat{T}). \tag{11}$$

With commodity prices adjusting to the initial output changes brought about by the change in factor endowments, the composition of outputs may, in the end, not change by as much, relatively, as the factor endowments. This clearly depends upon whether the "elasticity" expression, $\sigma_D/(\sigma_S + \sigma_D)$, is smaller than the "factor-intensity" expression, $|\lambda|$. Although it is *large* values of σ_S (and the underlying elasticities of factor substitution in each industry, σ_M and σ_F) that serve to dampen the spread of outputs, it is *small* values of σ_D that accomplish the same end. This comparison between elasticities on the demand and supply side is familiar to students of public finance concerned with questions of tax (or subsidy) incidence and shifting. I turn now to this problem.

The relationship between the change in factor prices and subsidies is given by (3c) and (4c). Solving for the change in the ratio of factor prices,

$$(\hat{w} - \hat{r}) = \frac{1}{|\theta|}\{(\hat{p}_M - \hat{p}_F) + (\hat{s}_M - \hat{s}_F)\}. \tag{12}$$

Consider factor endowments to be fixed. Any change in factor prices will nonetheless induce a readjustment of commodity outputs. On the supply side,

$$(\hat{M} - \hat{F}) = \sigma_S\{(\hat{p}_M + \hat{p}_F) + (\hat{s}_M - \hat{s}_F)\}.$$

The relative commodity price change that equates supply and demand is

$$(\hat{p}_M - \hat{p}_F) = -\frac{\sigma_S}{\sigma_S + \sigma_D}(\hat{s}_M - \hat{s}_F). \tag{13}$$

Substituting back into the expression for the change in the factor-price ratio yields

$$(\hat{w} - \hat{r}) = \frac{1}{|\theta|}\frac{\sigma_D}{\sigma_S + \sigma_D}(\hat{s}_M - \hat{s}_F). \tag{14}$$

This is a familiar result. Suppose M is subsidized more heavily than F. Part of the subsidy is shifted backward, affecting relatively favorably the factor used intensively in the M-industry (labor). Whether labor's relative return expands by a greater proportion than the spread in subsidies depends upon how much of the subsidy has been passed forward to consumers in the form of a relatively lower price for M. And this, of course, depends upon the relative sizes of σ_S and σ_D.

Notice the similarity between expressions (11) and (14). Factors produce commodities, and a change in endowments must result in an altered composition of production, by a magnified amount at unchanged prices. By analogy, subsidies "produce" returns to factors, and a change in the pattern of subsidies alters the distribution of income. In each case, of course, the extent of readjustment required is eased if commodity prices change, by a factor depending upon the relative sizes of demand and supply elasticities of substitution.

6. The Aggregate Elasticity of Substitution

The analysis of a change in factor endowments leading up to equation (11) has a direct bearing on a recent issue in the neoclassical theory of economic growth. Before describing this issue it is useful to introduce yet another elasticity concept—that of an economy-wide elasticity of substitution between factors.[12] With no subsidies, the relationship between the change in the factor price ratio and the change in endowments can be derived from (10). Thus,

$$(\hat{w} - \hat{r}) = -\frac{1}{|\lambda| |\theta| (\sigma_S + \sigma_D)}(\hat{L} - \hat{T}). \tag{15}$$

By analogy with the elasticity of substitution in a particular sector, define σ as the percentage rise in the land/labor endowment ratio required to raise the wage/rent ratio by 1%. Directly from (15),

$$\sigma = |\lambda| |\theta| (\sigma_S + \sigma_D).$$

But recall that σ_S is itself a composite of the two elasticities of substitution in each industry, σ_M and σ_F. Thus, σ can be expressed in terms of the three *primary* elasticities of substitution in this model:

$$\sigma = Q_M\sigma_M + Q_F\sigma_F + Q_D\sigma_D,$$

where

$$Q_M = \theta_{LM}\lambda_{TM} + \theta_{TM}\lambda_{LM},$$

$$Q_F = \theta_{LF}\lambda_{TF} + \theta_{TF}\lambda_{LF},$$

$$Q_D = |\lambda| \cdot |\theta|.$$

Note that σ is not just a linear expression in σ_M, σ_F, and σ_D—it is a weighted average of these three elasticities as $\Sigma Q_i = 1$. Note also that σ can be positive even if the elasticity of substitution in each industry is zero, for it incorporates the effect of intercommodity substitution by consumers as well as direct intracommodity substitution between factors.

Finally, introduce the concept, σ, into expression (11) for output changes:

$$(\hat{M} - \hat{F}) = \frac{|\theta|\sigma_D}{\sigma}(\hat{L} - \hat{T}),\tag{11a}$$

and into expression (14) for the change in factor prices in the subsidy case:

$$(\hat{w} - \hat{r}) = \frac{|\lambda|\sigma_D}{\sigma}(\hat{s}_M - \hat{s}_F).\tag{14a}$$

One consequence is immediately apparent: if the elasticity of substitution between commodities on the part of consumers is no greater than the overall elasticity of substitution between factors, the *magnification* effects discussed in section 4 are more than compensated for by the dampening effect of price changes.

7. Convergence to Balanced Growth

The two-sector model of production described in sections 1–6 can be used to analyze the process of economic growth. Already I have spoken of increases in factor endowments and the consequent "growth" of outputs. But a more satisfactory growth model would allow for the growth of at least one factor of production to be determined by the system rather than given parametrically. Let the factor "capital" replace "land" as the second factor in the two-sector model (replace T by K). And let M stand for machines rather than manufacturing goods. To simplify, I assume capital does not depreciate. The new feedback element in the system is that the rate of increase of the capital stock, $\hat{K}$, depends on the current output of machines, M. Thus $\hat{K} = M/K$. The "demand" for M now represents savings.

Suppose the rate of growth of the labor force, $\hat{L}$, is constant. At any moment of time the rate of capital accumulation, $\hat{K}$, either exceeds, equals, or falls short of $\hat{L}$. Of special interest in the neoclassical theory of growth (with no technological progress) is the case of balanced growth where $\hat{L} = \hat{K}$. Balance in the growth of factors will, as we have seen, result in balanced growth as between the two commodities (at the same rate). But if $\hat{L}$ and $\hat{K}$ are not equal, it becomes necessary to inquire whether they tend toward equality (balanced growth) asymptotically or tend to diverge even further.

If machines are produced by labor-intensive techniques, the rate of growth of machines exceeds that of capital if labor is growing faster than capital, or falls short of capital if capital is growing faster than labor. (This is the result in section 4, which is dampened, but not reversed, by the price changes discussed in section 5.) Thus, the rate of capital accumulation, if different from the rate of growth of the labor supply, falls or rises toward it. The economy tends toward the balanced-growth path.

The difficulty arises if machines are capital intensive. If there is no price change, the change in the composition of outputs must be a magnified reflection of the spread in the growth rates of factors. Thus, if capital is growing more rapidly than labor, machine output will expand at a greater rate than either factor, and this only serves to widen the spread between the rates of growth of capital and labor even further.[13] Once account is taken of price changes, however, the change in the composition of outputs may be sufficiently dampened to allow convergence to balanced growth despite the fact that machines are capital intensive.

Re-examine equation (11a), replacing $\hat{T}$ by $\hat{K}$ and recognizing that $|\theta|$ is negative if machines are capital intensive. If σ exceeds $-|\theta|\sigma_D$, on balance a dampening of the ratio of outputs as compared to factor endowments takes place. This suggests the critical condition that must be satisfied by σ, as compared with σ_D and $|\theta|$, in order to insure stability. But this is not precisely the condition required. Rather, stability hinges upon the *sign* of $(\hat{M} - \hat{K})$ being opposite to that of $(\hat{K} - \hat{L})$. There is a presumption that when $(\hat{M} - \hat{F})$ is smaller than $(\hat{K} - \hat{L})$ (assuming both are positive) the output of the machine sector is growing less rapidly than is the capital stock. But the corresponding is not exact.

To derive the relationship between $(\hat{M} - \hat{K})$ and $(\hat{M} - \hat{F})$ consider the two ways of expressing changes in the national income (Y). It can be viewed as the sum of returns to factors or the sum of the values of output in the two sectors. Let θ_i refer to the share of factor i or commodity i in the national income. In terms of rates of change,

$$\hat{Y} = \theta_L(\hat{w} + \hat{L}) + \theta_K(\hat{r} + \hat{K}) = \theta_M(\hat{p}_M + \hat{M}) + \theta_F(\hat{p}_F + \hat{F}).$$

But the share of a factor in the national income must be an average of its share in each sector, with the weights given by the share of that sector in the national income. This, and equations (3b) and (4b), guarantee that

$$\theta_L \hat{w} + \theta_K \hat{r} = \theta_M \hat{p}_M + \theta_F \hat{p}_F.$$

That is, the rates of change of the financial components in the two expressions for $\hat{Y}$ balance, leaving an equality between the physical terms:

$$\theta_L \hat{L} + \theta_K \hat{K} = \theta_M \hat{M} + \theta_F \hat{F}.$$

The desired relationship is obtained by observing that θ_K equals $(1 - \theta_L)$ and θ_M is $(1 - \theta_F)$. Thus,

$$(\hat{M} - \hat{K}) = \theta_F(\hat{M} - \hat{F}) - \theta_L(\hat{K} - \hat{L}).$$

With this in hand it is easy to see that (from (11a)) $(\hat{M} - \hat{K})$ is given by

$$(\hat{M} - \hat{K}) = \frac{\theta_L}{\sigma}\left\{-\frac{\theta_F|\theta|}{\theta_L}\sigma_D - \sigma\right\}(\hat{K} - \hat{L}). \tag{16}$$

It is not enough for σ to exceed—$|\theta|\sigma_D$, it must exceed—$(\theta_F/\theta_L)|\theta|\sigma_D$ for convergence to balanced growth.[14] It nonetheless remains the case that σ greater than σ_D is sufficient to insure that the expression in brackets in (16) is negative. For (16) can be rewritten as (16a):

$$(\hat{M} - \hat{K}) = -\frac{\theta_L}{\sigma}\left\{\sigma - \left[1 - \frac{\theta_{LM}}{\theta_L}\right]\sigma_D\right\}(\hat{K} - \hat{L}). \tag{16a}$$

Thus, it is overly strong to require that σ exceed σ_D.[15]

8. Savings Behavior

A popular assumption about savings behavior in the literature on growth theory is that aggregate savings form a constant percentage of the national income. (See, for example, Solow [20].) This, of course, implies that σ_D is unity. In this case it becomes legitimate to inquire as to the values of σ or σ_M and σ_F as compared with unity. For example, if each sector's production function is Cobb-Douglas (σ_M and σ_F each unity), stability is guaranteed. But the value "unity" that has a crucial role in this comparison only serves as a proxy for σ_D. With high σ_D even greater values for σ_M and σ_F (and σ) would be required.

If σ_D is unity when the savings ratio is constant, is its value higher or lower than unity when the savings ratio depends positively on the rate of profit? It turns out that this depends upon the technology in such a way as to encourage convergence to balanced growth precisely in those cases where factor intensities are such as to leave it in doubt.

The capital goods, machines, are demanded not for the utility they yield directly, but for the stream of additional future consumption they allow. This is represented by the rate of return (or profit), which is linked by the technology to the relative price of machines according to the magnification effects implicit in the Stolper-Samuelson theorem. The assumption that the savings ratio (the fraction of income devoted to new machines) rises as the rate of profit rises implies that the savings ratio rises as the relative price of machines rises (and thus that σ_D is less than unity) if and only if machines are capital intensive. Of course the savings assumption also implies that σ_D exceeds unity (that is, that the savings ratio falls as the relative price of machines rises) if machines are labor intensive, but convergence to balanced growth is already assured in this case.[16]

9. The Analysis of Technological Change

The preceding sections have dealt with the structure of the two-sector model of production with a given technology. They nonetheless contain the ingredients necessary for an analysis of the effects of technological progress. In this concluding section I examine this problem and simplify by assuming that factor endowments remain unchanged and subsidies are zero. I corcentrate on the impact of a change in production conditions on relative prices. The effect on outputs is considered implicitly in deriving the price changes.

Consider a typical input coefficient, a_{ij}, as depending both upon relative factor prices and the state of technology:

$$a_{ij} = a_{ij}(w/r, t).$$

In terms of the relative rates of change, $\hat{a}_{ij}$ may be decomposed as

$$\hat{a}_{ij} = \hat{c}_{ij} - \hat{b}_{ij}.$$

$\hat{c}_{ij}$ denotes the relative change in the input–output coefficient that is called forth by a change in factor prices as of a given technology. The $\hat{b}_{ij}$ is a measure of technological change that shows the alteration in a_{ij} that would take place at constant factor prices. Since technological progress usually involves a *reduction* in the input requirements, I define $\hat{b}_{ij}$ as $-(1/a_{ij})\partial a_{ij}/\partial t$.

The $\tilde{b}_{ij}$ are the basic expressions of technological change. After the discussion in section 3 it is not surprising that it is the λ and θ weighted averages of the $\hat{b}_{ij}$ that turn out to be important. These are defined by the following set of π's:

$$\pi_j = \theta_{Lj}\hat{b}_{Lj} + \theta_{Tj}\hat{b}_{Tj}, \quad j = M, F;$$

$$\pi_i = \lambda_{iM}\hat{b}_{iM} + \lambda_{iF}\hat{b}_{iF}, \qquad i = L, T.$$

If a $\hat{B}$ matrix is defined in a manner similar to the original A matrix, π_M and π_F are the sums of the elements in each column weighted by the relative factor shares, and π_L and π_T are sums of the elements in each row of $\hat{B}$ weighted by the fractions of the total factor supplies used in each industry. Thus, π_M, assumed non-negative, is a measure of the rate of technological advance in the M-industry and π_L, also assumed non-negative, reflects the overall labor-saving feature of technological change.

Turn now to the equations of change. The $\hat{c}_{ij}$ are precisely the $\hat{a}_{ij}$ used in equations (6)–(9) of the model without technological change. This subset can be solved, just as before, for the response of input coefficients to factor price changes. After substitution, the first four equations of change (equations (1a)–(4a)) become

$$\lambda_{LM}\hat{M} + \lambda_{LF}\hat{F} = \pi_L + \delta_L(\hat{w} - \hat{r}), \tag{1d}$$

$$\lambda_{TM}\hat{M} + \lambda_{TF}\hat{F} = \pi_T - \delta_T(\hat{w} - \hat{r}), \tag{2d}$$

$$\theta_{LM}\hat{w} + \theta_{TM}\hat{r} = \hat{p}_M + \pi_M, \tag{3d}$$

$$\theta_{LF}\hat{w} + \theta_{TF}\hat{r} = \hat{p}_F + \pi_F. \tag{4d}$$

The parameters of technological change appear only in the first four relationships and enter there in a particularly simple form. In the first two equations it is readily seen that, in part, technological change, through its impact in reducing input coefficients, has precisely the same effects on the system as would a change in factor endowments. π_L and π_T replace $\hat{L}$ and $\hat{T}$, respectively. In the second pair of equations the improvements in industry outputs attributable to technological progress enter the model precisely as do industry subsidies in equations (3c) and (4c) of section 4. Any general change in technology or in the quality of factors (that gets translated into a change in input coefficiencies) has an impact on prices and outputs that can be decomposed into the two kinds of parametric changes analyzed in the preceding sections.

Consider the effect of progress upon relative commodity and factor prices. The relationship between the changes in the two sets of prices is the same as in the subsidy case (see equation (12)):

$$(\hat{w} - \hat{r}) = \frac{1}{|\theta|}\{(\hat{p}_M - \hat{p}_F) + (\pi_M - \pi_F)\}. \tag{17}$$

Solving separately for each relative price change,

$$(\hat{p}_M - \hat{p}_F) = -\frac{|\theta|}{\sigma}\{(\pi_L - \pi_T) + |\lambda|\sigma_S(\pi_M - \pi_F)\}, \tag{18}$$

$$(\hat{w} - \hat{r}) = -\frac{1}{\sigma}\{(\pi_L - \pi_T) - |\lambda|\sigma_D(\pi_M - \pi_F)\}. \tag{19}$$

For convenience I refer to $(\pi_L - \pi_T)$ as the "differential factor effect" and $(\pi_M - \pi_F)$ as the "differential industry effect".[17]

Define a change in technology as "regular" if the differential factor and industry effects have the same sign.[18] For example, a change in technology that is relatively "labor-saving" for the economy as a whole ($\pi_L - \pi_T$ positive) is considered "regular" if it also reflects a relatively greater improvement in productivity in the labor-intensive industry. Suppose this to be the case. Both effects tend to depress the relative price of commodity M: the "labor-saving" feature of the change works exactly as would a relative increase in the labor endowment to reduce the relative price of the labor-intensive commodity (M). And part of the differential industry effect, like a relative subsidy to M, is shifted forward in a lower price for M.

Whereas the two components of "regular" technological change reinforce each other in their effect on the commodity price ratio, they pull the factor price ratio in opposite directions. The differential factor effect in the above case serves to depress the wage/rent ratio. But part of the relatively greater improvement in the labor-intensive M industry is shifted backward to increase, relatively, the return to labor. This "backward" shift is more pronounced the greater is the elasticity of substitution on the demand side. There will be some "critical" value of σ_D, above which relative wages will rise despite the downward pull of the differential factor effect:

$$(\hat{w} - \hat{r}) > 0 \text{ if and only if } \sigma_D > \frac{(\pi_L - \pi_T)}{|\lambda|(\pi_M - \pi_F)}.$$

If technological progress is not "regular" these conclusions are reversed. Suppose $(\pi_L - \pi_T) > 0$, but nonetheless $(\pi_M - \pi_F) < 0$. This might be the result, say, of technological change where the primary impact is to reduce labor requirements in food production. Labor is now affected relatively adversely on both counts, the differential factor effect serving to depress wages as before, and the differential industry effect working to the relative advantage of the factor used intensively in food production—land. On the other hand, the change in relative commodity prices is now less predictable. The differential factor effect, in tending to reduce M's relative price, is working counter to the differential industry effect, whereby the F industry is experiencing more rapid technological advance. The differential industry effect will, in this case, dominate if the elasticity of substitution between goods on the supply side is high enough:

$$(\hat{p}_M - \hat{p}_F) > 0 \text{ if and only if } \sigma_S > -\frac{\pi_L - \pi_T}{|\lambda|(\pi_M - \pi_F)}.$$

The differential factor and industry effects are not independent of each other. Some insight into the nature of the relationship between the two can be obtained by considering two special cases of "neutrality".

Suppose, first, that technological change is "Hicksian neutral" in each industry, implying that, at unchanged factor prices, factor proportions used in that industry do not change (see Hicks [8]). In terms of the $\hat{B}$ matrix, the rows are identical ($\hat{b}_{Lj} = \hat{b}_{Tj}$). As can easily be verified from the definition of the π, in this case

$$(\pi_L - \pi_T) = |\lambda|(\pi_M - \pi_F),$$

and technological change must be "regular". If, overall, technological change is "labor-saving" (and note that this can happen even if it is Hicksian neutral in each industry), the price of the relatively labor-intensive commodity must fall. Relative wages will, nonetheless, rise if σ_D exceeds the critical value shown earlier, which in this case reduces to unity.

The symmetrical nature of this approach to technological change suggests an alternative definition of neutrality, in which the columns of the $\hat{B}$ matrix are equal. This type of neutrality indicates that input requirements for any factor, i, have been reduced by the same relative amount in every industry. The relationship between the differential factor and industry effects is given by

$$(\pi_M - \pi_F) = |\theta|(\pi_L - \pi_T).$$

Again, technological change must be "regular". If the reduction in labor coefficients in each industry exceeds the reduction in land coefficients, this must filter through (in dampened form unless each industry uses just one factor) to affect relatively favorably the labor-intensive industry. The remarks made in the case of Hicksian neutrality carry over to this case, except for the fact that the critical value which σ_D must exceed in order for the differential industry effect to outweigh the factor effect on relative wages now becomes higher. Specifically, σ_D must exceed $1/|\lambda||\theta|$, which may be considerably greater than unity. This reflects the fact that in the case of Hicksian neutrality $(\pi_L - \pi_T)$ is smaller than $(\pi_M - \pi_F)$, whereas the reverse is true in the present case.

With Hicksian neutrality the paramount feature is the difference between rates of technological advance in each industry. This spills over into a differential factor effect only because the industries require the two factors in differing proportions. With the other kind of neutrality the basic change is that the input requirements of one factor are cut more than for the other factor. As we have just seen, this is transformed into a differential industry effect only in dampened form.

These cases of neutrality are special cases of "regular" technological progress. The general relationship between the differential factor and industry effects can be derived from the definitions to yield

$$(\pi_L - \pi_T) = Q_M \beta_M + Q_F \beta_F + |\lambda| (\pi_M - \pi_F) \tag{20}$$

and

$$(\pi_M - \pi_F) = Q_L \beta_L + Q_T \beta_T + |\theta| (\pi_L - \pi_T). \tag{21}$$

In the first equation the differential factor effect is broken down into three components; the labor-saving bias of technical change in each industry (β_j is defined as $\hat{b}_{Lj} - \hat{b}_{Tj}$) and the differential industry effect.[19] In the second expression the differential industry effect is shown as a combination of the relatively greater saving in each factor in the M industry (β_L, for example, is $\hat{b}_{LM} - \hat{b}_{LF}$) and the differential factor effect.[20] With these relationships at hand it is easy to see how it is the possible asymmetry between the row elements and/or the column elements of the $\hat{B}$ matrix that could disrupt the "regularity" feature of technical progress.[21]

For some purposes it is useful to make the substitution from either (20) or (21) into the expressions for the changes in relative factor and commodity prices shown by (17)–(19). For example, if technological change is 'neutral' in the sense described earlier, where the reduction in the input coefficient is the same in each industry (although different for each factor), β_L and β_T are zero in (21) and the relationship in (17) can be rewritten as

$$(\hat{w} - \hat{r}) = \frac{1}{|\theta|} (\hat{p}_M - \hat{p}_F) + (\pi_L - \pi_T).$$

To make things simple, suppose π_T is zero. The uniform reduction in labor input coefficients across industries might reflect, say, an improvement in labor quality attributable to education. Aside from the effect of any change in commodity prices on factor prices (of the Stolper-Samuelson variety), relative wages are directly increased by the improvement in labor quality.

Alternatively, consider substituting (20) into (19), to yield (19a):

$$(\hat{w} - \hat{r}) = -\frac{1}{\sigma}\left\{Q_M\beta_M + Q_F\beta_F + Q_D(1 - \sigma_D)\frac{\pi_M - \pi_F}{|\theta|}\right\}. \tag{19a}$$

Will technological change that is Hicks neutral in every industry leave the factor-price ratio unaltered at a given ratio of factor endowments? Equation (19a) suggests a negative answer to this query unless progress is at the same rate in the two industries ($\pi_M = \pi_F$) or unless σ_D is unity.[22]

There exists an extensive literature in the theory of international trade concerned with (a) the effects of differences in production functions on pre-trade factor and commodity price ratios (and thus on positions of comparative advantage), and (b) the impact of growth (in factor supplies) or changes in technological knowledge in one or more countries on the world terms of trade.[23] The analysis of this paper is well suited to the discussion of these problems. The connection between (a) and expressions (17)–(19) is obvious. For (b) it is helpful to observe that the impact of any of these changes on world terms of trade depends upon the effect in each country separately of these changes on production and consumption at constant commodity prices. The production effects can be derived from the four equations of change for the production sector (equations (1a)–(4a) or later versions) and the consumption changes from equation (5a).[24] The purpose of this paper is not to reproduce the results in detail but rather to expose those features of the model which bear upon all of these questions.

I am indebted to the National Science Foundation for support of this research in 1962–1964. I have benefited from discussions with Hugh Rose, Robert Fogel, Rudolph Penner, and Emmanuel Drandakis. My greatest debt is to Akihiro Amano [1], whose dissertation was a stimulus to my own work.

References

[1] Amano, A., *Neo-Classical Models of International Trade and Economic Growth* (University of Rochester, New York, 1963).

[2] Amano, A., "Determinants of Comparative Costs: A Theoretic Approach", *Oxford Economic Papers* (November 1964).

[3] Amano, A., "A Two-Sector Model of Economic Growth Involving Technical Progress" (unpublished).

[4] Bhagwati, J. and H. Johnson, "Notes on Some Controversies in the Theory of International Trade", *Economic Journal* (March 1960).

[5] Dorfman, R., P. A. Samuelson and R. M. Solow, *Linear Programming and Economic Analysis* (McGraw-Hill, New York, 1958).

[6] Drandakis, E., "Factor Substitution in the Two-Sector Growth Model", *Review of Economic Studies* (October 1963).

[7] Findlay, R. and H. Grubert, "Factor Intensities, Technological Progress and the Terms of Trade", *Oxford Economic Papers* (February 1959).

[8] Hicks, J. R., *The Theory of Wages* (Macmillan, New York, 1932).

[9] Hicks, J. R., "Linear Theory", *Economic Journal* (December 1960).

[10] Inada, Ken-ichi, "On Neoclassical Models of Economic Growth", *Review of Economic Studies* (April 1965).

[11] Johnson, H., "Economic Expansion and International Trade", *Manchester School of Economic and Social Studies* (May 1955).

[12] Johnson, H., "Economic Development and International Trade", in: *Money, Trade, and Economic Growth* (George Allen & Unwin, London, 1962) ch. 4.

[13] Jones, R. W., "Stability Condition in International Trade: A General Equilibrium Analysis", *International Economic Review* (May 1961).

[13a] Jones, R. W., *International Trade: Essays in Theory* (North-Holland, 1979) ch. 1.

[14] Kemp, C. M., *The Pure Theory of International Trade* (Prentice-Hall, Englewood Cliffs, 1964) pp. 10–11.

[15] Meade, J. E., *A Neo-Classical Theory of Economic Growth* (Allen & Unwin, London, 1961) pp. 84–86.

[16] Meier, G. M., *International Trade and Development* (Harper & Row, New York, 1963) ch. 1.

[17] Rybczynski, T. M., "Factor Endowments and Relative Commodity Prices", *Economica* (November 1955).

[18] Samuelson, P. A., "Prices of Factors and Goods in General Equilibrium", *Review of Economic Studies*, 21 (1) (1953–1954).

[19] Shinkai, Y., "On Equilibrium Growth of Capital and Labor", *International Economic Review* (May 1960).

[20] Solow, R., 'A Contribution to the Theory of Economic Growth', *Quarterly Journal of Economics* (February 1956).

[21] Stolper, W. F., and P. A. Samuelson, "Protection and Real Wages", *Review of Economic Studies* (November 1941).

[22] Takayama, A., "On a Two-Sector Model of Economic Growth: A Comparative Statics Analysis", *Review of Economic Studies* (June 1963).

[23] Takayama, A., "Economic Growth and International Trade", *Review of Economic Studies* (June 1964).

[24] Uzawa, H., "On a Two-Sector Model of Economic Growth", *Review of Economic Studies* (October 1961).

[25] Uzawa, H., "On a Two-Sector Model of Economic Growth—II", *Review of Economic Studies* (June 1963).

INTERNATIONAL ECONOMIC REVIEW
Vol. 10, No. 3, October, 1969

FACTOR PRICE EQUALIZATION AND THE STOLPER-SAMUELSON THEOREM*

BY JOHN S. CHIPMAN[1]

THE FACTOR PRICE EQUALIZATION theorem (Samuelson [11, (16)]) asserts that there is a one-to-one correspondence between commodity prices and factor prices. On the other hand, the Stolper-Samuelson theorem [13, (63–66)] asserts the existence of a special relationship between commodity and factor prices: namely, that an increase in the price of a commodity will bring about a more than proportionate increase in the price of the corresponding "intensive" factor.

It is important at the outset to remove an ambiguity in the statement just made. It is one thing to say that, given any initial equilibrium position, there exists a one-to-one association between commodities and factors such that a change in any commodity price will lead to a more than proportionate change (in the same direction) in the corresponding factor price. It is quite another thing to state that it is possible to find a one-to-one association between goods and factors *in advance* such that, starting from any equilibrium, a change in any commodity price will lead to a more than proportionate change in the price of the *already specified* factor. The first may be called the *local* version of the Stolper-Samuelson theorem, and the second the *global* version.

Another distinction must be made. In the case of two factors and two commodities (the only case treated rigorously by Stolper and Samuelson), it turns out that if, as a result of an increase in the price of a good, one of the factor prices rises more than proportionately, then the other factor price must actually fall. In generalizing the theory to more than two commodities and two factors, it no longer holds that a more than proportionate increase in one factor price entails a fall in *all* the remaining factor prices. The case in which this does occur will be referred to as the *strong* form of the Stolper-Samuelson theorem, whereas the more general case will be called the *weak* form.

We shall explore the various ways in which the theory first set forth by Stolper and Samuelson may be extended to n goods and factors. The main conclusions can be summarized as follows (the wording is necessarily vague, inasmuch as it constitutes a translation of mathematical conditions): (1) The Stolper-Samuelson theorem (strong, as well as weak form) is true *locally* (almost everywhere) for $n = 2$, and *globally* whenever reversal of factor intensity is ruled out, as is, by now, quite well known. However, it is no longer true for $n > 2$, even under conditions which guarantee full factor price equalization. (2) Under certain special conditions, the weak form of

---

* Manuscript received September 1, 1967.

[1] Originally presented at the Cleveland meetings of the Econometric Society, September 5, 1963. An abstract appeared in *Econometrica*, XXXII (October, 1964), 682–83.

JOHN S. CHIPMAN

the Stolper-Samuelson theorem, as well as full factor price equalization, holds globally for $n \leq 3$, but these conditions are no longer sufficient when $n \geq 4$. (3) If the strong form of the Stolper-Samuelson condition is assumed as a postulate, full factor price equalization is guaranteed (provided always that specialization is incomplete). Whether the weak form is also sufficient for this seems to be an open question.

This paper has been stimulated principally by the recent contributions by Gale [4], as well as by those of Nikaidô [10], Gale and Nikaidô [5], and McKenzie [9].

1. GENERAL FORMULATION

Let y_i be the output of the i-th commodity and x_{ij} the amount of the j-th factor used in the production of the i-th commodity, where $i, j = 1, 2, \cdots, n$. The production functions in a given country are given by

$$(1.1) \qquad y_i = f_i(x_{i1}, x_{i2}, \cdots, x_{in}) , \qquad\qquad i = 1, 2, \cdots, n$$

and are assumed to be concave and homogeneous of degree one, and to possess continuous first-order partial derivatives. Given a vector $w = (w_1, w_2, \cdots, w_n)$ of factor prices, the input demand functions which minimize costs for any given output are of the form

$$(1.2) \qquad x_{ij} = y_i a_{ij}(w_1, w_2, \cdots, w_n) , \qquad\qquad i, j = 1, 2, \cdots, n ,$$

where the functions $a_{ij}(w)$ are homogeneous of degree zero in the factor prices (see Shephard [12]). The corresponding minimum unit cost functions,

$$(1.3) \qquad c_i = \sum_{j=1}^{n} w_j a_{ij}(w) = g_i(w_1, w_2, \cdots, w_n) , \qquad\qquad i = 1, 2, \cdots, n ,$$

are, by Shephard's duality theorem, also homogeneous of degree one, and are concave.

We shall assume throughout that conditions are such that all n goods are produced in positive amounts, so that minimum unit costs c_i are equal to the respective prices p_i, which are assumed to be positive. Let $p = (p_1, p_2, \cdots, p_n)$; then we have a mapping

$$(1.4) \qquad p = g(w)$$

defined on the semi-positive orthant (that is, non-negative orthant excluding the origin) of n-dimensional Euclidean space. We denote its Jacobian matrix by $g'(w) = \partial g/\partial w = [\partial g_i/\partial w_j]$.

The elements of the Jacobian matrix are the input-output coefficients a_{ij}, since from (1.3) we have

$$(1.5) \qquad \partial g_i/\partial w_j = a_{ij}(w) + \sum_{k=1}^{n} w_k \frac{\partial a_{ik}(w)}{\partial w_j} ,$$

and the last term vanishes by the fundamental envelope theorem of production theory (see Shephard [12, (11)], Samuelson [11, (15)] and McKenzie [8, (54)]).

We may now distinguish three problems, each having a local and a global aspect:

(1) *The univalence problem.* g is locally univalent (one-to-one) in a neighborhood $N(w^0)$ of w^0 if $g(w) = g(w')$ implies $w = w'$ for all $w, w' \in N(w^0)$. It is well known that a sufficient condition for this is that the Jacobian determinant be nonvanishing at this point, i.e., $|g'(w^0)| \neq 0$.[2] However, even if $|g'(w)| \neq 0$ for all w, g need not be globally univalent. Even Samuelson's stronger condition [11, (16)] that the successive principal minors of $g'(w)$ be nonvanishing was shown by Nikaidô [10] to be insufficient. McKenzie [9] has shown that the condition $|g'(w)| \neq 0$ is not sufficient, even when the properties of concavity and homogeneity of g are taken into account. Gale [4] has shown, however, that a sufficient condition for the global univalence of g is that $g'(w)$ have all its principal minors positive; Nikaidô [10] has strengthened this to allow for the principal subminors (other than $|g'(w)|$ itself) to be non-negative.

(2) *The weak Stolper-Samuelson criterion.* If $g(w)$ is locally invertible at $w = w^0$, the weak Stolper-Samuelson criterion states that an increase in any commodity price p_i will lead to a more than proportionate increase in the corresponding factor price w_i. That is, according to the *local* version of the criterion, for some given w^0 such that $|g'(w^0)| \neq 0$, there is some association between commodities and factors such that, in a neighborhood $N(w^0)$, for all p in the image neighborhood $g(N(w^0))$ we have $\partial \log w_i / \partial \log p_i > 1$ for $i = 1, 2, \cdots, n$. This expresses the fact that the i-th factor price will increase proportionately more than the i-th commodity price, which is equivalent to the condition that it rise relative to all commodity prices; this is the criterion which makes it possible to avoid the index number problem. Note that the association between commodities and factors depends on w^0; in the global version, on the other hand, the same association between commodities and factors must apply for all w (which of course implies, for the condition to be meaningful, that the Jacobian be nonvanishing wherever it is defined).

(3) *The strong Stolper-Samuelson criterion.* This states that, given the association between goods and factors, $i \neq j$ implies $\partial w_i / \partial p_j < 0$. Again, this has its local and global versions.

The criterion $\partial \log w_i / \partial \log p_i > 1$ makes it natural to deal with the mapping from the logarithms of factor prices to the logarithms of commodity prices. Denote $\omega = \log w$ and $\pi = \log p$; then we obtain the mapping

$$(1.6) \qquad \pi \equiv \log p = \log g(e^\omega) \equiv \phi(\omega) \ .$$

Let $\hat{p}$ and $\hat{w}$ be diagonal matrices whose diagonal elements are the components of p and w respectively. Then, since

$$(1.7) \qquad \alpha_{ij} = \frac{\partial \log g_i}{\partial \log w_j} = \frac{w_j}{g_i} \frac{\partial g_i}{\partial w_j} = \frac{w_j}{g_i} a_{ij} \ ,$$

it follows that the Jacobian matrix $\phi'(\omega)$ of (1.6) is related to that of (1.4) by

$$(1.8) \qquad \phi'(\omega) = \hat{p}^{-1} g'(w) \hat{w} \ .$$

---

[2] See, for example, Apostol [2, (144)].

We now assert that $\psi'(\omega)$ *is a stochastic matrix*, that is, $\alpha_{ij} \geqq 0$ and $\sum_{j=1}^{n} \alpha_{ij} = 1.$[3] Clearly $\alpha_{ij} = x_{ij}/y_i \geqq 0$ for all i, j; and since prices are non-negative we have $\alpha_{ij} \geqq 0$. The fact that the rows of $\psi'(\omega)$ add up to unity is an immediate consequence of the homogeneity of g. From Euler's theorem,

$$(1.9) \qquad \sum_{j=1}^{n} \alpha_{ij} = \sum_{j=1}^{n} \frac{\partial \log g_i}{\partial \log w_j} = \frac{1}{g_i} \sum_{j=1}^{n} w_j \frac{\partial g_i}{\partial w_j} = 1 \; .$$

It has already been remarked that, to be meaningful, the Stolper-Samuelson criterion requires that the inverse partial derivatives $\partial w_i/\partial p_j$ be defined. This means that the Jacobian must be assumed to be nonvanishing everywhere. Hence the weak Stolper-Samuelson criterion can be stated thus: the stochastic matrix $\psi'(\omega) = [\alpha_{ij}(\omega)]$ has an inverse wherever it is defined, with diagonal elements greater than unity.

It is easy to see that the inverse of a stochastic matrix, when it exists, also has row sums equal to unity. Let 1 be the (column) vector consisting of n ones; then if the $n \times n$ matrix A has row sums equal to unity, we have $A1 = 1$, whence

$$(1.10) \qquad A^{-1}1 = A^{-1}(A1) = (A^{-1}A)1 = I1 = 1 \; .$$

Thus if the off-diagonal elements of A^{-1} are negative, the diagonal elements are greater than unity. Hence the strong Stolper-Samuelson criterion implies the weak one.

2. THE CASE $n \leq 3$

The case $n = 2$ is extremely simple. Let the stochastic matrix

$$\begin{bmatrix} \alpha_{11} & \alpha_{12} \\ \alpha_{21} & \alpha_{22} \end{bmatrix}$$

be nonsingular. Then its determinant is either positive or negative; if negative, then interchanging the rows will make it positive. Assuming this, then since its adjoint has non-positive off-diagonal elements, its inverse also has, which therefore has diagonal elements greater than or equal to unity. This, essentially, is the Stolper-Samuelson theorem.

That this does not generalize to higher dimensions may be seen from the following counterexample:

$$(2.1) \qquad \begin{bmatrix} 0.55 & 0.40 & 0.05 \\ 0.05 & 0.50 & 0.45 \\ 0.25 & 0.35 & 0.40 \end{bmatrix} = \begin{bmatrix} 0.77 & -2.59 & 2.82 \\ 1.68 & 3.77 & -4.45 \\ -1.95 & -1.68 & 4.64 \end{bmatrix} \; .$$

In this example, the stochastic matrix on the left of (2.1) has positive principal minors, so Gale's conditions are fulfilled and $\psi(\omega)$ is univalent. Thus conditions are satisfied which lead to full factor price equalization, yet the Stolper-Samuelson theorem does not hold.

The following theorem provides a sufficient condition for both the weak

---

[3] See, for instance, Gantmacher [6].

Stolper-Samuelson criterion and the Gale conditions on the principal minors.

THEOREM. *Let* $A = [a_{ij}]$ *be a* 3×3 *matrix, with* $i, j = 0, 1, 2,$ *such that* (i) $a_{ij} > 0$; (ii) $\sum_{j=0}^{2} a_{ij} = 1$; *and* (iii) $a_{ii} > a_{ji}$ *for* $j \neq i$. *Then* A *is nonsingular and*

$$(2.2) \qquad 1 > a_{ii} > \begin{vmatrix} a_{ii} & a_{ij} \\ a_{ji} & a_{jj} \end{vmatrix} > \begin{vmatrix} a_{00} & a_{01} & a_{02} \\ a_{10} & a_{11} & a_{12} \\ a_{20} & a_{21} & a_{22} \end{vmatrix} > 0 .$$

Thus the diagonal elements of A^{-1} *are greater than unity.*

PROOF. The last assertion follows immediately from the last two inequalities of (2.2). The first two inequalities are obvious. The proof will be accomplished by establishing (1) the nonsingularity of A; (2) the last inequality of (2.2); and (3) the second-to-last inequality.

(1) If A is singular, then for some (row) vector $\lambda \neq 0$ we have $\lambda A = 0$ where $\lambda A 1 = \lambda 1 = 0$, i.e., $\lambda_0 + \lambda_1 + \lambda_2 = 0$. Two of the λ_i will not have opposite signs, say λ_1 and λ_2, whence $\lambda_0 \neq 0$ and $a^0 = \mu_1 a^1 + \mu_2 a^2$ (where a^i is the i-th row of A and $\mu_1 = -\lambda_1/\lambda_0$, $\mu_2 = -\lambda_2/\lambda_0$, $\mu_1 + \mu_2 = 1$, and $\mu_1 \geqq 0$, $\mu_2 \geqq 0$ since λ_1 and λ_2 have opposite sign to λ_0). From $a^0 = \mu_1 a^1 + \mu_2 a^2$ we then have, in particular, $a_{00} = \mu_1 a_{10} + \mu_2 a_{20}$. Thus $\mu_1 a_{10} + (1 - \mu_1) a_{20} = a_{00}$, so $\mu_1 (a_{10} - a_{20}) = a_{00} - a_{20} > 0$ by assumption (iii), whence $a_{10} > a_{20}$. Similarly $(1 - \mu_2) a_{10} + \mu_2 a_{20} = a_{00}$, so $\mu_2 (a_{20} - a_{10}) = a_{00} - a_{10} > 0$ by assumption (iii), whence $a_{20} > a_{10}$. This is a contradiction, so A is nonsingular.[4]

(2) Define

$$A(t) = \begin{vmatrix} s a_{00} & t a_{01} & t a_{02} \\ a_{10} & a_{11} & a_{12} \\ a_{20} & a_{21} & a_{22} \end{vmatrix} = \begin{vmatrix} 1 & t a_{01} & t a_{02} \\ 1 & a_{11} & a_{12} \\ 1 & a_{21} & a_{22} \end{vmatrix},$$

where

$$s = \frac{1 - t(a_{01} + a_{02})}{a_{00}},$$

where, from the assumptions imposed, necessarily $a_{00} > 0$. Then for all t in the interval $0 \leqq t \leqq 1$, $A(t)$ satisfies the postulates of the theorem, and is therefore nonsingular from (1). Denoting its determinant by $D(t)$, it is a continuous (in fact linear) function of t, and $D(t) \neq 0$ for $0 \leqq t \leqq 1$. Since clearly $D(0) > 0$, it follows that $D(1) > 0$.

(3) As indicated above, since A is stochastic, if the unit vector is subtracted from any of its columns (say the 0-th) the resulting matrix is singular; thus

$$\begin{vmatrix} a_{00} & a_{01} & a_{02} \\ a_{10} & a_{11} & a_{12} \\ a_{20} & a_{21} & a_{22} \end{vmatrix} = \begin{vmatrix} 1 & a_{01} & a_{02} \\ 1 & a_{11} & a_{12} \\ 1 & a_{21} & a_{22} \end{vmatrix} .$$

The first diagonal element a^{00} of A^{-1} is therefore

---

[4] I am indebted to Charles Weaver for suggesting this proof.

404   JOHN S. CHIPMAN

$$a^{00} = \frac{\begin{vmatrix} a_{11} & a_{12} \\ a_{21} & a_{22} \end{vmatrix}}{\begin{vmatrix} a_{11} & a_{12} \\ a_{21} & a_{22} \end{vmatrix} - \begin{vmatrix} a_{01} & a_{02} \\ a_{21} & a_{22} \end{vmatrix} + \begin{vmatrix} a_{01} & a_{02} \\ a_{11} & a_{12} \end{vmatrix}}.$$

We are to show that $a^{00} > 1$. The numerator of the above expression is positive, since $a_{11} > a_{21} > 0$ and $a_{22} > a_{12} > 0$ by assumption. The denominator is positive (from (2)), being the determinant of A. Therefore $a^{00} > 1$ if and only if

$$\begin{vmatrix} a_{01} & a_{02} \\ a_{11} & a_{12} \end{vmatrix} - \begin{vmatrix} a_{01} & a_{02} \\ a_{21} & a_{22} \end{vmatrix} = \begin{vmatrix} a_{01} & a_{02} \\ a_{11} - a_{21} & a_{12} - a_{22} \end{vmatrix} < 0.$$

This is indeed the case, since $a_{11} - a_{21} > 0$ and $a_{12} - a_{22} < 0$ from assumption (iii). Similarly $a^{11} > 1$ and $a^{22} > 1$.   Q.E.D.

That the theorem is no longer true when $n > 3$ may be seen from the following example:[5]

$$\begin{bmatrix} 0.9 & 0.1 & 0 & 0 \\ 0 & 0.4 & 0.3 & 0.3 \\ 0.6 & 0 & 0.4 & 0 \\ 0.6 & 0 & 0 & 0.4 \end{bmatrix}^{-1} = \begin{bmatrix} \frac{8}{9} & -\frac{2}{9} & \frac{1}{6} & \frac{1}{6} \\ 2 & 2 & -1\frac{1}{2} & -1\frac{1}{2} \\ -1\frac{1}{3} & \frac{1}{3} & 2\frac{1}{4} & -\frac{1}{4} \\ -1\frac{1}{3} & \frac{1}{3} & -\frac{1}{4} & 2\frac{1}{4} \end{bmatrix}.$$

The crucial part of the above proof, which does not carry over to $n > 3$, is part (1). It rests on the following geometric fact: if three points lie on a line, one of them must be between the other two. But it is not true that if four points lie on a plane, one of them must be in the convex hull of the other three.

To complete this section, we remark that the above conditions do not imply the strong Stolper-Samuelson condition, as the following example shows:

$$\begin{bmatrix} 0.8 & 0.2 & 0 \\ 0.2 & 0.6 & 0.2 \\ 0 & 0.2 & 0.8 \end{bmatrix}^{-1} = \begin{bmatrix} 1\frac{3}{8} & -\frac{1}{2} & \frac{1}{8} \\ -\frac{1}{2} & 2 & -\frac{1}{2} \\ \frac{1}{8} & -\frac{1}{2} & 1\frac{3}{8} \end{bmatrix}.$$

Indeed the stochastic matrix on the left enjoys the stronger property of having a dominant diagonal[6] (see McKenzie [8]), yet its inverse does not have negative off-diagonal elements. Conversely, the example

$$\begin{bmatrix} 16/29 & 7/29 & 6/29 \\ 9/29 & 13/29 & 7/29 \\ 10/29 & 8/29 & 11/29 \end{bmatrix}^{-1} = \begin{bmatrix} 3 & -1 & -1 \\ -1 & 4 & -2 \\ -2 & -2 & 5 \end{bmatrix},$$

illustrates the case of a stochastic matrix which has positive principal minors

[5] This is similar to a counterexample for $n = 5$ which was furnished to the author by A. J. Hoffman.

[6] A matrix A is said to have a dominant diagonal in the strict sense if each of its diagonal elements exceeds in absolute value the sum of the absolute values of the remaining elements in the same column. A is said to have a dominant diagonal in the general sense (of McKenzie [8]) if DA has a dominant diagonal in the strict sense, where D is a diagonal matrix with positive diagonal elements.

and an inverse with the strong Stolper-Samuelson property, yet it does not have a dominant diagonal.

3. THE STRONG STOLPER-SAMUELSON PROPERTY

The case of the strong Stolper-Samuelson criterion brings out in rather remarkable form the formal unity of economic theory. For it turns out that in this case, the inverse of the Jacobian matrix is a Leontief matrix, and sufficient conditions for full factor price equalization follow from the well-known Hawkins-Simon conditions [7] and their recent generalization by Gale and Nikaidô, upon application of Jacobi's theorem on determinants.

At this point, it will be convenient to introduce some terminology. A matrix will be called *partially positive* if all its principal minors are positive.[7] If the strong Stolper-Samuelson property holds, the inverse of the Jacobian matrix has negative off-diagonal elements and positive diagonal elements, which are the formal properties of Leontief matrices. These properties are preserved after pre- or post-multiplication by diagonal matrices with positive diagonal elements, so that we may now conduct the argument just as well in terms of the original Jacobian matrix, $A = g'(w)$.

The Hawkins-Simon conditions state, essentially, that if a matrix B has positive diagonal and negative off-diagonal elements, then $B^{-1} \geq 0$ if and only if B is partially positive. In the present case, we have $B = A^{-1}$, and we know that $A \geq 0$, so it follows that B is partially positive. This in turn implies that A is partially positive. Thus the strong Stolper-Samuelson condition implies the Gale condition.

Since the Hawkins-Simon conditions [7] were not stated exactly in the above form, the following proof may be supplied, which rests on well-known theorems by Frobenius and others on nonnegative matrices. Denote $A^{-1} = [a_{ij}]^{-1} = [a^{ij}]$, and assume $a^{ij} < 0$ for $i \neq j$. We know in this case that $a^{ii} > 0$ for $i = 1, 2, \cdots, n$. Let $\mu = \text{Max}_i\, a^{ii}$, and define $M = \mu I - A^{-1}$. Then $M \geq 0$. Let ρ be the maximal characteristic root of M. Since $(\mu I - M)^{-1} = A \geq 0$ by assumption, it follows that $\mu > \rho$ (see Debreu and Herstein [3, (601, Theorem III*)]), and this in turn implies ([3, (602, Theorem IV)]) that the principal minors of $\mu I - M = A^{-1}$ are all positive. From Jacobi's theorem (see Aitken [1, (98)]) it follows that principal minors of A are all positive.

Gale and Nikaidô [5, (9)] have extended these results from nonnegative matrices to monotone increasing mappings. The essential property is that of the monotone increasing property of the mapping $g(w)$ from factor prices to commodity prices, from which follows, in combination with the assumption that $[g'(w)]^{-1}$ is a Leontief matrix, that $g'(w)$ is partially positive, hence $g(w)$ is univalent.

It may finally be remarked that it is an immediate consequence of McKenzie's results [8, (50, 60)] that the strong Stolper-Samuelson condition implies that $[g'(w)]^{-1}$ has a dominant diagonal; whereas McKenzie originally suggested [8,

---

[7] Gale [4] uses the term "*P*-matrix." The above terminology was suggested by Gantmacher's concept ([6, vol. 2, (98)]) of a "totally positive matrix," all of whose minors are positive.

406   JOHN S. CHIPMAN

(54)] imposing this condition on the Jacobian matrix $g'(w)$ itself. The former procedure would now seem more appropriate, but even so, such an assumption is very strong, and is hardly likely to be realized in practice.

University of Minnesota, U.S.A.

REFERENCES

[1]   AITKEN, A. C., *Determinants and Matrices* (Edinburgh: Oliver & Boyd, 1948).
[2]   APOSTOL, T. M., *Mathematical Analysis* (Reading, Mass.: Addison Wesley, 1957).
[3]   DEBREU, G. and I. N. HERSTEIN, "Nonnegative Square Matrices," *Econometrica*, XXI (October, 1953), 597-607.
[4]* GALE, DAVID, "Univalence Theorems for Differentiable Mappings," Discussion Paper No. 29, Institute of Social and Economic Research, Osaka University (November, 1962).
[5]* ———— and HUKUKANE NIKAIDÔ, "The Jacobian Matrix and Global Univalence of Mappings," *Mathematische Annalen*, CLIX (1965), 81-93.
[6]   GANTMACHER, F. R., *The Theory of Matrices*, two volumes (New York: Chelsea Publishing Company, 1960).
[7]   HAWKINS, DAVID and HERBERT A. SIMON, "Note: Some Conditions of Macroeconomic Stability," *Econometrica*, XVII (July-October, 1949), 245-48.
[8]   MCKENZIE, LIONEL W., "Matrices with Dominant Diagonals and Economic Theory," in K. J. ARROW, S. KARLIN, and P. SUPPES, eds., *Mathematical Methods in the Social Sciences* (Stanford: Stanford University Press, 1960), 47-62.
[9]   ————, "The Inversion of Cost Functions: A Counter-Example," *International Economic Review*, VIII (October, 1967), 271-8.
[10]* NIKAIDÔ, HUKUKANE, "Uniqueness of Solution of Certain Equations, I, II," Discussion Papers Nos. 28, 30, Institute of Social and Economic Research, Osaka University (November, 1962).
[11] SAMUELSON, PAUL A., "Prices of Factors and Goods in General Equilibrium," *Review of Economic Studies*, XXI (No. 1, 1953), 1-20.
[12] SHEPHARD, RONALD W., *Cost and Production Functions* (Princeton: Princeton University Press, 1953).
[13] STOLPER, WOLFGANG F. and PUAL A. SAMUELSON, "Protection and Real Wages," *Review of Economic Studies*, IX (November, 1941), 58--73.

---

* Cited with the kind permission of the authors.

INTERNATIONAL ECONOMIC REVIEW
Vol. 10, No. 3, October, 1969

ON THE RELATION BETWEEN COMMODITY PRICES
AND FACTOR REWARDS*

By Murray C. Kemp and Leon L. F. Wegge[1]

1. INTRODUCTION

1.1. Consider a competitive economy with two commodities produced in positive amounts, two non-produced factors of production, and production functions concave and homogeneous of degree one. According to the Stolper-Samuelson Theorem [12], an autonomous increase in the price of one product gives rise to an increase in the real reward of one factor and to a decline in the real reward of the other. Specifically, an increase in the price of the i-th product results in an increase in the real reward of whichever factor is used with greater relative intensity in the i-th industry; and since one is free to number factors in any order, it is possible to associate the i-th factor with the i-th product (at least in a sufficiently small neighborhood of an initial equilibrium).

1.2. This is an exceedingly useful theorem. In a two-by-two model one finds oneself appealing to it in just about every exercise involving the distribution of income. The original article by Stolper and Samuelson was devoted to a single application of the theorem, the relation between tariff protection and real wages.[2] But the theorem plays an equally important role in determining the incidence of a sales tax in a closed economy ([1], [4], [5]), and in making clear the distributional implications of capital accumulation [11].

The theorem would be even more useful if it could be extended to the case of n products and n factors. Can we in that more general case claim that an increase in the price of the i-th good results in an unambiguous increase

---

* Manuscript received October 19, 1966, revised July 23, 1968. .

[1] We are very greatly indebted to Professor and Mrs. George Szekeres for mathematical assistance, and to Michio Morishima for suggesting a proof of Theorem 3 much shorter than the one we had constructed. We should like to acknowledge also numerous helpful conversations with Ken-ichi Inada. Finally, we wish to acknowledge the general stimulation of Paul Samuelson's fundamental papers on trade theory and on the principle of Le Chatelier, especially [9] and [10].

We have enjoyed privileged access to unpublished papers by John Chipman [2] and Yasuo Uekawa [13]. The present paper is a revised version of part of an earlier paper of the same title referred to by Uekawa. It differs from its predecessor in omitting a section dealing with a general sufficient condition for the Stolper-Samuelson conclusions (a condition which has been weakened by Uekawa) and two sections dealing with cases in which products and factors are unequal in number.

Finally, we should like to acknowledge that Harold Kuhn [7] has independently stated Condition (7) and Theorem 2 of the present paper. Kuhn's paper became known to us only after our own work had been completed.

[2] Hence their classification of factors into "scarce" and "abundant." From our more general point of view the scarcity or abundance of a factor is irrelevant.

in the real reward of that factor (the i-th) which is used relatively intensively in the i-th industry, and in an unambiguous decline in the real rewards of all other factors?

The answer to this question depends on the way in which one generalizes the concept of relative factor intensity and on the related restriction on the matrix of input-output coefficients. If one adopts what seems to us to be the most natural generalization, the Stolper-Samuelson conclusions carry over in full strength if $n=3$ and in weakened form if $n=4$. For $n>1$, moreover, the proposed restriction is implied by the Stolper-Samuelson conclusions.

The bulk of the paper is devoted to a justification of these assertions.

2. THE MODEL

In the present section we set out the assumptions, notation and basic relationships to be used throughout the paper.[3]

Notation:

> y_i=amount of commodity i produced
>
> a_{ij}=amount of factor j used in the production of one unit of product i
>
> w_j=money reward (rental) of the j-th factor
>
> p_i=money price of the i-th product.

It will be assumed that all of these quantities are positive.

Given $w=(w_1, w_2, \cdots, w_n)$, producers select those a_{ij}'s which minimize the unit cost c_i of product i. Thus $a_{ij}=a_{ij}(w)$, where $a_{ij}(w)$ is homogeneous of degree zero; and $c_i=\sum_j w_j a_{ij}(w)=g_i(w)$, say, where g_i is homogeneous of degree one and concave. Moreover, $\partial g_i/\partial w_j=a_{ij}$ ([9, (15)]). Under competition, with all goods produced, therefore,

$$(1) \qquad c_i= \sum_{j=1}^{n} w_j a_{ij}(w)=g_i(w)=p_i$$

or, in vector notation,

$$(2) \qquad p=g(w)$$

with the Jacobian

$$(3) \qquad \partial g/\partial w=[a_{ij}]\equiv A\,.$$

It will, however, be more convenient to work with the logarithms of prices. Introducing the notation $\pi=\ln p$ and $\omega=\ln w$, we may rewrite (2) and (3) as

$$(2') \qquad \pi=\ln g(e^\omega)=\phi(\omega)$$

and

$$(3') \qquad \partial\phi/\partial\omega\equiv\phi'(\omega)=\hat{p}^{-1} A\hat{w}\,,$$

where $\hat{p}$ and $\hat{w}$ are diagonal matrices, so that the ij-th element of ϕ' is

$$(4) \qquad \alpha_{ij}=w_j a_{ij}/p_i\,.$$

Let $[\alpha_{ij}]$, the matrix of distributive shares, be denoted by S. It is obvious

---

[3] This section follows Chipman [2] closely.

that the row sums of S are one; that is, S is a stochastic matrix. It follows that the inverse S^{-1} also has unit row sums.[4]

In terms of this notation one can say that an increase in the price of the i-th product gives rise to an unambiguous increase in the real reward of the i-th factor and to an unambiguous decline in the real reward of the j-th factor ($j \neq i$) if and only if the inverse matrix S^{-1} possesses negative off-diagonal elements and diagonal elements in excess of unity.

3. EXTENSIONS OF THE STOLPER-SAMUELSON THEOREM

3.1. Stolper and Samuelson, in their consideration of the two-by-two case, assumed that

$$(5) \qquad \frac{a_{11}}{a_{12}} > \frac{a_{21}}{a_{22}} \quad \text{and} \quad \frac{\alpha_{11}}{\alpha_{12}} > \frac{\alpha_{21}}{\alpha_{22}} .$$

In words, the first factor is used relatively intensively in the first industry, and the second factor is used relatively intensively in the second. Moreover, it follows from a remark of Section 1.1 that it is always possible to number the factors in such a way that the inequality has the sense of (5), so that it is not necessary to consider the possibility that the first factor is used relatively intensively in the second industry, etc.

From (5) it follows that A^{-1} and S^{-1} possess negative off-diagonal elements and positive diagonal elements. And since the row sums of S^{-1} are equal to one, the diagonal elements must be greater than one. In fact, (5) is necessary as well as sufficient for the Stolper-Samuelson result.

3.2. Our first problem is to generalize the concept of relative factor intensity; that is, we need to generalize (5) so that it may be interpreted as requiring that the i-th factor is used relatively intensively in the i-th industry. Evidently non-singularity of the matrix S is not enough; further restrictions are necessary. There are several ways in which the concept might be generalized;[5] however, it seems most natural to say that factor i is used relatively intensively in the i-th industry, and is associated with that industry, if and only if

$$(6) \qquad \max \left(\frac{\alpha_{si}}{\alpha_{sj}} \right) = \frac{\alpha_{ii}}{\alpha_{ij}} , \qquad\qquad j = 1, \cdots, n .$$

If (6) holds for all i, so that[6]

---

[4] Let 1 be the column vector consisting of n ones. Then if the $n \times n$ matrix S has row sums equal to unity, $S1 = 1$, whence $S^{-1}1 = S^{-1}(S1) = (S^{-1}S)1 = 1$. The proof is Chipman's [2].

[5] Cf. [2], [13]. Johnson ([3, (30)]) seems to deny the possibility of generalization.

[6] For $n > 2$ condition (7) may be written more compactly as

$$\frac{\alpha_{ii}}{\alpha_{ij}} > \frac{\alpha_{si}}{\alpha_{sj}} , \qquad\qquad i \neq j \neq s; \quad i = 1, \cdots, n .$$

The "missing" relation, with $s = j$, follows from $\alpha_{ii}/\alpha_{ij} > \alpha_{si}/\alpha_{sj}$ and $\alpha_{jj}/\alpha_{ji} > \alpha_{sj}/\alpha_{si}$. Thus (7) contains just $n(n-1)(n-2)$ independent relations.

It is worth noting also that (7) holds if and only if

$$\frac{\alpha_{ii}}{\alpha_{ji}} > \frac{\alpha_{is}}{\alpha_{js}} , \qquad\qquad j \neq i, \ s \neq i; \quad i = 1, \cdots, n .$$

410   MURRAY C. KEMP AND LEON L. F. WEGGE

(7) $\dfrac{\alpha_{ii}}{\alpha_{ij}} > \dfrac{\alpha_{si}}{\alpha_{sj}}$, $j \neq i,\ s \neq i;\ i = 1, \cdots, n$,

we have the required generalization. In the special two-by-two case (7) reduces to (5).

3.3. A necessary and sufficient condition for the Stolper-Samuelson conclusions is that S^{-1} be a strong irreducible Minkowski matrix. Hence all *necessary* conditions for the Stolper-Samuelson conclusions are properties of such matrices. Among these properties the following are of special interest:
(i) S is a P-matrix,
(ii) the inequalities (7) are satisfied,
(iii) $\alpha_{ii} > \alpha_{ji}$, $j \neq i$.
Property (i) has been established by Chipman [2].[7] It remains to establish (ii) and (iii).

THEOREM 1. *If S^{-1} has positive diagonal elements and negative off-diagonal elements, condition (7) is satisfied.*

PROOF. Suppose that S^{-1} has the required sign pattern and is therefore a strong irreducible Minkowski matrix. Then every principal sub-matrix of S^{-1} is a strong irreducible Minkowski matrix. Hence S, and the inverse of every principal sub-matrix of S^{-1}, is positive. From Jacobi's theorem, for any determinant Δ and its minors

$$\Delta_{11}\Delta_{js} - \Delta_{1s}\Delta_{j1} = \Delta_{11,js}\Delta .$$

Hence

(8) $\dfrac{\Delta_{11}}{\Delta} \cdot \dfrac{(-1)^{j+s}\Delta_{js}}{\Delta} - \dfrac{(-1)^{1+s}\Delta_{1s}}{\Delta} \cdot \dfrac{(-1)^{1+j}\Delta_{j1}}{\Delta} = \dfrac{(-1)^{j+s}\Delta_{11,js}}{\Delta_{11}} \cdot \dfrac{\Delta_{11}}{\Delta} .$

Applying (8) to S^{-1}, and noting that $(-1)^{j+s}\Delta_{11,js}/\Delta_{11}$ is an element of the inverse of an $(n-1)$-dimensional principal sub-matrix of S^{-1} and therefore positive, we conclude that $\alpha_{11}\alpha_{sj} - \alpha_{s1}\alpha_{1j} > 0$. The same argument may be applied to each principal sub-matrix of S^{-1}.   Q.E.D.

THEOREM 2. *If S^{-1} has positive diagonal elements and negative off-diagonal elements, $\alpha_{ii} > \alpha_{ji}$ ($j \neq i$).*

PROOF. From Theorem 1, (7) is satisfied. Hence

$$\alpha_{ii}\alpha_{js} - \alpha_{is}\alpha_{ji} > 0 ,\qquad\qquad s \neq i,\ j \neq i .$$

Summing over $s \neq i$,

$$\alpha_{ii} \sum_{\substack{s=1 \\ s \neq i}}^{n} \alpha_{js} - \alpha_{ji} \sum_{\substack{s=1 \\ s \neq i}}^{n} \alpha_{is} > 0 .$$

That is, $\alpha_{ii}(1-\alpha_{ji}) - \alpha_{ji}(1-\alpha_{ii}) > 0$. Hence $\alpha_{ii} > \alpha_{ji}$.   Q.E.D.

3.4. In this section we prove two *sufficiency* theorems, one for the case $n = 3$, the other for the case $n = 4$.

---

[7] An alternative proof could make use of the known relationship between the minors of a non-singular matrix and the complementary cofactors of the inverse.

THEOREM 3. *For* $n=3$, (7) *implies that* S^{-1} *has negative off-diagonal elements and diagonal elements greater than one.*

PROOF. From (7), the cofactors of the diagonal elements of S are positive and the cofactors of the off-diagonal elements are negative. It therefore suffices to show that S has a positive determinant. Now

$$|S| = \begin{vmatrix} \alpha_{11} & \alpha_{12} & \alpha_{13} \\ \alpha_{21} & \alpha_{22} & \alpha_{23} \\ \alpha_{31} & \alpha_{32} & \alpha_{33} \end{vmatrix} = \frac{1}{\alpha_{23}} \begin{vmatrix} \alpha_{11}\alpha_{23}-\alpha_{21}\alpha_{13} & \alpha_{12}\alpha_{23}-\alpha_{13}\alpha_{22} & 0 \\ \alpha_{21} & \alpha_{22} & \alpha_{23} \\ \alpha_{31} & \alpha_{32} & \alpha_{33} \end{vmatrix}.$$

From (7), however, $\alpha_{11}\alpha_{23}-\alpha_{21}\alpha_{13}>0$ and $\alpha_{12}\alpha_{23}-\alpha_{13}\alpha_{22}<0$; moreover, the cofactors associated with these two elements are respectively positive and negative. Hence $|S|>0$. Q.E.D.

From Theorems 1 and 3 we infer that for $n=3$ condition (7) is both necessary and sufficient for the Stolper-Samuelson conclusions.

At the outset of our investigations we had hoped that, for $n\geqq4$ also, (7) would yield the Stolper-Samuelson conclusions. Our hopes were, however, soon frustrated. When $n=4$, (7) no longer ensures that the off-diagonal elements of S^{-1} are negative. Consider the counterexample

$$S=\frac{1}{22}\begin{pmatrix} 8 & 1 & 6.5 & 6.5 \\ 6.2 & 1.8 & 7 & 7 \\ 7 & 1 & 8 & 6 \\ 7 & 1.05 & 6 & 7.95 \end{pmatrix}.$$

The matrix satisfies (7) and has unit row sums; but the first column of S^{-1} is $(22/32.78)\times(21.33, 22.43, -11.89, -12.77)$, whence the $(2,1)$-th element of S^{-1} is positive and larger than the $(1,1)$-th element.

There is no way to negate a counter example. However, we were reluctant to concede that nothing at all can be said about the case $n=4$. In the above example, and in all others we have constructed, not only are the diagonal elements of the inverse greater than one, but at least two off-diagonals are negative in each column and the diagonal element is larger in absolute value than the negative elements in the same column. We can prove that this is always so for four-by-four matrices satisfying (7). The economic sense of this is as follows: given the factor intensity condition (7), an increase in the price of the i-th product results in an unambiguous increase in the real reward of the associated factor (the i-th); the real reward of at least two other factors must decline, but at a rate which is less than the rate of increase in the reward of the i-th factor.

More formally, we have been able to prove

THEOREM 4. *For* $n=4$, (7) *implies* (a) *that the determinant and therefore all principal minors of* S *are positive (so that* S *is a P-matrix and factor-price equalization is assured),* (b) *that the diagonal elements of* S^{-1} *are greater than one,* (c) *that in each column of* S^{-1} *at least two elements are negative,* (d) *that in each column of* S^{-1} *the diagonal element is larger in absolute value than the negative elements, but may be smaller than the other positive element, if there is one.*

Here we prove (b) only. Proofs of (a), (c) and (d) will be provided in [6].

PROOF OF THEOREM 4 (b). It suffices to show that the first diagonal element of S^{-1} is greater than one. Let the ij-th cofactor of S be represented by S_{ij}. Then

$$|S| = \begin{vmatrix} 1 & \alpha_{12} & \alpha_{13} & \alpha_{14} \\ 1 & \alpha_{22} & \alpha_{23} & \alpha_{24} \\ 1 & \alpha_{32} & \alpha_{33} & \alpha_{34} \\ 1 & \alpha_{42} & \alpha_{43} & \alpha_{44} \end{vmatrix} \quad \text{[Add all other columns to the first and recall that } S \text{ is a stochastic matrix.]}$$

$$= \begin{vmatrix} 1 & \alpha_{12} & \alpha_{13} & \alpha_{14} \\ 0 & \alpha_{22}-\alpha_{12} & \alpha_{23}-\alpha_{13} & \alpha_{24}-\alpha_{14} \\ 0 & \alpha_{32}-\alpha_{12} & \alpha_{33}-\alpha_{13} & \alpha_{34}-\alpha_{14} \\ 0 & \alpha_{42}-\alpha_{12} & \alpha_{43}-\alpha_{13} & \alpha_{44}-\alpha_{14} \end{vmatrix} \quad \text{[Subtract the first row from each of the remaining rows.]}$$

$$= \begin{vmatrix} \alpha_{22} & \alpha_{23} & \alpha_{24} \\ \alpha_{32} & \alpha_{33} & \alpha_{34} \\ \alpha_{42} & \alpha_{43} & \alpha_{44} \end{vmatrix} - \alpha_{12} \begin{vmatrix} 1 & \alpha_{23} & \alpha_{24} \\ 1 & \alpha_{33} & \alpha_{34} \\ 1 & \alpha_{43} & \alpha_{44} \end{vmatrix}$$

$$- \alpha_{13} \begin{vmatrix} \alpha_{22} & 1 & \alpha_{24} \\ \alpha_{32} & 1 & \alpha_{34} \\ \alpha_{42} & 1 & \alpha_{44} \end{vmatrix} - \alpha_{14} \begin{vmatrix} \alpha_{22} & \alpha_{23} & 1 \\ \alpha_{32} & \alpha_{33} & 1 \\ \alpha_{42} & \alpha_{43} & 1 \end{vmatrix}$$

$$= S_{11} - \alpha_{12} B_{12} - \alpha_{13} B_{13} - \alpha_{14} B_{14}$$

say. Now the first diagonal element of S^{-1} is $S_{11}/|S|$. Evidently this element is greater than one if and only if $(\alpha_{12} B_{12} + \alpha_{13} B_{13} + \alpha_{14} B_{14})$ is positive. Adding the first two terms, we obtain

$$(9) \qquad \alpha_{12} B_{12} + \alpha_{13} B_{13} = (\alpha_{13} \alpha_{22} - \alpha_{12} \alpha_{23} + \alpha_{12} \alpha_{43} - \alpha_{13} \alpha_{42})(\alpha_{44} - \alpha_{34})$$
$$+ (\alpha_{12} \alpha_{33} - \alpha_{13} \alpha_{32} - \alpha_{12} \alpha_{43} + \alpha_{13} \alpha_{42})(\alpha_{44} - \alpha_{24}) .$$

The first of the four bracketed expressions may be written

$$\xi \equiv \alpha_{13} \alpha_{22}(1-\mu_2) - \alpha_{12} \alpha_{23}(1-\mu_3) ,$$

where $\mu_2 \equiv \alpha_{42}/\alpha_{22}$ and $\mu_3 \equiv \alpha_{43}/\alpha_{23}$. Now (7) implies that the diagonal element is the largest in each column (see the proof of Theorem 2); hence $\mu_2 < 1$. Moreover, it follows from (7) that $\mu_2 < \mu_3$. Evidently ξ is positive if $\mu_3 \geq 1$; but, from (7) and the fact that $(1-\mu_3) < (1-\mu_2)$, it is positive also if $\mu_3 < 1$. The third bracketed component of (9) has a structure similar to that of the first; hence it too is positive. The second and fourth bracketed expressions are already known to be positive. Hence $(\alpha_{12} B_{12} + \alpha_{13} B_{13})$ is positive. By similar reasoning, $(\alpha_{13} B_{13} + \alpha_{14} B_{14})$ and $(\alpha_{12} B_{12} + \alpha_{14} B_{14})$ are positive. It follows by addition that $(\alpha_{12} B_{12} + \alpha_{13} B_{13} + \alpha_{14} B_{14})$ is positive.   Q.E.D.

4. CONCLUDING REMARK

It is well-known that in the two-by-two case an increase in a country's

COMMODITY PRICES AND FACTOR REWARDS 413

endowment of the i-th factor, commodity prices held constant, will give rise to an increase in the output of that industry (the i-th) in which the i-th factor is used relatively intensively, and to a decline in the output of the other industry, ([8]). This result is dual to the Stolper-Samuelson relationship between commodity prices and factor rewards described in Section 3.1. In fact

(10) $$\partial y_i/\partial V_j = \partial w_j/\partial p_i \qquad i, j = 1, 2,$$

where V_j is the country's endowment of the j-th factor. We now know ([9, (10)]) that (10) holds for any i and j $(i, j = 1, \cdots, n)$. It follows that any conclusions we have established concerning the sign of the price relationship $\partial w_j/\partial p_i$ apply equally to the quantity relationship $\partial y_i/\partial V_j$.

University of New South Wales, Australia, and
University of California at Davis, U.S.A.

REFERENCES

[1] BENHAM, FREDERICK, "Taxation and the Relative Shares of Factors of Production," *Economica*, New Series, II (May, 1935), 198-203.

[2] CHIPMAN, JOHN S., "Factor Price Equalization and the Stolper-Samuelson Theorem," *International Economic Review* (forthcoming).

[3] JOHNSON, HARRY G., *International Trade and Economic Growth* (London: Allen and Unwin, 1958).

[4] ————, "The General Equilibrium Analysis of Sales Taxes: A Comment," *American Economic Review*, XLVI (March, 1956), 151-6.

[5] KEMP, MURRAY C., *The Pure Theory of International Trade* (Englewood Cliffs: Prentice-Hall, 1964).

[6] ————, *The Pure Theory of International Trade and Investment* (Englewood Cliffs: Prentice-Hall, 1969).

[7] KUHN, HAROLD, W., "On Two Theorems in International Trade," *Economia Matematica* (Rome, 1967).

[8] RYBCZYNSKI, T. N., "Factor Endowments and Relative Factor Prices," *Economica* New Series, XXII (November, 1955), 336-41.

[9] SAMUELSON, PAUL A., "Prices of Factors and Goods in General Equilibrium," *Review of Economic Studies*, XXI (October, 1953), 1-20.

[10] ————, "An Extention of the Le Chatelier Principle," *Econometrica*, XXXIIX (April, 1960), 368-79.

[11] SOLOW, ROBERT M., "Note on Uzawa's Two-Sector Model of Economic Growth," *Review of Economic Studies*, XXIV (October, 1961), 48-50.

[12] STOLPER, WOLFGANG F. and PAUL A. SAMUELSON, "Protection and Real Wages," *Review of Economic Studies*, IX (November, 1941), 58-73. Reprinted in H. S. ELLIS and L. A. METZLER, eds., *Readings in the Theory of International Trade* (Philadelphia: The Blakiston Co., 1949), 333-57.

[13] UEKAWA, YASUO, "On the Generalization of the Stolper-Samuelson Theorem," *Econometrica* (forthcoming).

Journal of International Economics 4 (1974) 199–206. © North-Holland Publishing Company

SOME OF THE THEOREMS OF INTERNATIONAL TRADE
WITH MANY GOODS AND FACTORS

Wilfred ETHIER*

University of Pennsylvania, Philadelphia, Penn. 19174, U.S.A.

The Heckscher–Ohlin model yields three important results beyond the Heckscher–Ohlin theorem itself: the Rybczynski, Stolper–Samuelson, and factor price equalization theorems. Recent years have witnessed many investigations of whether these results generalize to the case of n goods and n factors. This literature has succeeded both in clarifying our understanding of the neo-classical production model and in obtaining difficult and frequently elegant results. However, most of these results imply that the n by n generalizations of the simple and powerful 2 by 2 properties are true only subject to conditions on the relevant determinants that are at once stringent, complicated, and, frequently, economically arcane. A reader might not unnaturally conclude that the most significant implication is that the interesting 2 by 2 properties can not in practice be expected to hold in any essential way in the more general n by n environment and therefore reflect nothing more than the simplification to a world of two goods and two factors.[1] This I think would be a mistake. It is the primary intent of this note to argue that to a significant degree the powerful 2 by 2 results reflect essential properties of the neoclassical general equilibrium of production (as opposed to properties of a 2 by 2 model) and that therefore a central economic core of these results generalizes in a straightforward way to the n by n case.[2] These generalizations depend on no complicated matrix properties and indeed follow immediately from the most elementary properties of the model.

Secondarily, I shall argue that economic considerations suggest a somewhat different route for the n by n generalizations of the strongest properties than has thus far been taken, and I shall make some efforts in that direction.

---

*This paper owes much to the comments, criticisms, and suggestions of John Chipman and Murray Kemp; thanks are also due to David Humphrey and Ronald Jones.
    [1]This impression would be reinforced by the fact that the conditions for many of the n by n results to hold can be interpreted as requiring that the $n \times n$ case reduce in some sense to the 2×2 case. See in particular Kemp and Wegge (1969), Uekawa (1971), and Uekawa, Kemp and Wegge (1973).
    [2]For the contrary point of view see, for example, Pearce (1970).

G

Let me first present my notation by briefly setting out the basic model. All n goods are produced by means of the n factors according to strictly quasi-concave, linear homogeneous production functions: $1 = f_j(\theta_{1j}, \ldots, \theta_{nj})$, where $j = 1, \ldots, n$. θ_{ij} denotes the number of units of factor i being employed in the production of one unit of good j and depends upon factor prices: $\theta_{ij} = \theta_{ij}(w) \equiv \theta_{ij}(w_1, \ldots, w_n)$ for $i, j = 1, \ldots, n$, where w_j denotes the price of the jth factor. Assume always positive marginal products so that all resources are fully employed in equilibrium. Then if X, K, P, and w denote the (strictly positive) vectors of outputs, factor endowments, and commodity and factor prices respectively, and if all goods are produced,

$$K = \theta(w)X, \tag{1}$$

$$P = w\theta(w), \tag{2}$$

where $\theta(w)$ denotes the matrix of $\theta_{ij}(w)$'s. It can be shown [see, e.g., Samuelson (1953)] that

$$\left[\frac{\partial K_i}{\partial X_j}\right] = \theta(w), \tag{3}$$

$$\left[\frac{\partial P_j}{w_i}\right] = \theta(w), \tag{4}$$

or, in elasticity terms:

$$\left[\frac{X_j}{K_i}\frac{\partial K_i}{\partial X_j}\right] = \hat{K}^{-1}\left[\frac{\partial K_i}{\partial X_j}\right]\hat{X} = \hat{K}^{-1}\theta(w)\hat{X} \equiv [a_{ij}] \equiv A, \tag{5}$$

$$\left[\frac{w_i}{P_j}\frac{\partial P_j}{\partial w_i}\right] = \hat{w}\left[\frac{\partial P_j}{\partial w_i}\right]\hat{P}^{-1} = \hat{w}\theta(w)\hat{P}^{-1} \equiv [b_{ij}] \equiv B, \tag{6}$$

where $\hat{X}$ etc. denote the diagonal matrices formed from the vectors X etc. (i.e, $\hat{X}_{ii} = X_i, \hat{X}_{ij} = 0$ if $i \neq j$). It is easily seen that a_{ij} equals the proportion of the total supply of factor i devoted to industry j so that eq. (1) implies that $\Sigma_j a_{ij} = 1$ and so A is row stochastic. Similarly b_{ij} equals the distributive share of factor i in industry j so that as a consequence of Euler's theorem on homogeneous functions B is column stochastic. I shall assume that θ, A, and B have all strictly positive elements; the implications of zeroes are easily deduced.

In the 2 by 2 case[3] the Stolper–Samuelson and Rybczynski theorems are easily derived directly from eqs. (5) and (6). Since A and B are stochastic matrices A^{-1} and B^{-1} must each have one negative term and one term exceeding

---

[3]See, for example, Jones (1965) for an analysis of the 2 by 2 model. Also Ethier (1972) has a discussion of how these theorems are affected by nontraded goods.

unity in each row and each column. Thus it is possible to assign the goods and factors to each other in such a way that an increase in one commodity price increases by a greater proportion the corresponding factor reward while reducing absolutely the reward to the other factor, etc. The only condition is that A^{-1} and B^{-1} exist, i.e., that $\theta(w)$ be non-singular.

In the n by n case it is likewise desirable to know whether associations of factors and goods exist which lead to similar conclusions. But many different criteria are possible. Chipman (1969) has suggested two. The first, dubbed by Chipman the weak Stolper–Samuelson property, requires that for some numbering of goods and factors B^{-1} have diagonal elements that all exceed unity. Thus an increase in any commodity price would induce a change in the corresponding factor reward independent of index number considerations. Alternatively the strong Stolper–Samuelson property, as defined by Chipman, requires that for some numbering of goods and factors B^{-1} have elements exceeding unity along the diagonal and have all other elements negative, i.e., an increase in any commodity price must increase by a greater proportion the reward of the associated factor while reducing absolutely the rewards of all other factors. Inada (1971) has pointed out that an alternative non-equivalent strong property would be for B^{-1} to have negative elements along the diagonal and all other elements positive.

Considerable effort has been devoted to deriving necessary and sufficient conditions for these criteria.[4] However, it will be useful to first look more closely at the fundamental economic issues involved.

The basic problem is to establish the existence of one or more associations of *each* factor with *some* good and of one or more associations of *each* good with *some* factor that possess certain comparative statics properties of economic interest. I shall use S to refer to an association of each good (price) with some factor (price) and R to refer to an association of each factor (quantity) with some good (quantity). Also an association will be termed intensive if the changes in associated goods and factors are in the same direction, non-intensive if they are in opposite directions.

Taking the 2 by 2 case as an analogy, there seem to be two distinct economic properties that are of interest. First an association should be *unambiguous*. I call an S association, for example, unambiguous if an increase in any commodity price causes a change in the associated factor price that is independent of index number considerations, i.e., if the appropriate element of B^{-1} does not lie between zero and unity.

The second property of interest is *duality*. I say that an S intensive association, for example, is dual if an increase in any commodity price induces an unambiguous increase in the associated factor price *and* if, at constant prices, an increase in the supply of that factor induces an unambiguous rise in the output

[4]See in particular Chipman (1969), Kemp and Wegge (1969), Kemp (1969), Uekawa (1971), Wegge and Kemp (1969), Inada (1971), and Uekawa, Kemp and Wegge (1973).

of that commodity, i.e., the corresponding elements of A^{-1} and of B^{-1} both exceed unity.[5]

Chipman's weak criterion is concerned only with the first of these two properties and implies nothing about duality. The economic essence of this criterion seems to be that some unambiguous S association exist. Now, whereas the weak criterion in the specific matrix form originally stated by Chipman is not implied simply by the non-singularity of θ as in the 2 by 2 case, but instead requires strict additional conditions on B, it is true that a property actually stronger than the above general reformulation of the weak criterion does hold and that this property follows directly from eqs. (5) and (6) in as simple a fashion as in the 2 by 2 case.[6]

Theorem 1. Let $\theta(w)$ be non-singular. Then there exist:

(a)   unambiguous, dual R-non-intensive and S-non-intensive associations,

(b)   unambiguous, R-intensive and unambiguous, S-intensive associations.

Proof. Since θ is non-singular $AA^{-1} = I$, where I denotes the indentity matrix. Since A is row stochastic some positive weighted average of each column of A^{-1} equals zero; thus each such column must contain a negative element. Also some positive weighted average of each column equals unity; this together with a negative element in each column implies an element exceeding unity in each column. In like manner B^{-1} has a negative element and an element exceeding unity in each row. Finally, since $\hat{K}^{-1}$, $\hat{X}$, $\hat{w}$, and $\hat{P}^{-1}$ have strictly positive diagonals, θ^{-1}, A^{-1}, and B^{-1} have the same sign pattern.

Theorem 1 appears to me to be the strongest result obtainable without additional restrictions.[7] Immediate implications are that A has a dual R-intensive association if for some S-intensive association the total reward to each factor is at least as great as the output of its S-intensive good, and that B has a dual S-intensive association if for some R-intensive association the value of the total output of each good is at least as great as the total reward to its R-intensive factor.

Whereas I have thus far discussed 'weak' questions concerned with whether each good can be associated with some factor, etc., one can also follow the

[5]Duality and unambiguity represent the two general ideas that seem to be of interest although one could of course instead consider somewhat stronger or weaker alternative specific definitions. A stronger version of duality, for example, would be to require an S-intensive association to be the inverse of an R-intensive; a weaker version would be to require each factor to be S-intensive in some good.
[6]Murray Kemp has informed me that much of Theorem 1 was deduced by James Meade in private correspondence in 1968.
[7]Murray Kemp has shown that much of the theorem can be extended to the case of unequal numbers of goods and factors; see Kemp (1973). Also for a further discussion of duality see Kemp and Ethier (1973).

spirit of Chipman's discussion and investigate 'strong' questions concerned with whether each good can be associated with each factor, etc. Accordingly I say that a technology is strongly R-unambiguous if A^{-1} has no elements between zero and unity, strongly S-unambiguous if B^{-1} has no elements between zero and unity, and strongly dual if in addition all associations are dual. Note that a technology can be strongly R-unambiguous but neither strongly S-unambiguous nor strongly dual. However, since A^{-1} and B^{-1} must always have the same sign pattern, strong duality is equivalent to a technology being both strongly R-unambiguous and strongly S-unambiguous.

Now Chipman's strong criterion applied to B^{-1} is of course a particular example of a strongly S-unambiguous technology. But it also implies that the technology is strongly R-unambiguous and thus dual as well. This follows from the facts that A^{-1} must have the same sign pattern as B^{-1} and that the inverse of a row stochastic matrix also has unit row sums ($Au = u$ implies $u = A^{-1} u$, where u denotes the vector of ones) so that the positive diagonal elements of A^{-1} must also exceed unity. Thus Chipman's strong property is quite strong indeed.

It should be emphasized that the situation regarding Inada's alternative is, surprisingly enough, radically different from an economic point of view, despite a symmetry of mathematical results [for the latter see Inada (1971), and Uekawa, Kemp and Wegge (1973)]. For if B^{-1} has negative diagonal elements and positive off-diagonal elements the positive elements need not exceed unity (if n is greater than two) and thus B^{-1} need not be strongly S-unambiguous. And even if the positive elements are assumed to be greater than unity it does not follow that the technology is dual or strongly R-unambiguous. Thus despite the severe mathematical conditions necessary to establish Inada's criterion it is basically a 'weak' rather than a 'strong' result and indeed gives economic information of about the same value as that which Theorem 1 yields in 'almost all' cases.[8]

'Strong' properties need not hold 'almost always' and so additional necessary and sufficient conditions must be considered. Such conditions tend to be complicated and need not be of any interest because if they require one to perform tests involving an entire matrix one might just as well simply calculate the inverse in the first place. Attention thus focuses on conditions which can be given some intuitive interpretation, such as that the economy reduce to a 2 by 2 economy in some sense. Following Uekawa (1971), such a condition will be presented for the technology to be strongly unambiguous. In the 2 by 2 case good one is said to be intensive in factor one if $\theta_{11}/\theta_{21} > \theta_{12}/\theta_{22}$. An alternative statement of this condition would be to require that for each factor (say the first) there exists some good (in this case the first) and some positive proportional increases y_1 and y_2 in the present output levels X_1 and X_2 such that $\theta_{21}X_1y_1 = \theta_{22}X_2y_2$, $\theta_{11}X_1y_1 > \theta_{12}X_2y_2$ and $\theta_{11}X_1(y_1-\delta) < \theta_{12}X_2(y_2+\delta)$ for some positive $\delta \leq y_1$.

[8]Inada's criterion is weaker than Theorem 1 in that it says nothing about intensive associations, stronger in that the nonintensive is unique and one to one.

It is in the context of this formulation of the factor intensity condition that the n by n economy will be required in a sense to reduce to a 2 by 2 economy. The following result is obtained easily enough.

Theorem 2. *A non-singular positive $\theta(w)$ is strongly R-unambiguous if and only if for each factor k there exists some decomposition of the n goods into two groups J and $\bar{J}$ and some positive vector y such that if each industry output X_j is increased in the proportion y_j, then*

(a) *the goods in J will together require exactly as much additional input of each factor other than k as will the goods in $\bar{J}$ together,*

(b) *the goods in J will together increase their use of factor k more than will the goods in $\bar{J}$ together,*

(c) *for some uniform reduction in the y_j of the J goods and increase in the y_j of the $\bar{J}$ goods, the latter will together require more additional units of k than will the former.*

Proof. The condition means that for some decomposition $J, \bar{J}$ of $\{1, \ldots, n\}$ and some positive y

$$\sum_{j \in J} a_{ij} y_j = \sum_{j \in \bar{J}} a_{ij} y_j, \quad i \neq k, \tag{7}$$

$$\sum_{j \in J} a_{kj} y_j > \sum_{j \in \bar{J}} a_{kj} y_j, \tag{8}$$

$$\sum_{\in J} a_{kj}(y_j - \delta) < \sum_{j \in \bar{J}} a_{kj}(y_j + \delta), \quad \text{where } y_j - \delta \geqq 0, j \in J. \tag{9}$$

Since A is row stochastic, eq. (9) can be rewritten as

$$\delta > \sum_{j \in J} a_{kj} y_j - \sum_{j \in \bar{J}} a_{kj} y_j,$$

or $\quad\quad 1 > \sum_{j \in J} a_{kj}\left(\frac{y_j}{\delta}\right) - \sum_{j \in \bar{J}} a_{kj}\left(\frac{y_j}{\delta}\right) \equiv m,$

or $\quad\quad 1 = \sum_{j \in J} a_{kj} z_j - \sum_{j \in \bar{J}} a_{kj} z_j, \quad \text{where} \quad z_j = y_j/\delta m. \tag{9'}$

Now eq. (8) implies that $1 > m > 0$, which together with $y_j - \delta \geqq 0$ for $j \in J$ implies that $z_j > 1$ for $j \in J$. Let x be the vector such that $x_j = z_j$ for $j \in J$ and $x_j = -z_j$ for $j \in \bar{J}$. Thus eqs. (7) and (9') are equivalent to $Ax = e_k$, where e_k denotes the vector with the kth component equal to unity and all others zero. Then $A^{-1} e_k = x$, where x has no component between zero and unity. As the argument applies to each k this proves that the condition of the theorem is equivalent to A^{-1} having no element between zero and unity.[9]

---

[9]The method of Theorem 2 can also be applied to obtain an analogous condition for θ to be strongly S-unambiguous. Strong duality requires that the two conditions hold simultaneously.

In order to give some idea of how these 'strong' properties compare with Chipman's formulation of the strong criterion, it is desirable to have conditions for the latter based on that concept of factor intensity which motivated Theorem 2. The proof of this theorem immediately implies that A^{-1} has an element exceeding unity in each row and column and all other elements negative if and only if the set J in Theorem 2 has precisely one good. Also A^{-1} has a negative element in each row and column and all other elements greater than unity (i.e., the strengthened form of Inada's criterion) if and only if the set $\bar{J}$ in Theorem 2 has precisely one good.[10] Finally, it can easily be shown that a technology possesses Chipman's strong property if and only if for any set J of factors there exists a corresponding equal-sized set of goods and a positive vector y of proportional changes in outputs for which the goods in J will together use exactly as much additional input of each factor in $\bar{J}$ and uniformly more additional input of each factor in J than will the goods in $\bar{J}$ together.

I now turn briefly to the factor price equalization property. Most n by n treatments have been concerned[11] with the global univalence of the cost function (2). This problem is of interest in its own right and is central to whether complete diversification implies factor price equalization. But it is not relevant to what seems to me to be the essential message of factor price equalization: if trading countries have 'sufficiently similar' factor endowments commodity trade will completely substitute for factor movements whereas if the endowments are not 'sufficiently similar' factor prices can not possibly be equalized by trade regardless of the actual pattern of specialization. This result does not depend upon the global properties of the cost function and can easily be shown to generalize in full strength to the n by n case:

(a) For any P such that eq. (2) holds for some w there exists some closed cone $H(P)$ such that all countries with non-zero endowments in $H(P)$ will have equal factor prices if engaged in free trade at world prices P.

(b) For any K there exists a closed cone $G(K)$ such that for any positive $K' \in G(K)$ there exists a closed cone $M(K, K')$ such that countries with positive endowments K and K' will have equal factor prices if engaged in free trade at any world prices $P \in M(K, K')$.

(c) The cones $H(P)$ and $G(K)$ can be made exhaustive in the sense that $K \in H(P)$ and $K' \notin H(P)$ imply that countries with endowments K and K' can not have equal factor prices when trading at commodity prices P and that $K' \notin G(K)$ implies that countries with endowments K and K' can never have equal factor prices.[12]

[10]Note that if J contains but one good then part (c) of Theorem 2 must be trivially satisfied, i.e., it becomes a restriction only when J contains at least two goods.

[11]See, for example, Samuelson (1953, 1967), McKenzie (1955, 1960, 1967), Gale and Nikaido (1965), Pearce (1967), and Chipman (1969). For a notable exception see McKenzie (1955) and cf. also Pearce (1970, chs. 12 and 16).

[12]Proposition (a) is essentially McKenzie's (1955) Theorem 1 and propositions (b) and (c) can be proved in roughly similar fashion.

I have argued that the 2 by 2 Heckscher–Ohlin model is quite robust in the specific sense that an essential core of basic results generalizes in a straightforward way to the n by n case. Indeed it is the Heckscher–Ohlin theorem itself which is apparently the least robust (and recall that this is quite fragile in the 2 by 2 case; see Jones' classic paper (1956–57) for example). Of course it must be a matter of opinion as to what is called the 'essential core'. But, once it is known that the strongest possible interpretations do not generalize without additional restrictions, there is reason to point out what does.

References

Chipman, S., 1969, Factor price equalization and the Stolper–Samuelson theorem, International Economic Review 10, 399–406.

Ethier, W., 1972, Non-traded goods and the Heckscher–Ohlin model, International Economic Review 13, 132–147.

Gale, D. and H. Nikaido, 1965, The Jacobian matrix and global univalence of mappings, Mathematische Annalen 159, 81–93.

Inada, Ken-Ichi, 1971, The production coefficient matrix and the Stolper–Samuelson condition, Econometrica 39, 219–240.

Jones, R.W., 1956–57, Factor proportions and the Heckscher–Ohlin theorem, Review of Economic Studies 24, 1–10.

Jones, R.W., 1965, The structure of simple general equilibrium models, Journal of Political Economy 73, 557–572.

Kemp, M.C., 1969, The pure theory of international trade and investment (Prentice-Hall, Englewood Cliffs).

Kemp, M.C., 1973, Relatively simple generalizations of the Stolper–Samuelson and Samuelson–Rybczynski theorems, unpublished.

Kemp, M. C. and W. Ethier, 1973, A note on joint production and the theory of international trade, Department of Economics Discussion Paper no. 265 (University of Pennsylvania, Philadelphia).

Kemp, M.C. and L.L. Wegge, 1969, On the relation between commodity prices and factor rewards, International Economic Review 10, 407–413.

McKenzie, L.W., 1955, Equality of factor prices in world trade, Econometrica 23, 239–257.

McKenzie, L.W., 1960, Matrices with dominant diagonals and economic theory, in: Arrow, Karlin and Suppes, eds., Mathematical methods in the social sciences, 1959 (Stanford University Press, Stanford) 47–62.

McKenzie, L.W., 1967, The inversion of cost functions: A counter-example, International Economic Review 8, 271–278.

Pearce, I., 1967, More about factor price equalization, International Economic Review 8, 255–270.

Pearce, I., 1970, International trade (Norton, New York).

Samuelson, P.A., 1953, Prices of factors and goods in general equilibrium, Review of Economic Studies 21, 1–20.

Samuelson, P.A., 1967, Summary on factor price equalization, International Economic Review 8, 286–295.

Uekawa, Y., 1971, Generalization of the Stolper–Samuelson theorem, Econometrica 39, 197–218.

Uekawa, Y., M.C. Kemp and L.L. Wegge, 1973, *P*- and *PN*-matrices, Minkowski- and Metzler-matrices, and generalization of the Stolper–Samuelson and Samuelson–Rybczynski theorems, Journal of International Economics 3, 53–76.

Wegge, L.L. and M.C. Kemp, 1969, Generalizations of the Stolper–Samuelson and Samuelson–Rybczynski theorems in terms of conditional input–output coefficients, International Economic Review 10, 414–425.

The Relevance of the Two-Sector Production Model in Trade Theory

---

Ronald W. Jones

University of Rochester

José A. Scheinkman

University of Chicago

This paper examines how well the basic properties of the traditional 2 × 2 model of a competitive economy, commonly used in much of the pure theory of international trade, generalize when more goods and factors are considered. The notion of factor intensity and the Hekscher-Ohlin, Stolper-Samuelson, and Rybczynski theorems are discussed. The role played by the no-joint-production assumption as opposed to small dimensionality in the latter two results is stressed. The mathematical appendix provides a compact and formal statement of the properties discussed in the text.

The two-sector, two-factor model of a competitive economy is by now standard fare in a number of fields in economics. In particular, the pure theory of international trade has made extensive use of the "2 × 2" model. As in any body of theory, the results and theorems obtained rest upon the entire set of assumptions. How crucial is the assumption limiting the number of factors and commodities to two apiece? The widespread use of the model suggests that the prevailing belief is that basic properties and theorems in some sense are capable of generalization. On the other hand, there are those who are strongly critical of the simple model precisely because its dimensionality is limited to the 2 × 2 case.

Consider the following sample of critical opinion. We begin with Ivor

We wish to thank Ikushi Egawa, Winston Chang, Trout Rader, and Harry Johnson for comments on this paper as well as Bill Ethier and Murray Kemp for earlier remarks in 1973 on preliminary work. A recent paper by Diewert and Woodland (1977) provides an elegant model with some results in common with our own paper. This research was supported by the National Science Foundation.

[*Journal of Political Economy*, 1977, vol. 85, no. 5]

Pearce (1970), who devotes much of his book to challenging the usefulness and general validity of the simple traditional trade models. Thus ". . . we shall again and again argue that it is in fact not possible to study problems involving factor prices *in anything like a realistic way* until at least three commodities and three factors are introduced," or, further on, ". . . many textbooks of international trade theory (even the most advanced) lay a great deal too much emphasis upon *propositions which are true only for models with two commodities and two factors of production*" (p. 320, italics supplied). The latter quote is quite explicit in saying that at least some of the standard propositions are false for economies with more than two commodities and factors. This of course goes further than the remark that it may be difficult to prove results in the case of many goods and factors without adding further assumptions. Murray Kemp (1971), in a review of Pearce's book, states with approval, "He shows that many of the familiar propositions of two-by-two-by-two trade theory do not carry over to larger and, from a policy-making point of view, more relevant systems" (p. 251). Finally, consider the following remark by Frank Hahn (1973): "It is well known that an economy with only two goods has a number of important properties which do not carry over to the general case" (p. 297).

The purpose of this paper is to respond to these charges by considering how well or poorly the basic properties of the 2×2 model generalize. In the first section of the paper, we present the basic set of four propositions in the pure theory of international trade as typically set out for the standard model. This is followed by a section discussing a generalized notion of factor intensity, a concept central to the Heckscher-Ohlin theorem about trade flows. Section III establishes a general form of the dual Stolper-Samuelson and Rybczynski theorems and points out that the crucial assumption upon which these properties rest is *not* small dimensionality but, rather, the lack of joint production.

Two features concerning dimensionality are found in the 2×2 model. The first is that 2 is a small number. The second is that the number of factors is the same as the number of commodities. Section IV of the paper discusses those properties of a general model that hold if the number of factors and commodities are the same (the "even" case) but may not hold if there are more factors than commodities (the "uneven" case). The concluding section discusses some basic properties found not only in the 2×2 case but in much more general settings as well—in both "even" and "uneven" cases and in cases in which joint production appears.

The discussion in the body of the paper is kept deliberately nonmathematical, primarily to establish that the properties being discussed rest upon simple assumptions about technology. The Appendix reconsiders some of this material in a more compact matrix format.

I. The Basic Trade Model

The standard Heckscher-Ohlin model of international trade incorporates a set of propositions that reveal essential properties of the two-commodity, two-factor general equilibrium model of production. Of these propositions, four are central:[1]

i) The *Heckscher-Ohlin theorem* links the pattern of trade to factor intensities and factor endowments. A country exports that commodity which uses intensively the factor which is relatively cheap prior to trade.

ii) The *Factor-Price Equalization theorem* suggests that free trade in commodities is sufficient to cause factor prices to be equalized between countries even if factor supplies cannot cross national boundaries.

iii) The *Stolper-Samuelson theorem* states that an increase in the price of some commodity (through tariff policy, e.g.) must unambiguously raise the real reward to some factor of production.

iv) The *Rybczynski theorem* points out that, if prices are kept constant but the endowment of some factor rises, not all outputs can expand. The production of some commodity must fall.

It is convenient to group (i) and (ii) together and (iii) and (iv) together. At a superficial level, the Heckscher-Ohlin theorem and Factor-Price Equalization theorem seem to rely heavily upon an assumption that countries share identical technologies, whereas the Stolper-Samuelson and Rybczynski theorems stress the internal structure of a single economy, quite apart from levels of technology abroad. Indeed this seems especially true of the Factor-Price Equalization theorem, which is a razor's-edge kind of result. If two countries have dissimilar technologies, any basis for an exact equivalence in factor-pricing structure (in the absence of international factor mobility) quite obviously disappears. In similar though less exact fashion, any strong difference in the quality of technologies between countries could outweigh factor endowment differences and upset the Heckscher-Ohlin theorem.

At a deeper level, however, the essence of propositions (i) and (ii) is the link between factor and commodity prices in any particular country. The Heckscher-Ohlin theorem rests upon an assumption that unit costs can be disaggregated into components (labor costs, capital costs) and that changes in factor prices influence unit costs of various commodities differently, depending upon factor proportions. The Factor-Price Equalization theorem, in turn, depends upon the delicate mathematical property of uniqueness of a factor-price vector for a given set of commodity prices for a single economy.[2] The international trade application then follows

---

[1] These are the same four propositions singled out by Ethier (1974) in a classic paper.

[2] For this reason we do not pursue an analysis of the Factor-Price Equalization theorem in the remainder of the paper. For discussion of this topic, see, e.g., Chipman (1969).

from the assumption that trade equalizes commodity prices between countries and, of course, that countries share a common technology.

It is important also to point out that the standard Heckscher-Ohlin theory in the simple two-commodity, two-factor case does *not* argue that these theorems *must* hold. Even the simple two-dimensional theory allows these theorems to be violated. For example, if the ranking of commodities by factor intensities does not correspond between countries (the "factor-intensity reversal" phenomenon), the Factor-Price Equalization theorem cannot be satisfied, and the Heckscher-Ohlin theorem must be violated for at least one country.[3] Difficulties of this kind obviously do not go away in higher-dimensional cases. The point that is relevant here, however, is that the assumption of small scale (2 × 2) does not preclude a richer variety of results.

The Stolper-Samuelson and Rybczynski theorems seem more robust. They depend only upon the assumption that each commodity is produced by combining the two factors in proportions that differ between sectors. Each is a different reflection of the *magnification effect* whereby factor prices and commodity output changes are more widespread than commodity price and factor endowment changes, respectively (see Jones 1965a, 1965b; or Caves and Jones 1973, chaps. 8, 9). Properly qualified, this magnification effect does not depend upon the number of sectors in the economy.

II. Factor Intensities and the Heckscher-Ohlin Theorem

In the 2 × 2 model with labor and capital the two productive factors, one commodity is said to be relatively labor intensive if the ratio of labor to capital employed in producing that commodity is greater than the labor/capital ratio used in the other sector. A double bilateral comparison is involved: a ratio of two factors compared between two industries. Such a concept of factor intensity can be carried over readily to a model incorporating many factors and commodities. Just pick a pair of factors and a pair of commodities, and compare the ratio of factor use for the two industries.

However, it proves more instructive to proceed along different lines. In the 2 × 2 model, alternative but equivalent expressions of the factor-intensity ranking were provided, on the one hand, by a comparison of the distributive share of labor in the two industries (θ_{L1} and θ_{L2}) or, on the other, by a comparison of the fraction of the total supply of each of the two factors employed in the first industry (λ_{L1} with λ_{K1}). If the first industry employs a higher labor/capital ratio than does the second, then θ_{L1}

---

[3] That is, with intensities reversed, either each country exports the commodity which, to it, is labor intensive, or each country exports its capital-intensive good. See Jones (1956).

exceeds θ_{L2}, and, as well, the fraction of the labor force used in the first industry (λ_{L1}) exceeds the fraction of the capital stock employed by the first industry (λ_{K1}). It is a variation on these comparisons rather than physical bilateral proportions that usefully generalizes.

The intensity with which any sector uses a particular factor can be compared with the average for the economy. Let α^i represent factor i's distributive share in the economy as a whole. In contrast, θ_{ij} is factor i's distributive share in the jth sector. Let

$$z_{ij} \equiv \frac{\theta_{ij}}{\alpha^i}, \tag{1}$$

so that, if z_{ij} exceeds unity, the jth sector is said to be "intensive" in its use of factor i. If each z_{ij} were weighted by the importance of factor i in the national income (α^i), the weighted average for *all* factors used in the jth industry,

$$\sum_i \alpha^i z_{ij},$$

would of course be unity.

Along parallel lines, compare the fraction of factor i used in industry j, λ_{ij}, with the fraction of the national income represented by the output of industry j, α_j. (Literally α_j is $p_j x_j / Y$, where p_j is price, x_j is output, and Y is the value of national income.) Industry j might be termed "intensive" in its use of factor i if λ_{ij} exceeds α_j. Indeed, as it is easy to verify, the ratio λ_{ij}/α_j is equal to z_{ij}.

The Z-matrix thus summarizes information about factor intensities. If an entry, z_{ij}, exceeds unity, industry j uses factor i intensively.[4] The z_{ij} can be compared with any other element in row i or column j. Each column refers to a particular industry's use of each and every productive factor. Thus z_{ij} exceeds z_{hj} if λ_{ij} exceeds λ_{hj}. If so, industry j is intensive in its use of factor i relative to its use of factor h. Such a comparison would be useful in answering the following question: If factor prices are given and the jth output rises (all other outputs constant), does the demand for factor i rise relatively more or less than the demand for factor h? The answer is more, if z_{ij} exceeds z_{hj}.[5]

It is a comparison of elements in a row of the Z-matrix that supports the extension of the Heckscher-Ohlin theorem to a world of many factors

---

[4] Dual interpretations of this concept of intensity are discussed in Section V.

[5] Let a_{ij} denote the amount of factor i used per unit output of commodity j. If factor prices are given, a_{ij} is determined. The total amount of factor i used in the economy, V_i, is

$$\sum_i a_{il} x_l.$$

Therefore, if only output j rises (and factor prices are fixed), $\hat{V}_i = \lambda_{ij} \hat{x}_j$, where $\hat{\ }$ over a variable denotes a relative change ($\hat{x}$ is dx/x).

and commodities. The underlying rationale for the Heckscher-Ohlin theorem is the connection between factor prices and unit costs. Unit costs (c_j) are equal to the sum of factor components. Thus

$$a_{1j}w_1 + a_{2j}w_2 + \cdots + a_{rj}w_r = c_j. \tag{2}$$

Taking small changes (and letting $\hat{x}$ be defined as dx/x),

$$\theta_{1j}\hat{w}_1 + \cdots + \theta_{rj}\hat{w}_r = \hat{c}_j. \tag{3}$$

This result presupposes that firms attempt to minimize costs. For any set of factor prices, c_j is minimized when

$$\sum_i \theta_{ij}\hat{a}_{ij}$$

is reduced to zero. Now suppose all we know about two economies before trade is that in the first of them the return to factor 17, w_{17}, is lower than in the other. Then industries can be ranked from highest $\theta_{17,j}$ to lowest $\theta_{17,j}$, and such a factor-intensity ranking would serve as best guide to the extent to which c_j differs in the two countries before trade and thus to the pattern of trade. This of course is only a partial analysis, as differences in other factor prices also affect costs. But the rationale for each factor-price difference between countries affecting unit costs is the same. The impact on costs and the trade pattern depends upon factor-intensity rankings precisely as in the 2 × 2 model.

III. The Magnification Effect: Stolper-Samuelson and Rybczynski Theorems

In the 2 × 2 model, an increase in the price of one commodity causes one factor return to rise relatively more than this price and another factor return to fall. This Stolper-Samuelson version of the magnification effect of commodity-price changes on factor prices holds *regardless* of the number of factors and commodities in the model, as long as there is no joint production. That is, this much-cited feature of the 2 × 2 model is based on a commonly assumed feature of technology: that each productive process combines more than one input to produce only one output. The productive structure is pyramidical (see fig. 1).

No complicated mathematics is required to establish this assertion. Consider equation (3) for all those commodities actually produced, so that unit costs, c_j, represent prices, p_j. Equation (3) states that each price change, $\hat{p}_j$, is a positive weighted average of all factor-price changes. That is, each $\hat{p}_j$ must be trapped between the largest and the smallest of the $\hat{w}_i$'s. Such a relationship holds for every commodity produced in

TWO-SECTOR PRODUCTION MODEL 915

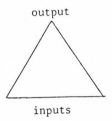
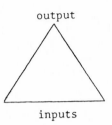

Fig. 1

positive quantities. Thus, if commodities are numbered so that $\hat{p}_1 > \hat{p}_2 > \cdots > \hat{p}_n$, there must exist at least two factors, i and h, such that

$$\hat{w}_i > \hat{p}_1 > \cdots > \hat{p}_n > \hat{w}_h. \tag{4}$$

This proposition is in no way limited to 2×2 models.[6]

As a special case, suppose that only one commodity price rises and all other commodity prices remain constant. Then at least one factor of production finds its real reward unambiguously raised, and at least one other factor reward falls. This basic generalization of the Stolper-Samuelson result follows directly from the assumption of no joint production and is independent of the dimensionality assumption as to the number of factors and commodities.[7] Of course we would like to know more—*which* factor prices rise and which do not. Answers to these detailed compositional questions depend upon a description of the technology for each and every commodity-factor share and (in cases in which the number of factors exceeds the number of commodities) elasticities of substitution between factors. Chipman (1969), Kemp and Wegge (1969), Inada (1971), Uekawa (1971), and others have investigated special sets of restrictions that allow detailed results in the $n \times n$ case to correspond to those in the 2×2 case. The basic "magnification effect" for prices is independent of such restrictions.

If joint production takes the special form in which a single input produces many outputs (see fig. 2), the Stolper-Samuelson type of result would be reversed: the distribution of output prices would be wider than that of input prices. Each input-price change would be a positive weighted

[6] In some special cases the strict inequality at the beginning or end of this chain would not hold. The Appendix explains more carefully the conditions required to ensure strict inequalities here and subsequently in the text. As the emphasis on the lack of joint production may suggest, we assume that at least two factors are employed in each productive activity (and, further, that every factor is employed in at least two sectors).

[7] A simple proof for the "even" case ($n \times n$) involving the share matrix and its inverse is provided in Ethier (1974). In these remarks we continue to assume that any commodity whose price changes continues to be produced.

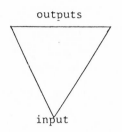
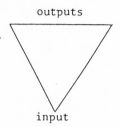

FIG. 2

average of commodity-price changes.[8] Again, it is the asymmetry between inputs and outputs in the productive structure that accounts for the basic theorem establishing asymmetry between the changes in input and output prices.[9]

The magnification effect linking changes in commodity and factor prices is also revealed in the dual ranking of endowment and output changes in the basic 2 × 2 model. The special case in which the endowment of only one factor changes leads to the Rybczynski result: if prices are constant, the output of some commodity must fall.[10] But there is a potential ambiguity in the preceding statement of the theorem. Which set of prices is assumed constant? In the 2 × 2 world, commodity and factor prices are *locally* uniquely linked so that, if one set of prices is held constant, so is the other. Fairly weak conditions suffice to establish in the *n* × *n* case that *locally* factor prices and commodity prices are uniquely linked (as opposed to the stronger conditions needed for global factor-price equalization, as in Gale and Nikaido [1965] and Chipman [1969]).

The ambiguity arises in the case in which the number of factors exceeds the number of produced commodities. Suppose commodity prices are fixed in such a model. Let the endowment of some factor rise. This results in an outward shift in the transformation surface and (at the given commodity prices) a unique change in outputs. But factor prices are also disturbed and with them techniques. Thus holding commodity prices constant is different from holding factor prices (and all techniques) constant.

---

[8] There is a branch of economics that employs the basic assumption that each input produces many outputs. This is the "new" theory of demand associated with the work of Lancaster (1971), in which each commodity (input) provides a variety of characteristics (outputs) of value to consumers.

[9] Joint production may not involve such asymmetries: many inputs may be required to produce, jointly, many outputs. But an asymmetry can be created by focusing on the concept of a production process (one) involving many inputs and many outputs. Indeed, a central issue for trade theory would be the question of where the *processes* are located and how factor intensities and factor endowments are instrumental in determining location patterns.

[10] The basic reference is Rybczynski (1955). See also Jones (1956). Duality to the Stolper-Samuelson result is discussed in Jones (1965a).

To see why this is an important issue, consider the basic relationship between outputs and a typical factor endowment (V_i), if that factor is fully employed:

$$a_{i1}x_1 + a_{i2}x_2 + \cdots + a_{in}x_n = V_i. \tag{5}$$

Let the initial equilibrium be disturbed by a change in factor endowments, with no restriction on factor prices. If full employment can still be maintained,

$$\lambda_{i1}\hat{x}_1 + \lambda_{i2}\hat{x}_2 + \cdots + \lambda_{in}\hat{x}_n = \hat{V}_i - \left(\sum_j \lambda_{ij}\hat{a}_{ij}\right). \tag{6}$$

Each λ_{ij} represents the fraction of factor i that is employed in the jth industry. If factor prices are kept constant, the term

$$\sum_j \lambda_{ij}\hat{a}_{ij}$$

disappears as techniques are unaltered. If such is the case, the form of (6) looks much like that of (3). Each endowment change, $\hat{V}_i$, would be a positive weighted average of all the output changes, and this would once again reflect the assumption of no joint production.

These remarks suggest that, if the factor price–commodity price link is not unique, the generalization of the Rybczynski theorem should be phrased in terms of constant factor prices. This would, we feel, be inappropriate for the following two reasons. First, if the number of factors exceeds the number of commodities and *if factor prices are held constant*, relationships such as (6) cannot hold for all factors. Even if all factors are initially fully employed, they cannot remain so unless all factor endowments expand in proportion. Second, the remarkable *reciprocity* relationship shown in (7), which serves as the basis

$$\frac{\partial w_i}{\partial p_j} = \frac{\partial x_j}{\partial V_i} \tag{7}$$

for the dual relationship between the Stolper-Samuelson and Rybczynski results, assumes (in the $\partial x_j/\partial V_i$ term) that all *commodity prices* are held constant.[11] We postpone until Section V a proof of this relationship.

The case in which the number of commodities exceeds the number of factors is different. If commodity prices are arbitrarily chosen, with no link to local technology, the economy would tend to specialize to produce no more commodities than factors. On the other hand, a closed economy consuming and producing all commodities has its commodity prices reflecting local costs. For example, consider a Ricardian (one-factor) economy producing n goods on the interior of a flat transformation surface. Suppose that the labor endowment expands but commodity

---

[11] This relationship was stated and proved by Samuelson (1953).

prices stay constant. Without information about tastes, of course, output changes are not uniquely determined. But for *any* feasible output changes it must be the case that the relative change in the labor endowment is a positive weighted average of the relative changes in outputs. Outputs either all rise in the same proportion as labor, or some rise more and others less. If there should be more than one factor (but still many more goods) and the endowment of one of them does not change, at least one output falls.

IV. "Even" versus "Uneven" Cases

The 2×2 model is "even"—the same number of factors and commodities. Generalizations to higher dimensions need to account not only for "even" $n \times n$ versions but also for cases in which the number of commodities, n, differs from the number of productive factors, r. Given the tendency to specialize in open economies if $n > r$, here we restrict ourselves to the "uneven" case in which $r > n$.

The Stolper-Samuelson generalization discussed in the preceding section was not restricted to the $n \times n$ case. A relationship like (4) reflects the absence of joint production. For example, if just one commodity price, p_j, rises, some factor price must rise in greater proportion, and some other factor price must fall. But must each factor in turn play these extreme roles for some commodity-price changes?

In examining this question, consider a simple version of an "uneven" case. It is the "specific-factors" model or what Samuelson has termed the "Ricardo-Viner" model.[12] Restrict the number of commodities to two, and suppose that one sector uses capital and labor and the other uses land and labor. Capital and land are each specific to one sector, while labor is mobile—it can be used in either sector and earns the same return in each. Now consider how the wage rate is affected by a rise in either commodity price. Labor is attracted to whichever sector benefits from the price rise. Therefore labor's marginal product must rise in the sector in which price is constant (since the ratio of labor to the specific factor there falls). The wage rate must therefore rise. But in real terms the wage rate falls in the sector where price has risen. To be explicit, if $\hat{p}_1 > \hat{p}_2$,

$$\hat{p}_1 > \hat{w} > \hat{p}_2.$$

Labor plays an "intermediate" role. It is never the extreme factor.

In the even $n \times n$ case, with perhaps all factors mobile from sector to sector, this kind of behavior cannot arise. In particular, the following result can easily be proved: *if the number of factors equals the number of*

---

[12] This model is discussed in Jones (1971, 1975), Samuelson (1971), Mayer (1974), and Mussa (1974).

commodities, every factor has at least one natural enemy. That is, pick a factor i. It is always possible to find a commodity, j, such that, if the price of j rises and no other commodity prices change, w_i must fall. In this sense industry j is a "natural enemy" of factor i.

The proof is simple and makes use of the reciprocity relationship, (7). In the "even" case, ask what happens if, at constant commodity prices, the endowment of factor i, V_i, should expand, all other endowments constant. Because $n = r$, factor prices and techniques are also constant. From relationships like (6), simplified now with every $\hat{a}_{ij}$ zero, we know that for some j, k,

$$\hat{x}_k > \hat{V}_i > 0 > \hat{x}_j. \tag{8}$$

Each factor endowment change is trapped between output changes. Since all endowments other than V_i are constant, some x_j must fall. The reciprocity relationship, (7), then ensures that, if commodity j experiences a price rise (all other prices constant), the return to factor i would fall. In the even case, every factor has at least one natural enemy. And, as the specific factors model reveals, this is a peculiarity of even cases not necessarily shared by the uneven cases.

If in the even case every factor has a natural enemy, does each factor as well have at least one unambiguous natural friend? That is, for each factor, i, is it possible to find at least one industry, k, for which $\hat{w}_i > \hat{p}_k$ if p_k rises with all other commodity prices constant? Can dual relationship (8) be used to establish this? No. What (8) proves is that for each factor, i, there is some industry, k, such that, if V_i rises (all other endowments constant),

$$\frac{\partial x_k}{\partial V_i} > \frac{x_k}{V_i}.$$

Reciprocity relationship (7) identifies $\partial x_k/\partial V_i$ with $\partial w_i/\partial p_k$. Thus

$$\frac{\partial w_i}{\partial p_k} > \frac{x_k}{V_i},$$

or, in relative terms,

$$\frac{\hat{w}_i}{\hat{p}_k} > \frac{\alpha_k}{\alpha^i},$$

where, as before, α^i is factor i's share of the national income and α_k is the share of commodity k's output in the national income.[13] If factor i is *unimportant* enough, in the sense of a low factor share, α^i, compared with α_k, then indeed commodity k is a natural friend in the sense that $\hat{w}_i$

---

[13] For a discussion of the relationship between Stolper-Samuelson terms such as $\hat{w}_i/\hat{p}_k$ and Rybczynski terms such as $\hat{x}_k/\hat{V}_i$, see Ethier (1974) and Ruffin and Jones (1977).

would exceed $\hat{p}_k$. But no general proof along these lines can be constructed.

To establish this, consider the following counterexample.[14] Let

$$\theta' = \begin{bmatrix} \frac{8}{10} & 0 & \frac{2}{10} \\ \frac{7}{20} & \frac{7}{20} & \frac{6}{20} \\ 0 & \frac{6}{15} & \frac{9}{15} \end{bmatrix}$$

be the matrix of distributive shares in a case of three factors and three commodities. Elements in each row refer to the factor shares in a particular industry and thus must add to unity. The inverse of this matrix is

$$(\theta')^{-1} = \begin{bmatrix} \frac{9}{10} & \frac{4}{5} & -\frac{7}{10} \\ -\frac{21}{10} & \frac{24}{5} & -\frac{17}{10} \\ \frac{7}{5} & -\frac{16}{5} & \frac{14}{5} \end{bmatrix}.$$

Each row shows what would happen to a particular factor price if each commodity price, in turn, were raised. For example, the $\frac{7}{5}$ entry in the third row, first column, shows that, if the price of the first commodity were to rise by 10 percent, other commodity prices constant, the return to the third factor would rise by 14 percent. Now focus on the first row. No entry exceeds unity. It is not possible to find an industry for which protection (a price rise) would unambiguously raise the real return to the first factor. *Some* return would have to rise—for example, that of the second factor if the second price rises. Note also that each row has a negative entry—every factor has a natural enemy.

In the original literature, the Stolper-Samuelson result aimed at establishing an unambiguous winner when a commodity price rises. There will always be at least one, but, as shown above, not every factor can rely upon some commodity-price rise (or combination of price rises) to improve its real position. Thus carte blanche in imposing tariffs may not prove sufficient to raise the real wage of some factors, even in the $n \times n$ (even) case.

In contrast, consider the Rybczynski result. It purported to show some output *falling* when the endowment of some factor increases, other endowments (and commodity prices) held constant. This must be the case if the number of factors equals the number of commodities—this was shown by (8). But if factors exceed commodities in number, no output need fall as one endowment rises. The specific-factors model again provides the illustration: at constant prices an increase in mobile labor causes all outputs to rise. Nevertheless, the following Rybczynski result does generalize: for each output, j, it is possible to find a factor of production, i, such that if V_i increases (other V's and p's constant) x_j must fall. In this sense each *industry* has a natural enemy. *Proof:* for each commodity, j,

[14] This matrix appears in Uekawa (1971).

there is some factor, i, such that w_i falls if p_j rises. Using the reciprocity relationship(7), an increase in V_i must reduce x_j. The number of factors may exceed the number of commodities.

V. General Properties of Production Models

Some properties of the 2×2 model hold in a wide variety of cases, including both even and uneven cases (still assuming $r \geq n$) with large numbers of factors and commodities as well as cases involving joint production. To conclude this paper we consider three such properties, the last of them the basic reciprocity relationship already stated in equation (7).

The appropriate degree of generality is attained by considering a set of productive activities. The unit level of activity j involves a set of inputs, a_{ij}, and a set of outputs, b_{kj}. The competitive profit conditions maintain that in equilibrium unit costs cannot fall short of the value of operating the activity at unit level. Thus

$$\sum_i a_{ij} w_i \geq \sum_k b_{kj} p_k. \tag{9}$$

If actual losses are made, the level of the activity, s_j, would be reduced to zero. For activities involving positive production, unit costs are reduced to a minimum by appropriate choice of techniques. This entails

$$\sum_i w_i \, da_{ij} - \sum_k p_k \, db_{kj} = 0. \tag{10}$$

Therefore, differentiating (9), we obtain

$$\sum_i a_{ij} \, dw_i \gtreqqless \sum_k b_{kj} \, dp_k. \tag{11}$$

The equality sign holds if production level s_j is positive. The inequalities to not disturb matters, since each relationship in (11) is now multiplied by the activity level. Summing over all j,

$$\sum_j s_j \sum_i a_{ij} \, dw_i = \sum_j s_j \sum_k b_{kj} \, dp_k, \tag{12}$$

or

$$\sum_i V_i \, dw_i = \sum_k x_k \, dp_k. \tag{13}$$

This can also be written in relative terms as

$$\sum_i \alpha^i \hat{w}_i = \sum_k \alpha_k \hat{p}_k, \tag{14}$$

where the α^i are input shares in the national income and the α_k are output shares.

Expression (14) states a widespread property of any general equilibrium model in which monetary factors are excluded so that the prive *level* has no real impact. It accommodates an equal proportional change in all output and input prices.

The second general property is similar to (14) except in involving physical outputs and inputs instead of prices. It states,

$$\sum_i \alpha^i \hat{V}_i = \sum_j \alpha_j \hat{x}_j. \tag{15}$$

Assuming there is no technical progress, (15) asserts that any changes in factor endowments are matched, in the aggregate, by a change in physical outputs. The weights are once again the input and output shares in the national income. Relationship (15) is derived by considering the equality between the two ways of expressing national income:

$$\sum w_i V_i = \sum p_j x_j. \tag{16}$$

Differentiate (16) and cancel the price variations by using (14) to obtain (15).

A special case of (15) involves a general statement of the marginal productivity relationship. Suppose only one factor endowment, V_i, changes. Then (15) can be written as

$$w_i = \left(\sum_j p_j \, dx_j \right) \Big/ dV_i. \tag{17}$$

This identifies the competitive return to factor i as the change in the value of aggregate output at initial prices that would accompany an increase in V_i of one unit. The remarkable feature of (17) is that prices are not necessarily being held constant, nor are techniques of production necessarily smoothly flexible, nor indeed is joint production ruled out.

Section II of this paper alluded to dual interpretations of the concept of factor intensity embodied in the Z-matrix where z_{ij} referred either to θ_{ij}/α^i or to λ_{ij}/α_j.[15] Industry j was said to use factor i intensively if z_{ij} exceeded unity. This involves a comparison of j with the economy as a whole. Suppose that endowments are held constant but w_i is raised by 1 percent. As (14) suggests, the aggregate price *level* is in this case raised by the fraction α^i of 1 percent. In contrast, single price p_j is raised by the fraction θ_{ij} of 1 percent. Industry j is deemed to be intensive in its use of factor i if a given change in w_i has a relatively stronger impact on the price of commodity j than it does on the aggregate price level.

The dual interpretation of z_{ij} utilizes (15). Suppose the economy wishes to expand output in the jth sector by 1 percent, without reducing output in any other sectors and without changing techniques. This would require

---

[15] We assume now that there is no joint production.

an increase in the economy's factor endowments. As (15) states, the output share, α_j, would express the fraction of 1 percent by which demand for all productive factors rises. The λ_{ij}, the fraction of V_i used in the jth industry, expresses the fraction of 1 percent by which demand for factor i is increased when x_j expands by 1 percent. If z_{ij} is greater than unity, an expansion of j's output increases demand for factor i by a greater relative amount than it does for resources on average. In this sense j is factor-i intensive.

Both properties (14) and (15) are crucial in establishing the basic reciprocity relationship captured by (7). National income, Y, is expressed either as the sum of factor payments,

$$\sum_h w_h V_h,$$

or as the aggregate value of output,

$$\sum_k p_k x_k.$$

Differentiate the latter expression with respect to p_j, holding all other commodity prices and all factor endowments constant. This yields

$$\frac{\partial Y}{\partial p_j} = x_j + \sum p_k \frac{dx_k}{dp_j}.$$

Such a price change in general causes outputs to respond along the transformation schedule. But relationship (15) states that, if all endowments are fixed, the aggregate value of output changes at initial prices, $\sum p_k \, dx_k$, must vanish. Therefore

$$\frac{\partial Y}{\partial p_j} = x_j. \tag{18}$$

In similar fashion, differentiate Y expressed as

$$\sum_h w_h V_h$$

with respect to V_i, holding all commodity prices and all other factor endowments constant. Thus

$$\frac{\partial Y}{\partial V_i} = w_i + \sum_h V_h \frac{dw_h}{dV_i}.$$

In special cases (the $n \times n$ case) each factor-price change is zero because commodity prices are being held constant. But in any event the sum

$$\sum_h V_h \, dw_h$$

must vanish by (14) if each commodity price is held fixed. Thus

$$\frac{\partial Y}{\partial V_i} = w_i. \tag{19}$$

The reciprocity relationship, (7), follows by differentiating (18) with respect to V_i and (19) with respect to p_j and equating the second partials of income with respect to p_j and V_i regardless of the order of differentiation. This relationship can also be used to link *relative* changes in factor and commodity prices (the Stolper-Samuelson terms) on the one hand and *relative* changes in outputs and endowments (the Rybczynski terms) on the other:[16]

$$\alpha^i \cdot \frac{\hat{w}_i}{\hat{p}_j} = \alpha_j \frac{\hat{x}_j}{\hat{V}_i}. \tag{20}$$

This relationship underlies the asymmetry established in the preceding section: in the $n \times n$ case each factor had a "natural enemy," since a negative $\hat{x}_j/\hat{V}_i$ implies a negative $\hat{w}_i/\hat{p}_j$. But each factor need not, in general, have a "natural friend," since a value of $\hat{x}_j/\hat{V}_i$ greater than unity is no guarantee that $\hat{w}_i/\hat{p}_j$ also exceeds unity. Factor and output shares are also involved.

VI. Concluding Remarks

The two-sector model of production as used in the theory of international trade has a rich variety of properties. This paper has shown that relatively few of them are directly dependent upon the small dimensionality represented by two commodities and two factors. The concept of factor intensity and the rationale of the Heckscher-Ohlin theorem generalize readily to higher-dimensional cases. The crucial assumption supporting the Stolper-Samuelson and Rybczynski theorems is the absence of joint production. Identifying the detailed composition of output and factor-price changes is difficult, in higher dimensions, but the existence of magnification effects, especially in the even case in which the number of factors equals the number of goods, is easy to establish. Throughout, the argument has deliberately been kept free of formal mathematics. The Appendix provides an alternative formal treatment of the general model.

Mathematical Appendix

Let technology be summarized by an $r \times n$ nonnegative matrix of input-output coefficients, A. The number of factors, r, is greater than or equal to the number of commodities, n. Each element of A, a_{ij}, is assumed to be a unique zero

---

[16] This relationship is also discussed in Ruffin and Jones (1977). Note that endowments and all p_k, $k \neq j$, are held constant in $(\hat{w}_i/\hat{p}_j)$ and all commodity prices and all V_h, $h \neq i$, are held constant in $(\hat{x}_j/\hat{V}_i)$.

homogeneous function of all factor prices:

$$a_{ij} = a_{ij}(w_1, \ldots, w_r). \tag{A1}$$

We assume this can be differentiated to yield

$$da_{ij} = \sum_{k=1}^{r} a_{ij}^k \, dw_k, \tag{A2}$$

where a_{ij}^k is defined as $\partial a_{ij}/\partial w_k$. Of course each a_{ij}^i is negative (or zero), and

$$\sum_k w_k a_{ij}^k = 0.$$

Suppose that the technology possesses sufficient flexibility to allow full employment. With joint production ruled out and with x representing the vector of outputs and V the vector of factor endowments, the full-employment conditions can be stated as

$$Ax = V. \tag{A3}$$

Consider the ith factor. For small changes,

$$\sum_j x_j \, da_{ij} + \sum_j a_{ij} \, dx_j = dV_i. \tag{A4}$$

Substitute (A2) for da_{ij} to obtain

$$\sum_k s_{ik} \, dw_k + \sum_j a_{ij} \, dx_j = dV_i, \tag{A5}$$

where s_{ik} is defined as

$$s_{ik} \equiv \sum_j x_j a_{ij}^k.$$

The s_{ik} shows how the economy's demand for factor i would respond at unchanged outputs as the return to factor k rises. Each s_{ii} is negative (or zero), and

$$\sum_k w_k s_{ik} = 0.$$

In matrix notation, the differentiated full-employment conditions can be written as

$$S \, dw + A \, dx = dV, \tag{A6}$$

where S is the $r \times r$ matrix $[s_{ik}]$, dw the r-element column vector $\langle dw_i \rangle$, and dx the n-element column vector $\langle dx_j \rangle$.

The dual competitive profit conditions, assuming that all industries operate at positive levels, are shown by

$$A' \cdot w = p. \tag{A7}$$

With technology sufficiently flexible to yield full employment, we now assume that all factor prices and commodity prices are strictly positive. Cost minimization in each industry ensures that

$$\sum_i w_i \, da_{ij} = 0,$$

so that the equations of change, in matrix notation, are

$$A' \cdot dw = dp. \tag{A8}$$

It proves convenient to write equation sets (A6) and (A8) together as

$$\begin{bmatrix} S & \vdots & A \\ \hdashline A' & \vdots & 0 \end{bmatrix} \cdot \begin{bmatrix} dw \\ \hdashline dx \end{bmatrix} = \begin{bmatrix} dV \\ \hdashline dp \end{bmatrix}. \tag{A9}$$

Properties of this partitioned matrix and its inverse are discussed below. For easy reference, let

$$B \equiv \begin{bmatrix} S & \vdots & A \\ \hdashline A' & \vdots & 0 \end{bmatrix}. \tag{A10}$$

The substitution matrix S is symmetric and negative semidefinite. We will assume that we have a regular minimum of the cost function (see Samuelson 1947, p. 68); that is, the corresponding substitution matrix S^j for each commodity satisfies $u'S^j u < 0$ for every nonzero u not proportional to w.[17] Hence we have

$$u'Su < 0 \qquad \text{for } u \text{ not proportional to } w, u \neq 0. \tag{A11}$$

In particular, S has rank $r - 1$ and a negative diagonal, since w is a strictly positive vector.

Also, since p is a positive vector, (A7) implies that, if $u \neq 0$ and $A'u = 0$, then u is not proportional to w. Hence, if $u \neq 0$ and $A'u = 0$, by (A11), $u'Su < 0$. Hence B is a bordered matrix that represents a quadratic form which is negative definite under constraints. In particular, if $r \geq n$, B has full rank $n + r$, since the rank of A is n (see Caratheodory 1967, pp. 195–96; and Samuelson 1947, pp. 378–79). Its inverse is written as in (A12):

$$B^{-1} \equiv \begin{bmatrix} S & \vdots & A \\ \hdashline A' & \vdots & 0 \end{bmatrix}^{-1} \equiv \begin{bmatrix} K & \vdots & G \\ \hdashline G' & \vdots & L \end{bmatrix} \tag{A12}$$

The inverse of B has some known properties (see, once again, Caratheodory 1967; and Samuelson 1947). In particular, K is symmetric and negative semidefinite with rank $r - n$.

Solving for (dw, dx), we obtain

$$\begin{bmatrix} dw \\ \hdashline dx \end{bmatrix} = \begin{bmatrix} K & \vdots & G \\ \hdashline G' & \vdots & L \end{bmatrix} \begin{bmatrix} dV \\ \hdashline dp \end{bmatrix}. \tag{A13}$$

It is clear that the K-matrix answers the following question: What is the impact of a change of factor endowments on factor prices if commodity prices are kept constant? Since K has rank $r - n$, it is clear that in the even case, $n = r$, the K-matrix reduces to a zero matrix. This is the factor-price equalization result. But if $r > n$, factor endowments would have an impact on factor prices. However, it is not true that K must have a negative diagonal. That is, even with $r > n$, an increase in a factor endowment does not have to lower (although it cannot raise) that factor's price at constant commodity prices. For instance, if a good uses only one factor of production, that factor's price cannot change no matter what happens to its endowment, since the commodity price is being held constant.

---

[17] This restriction on the values of u is necessary because the homogeneity property requires that

$$\sum_k w_k s_{lk} = 0.$$

More about K can be learned by writing explicitly the equation $BB^{-1} = I$, as in (A14):

$$\begin{bmatrix} S & A \\ \hline A' & 0 \end{bmatrix} \cdot \begin{bmatrix} K & G \\ \hline G' & L \end{bmatrix} = \begin{bmatrix} I & 0 \\ \hline 0 & I \end{bmatrix}. \tag{A14}$$

Notice that $0 = A'K \equiv KA$. Hence all vectors of endowment changes which are linear combinations of columns of A leave factor prices unchanged.[18] Furthermore, since the rank of K is $r - n$ and the rank of A is n, those are the only vectors of endowment changes that leave factor prices unchanged. Hence (A15) holds:

$$Ku = 0 \qquad \text{iff } u = Aq \text{ for some } n\text{-vector } q. \tag{A15}$$

It follows that, *if every* $r - 1$ *rows of* A *contain* n *linearly independent vectors, then the diagonal elements of* K *are negative.* To see this, observe that, since K is symmetric and negative semidefinite, if $u'Ku = 0$, then $Ku = 0$. Let e_i denote the r-vector whose ith coordinate is 1, and all other coordinates are zero. If $K_{ii} = e_i'Ke_i = 0$, then $Ke_i = 0$, and by (A15) there exists $q \neq 0$ such that $Aq = e_i$. Such q is then perpendicular to every row of A except the ith row. By assumption, there exist n linearly independent n-vectors among those $r - 1$ rows of A. Hence q is an n-vector perpendicular to n linearly independent n-vectors, and hence $q = 0$. But this contradicts $Aq = e_i$.

If the condition stated above is not satisfied, then a change in the endowment of one factor may not affect that factor's price. To see this, consider

$$A = \begin{bmatrix} 1 & 2 \\ 1 & 1 \\ 1 & 1 \end{bmatrix}.$$

If $q = (-1, 1)$, then $Aq = e_1$. Hence $Ke_1 = KAq = 0$, since $KA = 0$. Hence a change in the first factor endowment does not change any factor prices. But notice that in this case, if we leave out the first row of A, we obtain a matrix of rank 1, and hence the hypothesis of the theorem is not satisfied. This illustrates the importance of looking at the rows of A, that is, how each particular factor enters the input-output matrix.

A simple diagram can point out the importance of the rows of A. Suppose that all factors are fully employed in a three-factor, two-commodity model. The ith row of A shows how the two outputs are constrained by the limitation of factor V_i. This constraint is linear, and for full employment all three constraints must intersect at the same point, as in figure 3. Clearly a change in any single factor endowment would no longer entail a common intersection point. Therefore factor prices would have to change. However, suppose that rows 2 and 3 of A were linearly dependent. In such a case the V_2 and V_3 constraint lines in the diagram would be parallel—and full employment would necessitate their lying on top of each other. A change in the endowment of factor 1 could thus be accommodated by output changes without the necessity of any change in factor prices. Note also that, if all endowments expand proportionally to the input requirements in x_1,

---

[18] Suppose that endowment changes are proportional to the input requirements for commodity j. Then at constant commodity prices these endowment changes can be exactly absorbed by changes in j's output without requiring other outputs to adjust or techniques (through changes in factor prices) to be altered. To see that only j's output changes, note that (A14) provides that $A'G = I = G'A$ and that, by (A13), $dx = G'dV$ at constant commodity prices. Therefore, if dV (nonnegative) is proportional to the jth column of A, dx_j is positive, and $dx_k = 0$ for all $k \neq j$.

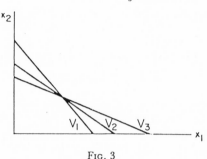

FIG. 3

the common intersection point shifts to the right—an increase in x_1 output alone can maintain full employment without any change in factor prices.[19]

The $n \times n$ submatrix L relates output changes along a given transformation surface to commodity-price changes. From (A14), we have

$$SG + AL = 0.$$

Therefore

$$AL = -SG,$$

or

$$G'AL = -G'SG.$$

But, when the second row of the B-matrix is multiplied by the second column of B^{-1}, we obtain

$$A'G = I, \tag{A16}$$

or, what is the same thing,

$$G'A = I.$$

Therefore

$$L = -G'SG.$$

Pre- and postmultiply by a vector, x, to obtain

$$x'Lx = -(Gx)'S(Gx). \tag{A17}$$

The negative semidefiniteness of S establishes that L is a *positive semidefinite* matrix. Using the fact that the rank of S is assumed to be $r - 1$, one can show that L has a *positive* diagonal whenever $n \geq 2$. For if $L_{ii} = 0$, we have (using [A17]) $0 = -(Ge_i)'S(Ge_i)$. By (A11) this means that $Ge_i = \alpha w$ for some real number α. However, (A16) and (A17) (together with [A7]) imply that $e_i = A'Ge_i = A'\alpha w = \alpha p$. If $n \geq 2$, this means that some coordinate of the price vector is zero, which contradicts our assumptions. Thus, as we would expect, a rise in any commodity price must increase the output of that commodity along the (strictly bowed out) transformation surface.[20]

Note the roles of G and G', as shown by (A13). The G-matrix reveals how a change in commodity prices affects factor prices as of given factor endowments. The G'-matrix links endowment changes (at constant commodity prices) to

[19] See the discussion in n. 18 above.

[20] If $n = 1$ and factor endowments are constant, output cannot respond to price. A positive diagonal for L presupposes the existence of at least one other sector from which resources can be drawn when the price of some given sector rises.

output changes. That these matrices are indeed the transposes of each other confirms the Samuelson *reciprocity* relation. It proves convenient to alter the B-matrix so that the relationship between $\hat{V}$ and $\hat{p}$, on the one hand, and $\hat{w}$ and $\hat{x}$, on the other, can be displayed. Both the Stolper-Samuelson and the Rybczynski results deal in these *relative* changes.

Return to the basic equation set (A9). Rewriting in terms of relative changes yields

$$\begin{bmatrix} \sigma & \vdots & \lambda \\ \hline \theta' & \vdots & 0 \end{bmatrix} \cdot \begin{bmatrix} \hat{w} \\ \hline \hat{x} \end{bmatrix} = \begin{bmatrix} \hat{V} \\ \hline \hat{p} \end{bmatrix}. \tag{A18}$$

The σ_{ij} is the element $(w_j \cdot s_{ij})/V_i$. It is a substitution elasticity, showing the percentage of change in the economy's use of factor i (at unchanged outputs) associated with a 1 percent increase in the jth factor price. The σ has a negative diagonal and zero row sums. The λ is the $r \times n$ matrix of factor-allocation coefficients. Thus λ_{ij} is $a_{ij}x_j/V_i$, the fraction of the ith factor employed in the jth industry. The λ is a nonnegative row-stochastic matrix. The θ' is $n \times r$, a matrix of distributive shares. The θ_{ij} is, of course, $w_i a_{ij}/p_j$. The θ' is also row stochastic, so that the entire matrix is row stochastic. We are primarily concerned with the properties of the inverse matrix:[21]

$$\begin{bmatrix} \hat{w} \\ \hline \hat{x} \end{bmatrix} = \begin{bmatrix} M & \vdots & N \\ \hline Q & \vdots & R \end{bmatrix} \begin{bmatrix} \hat{V} \\ \hline \hat{p} \end{bmatrix}. \tag{A19}$$

The M- and R-matrices are closely related to the K- and L-matrices already discussed. They serve to put factor endowment–factor price and commodity price–commodity output relationships into elasticity form. Stolper-Samuelson results are displayed by N and Rybczynski results by Q. It is to these we now turn. We assume at the outset sufficient richness in the technology so that every factor is used in positive quantities by at least two industries and every industry employs positive amounts of at least two factors.

Consider what can be said in general terms about N and Q by assuming $r \geq n$ and writing explicitly,

$$\begin{bmatrix} \sigma & \vdots & \lambda \\ \hline \theta' & \vdots & 0 \end{bmatrix} \cdot \begin{bmatrix} M & \vdots & N \\ \hline Q & \vdots & R \end{bmatrix} = \begin{bmatrix} I & \vdots & 0 \\ \hline 0 & \vdots & I \end{bmatrix}. \tag{A20}$$

Multiply the second row of the first matrix by the second column of the second to obtain

$$\theta' \cdot N = I. \tag{A21}$$

Ethier (1974) used this relationship in the $n \times n$ case (in which also all a_{ij} were assumed strictly positive) to establish that every column of the N-matrix has at least one negative element. His method of proof extends more generally to the $r \geq n$ case.

Consider the jth column of N. By (A21) this column must be nonzero, so that there exists some k such that $N_{kj} \neq 0$. If the jth column of N is premultiplied by any ith row of θ', (A21) reveals the product to be zero as long as $i \neq j$. We wish to choose row i so that $\theta'_{ik} > 0$. This is possible since every factor k, is by assumption used in at least two industries, and even if one of these should be industry j there will exist some $i \neq j$ for which θ'_{ik} is positive. Therefore $\theta'_{ik} N_{kj} \neq 0$. Now N_{kj} is either negative or positive. If $N_{kj} > 0$, there must exist at least one other

---

[21] The existence of the inverse is obviously guaranteed by the invertibility of B.

element of the jth column of N, $N_{h j}$, $h \neq k$, such that $N_{h j} < 0$, since

$$\sum_k \theta'_{ik} N_{kj} = 0 \qquad \text{for } i \neq j.$$

Therefore at least one element in every column of N must be negative.

Ethier was also able to establish that every column of N must contain at least one element greater than unity. Here his assumption that all a_{ij} are strictly positive turns out to be crucial. Premultiplying the jth column of N by the jth row of θ' yields unity. Therefore, if all θ'_{jk} are positive, at least one N_{kj} must exceed unity, since at least one other element in the jth column of N has been proved to be negative, and θ' is row stochastic. The following 3×3 example shows wherein this result can break down if all factors are not assumed to be positively employed in all industries. Suppose that

$$\theta' = \begin{bmatrix} 0 & \frac{1}{2} & \frac{1}{2} \\ \frac{1}{2} & 0 & \frac{1}{2} \\ \frac{1}{2} & \frac{1}{2} & 0 \end{bmatrix}.$$

In this case, the inverse is

$$N = \begin{bmatrix} -1 & 1 & 1 \\ 1 & -1 & 1 \\ 1 & 1 & -1 \end{bmatrix}.$$

Although every column of N has at least one negative element, no column of N has any elements greater than unity. The jth column of N displays the relative impact on all factor prices of a change in the price of commodity j with all other commodity prices (and factor endowments) constant. If factor j is not used in industry j, an increase in p_j can be passed on uniformly to all factors $k \neq j$, as in this example, without driving any w_k up more than proportionally to p_j. The row-stochastic property of θ' guarantees that either the jth column of N has an element exceeding unity *or* the factor whose wage goes down when p_j rises (and there must be at least one such factor which loses) is not used in the production of the jth commodity.[22]

Must properties of this type characterize the *rows* of N when $r > n$? No. The paper described the specific-factors model as an illustration in which some row of N (the one showing the impact of each and every commodity-price rise on the wage rate) consisted entirely of positive fractions.

When the number of commodities *equals* the number of factors (the even case), more can be said about the rows of N. Rewrite (A20) as

$$\begin{bmatrix} M & \vdots & N \\ \hline Q & \vdots & R \end{bmatrix} \begin{bmatrix} \sigma & \vdots & \lambda \\ \hline \theta' & \vdots & 0 \end{bmatrix} = \begin{bmatrix} I & \vdots & 0 \\ \hline 0 & \vdots & I \end{bmatrix}. \qquad \text{(A22)}$$

In the even case, the M-matrix is the zero matrix—the local factor-price equalization result. Therefore multiplying the first row of the first matrix by the first column of the second yields

$$N\theta' = I.$$

Consider now the ith *row* of N. Postmultiplying by the kth column of θ' $(k \neq i)$ yields the result that every *row* of N must contain at least one negative element,

---

[22] Note that, in the 2×2 case, the assumption that every factor is used in at least two industries is sufficient to establish a positive θ' matrix.

TWO-SECTOR PRODUCTION MODEL 931

since the elements of θ' are nonnegative.[23] The ith *row* of N describes what happens to w_i as, in turn, each commodity price rises. At least one commodity-price rise must thus lower w_i. Each factor has at least one natural "enemy" in the even $(n = r)$ case. Note that multiplying the ith row of N by the ith column of θ' yields an inner product of unity. But this cannot be used to prove that some element of the ith row of N must exceed unity, because the ith *column* of θ' does not add to unity. The ith column of θ' refers to the shares of factor i in all the industries. If factor i is an "important" factor, little can be said, as the ith column would add to greater than unity.[24] But if it is unimportant (with column sum less than unity), then at least one element of the ith row of N must exceed unity. As suggested in the main body of the paper, a relatively unimportant factor could unambiguously be protected by some set of commodity price increases. *But it is not necessarily the case that the "important" factors each have a natural "friend."*

The Q-matrix, whose elements reveal the Rybczynski results, is not as strongly structured as is the Stolper-Samuelson N-matrix. This difference, to be developed below, is a basic reflection of the asymmetry in the two equation sets captured by (A18). The competitive profit conditions assume the simple form:

$$\theta'\hat{w} = \hat{p},$$

because of the envelope result expressed by the cost-minimization condition $\sum w_i \, da_{ij} = 0$. In contrast, the full-employment conditions are more complicated:

$$\sigma\hat{w} + \lambda\hat{x} = \hat{V}.$$

Even with commodity prices constant, factor prices can change in the case $r > n$.

If the number of factors exceeds the number of produced commodities, it is possible to prove that each *row* of Q has at least one negative element but not that it contains an element greater than unity. Nothing in general can be said about the columns of Q. To verify these remarks, multiply the second row of the first matrix in (A22) by the second column of the second matrix to obtain

$$Q\lambda = I.$$

The inner product of the ith row of Q with the kth column of λ $(k \neq i)$ is zero. Since all elements in the λ-matrix are nonnegative, some element in the ith row of Q must be negative.[25]

The elements in the *columns* of λ need not add to unity. The ith column of λ refers to the percentage of each and every factor used in the ith sector. If output i bulks large in the national income, the sum

$$\sum_h \lambda_{hi}$$

---

[23] Here we make use of the assumption that every row of θ' must contain at least two positive elements, i.e., that every good uses at least two distinct factors.

[24] As the preceding example illustrated (for the columns of N), having a column of θ' add exactly to unity here might not suffice to establish the existence of an element in the row of N actually exceeding unity. Formally, we define factor i as *important* if

$$\sum_i \theta'_{ij} = \sum_j \theta_{ij} \geq 1.$$

[25] The proof follows the lines used earlier in establishing the properties of the N matrix. It is necessary to assume, as we have, that each factor is used in the production of at least two commodities.

will greatly exceed unity, and it would not be possible to prove that any element of the ith row of Q would have to be larger than one. On the other hand, if the ith sector is a small part of the economy,

$$\sum_h \lambda_{hi}$$

would add to less than unity. This suffices to establish the existence of at least one q_{il} greater than unity. To see this, let $J = \{j \mid q_{ij} \geq 0\}$. Then

$$1 = \sum_j q_{ij}\lambda_{ji} \leq \sum_{j \in J} q_{ij}\lambda_{ji} \leq \max_{j \in J} \{q_{ij}\} \cdot \sum_{j \in J} \lambda_{ji} \leq \max_{j \in J} \{q_{ij}\} \sum_j \lambda_{ji}.$$

If

$$\sum_j \lambda_{ji}$$

is strictly less than unity (ith sector "unimportant" enough), some q_{il}, at least the

$$\max_{j \in J} \{q_{ij}\},$$

must exceed unity.

The ith row of Q shows what happens to output in the ith sector as each factor endowment rises in turn (and commodity prices are held constant). In general each industry has a "natural enemy" in the sense that for each industry, i, there exists some factor, j, such that industry i would have to contract if only factor j's supply expanded (at constant commodity prices). Of course this is the phenomenon at issue in the Rybczynski result—the actual decline in output as some endowment rises. If the ith sector is relatively unimportant, we have established above that there will be at least one factor which, if it grows, would cause an even greater relative expansion in the ith sector at constant commodity prices.

The columns of Q refer to the impact on all outputs of an increase in a particular V_i (at constant p). If $r > n$, nothing can be said about the columns. For example, consider again the specific-factors model. An increase in the endowment of mobile labor would, at constant p, serve to increase all outputs but perhaps none of them by as great a relative extent as labor.

Although Q is, in the sense described above, less structured than N if the number of factors exceeds the number of commodities, this asymmetry disappears if $n = r$. The reason is that now factor prices are constant if commodity prices do not change. The M-submatrix reduces to an $r \times r$ matrix of zeros. This helps add structure both to the Stolper-Samuelson N-matrix (as we proved above) and the Rybczynski Q-matrix, but primarily to the latter.

From (A20) it is clear that, if M is zero,

$$\lambda Q = I.$$

Since the row sums of λ all add to unity, the type of argument used above serves now to verify that in the even case every column of Q has at least one negative element and, subject to the type of conditions established earlier for N, one element greater than unity. The main body of the paper stated this result somewhat differently: with factor prices uniquely linked to commodity prices and commodity prices held constant, if only one endowment rises, some output must rise by at least a greater relative amount, and some other sector's output must decline.

Fɪɢ. 4

To conclude, it may prove useful to present two examples of sign patterns of the inverse matrix,

$$\left[\begin{array}{c|c} M & N \\ \hline Q & R \end{array}\right].$$

In the first example, let the number of commodities and factors be the same. Furthermore, impose a strong symmetry on the production structure by assuming that each sector j spends half its revenue on factor j and the other half evenly split among all remaining factors. The sheer symmetry of the case is sufficient to establish the sign and size pattern shown in figure 4. All the features of the two-sector sign pattern would be writ large.

As a second example, consider the $n + 1$ factor, n-commodity version of the specific-factors model, shown in figure 5.[26] The M-matrix has rank 1. The diagonal must be negative—the return to factor i is depressed by an increase in V_i with p held constant. The negative elements off the diagonal (except the last row and column) show that, as the endowment of any specific factor rises (at constant p), the return to *all* specific factors must fall. However, the return to the mobile factor (labor) rises with every positive $\hat{V}_i$ ($i \neq$ labor). This is shown by the first n elements of the last row of M. The last column of M (off-diagonal elements only) shows that an increase in the endowment of mobile labor at constant p must raise the returns to all specific factors.

The R-matrix in this case is especially simple and displays strong gross substitute relationships for outputs along the transformation surface. A rise in p_j increases x_j and reduces all other outputs. (All sectors lose labor to the jth sector.)

The N-matrix shows the Stolper-Samuelson elements. The general result (following from the lack of joint production) is verified: every column of N has at least one element greater than unity (in this case only one) and at least one element negative. The jth column of N shows that, as p_j rises, the return to the factor used specifically in j rises by a greater proportional amount, and the returns to all other specific factors must fall. The positive fractions in the $(n + 1)$st row of N show that each rise in p_j raises the wage rate, but relatively not as much. In the even ($r = n$) case, each *row* of N would have to contain at least one negative element. In the specific-factors model, the $(n + 1)$st row contains none.

The Rybczynski Q-matrix shows, in the first n columns, that an increase in the endowment of each specific factor would raise output in the sector using that

[26] This version was described in Jones (1975).

$$\begin{bmatrix} M & | & N \\ -- & | & -- \\ Q & | & R \end{bmatrix} =$$

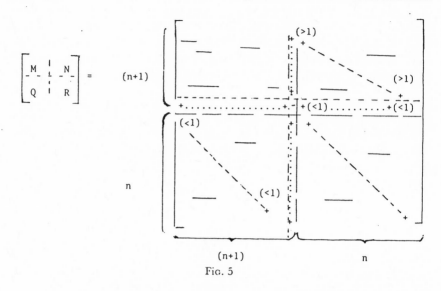

Fig. 5

factor and reduce outputs in all other sectors. However, no element is greater than unity. If V_i should rise by 10 percent, the ith sector will attract some labor. But since the wage has been driven up, the labor force in the ith sector will rise by less than 10 percent. Therefore output x_i must also rise by less than 10 percent. The last column consists of positive elements, each showing how a sector's output expands if mobile labor grows. A 10 percent increase in the supply of labor causes all sectors to expand. Some may expand by greater than 10 percent if the elasticity of demand for labor in those sectors is especially high. We confirm the general property that each row of Q must contain at least one negative element. In the even case ($n = r$), each *column* of Q would display at least one negative element and one element exceeding unity. In the specific-factors $(n + 1) \times n$ case, the first n columns have no element greater than unity, and the last column has no negative entries.

References

Caratheodory, C. *Calculus of Variations and Partial Differential Equations of the First Order. II. Calculus of Variations.* San Francisco: Holden Day, 1967.

Caves, Richard, and Jones, R. W. *World Trade and Payments—an Introduction.* Boston: Little, Brown, 1973.

Chipman, John. "Factor Price Equalization and the Stolper-Samuelson Theorem." *Internat. Econ. Rev.* 10 (October 1969): 399–406.

Diewert, W. E., and Woodland, A. D. "Frank Knight's Theorem in Linear Programming Revisited." *Econometrica* 45, no. 2 (March 1977): 375–99.

Ethier, Wilfred. "Some of the Theorems of International Trade with Many Goods and Factors." *J. Internat. Econ.* 4, no. 2 (May 1974): 199–206.

Gale, David, and Nikaido, H. "The Jacobian Matrix and Global Univalence of Mappings." *Math. Ann.* 159 (1965): 81–93.

Hahn, Frank. Review of *General Equilibrium Theory and International Trade*, by Takashi Negishi. *J. Internat. Econ.* 3, no. 3 (August 1973): 297–98.

Inada, Ken-ichi. "The Production Coefficient Matrix and the Stolper-Samuelson Condition." *Econometrica* 39 (March 1971): 219–39.

Jones, Ronald W. "Factor Proportions and the Heckscher-Ohlin Theorem." *Rev. Econ. Studies* 24 (October 1956): 1–10.

———. "Duality in International Trade: A Geometric Note." *Canadian J. Econ. and Polit. Sci.* 31 (August 1965): 390–93. (*a*)

———. "The Structure of Simple General Equilibrium Models." *J.P.E.* 73, no. 6 (December 1965): 557–72. (*b*)

———. "A Three-Factor Model in Theory, Trade and History." In *Trade, Balance of Payments and Growth,* edited by Jagdish Bhagwati, Ronald W. Jones, Robert Mundell, and Jaroslav Vanek. Amsterdam: North-Holland, 1971.

———. "Income Distribution and Effective Protection in a Multicommodity Trade Model." *J. Econ. Theory* 11, no. 1 (August 1975): 1–15.

Kemp, Murray. Review of *International Trade,* by Ivor Pearce. *J. Internat. Econ.* 1, no. 2 (May 1971): 251–54.

Kemp, Murray, and Wegge, L. "On the Relation between Commodity Prices and Factor Rewards." *Internat. Econ. Rev.* 10 (October 1969): 407–13.

Lancaster, Kevin. *Consumer Demand: A New Approach.* New York: Columbia Univ. Press, 1971.

Mayer, Wolfgang. "Short-Run and Long-Run Equilibrium for a Small Open Economy." *J.P.E.* 82, no. 5 (September/October 1974): 955–67.

Mussa, Michael. "Tariffs and the Distribution of Income: The Importance of Factor Specificity, Substitutability, and Intensity in the Short and Long Run." *J.P.E.* 82, no. 6 (November/December 1974): 1191–1203.

Pearce, Ivor. *International Trade.* New York: Norton, 1970.

Ruffin, Roy, and Jones, R. W. "Protection and Real Wages: The Neo-classical Ambiguity." *J. Econ. Theory* 14 (April 1977): 337–48.

Rybczynski, T. "Factor Endowment and Relative Commodity Prices." *Economica,* n.s. 22 (November 1955): 336–41.

Samuelson, Paul A. *The Foundations of Economic Analysis.* Cambridge, Mass.: Harvard Univ. Press, 1947.

———. "Prices of Factors and Goods in General Equilibrium." *Rev. Econ. Studies* 21, no. 1 (1953): 1–20.

———. "Ohlin Was Right." *Swedish J. Econ.* 39, no. 2 (December 1971): 365–84.

Uekawa, Yasuo. "Generalization of the Stolper-Samuelson Theorem." *Econometrica* 39, no. 2 (March 1971): 197–217.

Chapter Eight

THREE SIMPLE TESTS OF THE STOLPER–SAMUELSON THEOREM

Stephen P. Magee

1. Introduction

Second only in political appeal to the argument that tariffs increase employment is the popular notion that the standard of living of the American worker must be protected against the ruinous competition of cheap foreign labor.

Stolper and Samuelson (1941, p. 333).

HARRY JOHNSON made important contributions to many fields, particularly to the pure theory of international trade. His influence was especially significant on the theory of tariffs: witness the collection of classic papers in his *Aspects of The Theory of Tariffs* (1972). An important question in tariff theory is the effect of a tariff on the distribution of income. The Stolper and Samuelson (1941) theorem asserts that in a two-factor world with complete mobility of factors within a country, liberalization of international trade will lower the real income of one factor of production and increase the real income of the other. It is one of the four central propositions in the 2×2 theory of international trade, along with the factor price equalization, Heckscher–Ohlin and Rybczynski theorems.

The most extreme theoretical alternative to the Stolper–Samuelson theorem is the theory of noncompeting groups advanced by Cairnes (1874). It suggests that factors of production are industry-specific even in the long run so that trade liberalization would benefit all factors in the export industry (which enjoy increased demand) but hurt all factors in the import-competing industry (which faces increased import competition). Studies by Mayer (1974) and Mussa (1974) combine short-run immobility

STEPHEN P. MAGEE

with long-run factor mobility to yield intermediate results: one factor will, say, unambiguously, gain both in the short and in the long run while the other will gain in the short run but lose in the long run from trade liberalization. This intertemporal conflict could be resolved by present-value calculations, if the factors have sufficient information about the adjustment path. While these present-value calculations would be tedious, they could be done.

The intertemporal consideration highlights the difficulty of constructing direct statistical tests which would establish the empirical relevance of the Stolper–Samuelson vs. Cairnes models. The researcher would have to determine factor intensities, factor elasticities of substitution, all variables affecting inter-industry movements in the factors of production (moving costs and geographical dispersion of plants), discount rates, expectations of the likelihood of government adjustment assistance, etc. The enormity of this task explains the shortage of direct empirical tests of the two models.

The original Stolper–Samuelson article itself suggests an indirect approach. Tariffs are set by politicians. Recent work on the economics of special-interest politics indicates that tariffs can be thought of as prices which clear political markets (see Brock and Magee; 1978 and 1979). An important question, using this approach, is the manner in which coalitions form. Any theorem regarding the redistributional effect of a tariff also implies the way in which coalitions are likely to form for and against tariffs: Stolper–Samuelson suggests that lobbying activity will occur along factor lines (capital vs. labor) while Cairnes suggests that they will occur along industry lines (import-competing vs. export). This paper provides three tests of these contrasting forms of lobbying behavior. We assume that the factors of production base their lobbying on rational present-value calculations of their self interest. If the present value of their income streams (inclusive of non-pecuniary considerations and taking lobbying costs into account) would be increased by free trade, we can expect them to lobby for freer trade (and vice versa). This 'revealed-preference' approach to testing for the redistributive effects of tariffs shifts the voluminous amount of information required for an empirical test from the researcher to the representatives of the factors of production.

Three revealed-preference tests of the competing theorems are described and performed on 1973 United States data in Section 2. Section 3 discusses limitations, alternative interpretations and some implications of the tests. The results generally reject Stolper–

139

THREE SIMPLE TESTS OF THE STOLPER–SAMUELSON THEOREM

Samuelson and accept the Cairnes approach. This is consistent with the view that factors are less mobile between industries in advanced industrial societies because of sector-specific human capital and high-technology physical capital.[1] Another interpretation is that lobbying costs and free-rider problems are lower for industry lobbies than for factor lobbies.

2. *The Empirical Results*

> In other words, whatever will happen to wages in the wage good (labor intensive) industry will happen to labor as a whole. And this answer is independent of whether the wage good will be imported or exported . . .
> *Stolper and Samuelson (1941, p. 344).*

Simplicity, statistical methodology and data availability dictated that the tests be limited to two factors of production, capital and labor. The cost of this limitation is that we may be testing other relationships (e.g., substitutability or complementarity between two out of many factors) rather than the two competing theories.

Capital and production labor in the U.S. were chosen to illustrate the tests. The American labor movement has been actively engaged in lobbying on trade policy in the last decade. Most of the headlines have placed labor on the side of greater protection, although we shall see shortly that this position is far from unanimous. Similarly, management in many industries has lobbied actively. Since management is chosen by stockholders, I assume that management's interests coincide with the owners of the firm's physical capital. Regardless of the positions of the factors not considered here (land, skilled labor, etc.), it is of some interest whether production labor and capital are protagonists or antagonists on the question of freer United States trade.

The empirical evidence used in this paper is taken from the Summary of Testimony for the Hearings before the Committee on Ways and Means in the U.S. House of Representatives on the Trade Reform Act of 1973, May–June of 1973. These summaries revealed the preference of 29 trade associations (representing management) and 23 unions for either freer trade or greater protection. A summary of the results together with the related Standard Industrial Classification (SIC) codes are shown in Table 1. In cases where the information was ambiguous or where no information was given, the staff of the Ways and Means Committee and other experts in Washington were consulted. Table 1

Table 1: Positions of Groups on U.S. Trade Policy by Industry.

SIC	Industry	Trade Balance	Trade Associations — Name	Capital's Position†	Labor Unions — Labor's Position†	Labor Unions — Name
2015	Poultry	41	Poul. and Egg Instit. of Am.			
2026	Dairy	−1	Nat'l Milk Prod. Fed.			
2085	Distilling	−416	Dist. Spirits Counc.	F	P	Dist., Rect., Wine and Allied Wkrs
2092	Soybeans	320	Nat. Soyb. Processors	F		
21	Tobacco	130	Tobacco Institute	P	F	Tab. Int'l Workers Union
22	Textiles	−418	Am. Txt. Man. Inst.	P	P	Text. Wkrs Union of America
23	Apparel	−486	*	P	P	Amalg. Clothing Wkrs
26	Paper	−632	Am. Paper Inst.	F	F	United Papers Wkrs Int'l.
2815	Chemicals	81	Syn. Org. Chem. Man.	P	P–M	Int'l Chem. Wkrs Union
2821	Plastics	527	Society of the Plast.	P	P	United R.C.L. and Plast. Wkrs
2911	Petroleum	−505	Amer. Petrol. Inst.	F	F	Petroleum Wkrs Union
30	Rubber	92	Rubber Man. Assoc.	M	P–M	United Rubber Wkrs
3021	Rubber Shoes	−82	Rub. Man. Ass. – Footwear D.	P	P	United Rubber, C, L and P
31	Leather	−364	Tanners Coun. of Am.	P	P	Int'l Leath. Goods Wkrs
3141	Shoes	−471	Am. Footwear Assn.	P	P	United Shoewkr of America
32	Stone, etc.	12	Stone Glass & Clay C. Com.	P	P	Un. Glass and Ceramic Wkrs
331–2	Iron/Steel	−1923	Am. Iron and Steel Inst.	P	P	IAIW and Un. Steelw. of America
3732–3	Lead/Zinc	−137	Lead/Zinc Prod. Com.	M		
3334	Aluminum	−95	Alum Assn.	F	M	Alum. Wkrs Int'l Union
3421	Cutlery	−16	Nat. Ass. of Scissors M.	P	P?	*
3423	Hardware	38	Bldrs Hardw. Manuf.	P	P	Int'l Assn of Tool Craftsmen
35	Machinery	4029	Mach. and Allied Prod. Inst.	F	F	Int'l Assn of Machinists
3522	Tractors	146	Caterpillar Tractor	F	F?	
3541	Mach. Tools	25	Nat'l Mach. Tool Bldrs	M	P	Int'l Assn of Tool Craftsmen
3562	Bearings	23	Anti Fr. Bearing Man.	P	P?	*
3572	Bus. Eq.	−21	Comp. and BE Man. Assn	P	M?	
36	Electrical	701	Nat'l Electr. Man. Assn	M	P	Int'l Broth. of Eelct. Wkr
3711	Cars	−1730			P	United Auto Wkrs
3713	Trucks	1203	Hvy Duty Truck Man.	F	F	Transport Wkrs U. of America
3720	Aviation	1695	Gen. Aero Man. Assoc.	F	F	Int. Assn of Mach. and Aerospace
3751	Bicycles	−296	Cycle Parts and Acc. Ass.	P	P	Am. Watch Wkrs Union
3871	Watches	−126	Am. Watch Ass.	P	P	Int. U. of Dolls, Toys
3941	Toys	−51				

Source: U.S. Ways and Means (1973).
* Position determined from other sources.

† P = protectionist; F = free trade; M = intermediate (ambiguous).
† Trade balance given in millions of dollars.

THREE SIMPLE TESTS OF THE STOLPER–SAMUELSON THEOREM

should not be read in terms of each group's position on specific items in the 1973 trade bill but rather its general position on freer vs. more restricted trade. This position is presumed to reflect its preference both for itself and other industries since trade bills are seldom industry specific. 'P' stands for a protectionist position, 'F' for freer trade and 'M' for mixed positions (powerful subgroups within the organization on both sides).

The quotation from Stolper and Samuelson (1941) at the beginning of this section suggests three empirical implications of their theorem in a simple two-factor world.

1. *Capital and labor in a given industry will oppose each other on the issue of protection (or free trade) for that industry.*
2. *For the country as a whole, each factor will favor either free trade or protection but not both.*
3. *The position taken by capital or labor in an industry on the issue of protection will be independent of whether the industry is export or import-competing.*

These implications form the basis of the three tests.

TEST 1

The first implication suggests that we could test the competing hypotheses for two factors of production with a 2×2 contingency table, as shown in Table 2. Each industry can be placed in one of the four mutually exclusive and exhaustive cells, depending on the position of its capital and labor on trade policy.

Table 2: Contingency Table for the Probable Positions of Capital and Labor on Protection vs. Free Trade.

		Position of Labor	
		1. Protectionist	*2. Free Trade*
Position of Capital:	1. Protectionist	P_{11}	P_{12}
	2. Free Trade	P_{21}	P_{22}

The number of industries in each cell, when divided by the total number of industries, yield the probabilities shown. The first item, P_{11}, for example, is the probability that a randomly chosen industry will have both capital and labor lobby for protection. The sum of the four cell probabilities equals one.

The Stolper–Samuelson theorem asserts that capital and labor will oppose each other on trade policy: thus, the diagonal elements

STEPHEN P. MAGEE

should equal zero. Furthermore, all labor will support one policy while capital will do the reverse. Thus, one of the off-diagonal elements will equal 1 while the other will equal 0. In short, Stolper–Samuelson asserts that 3 of the 4 cells in Table 2 will contain zeros.

The Cairnes factor-specific model predicts sharply contrasting results. With immobility of both factors, the prices of capital and labor move with the price of industry output. Thus, capital and labor in an industry will work together on trade policy, implying that the only nonzero elements in the matrix will be in one of the two diagonal boxes: $p_{11} + p_{22} = 1$.

The results of this test for 21 of the industries in Table 1 are shown in Table 3. The term n_{ij} represents the number of industries falling into each cell. It is apparent from observation that the data are strongly supportive of the Cairnes factor specific model and

Table 3: A Classification of n = 21 Industries According to the Political Preferences of Capital and Labor.

	Position of Labor		
	1. Protectionist	*2. Free Trade*	
Position of Capital: 1. Protectionist	$n_{11} = 14$ ($p_{11} = 0.66$)	$n_{12} = 1$ ($p_{12} = 0.05$)	$P_1 = 0.71$
2. Free Trade	$n_{21} = 1$ ($p_{21} = 0.05$)	$n_{22} = 5$ ($p_{22} = 0.24$)	$P_2 = 0.29$
	($p_1 = 0.71$)	($p_2 = 0.29$)	

reject the Stolper–Samuelson hypothesis. In only 2 industries do labor and management oppose each other: management is for free trade in petroleum and protectionist in tobacco, with labor being the reverse.[2] *In 19 out of 21 industries, labor and management work together on the question of protection.* To perform a test of statistical significance would belabor the obvious.

TEST 2

The second implication of the Stolper–Samuelson theorem is that all of labor will favor either free trade or protection (similarly for capital). Test 2 provides a test of the degree of unanimity of each factor on one position or the other. Table 4 summarizes the data from Table 1 for capital and labor. (More observations are possible for capital here since its position does not have to be paired with knowledge of labor's position.)

THREE SIMPLE TESTS OF THE STOLPER–SAMUELSON THEOREM

Table 4.

	Number of Industries (1)	Proportion of Cases (2)	Value of z in a Normal Approximation of the Binomial (the hypothesis is rejected at this level of significance)	
			Hypothesis Tested	
			Stolper Samuelson (3)	Factor Specific (4)
Capital's Position:				
Protectionism	15	$p_1 = 0.63$	4.49	0.50
Free Trade	9	$p_2 = 0.37$	(0.000003)*	(0.31)
Labor's Position:				
Protectionism	16	$p_1 = 0.76$	2.10	4.01
Free Trade	5	$p_2 = 0.24$	(0.018)*	(0.000003)*

* Hypothesis rejected.

Notice that only 63 per cent of the industries selected show capital supporting the preferred alternative (protectionism). Stolper–Samuelson predicts that all capital would choose one alternative or the other (100 per cent vs. 0) and should not split this way (63 per cent vs. 37 per cent).

Since it is impossible to test the sample observations in Table 4 against the hypothesis that $p_1 = 1.0$ and $p_2 = 0$, we must set some arbitrary value of p_1 which is less than 1.0. I arbitrarily set $p_1 = 0.9$ and $0.2 = 0.1$ as the hypothesized Stolper–Samuelsons values. Thus, a sample which showed 90 per cent of capital supporting the preferred alternative (say, protection) and only 10 per cent supporting the other (free trade) would be consistent with the factor mobility assumption implicit in Stolper–Samuelson. Similarly, I arbitrarily set $p_1 = p_2 = 0.5$ as the hypothesized population values associated with the factor-specific model. Notice that we bias against acceptance of Stolper-Samuelson if p_1 is set too close to 1 and the test of factor specificity is influenced by the random breakdown of the sample between protectionists and free traders. If there is a tendency for only one group to lobby, there is also a tendency to reject the Cairnes model of factor specificity.

The test is conducted as follows. What is the probability that the sample proportions in column (2) of Table 4 would have been obtained if the true population proportions were those hypothesized ($p_1 = 0.9$ for Stolper–Samuelson and $p_1 = p_2 = 0.5$ for Cairnes?). We use the binomial distribution for the test. Since the number of trials exceeds 20 (n = 24 for capital and n = 21 for labor) an

STEPHEN P. MAGEE

approximation must be used. The Poisson distribution could be used but is recommended only when $p_1 = 0.05$. Thus, we must use the normal approximation. We transform the number of cases ($x = 15$ for capital and $x = 16$ for labor) apparently satisfying the hypothesis into the standardized normal random variable, z (see Freund; 1971, pp. 75 and 175):

$$(1) \qquad\qquad z = \frac{x - np_1}{\sqrt{np_1\,(1 - p_1)}}.$$

The tabulated values of z are shown in columns (3) and (4) of Table 4, along with their significance levels.

Consider capital. If the true population proportion is 0.9 (Stolper–Samuelson) the chances of obtaining a proportion of $p_1 = 0.63$ are only 0.0003 per cent, whereas the chances of getting $p_1 = 0.63$ are 31 per cent when the hypothesized value is 0.5 (Cairnes). Thus, for capital the results reject the factor mobility hypothesis implicit in Stolper–Samuelson and cannot reject the factor-specific Cairnes hypothesis. The sample proportion of labor favoring protection is 0.76: both Stolper–Samuelson and Cairnes are rejected, with the latter rejected more decisively. The results for labor are thus inconclusive. Notice that we biased the test in favor of Stolper–Samuelson by choosing the larger of the two sample proportions to compare with the hypothesized value of 0.9.

As an aside, the data in Table 4 permits a test of the Burgess (1976) result that American labor would gain at the expense of American capital with greater protection. If they were true, we should observe that labor would support protection in a larger proportion of the industries than capital. Using the test described in equation (1), we find that $p_1 = 0.76$ is significantly greater than 0.63 at the 0.11 level ($z = 1.25$) while 0.63 is significantly less than 0.76 at the 0.06 level ($z = 1.58$). Thus, the data here is not inconsistent with the Burgess results; it supports him using one test and almost confirms his result when the order of the test is reversed. I view these results as mixed, however, and turn instead to a third and stronger test of the factor mobility assumption than is provided by either Test 1 or 2.

TEST 3

Test 2 merely indicated the degree of unanimity (or lack thereof) which a factor has for a specific trade policy. Here we test whether or not a factor prefers a policy which is beneficial to the industry in which it is currently employed. If it does, factor specificity is

THREE SIMPLE TESTS OF THE STOLPER–SAMUELSON THEOREM

implied; if not, factor mobility (among other things) is more likely. Two versions of this test are presented: the first is a proportion test while the second allows continuous variation in the industry's trade balance.

Consider the data in Tables 5a and 5b. There are the same industries which were used in test 2[3]. However, the rows in Table 5 classify the industries according to whether they are export or import-competing. A tendency for dominant diagonality indicates Cairnes factor specificity while independence of the sectors and the trade positions is consistent with Stolper–Samuelson factor mobility. The usual test of association in these tables is a straightforward application of the Chi-square test, χ^2. While χ^2 is a good measure of the significance of the association, it is not useful as a measure of the degree of association between sectoral location and the factor's preferred trade policy (Fleiss (1973, p. 41)). The odds ratio does provide such a test (Fleiss (1973, pp. 43–46)). The sample odds ratio, 0, equals

$$(2) \qquad 0 = \frac{p_{11}/p_{12}}{p_{21}/p_{22}} = \frac{p_{11}\,p_{22}}{p_{12}\,p_{21}}.$$

Notice that the odds of a factor favoring protection relative to free trade are p_{11}/p_{12} if the factor is in the import-competing sector and p_{21}/p_{22} if it is in the export sector. If these odds are the same, then knowledge of the factor's sectoral location gives us no information about the factor's most likely policy preference. In this case, the numerator and denominator in (2) are equal and the odds ratio equals 1. Stolper – Samuelson predicts $0 = 1$ while factor specificity implies $0 > 1$. Let us test these hypotheses.

The standard error of 0, s.e. (0), is approximately:

$$(3) \qquad \text{s.e. } (0) = \frac{0}{\sqrt{n}}\sqrt{\frac{1}{p_{11}} + \frac{1}{p_{12}} + \frac{1}{p_{21}} + \frac{1}{p_{22}}}.$$

[Fleiss (1973, p. 45)). The values of 0 and s.e. (0) from (2) and (3) are reported in Tables 5a and 5b. The calculations indicate that the odds of capital in the import competing sector favoring protection are 4 times those of capital in the export sector; for labor, the same odds ratio is 8·8. The standard errors are 3·6 and 10·9, respectively. The significance tests should not be performed using just these standard errors. Rather, calculate the variable Y,

$$(4) \qquad Y = \left[\frac{0 - 0^h}{\text{s.e. } (0)/\sqrt{n}}\right]^2$$

146

Table 5a: Industries with Capital's Position on Free Trade Related to the Trade Sector (n = 24)

	Position of Capital		*Odds Ratio* (stand. error)	χ^2 (sig. level)
	1. Protectionist	*2. Free Trade*		
Sector of Industry				
1. Import-Competing	(n_{11} = 10) (p_{11} = 0.42)	n_{12} = 3 (p_{12} = 0.12)	4.0 (3.6)	4.1 (0.05)
2. Export	n_{21} = 5 (p_{21} = 0.21)	n_{22} = 6 (p_{22} = 0.25)		

Table 5b: Number of Industries with Labor's Position on Free Trade Related to the Trade Sector (n = 21)

	Position of Labor		*Odds Ratio* (stand. error)	χ^2 (sig. level)
	1. Protectionist	*2. Free Trade*		
Sector of Industry				
1. Import-Competing	n_{11} = 11 (p_{11} = 0.53)	n_{12} = 1 (p_{12} = 0.04)	8.8 (10.9)	3.3 (0.10)
2. Export	n_{21} = 5 (p_{21} = 0.24)	n_{22} = 4 (p_{22} = 0.19)		

See Appendix Table 1 for the SIC codes of the numbers in each cell.

THREE SIMPLE TESTS OF THE STOLPER–SAMUELSON THEOREM

which has a Chi-square distribution with 1 degree of freedom (Freund (1971, p. 214)). 0^h is the hypothesized value of the odds ratio against which we are testing the obtained sample value, 0.

The values of χ^2 computed from (4) for Y and their significance levels are shown in the last column of Tables 5a and 5b. Both capital and labor differ significantly from the hypothesized Stolper–Samuelson independence of lobbying positions and sectoral location: Stolper–Samuelson is refuted for capital at the 5 per cent level and labor at the 10 per cent level.

A limitation of the qualitative test just completed is that it does not consider the association between a factor's position on trade policy and the extent to which each industry is export or import-competing. We can remedy this problem partially by testing, for each factor, whether there are significant differences between the trade balances in industries containing free traders vs. industries containing protectionists. If more positive trade balances are associated with the free trade position, we can reject the Stolper–Samuelson theorem. If there is no significant difference in the trade balances, then the positions are independent of sectoral location and we can reject the Cairnes model. The results are shown in Table 6.

Notice that the average trade balance in industries in which capital supports free trade is $689 million while it is − $254 million if capital is protectionist. The difference is statistically significant using three different tests for equality of the trade balances of the two groups. The average trade balance in industries in which labor supports free trade is $985 million while it is − $321 million in labor-protectionist industries. These differences are significant for two out of three of the tests.

I conclude from both versions of test 3 that both capital and labor lobby for protection in ways consistent with the Cairnes model of factor immobility and inconsistent with the Stolper–Samuelson model of factor mobility.

3. Caveats and Conclusions

Tests 1 and 3 provide refutation of Stolper–Samuelson relative to Cairnes. In test 2, Stolper–Samuelson was rejected for capital while labor was impossible to classify as mobile or specific; this is not inconsistent with the *a priori* assumptions made in theoretical discussions by Mayer (1974) and Mussa (1974) that capital is *quasi*-fixed in the short run relative to labor. What conclusions

STEPHEN P. MAGEE

are we to derive from these results? We deal first with the possibility that they might have been obtained spuriously.

For the thirty-three industries in Table 1, there is no significant relationship between the trade balance and capital per man. However, this fact does not explain our failure to confirm the Stolper–Samuelson results. In fact, exactly the reverse is true. We know from the pure theory of international trade that with two products and two factors, the closer the factor intensities of the two sectors, the greater the magnification affect of product prices on factor prices. Hence, the closer the factor intensities in production, the greater the potential benefit to either factor from affecting relative product prices through legislation.

It is possible that the likelihood of foreign retaliation against greater protection in the United States might bias the results away from Stolper–Samuelson? No, foreign retaliation will help the scarce factor and hurt the abundant factor.[4] In the Stolper–Samuelson framework, if the scarce factor succeeds in raising its returns by increasing the home price of importables relative to exportables, then foreign retaliation will simply cause the product price ratio to increase further as foreign demand drops for United States exports. Again, this consideration would bias the results in favor of Stolper–Samuelson.

One clear empirical violation of the simple two factor Stolper–Samuelson assumption is the presence of other factors of production (land, skilled labor, etc.). If labor and capital are complementary, relative to these other factors, do we have an alternative explanation of the results presented here? This point seems reasonable but applies only to test 1: it cannot explain the results of test 3 in which each factor's lobbying position was significantly related to its sectoral location.

One explanation of the Leontief paradox which seemed consistent with the Stolper–Samuelson approach, was that the U.S. is skilled labor abundant and unskilled labor scarce. It is possible that the labor unions, in the tests above, represent unskilled labor in the industries favoring protection and skilled labor in the industries favoring free trade. If so, the approach would improperly aggregate two diverse groups of labor and spuriously reject Stolper–Samuelson. However, tests showed no significant difference in production wage rates between the two labor groups (those for and against freer trade). Thus, the labor groupings here appear to be homogeneous and avoid this pitfall.

Could the degree of unionization bias the tests, since unions

THREE SIMPLE TESTS OF THE STOLPER–SAMUELSON THEOREM

largely spoke for labor? A test of the average proportion of labor unionized between the two labor groups also found no significant difference (for those for and against freer trade). Thus, the position on free trade is independent of the degree of unionization. However, one could argue that labor leaders will not represent the 'true interests' of their constituency. The truth of this proposition is questionable in light of many voting models; the rational elected union official will take the position favored by the median union member. Thus, there should not be a tendency for him to work against the 'best interests' of union members.

However, the problem of how well union leaders represent their own constituency is probably less important than the question of wage differentials and the question of whether the interests of union labor also coincide with those of the nonunion labor. Wage differentials do not pose serious problems for the Stolper–Samuelson theorem: the theorem holds at all points in the Edgeworth–Bowley box so long as product factor intensities are defined in 'value rather than physical' terms (see the discussion in Magee (1976 pp. 25–32)). However, unionization is more likely to generate low labor turnover than a smoothly operating wage differential. (The average per cent of unionization is over 60 per cent in the industries in Table 1). Because of seniority systems coupled with positive union/nonunion wage differentials, union labor should be more industry-specific than nonunion labor. Since many unions are organized along industry lines because of organizational efficiency, one might think that the presence of union lobbying groups generate data favorable to labor specificity. However, their lobbying positions need not favor their industry if Stolper–Samuelson accurately describe labor's interests.

In comments on an earlier draft of this paper Harry Johnson suggested a reconciliation of these results with the Stolper–Samuelson theorem. Protection can benefit both factors in the short run in import-competing industries with short-run immobility. But if both factors are mobile in the long run, the position of one of the factors must ultimately deteriorate. Since many import-competing (standardized goods) industries in the U.S. are 'traditional industries', they use older labor. If standardized goods industries are also more capital intensive because of assembly-line type production (à la Leontief and Vernon), then labor would ultimately be hurt by their expansion through higher tariffs. But, if the long run is far enough away, this long-run deterioration is economically irrelevant. If all workers in the shoe industry were

STEPHEN P. MAGEE

old and the present value of the long-run Stolper–Samuelson effects did not dominate the (reverse) factor specific effects before their retirement, then these workers would lobby as if they were sector specific. Thus, even if the Stolper–Samuelson theorem were empirically valid, it might not be detectable in the presence of older workers for whom the long run never comes.

NOTES

* The author wishes to thank Robert Baldwin, William Brock, Franz Gehrels, Peter Gray, Ronald Jones, Rachel McCulloch, Tracy Murray, Carlos Rodriguez and especially Harry Johnson for comments on an earlier draft of this paper, which was first presented at the Eastern Economic Association Meetings in Bloomsburg, Pa., April 17, 1976; Harry Eisenstein, Stephen Thompson and Doug Van Ness for research assistance; and the Center for the Management of Public and Nonprofit Enterprise, Graduate School of Business, University of Chicago and the National Science Foundation for financial support.

1. Franz Gehrels suggested this point.

2. The petroleum case is weakened by the split between the major oil companies and the independents; the latter are opposed to free trade.

3. The composition of industries in Tables 5a and 5b also differs from those in Table 3. Table 3 was restricted to industries in which the position of both management and labor were known. Tables 5a and 5b require only that the position of one side be known. Also, two industries included in Table 3 were dropped from 5a and 5b because of inability to allocate them to one of the two trade sectors because of small trade balances (SIC 32 and 3421).

4. Ronald Jones suggested this point.

REFERENCES

Brock, William A. and Magee, Stephen P. 'The Economics of Special-Interest Politics: The Case of the Tariff,' *American Economic Review*, 68 (May 1978), pp. 246–250.

Brock, William A and Magee, Stephen P. 'Tariff Setting in a Democracy,' John Black and Brian Hindley, eds., *Current Issues in International Commercial Policy and Economic Diplomacy*. London: Macmillan Press, 1980.

Burgess, David F. 'Tariffs and Income Distribution: Some Empirical Evidence for the United States'. *Journal of Political Economy*, *84* (February 1976), pp. 17–46.

Cairnes, J. E. *Some Leading Principles of Political Economy*. London: Macmillan, 1874.

Fleiss, Joseph L. *Statistical Methods for Rates and Proportions*. New York: John Wiley, 1973.

Freund, John E. *Mathematical Statistics*, 2nd ed., Englewood Cliffs: Prentice-Hall, 1971.

THREE SIMPLE TESTS OF THE STOLPER–SAMUELSON THEOREM

Hays, William L. and Winkler, Robert L. *Statistics*. New York: Holt, Rinehart and Winston, 1971.

Johnson, Harry G. *Aspects of the Theory of Tariffs*. London: George Allen & Unwin, 1971.

Magee, Stephen. *International Trade and Distortions in Factor Markets*. New York: Marcel Dekker, 1976.

Mayer, Wolfgang. 'Short-Run and Long-Run Equilibrium for a Small Open Economy. *Journal of Political Economy*, *82* (October 1974), pp. 955–968.

Mussa, Michael. 'Tariffs and the Distribution of Income: The Importance of Factor Specificity, Substitutability, and Intensity in the Short and Long Run'. *Journal of Political Economy*, *82* (December 1974), pp. 1191–1203.

Stolper, Wolfgang and Samuelson, Paul A. 'Protection and Real Wages'. *Review of Economic Studies*, *9* (November 1941), pp. 58–73. Reprinted in AEA *Readings in the Theory of International Trade*. Homewood, Illinois: Richard D. Irwin, 1950, pp. 333–357.

United States Congress, Committee on Ways and Means, Hearings on HR: 6767, The Trade Reform Act of 1973 (15 Parts), May 9–June 15, 1973; Part 15, pp. 5171–5317, Washington: U.S. Government Printing Office, 1973.

Appendix

SIC Codes for the Industries in Tables 3, 5a and 5b in the Text.

Table 3.
Labor

		Protectionist	Free Trade
Management	Protectionist	2085, 22, 23, 2815, 2821, 3021, 31, 3141, 32, 331–2, 3421, 3423, 3562, 3871	21
	Free Trade	2911	26, 35, 3522, 2713, 3720

Table 5a
Management

	Protectionist	Free Trade
Import Competing	2085, 22, 23, 3021, 31, 3141, 3572, 3751, 3871, 331–2	26, 2911, 3334
Export	21, 2815, 2821, 3423, 3562	2015, 2092, 35, 3522, 3715, 3720

Table 5b
Labor

	Protectionist	Free Trade
Import Competing	2085, 22, 23, 3021, 3141, 2911, 31, 331–2, 3711, 3871, 3941	26
Export	2815, 2821, 30, 3423, 36	21, 35, 3713, 3720

A COMMENT ON MAGEE'S THREE SIMPLE TESTS

Christopher Bliss

STEPHEN MAGEE has undertaken a fascinating study and his results stand as a challenge to all those who have felt that simple trade models cannot say anything definite enough to be tested about the world, and particularly to those who have been rather grateful for that conclusion. After Leontief's elaborate attempt to test the Hecksher–Ohlin theory, this approach is marvellously simple and its clearly robust result is all the more impressive.

The main point that I want to mention is one which is not discussed in the paper and which provides a possible third model to add to the Stolper–Samuelson and Cairnes models which the author makes his main alternatives. The case that I have in mind is one in which there is a deficiency of overall effective demand. One would then usually assume that the imposition of tariffs or other protective measures would help to raise the level of home activity and would be likely to benefit both capital and labour, at least in the short run. This requires that factors be willing to accept a cut in their real rate of remuneration per unit after tariffs are imposed, where they would not have effected the same outcome directly by cuts in the money price of factor services, and hence be dismissed as 'irrational'. It also requires that the government be willing to impose tariffs to increase activity where fiscal and monetary policy of an appropriate kind would be a superior policy. Nevertheless the, no doubt irrational, view that imports cause unemployment and that they should be curtailed when unemployment is high, commands a lot of support and it may be behind some of the lobbying that the author has observed. If so, it would bias his findings towards what he has interpreted as the Cairnes outcome.

CHRISTOPHER BLISS

There is no point in detailing the many problems that arise because the Stolper–Samuelson model is extremely simple where reality is complicated. Most of these will have been remarked by Professor Magee's readers and his approach gains from going for the direct strong result rather than setting up alibis for the theory in various complications. One point however deserves mention.[1] The Stolper–Samuelson theory deals most naturally with perfectly-vertically integrated industries which use original factors to produce final output. The actual industries and trade unions whose spokesmen lobby the U.S. Congress typically use intermediate goods as inputs including some importable intermediates. One can extend the theorem to cover this case, but the results change somewhat. For example, both capital and labour may favour the lowering of the tariff on intermediates used by their industry. Ideally one would like to have to hand the results of an input-output study showing the direct factor-demand components of various imports and their substitutes. It might well emerge that the resultant factor interests were not organized as lobbies and the practical difficulty or expense of organizing real-world lobbies to approximate to Stolper–Samuelson factor groups may explain some of the author's findings.

NOTES

1 Emphasised in discussion by Professor Ann Krueger.

Economics Letters 10 (1982) 337–342
North-Holland Publishing Company

THE GENERAL ROLE OF FACTOR INTENSITY
IN THE THEOREMS OF INTERNATIONAL TRADE *

Wilfred J. ETHIER

University of Stockholm, S-106 91 Stockholm, Sweden

Received 1 April 1982

The pattern of factor intensities often allows predictions of directions of change in 2×2 trade theory, but the most general higher dimensional extensions have said little about analogous predictions. This paper obtains general results in an elementary way.

1. Introduction

The Stolper–Samuelson theorem (as does its Rybczynski analog) contains two assertions: that relative commodity price changes produce unambiguous changes in real factor rewards, and that the direction of the latter can be predicted from relative factor intensities. The Heckscher–Ohlin theorem likewise predicts trade flows on the basis of such intensities.

Higher dimensional generalization has followed two paths. That concerned with stronger results [1] has touched on both aspects of the theorems, with the existence of desired relations between goods and factors shown to be equivalent to the satisfaction of stringent factor intensity conditions. But the second, more general, path [2] has focused on the first aspect and ignored whether relative factor intensities allow a prediction

---

* Research for this paper was supported by the National Science Foundation. Lars Svensson and Avinash Dixit contributed valuable suggestions.
[1] See Uekawa (1971), and Kemp (1976, ch. 3).
[2] See Ethier (1974), Kemp (1976, chs. 4, 7), Jones and Scheinkman (1977) and Ethier (1983, app. One).

0165-1765/82/0000–0000/$02.75 © 1982 North-Holland

338   W.J. Ethier / Factor intensity in international trade theorems

of the direction of factor-reward responses or of trade flows. [3] This paper obtains general results in an elementary way.

2. Stolper–Samuelson type and Rybczynski type results

Allow any number of goods and factors. Consider a change in commodity prices, and denote by p^0 and p' the respective vectors of prices of those goods actually produced *both* before and after the change. Let $c(w) = wA(w)$ denote the cost functions of those goods, where w denotes the vector of factor rewards and $A(w)$ the matrix of least-cost techniques.

Thus $p^0 = c(w^0)$ and $p' = c(w')$. Define $b(w) = c(w)(p' - p^0)$. By the mean value theorem there exists some vector $\bar{w}$ of factor rewards such that

$$b(w') = b(w^0) + (w' - w^0)\,db(\bar{w}),$$ (1)

where $db(\bar{w})$, the Hessian matrix of b, equals $[A(\bar{w}) + \bar{w}dA(\bar{w})](p' - p^0)$. Now $\bar{w}dA(\bar{w}) = 0$ as a condition of cost minimization. Thus (1) can be written

$$[c(w') - c(w^0)](p' - p^0) = (w' - w^0)A(\bar{w})(p' - p^0).$$ (2)

Noting that $c(w') - c(w^0) = p' - p^0$, (2) implies

$$(w' - w^0)A(\bar{w})(p' - p^0) \geqslant 0.$$ (3)

This is the basic result: $(w' - w^0)$ is positively *correlated* with $A(\bar{w})(p' - p^0)$, or $(p' - p^0)$ is positively correlated with $(w' - w^0)A(\bar{w})$. Large values of $(w_i' - w_i^0)$ tend to accompany large values of a_{ij} and of $(p_j' - p_j^0)$; commodity price changes on average raise the most the rewards of the factors used most intensively by the goods whose prices increase the most, etc. In the two-by-two case (3) gives the usual rigid link, but when dimensionality increases the relation says nothing about the direction of change of individual factor rewards and merely describes *average* changes.

---

[3] Exceptions are Uekawa (1979), unrelated to the present paper, Deardorff (1981), and Dixit and Norman (1980), discussed below.

Note the great generality of (3). It follows directly from cost minimization without any special restriction on dimensionality, technology, or endowments. [4] The present proposition relates the direction of factor reward changes to the direction of changes in the prices of goods that continue to be produced. Goods not produced in either or both states contribute no information, although they would of course be relevant to the magnitude of changes in *real* rewards.

For sufficiently small changes, $\overline{w} = w^0$ will work in (3), but large changes could demand a $\overline{w}$ close to neither w^0 nor w', so that $A(\overline{w})$ could be quite distinct from observed techniques. But this is *not* a penalty of higher dimensions: the point can be grasped in a two-by-two world. Suppose that, because of a factor-intensity reversal, $p^0 = c(w^0) = c(w^{00})$, and $p' = c(w') = c(w'')$, with $w_2''/w_1'' > w_2^0/w_1^0 > w_2^{00}/w_1^{00} > w_2'/w_1'$. Then the movement from w^0 to w' involves the opposite direction of change of relative factor rewards to the movement from w^{00} to w''. $A\overline{w}$ satisfying (3) need imply the appropriate pattern of factor intensities in the former case, but the latter case requires a quite different $\overline{w}$ with the opposite intensity pattern. The ability to choose $\overline{w}$ appropriately is the reason I have a global Stolper–Samuelson-type result without ruling out factor intensity reversals or their higher dimensional analogs.

A similar Rybczynski type result is easily obtained. Let v^0 and v' be two endowment vectors and x^0 and x' the corresponding vectors of outputs of those goods actually produced in *both* states. Then, *if* $w^0 = w'$,

$$v' - v^0 = A(w^0)(x' - x^0) \tag{4}$$

and multiplying both sides by the vector $(v' - v^0)$

$$(v' - v^0)A(w^0)(x' - x^0) \geqslant 0. \tag{5}$$

This is a general Rybczynski-type result: on average, endowment changes cause the largest increases in the outputs of the goods which most intensively use the factors that have increased relatively the most in supply, etc. The requirement that $w^0 = w'$ limits applicability. The change $v' - v^0$ must not be large enough to depart from the relevant diversifica-

---

[4] Of course the mean value theorem must be applicable, so $b(w)$ should be continuously differentiable over some path of non-negative factor prices connecting w^0 and w'. But no restrictions are placed on production patterns over that path, endowments can change in any way between equilibria, and A need not even be non-singular. But constant returns to scale and no joint production are assumed.

tion cone. If $n \geqslant m$, where n and m denote the numbers of produced goods and factors, the factor-price-equalization theorem can be appealed to for $w^0 = w'$, and my result is again a direct consequence of cost minimization. But if $m > n$, the elements of $v' - v^0$ cannot be chosen at will: n of them may be specified arbitrarily, with the remaining $m - n$ then set to equilibrate factor markets at prices w_0 (as would be the case if $m - n$ factors were freely traded at world prices). This limits the result in a way not necessary with its Stolper–Samuelson analog. But such asymmetry should come as no surprise. [5]

3. Heckscher–Ohlin type theorems

Let w' and w^0 denote home and foreign autarky prices. Then define $d(w) = c(w)M$, where M denotes the vector of home free-trade imports. The same logic which produced (3) implies, for some $\bar{w}$,

$$(p' - p^0)M = (w' - w^0)A(\bar{w})M.$$

Now $(p' - p^0)M \geqslant 0$ by the general law of comparative advantage, [6] so

$$(w' - w^0)A(\bar{w})M > 0. \tag{6}$$

This correlation is a generalized price version of the Heckscher–Ohlin theorem: on average countries tend to import the goods most intensive in the use of the factors most abundant in a price sense, etc. [7] This is a very general result, depending only on cost minimization and requiring no restrictions on demand or on technology – including. no exclusion of higher-dimensional analogs of factor intensity reversals.

Turning to the quantity version, let v' and v^0 denote home and foreign endowments and suppose at least as many produced goods as factors. With endowments given, commodity prices uniquely relate to factor

---

[5] See, for example, Kemp (1976, ch. 4) or Jones and Scheinkman (1977).
[6] See Deardorff (1980), Dixit and Norman (1980, pp. 94–96) or Ethier (1983, app. One).
[7] Deardorff (1981) obtains in a different way a similar result with $A(\bar{w})$ replaced by a matrix A^0, which can be obtained by using in each column the technique actually employed in free trade in the country of export of the respective goods. Thus $A(\bar{w})$ has the advantage of consistent comparison across industries since its techniques would actually be chosen under some common factor rewards, and A^0 the advantage of being constructed from observed (post-trade) techniques. See also Ethier (1983, app. One).

prices [see McKenzie (1955)], so I can write $w = f(p, v)$. Define $h(p, v) = f(p, v)(v' - v^0)$ and proceed as above to obtain, for some $\bar{w} = f(\bar{p}, \bar{v})$,

$$g(p', v') - g(p^0, v^0) = (p' - p^0)f_p(\bar{p}, \bar{v})(v' - v^0)$$
$$+ (v' - v^0)f_v(\bar{p}, \bar{v})(v' - v^0),$$

where f_p and f_v denote the appropriate matrices of partial derivatives. Now $f_v(\bar{p}, \bar{v}) = 0$ by the factor price equalization theorem and $f_p(\bar{p}, \bar{v}) = A^{-1}(\bar{w})$, where $A(\bar{w})$ is made square, if necessary, by arbitrarily deleting enough goods. Also it is known [8] that $(w' - w^0)(v' - v^0) \leqslant 0$, with identical homothetic tastes. So

$$(p' - p^0)A^{-1}(\bar{w})(v' - v^0) \leqslant 0. \tag{7}$$

This correlation is a generalized quantity version: countries tend on average to have a comparative advantage in those goods that most intensively employ the most relatively abundant factors. [9] Note the relation between the concepts of relative factor intensity in my price and quantity generalizations: the former interprets factor intensity as a matter of the relative magnitude of the elements of A whereas the latter looks at the elements of A^{-1}, and the two are likely evaluated at different factor prices. These two concepts become distinct when the numbers of goods and factors exceed two.

Next, assume that all countries have identical homothetic tastes and that in free trade factor-price equalization holds. Then it is well-known that the *factor content* of trade will reflect relative factor abundance in a quantity sense, [10] but there are no results on commodity composition. To obtain one, define, in (5), $x^0 = (1 - g)x^H$, $x' = gx^F$, $v^0 = (1 - g)v^H$, $v' = gv^F$, where v^H and v^F denote the home and foreign endowment vectors, x^H and x^F home and foreign free trade outputs, and g a scalar:

$$\left[gv^F - (1 - g)v^H \right] A(\bar{w}) \left[gx^F - (1 - g)x^H \right] \geqslant 0. \tag{8}$$

Now if g is set equal to free trade home income as a fraction of world

---

[8] See Dixit and Norman (1980, p. 99) or Ethier (1983, app. One).

[9] Dixit and Norman (1980, p. 100) obtain a result like (7) on the strong assumption that $c(w)$ is globally invertible. The present approach demonstrates that such an assumption is unnecessary, and the discussion following (3) explains why.

[10] See, for example, Vanek (1968).

income, identical homothetic tastes imply that $M = g(x^H + x^F) - x^H = gx^F - (1-g)x^H$. Thus

$$\left[g(v^F + v^H) - v^H \right] A(\bar{w})M \geqslant 0. \tag{9}$$

This correlation says that on average a country tends to import those goods which make most intensive use of the country's relatively scarce factors, where factor scarcity is measured in a quantity sense by comparing the national endowment to the world endowment scaled down by the aggregate value of national factor service supplies as a fraction of the aggregate value of world supplies.

References

Deardorff, A.V., 1980, The general validity of the law of comparative advantage, Journal of Political Economy 88, 941–957.

Deardorff, A.V., 1981, The general validity of the Heckscher-Ohlin theorem, processed.

Dixit, A.K. and V. Norman, 1980, Theory of international trade (Nisbet, Cambridge, London).

Ethier, W., 1974, Some of the theorems of international trade with many goods and factors, Journal of International Economics 4, 194–206.

Ethier, W., 1983, Modern international economics (Norton, New York).

Jones, R.W. and J. Scheinkman, 1977, The relevance of the two-sector production model in trade theory, Journal of Political Economy 85, 909–935.

Kemp, M.C., 1976, Three topics in the theory of international trade (North-Holland, Amsterdam).

McKenzie, L.W., 1955, Equality of factor prices in world trade, Econometrica 23, 239–257.

Uekawa, Y., 1971, Generalization of the Stolper-Samuelson theorem, Econometrica 39, 197–218.

Uekawa, Y., 1979, On the concepts of factor intensities and the relation between commodity prices and factor rewards, in: J.R. Green and J.A. Scheinkman, eds., General equilibrium, growth, and trade (Academic, New York).

Vanek, J., 1968, The factor proportions theory: The n-factor case, Kyklos 21, 749–755.

Economics Letters 19 (1985) 47-49
North-Holland

CHAPTER 13

RELATIVE PRICES AND REAL FACTOR REWARDS
A Reinterpretation[*]

Ronald W. JONES
University of Rochester, Rochester, NY 14627, USA

Received 7 February 1985

Two devices are generally available to increase the reward of a productive factor: (i) a direct subsidy to the factor, and (ii) an alteration in relative commodity prices. The Stolper-Samuelson result, whereby method (ii) suffices to improve the *real* reward of a productive factor in a 2×2 setting with no joint production is shown to be valid in the *n*-commodity, *n*-factor model.

There seems to be some concensus in the international trade literature on how to interpret the Stolper-Samuelson theorem in an *n*-factor, *n*-commodity setting in which technology is characterized by constant returns to scale and the absence of joint production. The theorem, at least in its 'strong' form,[1] requires an association of factors with commodities such that an increase in any single commodity price raises the reward of the associated factor by a greater relative amount and reduces the return to all other factors. Although interpretations of these conditions have

---

[*] Research support has been provided by Grant SES 8309386 from the National Science Foundation.

[1] See Chipman (1969), Kemp and Wegge (1969) and Uekawa (1971).

been given [(Uekawa (1971,1979), Ethier (1984)], relatively few specific $n \times n$ cases satisfying the theorem have been put forward.[2] The object of this note is to re-interpret the original Stolper-Samuelson result so that a theorem emerges that is robust in the $n \times n$ non-joint production context.

The factoral distribution of income can generally be affected by a policy (i) of granting direct subsidies (or taxes) on factor earnings, or (ii) of changing relative commodity prices and thus, indirectly, affecting factor rewards. It was the contribution of Stolper and Samuelson to show that in a 2×2 trade model a factor's *real* reward could unambiguously be improved by a policy of just changing relative commodity prices. Indeed, although a tariff was the policy instrument chosen to alter relative commodity prices, Stolper and Samuelson showed how real wages could be improved without any recourse to a share of the tariff revenue. Results already available in the literature [e.g., Jones and Scheinkman (1977) or Ethier (1984)] support the following $n \times n$ generalization of this interpretation of the Stolper-Samuelson theorem: for *any* factor of production, a simple change in relative commodity prices, without any further redistribution of public revenues, suffices to raise the reward of that factor relative to *any* commodity price. Thus a move to higher dimensions *per se* does not damage the Stolper-Samuelson result even though much more structure needs to be added if one wants to insure that the real gains obtained by the factor in question are not shared by any other factor.

Before proceeding it is perhaps worthwhile to emphasize two well-known results. First, if the number of factors exceeds the number of commodities produced, such a result may fail to hold. The classic example is the specific-factors 3×2 model in which the change in the return to the mobile factor (assuming factor endowments constant) is a *positive* weighted average of all commodity price changes; a uniform rise in any subset of commodity prices must raise the reward of the mobile factor by relatively less. Secondly, it is the case that for any increase in a single commodity price in models which allow more factors than commodities there must be *some* factor of production whose real return

---

[2] For an exception see Jones and Marjit (1985).

has improved; this is the essence of the lack of joint production. However, there is no guarantee that *any* factor's real reward can be improved in this fashion.

In general the solution for any factor price change, $\hat{w}_i$, is a weighted average of all commodity price changes,[3]

$$\hat{w}_i = \sum_{j=1}^{n} \beta_{ij} \hat{p}_j, \qquad i = 1,...,n \quad \text{where} \quad \sum_{j} \beta_{ij} = 1. \quad (1)$$

The peculiarity of the $n \times n$ case is that at least one β_{ij} must be negative. This is most readily established by considering a different question: what is the effect on outputs of an increase in the endowment factor i, V_i, at given commodity prices? In the $n \times n$ case factor prices, and therefore production techniques, must be determined by these commodity prices. With full employment of all factors some outputs must rise and at least one output (say x_k) must fall since

$$\sum_{j=1}^{n} \lambda_{kj} \hat{x}_j = 0, \qquad k \neq i, \qquad \lambda_{kj} \equiv \frac{V_{kj}}{V_k}, \qquad \sum \lambda_{kj} = 1. \quad (2)$$

By Samuelson's reciprocity theorem,

$$\frac{\partial x_k}{\partial V_i} = \frac{\partial w_i}{\partial p_k}. \quad (3)$$

---

[3] If the number of factors matches the number of produced commodities, as assumed here, no qualification need be added about keeping factor endowments constant. In the more general setting with unmatched sets of factors and commodities, (1) holds, assuming endowment levels are fixed.

Thus any increase in the price of commodity k must lower the return to factor i. In expression (1) at least β_{ik} is negative, and perhaps this is true for more than one k.

Let the set J be the proper subset of commodities j for which $\beta_{ij} > 0$ for the given i. Let $\hat{p}_j = \hat{p} > 0$ for all $j \in J$ and $\hat{p}_j = 0$ for all $j \notin J$. Then

$$\hat{w}_i = \sum_{j \in J} \beta_{ij} \hat{p}.$$

This establishes the result since with $\sum_{j=1}^{n} \beta_{ij}$ equal to unity, the sum of the weights over all positive values must exceed unity. Such a (binary) change in relative commodity prices must suffice to raise unambiguously the real reward to any pre-selected factor in the $n \times n$ case.[4]

Of course it may not be the case that any factor, i, can have its real reward raised unambiguously by raising the price of any *single* commodity. But to round out this discussion I repeat a result contained in Jones and Scheinkman (1977). For pre-selected factor i there is at least one commodity, s, such that $\hat{x}_s / \hat{V}_i$ exceeds unity when V_i alone increases. Changing reciprocity relationship (3) into relative terms,

$$\frac{\hat{w}_i}{\hat{p}_s} = \frac{\theta_s}{\theta^i} \frac{\hat{x}_s}{\hat{V}_i}, \tag{5}$$

where θ_s refers to the share of commodity s in the national income and θ^i the share of factor i. Thus if factor i is relatively unimportant ($\theta^i < \theta_s$), an increase in a single commodity price (p_s) suffices to raise

---

[4] Jones and Scheinkman (1977) stated that every factor i need not have a 'natural friend' in the sense of some β_{ik} exceeding unity, but erred in suggesting further that no combination of price rises might unambiguously reward factor i. This error is also contained in Jones (1977).

factor *i*'s real return. The generalization of the Stolper-Samuelson result suggested here is that even if factor *i* looms large enough in the national income so that no single commodity price rise suffices to raise factor *i*'s return by relatively more, there is always some subset of commodities whose rise in price will accomplish the required increase in real income for factor *i* without recourse to direct subsidies.

References

Chipman, J., 1969, Factor price equalization and the Stolper-Samuelson theorem, International Economic Review 10, 399–406.

Ethier, W., 1984, Higher dimensional issues in trade theory, in: R.W. Jones and P.B. Kenen, eds., Handbook of international economics, Vol. 1, ch. 3 (North-Holland, Amsterdam) 131–184.

Jones, R.W., 1977, 'Two-ness' in trade theory: Costs and benefits, Special papers in international economics, no. 12 (Princeton University, Princeton, NJ).

Jones, R.W. and S. Marjit. 1985, A simple production model with Stolper-Samuelson properties, International Economic Review, forthcoming.

Jones, R.W. and J. Scheinkman, 1977, The relevance of the two-sector production model in trade theory, Journal of Political Economy 85, 909–935.

Kemp, M. and L. Wegge, 1969, On the relation between commodity prices and factor rewards, International Economic Review 10, 407–413.

Uekawa, Y., 1971, Generalization of the Stolper-Samuelson theorem. Econometrica 39, 197–217.

Uekawa, Y., 1979, On the concepts of factor intensities and the relation between commodity prices and factor rewards, in: J. Green and J. Scheinkman, eds., General equilibrium, growth and trade (Academic Press, New York).

Part IV

Reflections on the Stolper-Samuelson Theorem

CHAPTER 14

THE STOLPER-SAMUELSON THEOREM: THEN AND NOW

Jagdish Bhagwati

The celebration of the Stolper-Samuelson theorem is a splendid idea. I know of no major international economic theorist today who would not trade an arm and a leg and a sizeable fraction of his own research output for the authorship of this remarkable result.

The Stolper-Samuelson theorem has all the values of a major scientific construct in economics. It has the power of paradox: it demonstrated, contrary to earlier intuition, that one could unambiguously infer changes in real wages, resulting from goods price changes, without having to discover who consumed what. Then again, by the critical test of marginal productivity, it has been a roaring success: it has produced an unceasing flood of research, as scores of us have followed where the masters led.

Indeed, the Schumpeterian followers among us have wandered off in many directions. Following comparative advantage, mindful that familiarity breeds good science, and recognizing that others will describe the paths down which they went, I shall speak only of the three major ways in which I participated in the development of the Stolper-Samuelson analysis.

To place these developments into analytical perspective, it is useful to recall (Bhagwati 1959) that the Stolper-Samuelson theorem, stripped of the Hechscher-Ohlin Theorem baggage that led the authors to assume in their 2×2 model that imports used the scarce factor intensively, implied four propositions:

(1)   autarky, relative to free trade, raised the domestic (relative) price of the importable good;

(2)   the real wage of the factor used intensively in the importable good then went up, with the real wage of the other good falling;

(3)   the (domestic) production of the importable good rose
        with its price; and
(4)   since the real wage in employment was the entire source
        of real income for factors, the real income of the factor
        used intensively in the importable good also rose, and
        the real income of the other factor fell.

The Stolper-Samuelson analysis, as one would expect, is logically
tight, the results following strictly from the assumptions. The subsequent
developments come simply from changing one or more of the assumptions. The developments, detailed below, can essentially be seen further
as bearing intellectual affinity to the early contributions of Lloyd
Metzler, whose untimely death deprives this symposium of the one
economist who promptly saw the importance of the Stolper-Samuelson
analysis and opened the floodgates to other extensions with his two
remarkable articles (1949a,b).

The Metzler Paradox: Extensions

Metzler's major contribution was to extend the Stolper-Samuelson
analysis to a comparison of nonprohibitive protection with free trade,
under the assumption of monopoly power in trade. This immediately
opened up the possibility of the Metzler Price Paradox, undermining
proposition (1) in the list above: protection could now lower the domestic
(relative) price of the importable good.[1] In turn, this undermines
propositions (2) and (3).
        The condition for the Metzler paradox to arise depended, as he
showed, on whether the tariff revenue was assumed to be spent by the
government at tariff-exclusive prices or by the consumers at tariff-
inclusive prices: this being the main difference between his two articles.

---

[1] I distinguish here between the Metzler *Price* Paradox and the Metzler
Production Paradox, though (given the conventional specification of the
problem, chiefly the convexity of the production possibility set) one implied the
other and therefore it has been customary to talk only of *the* Metzler Paradox.

The focus of the research in the late 1950s was, therefore, to explore this condition further, by allowing into the Stolper-Samuelson-Metzler model new possibilities. For example, Kemp and Jones (1961) and Bhagwati and Johnson (1961) examined the effect of allowing factor supply to vary with real wages. Bhagwati and Johnson (1961) further considered the effects of demand disaggregation so as to permit redistribution of income in response to factor reward changes to affect overall demand, and also the effects of allowing consumer taste to depend on the amount of government expenditure.[2]

Real Wages versus Real Incomes

These extensions (including the important extensions of the Stolper-Samuelson theorem to higher dimensions by Chipman, Jones, and Kemp) took the problem as defined by Stolper-Samuelson: how would real *wages* of the factors be affected by protection?

But in Bhagwati (1959), I took the position that the true objective of the analysis could be defined as the effect on the real *incomes* of the factors. If the comparison were between free trade and autarky, real income coincided with real wage. But where protection was nonprohibitive, as in Metzler's analysis, tariff revenues arose. But then, the redistribution of these revenues to factors (*qua* households) would mean that changes in real incomes would reflect changes in real wages *and* in the tariff revenue received.

In Bhagwati (1959), this problem was analyzed.[3] Rao (1971), a student of Chipman, explored it yet further. The distinction plays a role in Mayer and Riezman's recent political-economy-theoretic work (1990)

---

[2] Also, the dependence of the Metzler condition for the paradox on whether the initial situation was one of free trade or a tariff was systematically investigated.

[3] In correspondence, Ethier (who analyzed the problem again in the early 1980s) argued that Metzler had already incorporated tariff revenues in the analysis. True, but irrelevant. Metzler analyzed the effect of tariff revenue disposal (as he necessarily had to) on real *wages*, not on real *incomes*.

on why the revealed political preference in pluralistic societies is for tariffs over subsidies in cases where subsidies should be preferred by a benign government over tariffs *a la* Bhagwati-Ramaswami (1963), Johnson (1965), Bhagwati (1971) and Corden (1974).

Evidently, for the political-economy-theoretic policy choice by economic agents seeking to maximize utility conventionally defined, real incomes matter and not real wages (which are only a component of one's total income when entitlements such as to tariff revenues are present).

The distinction is clearly also of relevance in public policy discussions of income distribution. Thus, the recent U.S. debate on what has happened, and why, to poverty relates to both the real wages of adult unskilled men (which have fallen somewhat throughout the 1980s) and the redistribution by the state (which, unlike in Canada, has failed to offset this decline).

Metzler Production Paradox

As soon as the analysis is extended to include induced production changes other than those in the Stolper-Samuelson-Metzler analysis, where they were exclusively in response to change in the domestic goods price-ratio so that proposition (1) implied proposition (3), it follows that the Metzler Paradox has to be split into two: the Metzler Price Paradox (where protection leads to a fall in the domestic production of the importable) and the Metzler Production Paradox (where protection leads to a fall in the domestic production of the importable).

But in the Bhagwati-Johnson (1961) and Kemp-Jones analysis of variable factor supply, for instance, this implication was not highlighted. The focus on the separateness of the paradoxes came with the analysis of revenue-seeking in Bhagwati and Srinivasan (1980).

There, the revenue-seeking was analyzed in a Komiya model as a resource-using nontraded activity with two tradables and two primary factors. In accommodating revenue-seeking into the tariff analysis of a small country, Bhagwati and Srinivasan showed that the revenue-seeking would have drawn resources away from the production of traded goods and that, even though a tariff for a small country would have raised the domestic price of the importable good (so that the Metzler Price Paradox was ruled out), and hence also raised the domestic production of the importable therewith, the added production effect from revenue-seeking could be to reduce importable production. The latter effect could outweigh the former, producing the Metzler Production Paradox (as in Figure 1). Yabuuchi (1989) has later analyzed the conditions, related to factor-intensities in the activities, under which this Metzler Production Paradox would arise.

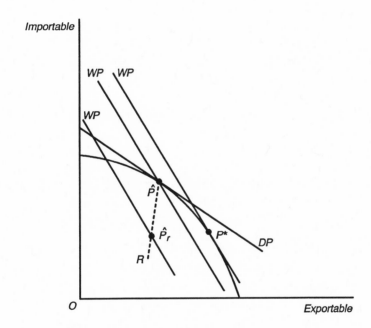

Figure 1

References

Bhagwati, J.N. 1959. "Protection, Real Wages, and Real Incomes," *Economic Journal* 69:733–748.

Bhagwati, J.N. 1971. "The Generalized Theory of Distortions and Welfare," in J.N. Bhagwati, R.A. Mundell, R.W. Jones, and J. Vanek (eds.), *Trade, Balance of Payments and Growth: Papers in International Economics in Honor of Charles P. Kindleberger.* Amsterdam: North-Holland.

Bhagwati, J.N. and H.G. Johnson. 1961. "A Generalized Theory of the Effects of Tariffs on the Terms of Trade," *Oxford Economic Papers* 13:225–253.

Bhagwati, J.N. and V.K. Ramaswami. 1963. "Domestic Distortions, Tariffs and the Theory of Optimum Subsidy," *Journal of Political Economy* 71:44–50.

Bhagwati, J.N. and T.N. Srinivasan. 1980. "Revenue Seeking: A Generalization of the Theory of Tariffs," *Journal of Political Economy* 88:1069–1087.

Corden, W.M. 1974. *Trade Policy and Economic Welfare.* Oxford: Oxford University Press.

Kemp, M. and R. Jones. 1961. "Variable Labour Supply and the Theory of International Trade," *Journal of Political Economy* 70:30–36.

Johnson, H.G. 1965. "Optimal Trade Intervention in the Presence of Domestic Distortions," in R.E. Caves, H.G. Johnson, and P.B. Kenen (eds.), *Trade, Growth and the Balance of Payments.* Amsterdam: North Holland.

Mayer, W. and R. Riezman. 1990. "Voter Preferences for Trade Policy Instruments," *Economics and Politics* 2:61–81.

Metzler, L. 1949a. "Tariffs, the Terms of Trade and the Distribution of National Income," *Journal of Political Economy* 57:1–29.

Metzler, L. 1949b. "Tariffs, International Demand and Domestic Prices," *Journal of Political Economy* 57:345–351.

Rao, V.S. 1971. "Tariffs and Welfare of Factor Owners: A Normative Extension of the Stolper-Samuelson Theorem," *Journal of International Economics* 1:401–415.

Stolper, W. and P.A. Samuelson. 1941. "Protection and Real Wages," *Review of Economic Studies* 9:58–73.

Yabuuchi, S. 1989. "Revenue Seeking and Metzler Paradoxes," *Economics and Politics* 2:187–201.

CHAPTER 15

THE GOLDEN ANNIVERSARY: STOLPER-SAMUELSON AT 50

Ronald W. Jones

It is a pleasure for me to lead off the panel discussion, a pleasure made double by the fact that it honors two of my former professors—Wolfgang Stolper for my first course in economics at Swarthmore in 1948 and Paul Samuelson at MIT four years later. We are here today to celebrate the 50th anniversary of the appearance of their joint paper, a celebration which by rights should have taken place earlier, and would have if this country's official house organ, the *American Economic Review*, had not rejected the piece. It all turned out well in the end, and I frequently cite this rejection to my students to prepare them for the real world.

Why has this paper attained such an important place in the literature? There are, I think, several strands to the answer. Initially, perhaps, because on its appearance it ran directly counter to received wisdom. Proponents of free trade, and at the occasion of the Smoot-Hawley tariff the number in the economics profession ran to over a thousand, were willing to concede that special interest groups might gain from protection, but hardly such an important group as labor. It also took general equilibrium theory off its lofty, pristine shelf and revealed how small-scale versions can usefully be harnessed in comparative statistics to reveal, in this case, firm answers to the question of the effects of commercial policy on the distribution of income. In doing so it introduced the applicability of the box diagram, already familiar to some for its uses in consumption and exchange models by Edgeworth and Bowley, to the allocation of resources for productive purposes. Readers could glance at this diagram and confirm for themselves the surprising conclusion that the ratio of land to labor used in every sector of the economy could rise even though the economy's overall endowment ratio did not change. This was the key to understanding the Stolper/Samuelson Theorem that protection would unambiguously improve the real wage,

227

regardless of taste patterns.[1] As well, a fuse was lit which in time would lead to a criticism directed at the small-scale dimensions of what became the standard trade model. Could the Stolper-Samuelson Theorem survive in a world of many commodities and factors? Let me pick up this theme now.

In the late sixties and early seventies several key papers on the issue of dimensionality were published. As sometimes happens, major contributions by John Chipman, on the one hand, and Murray Kemp and Leon Wegge, on the other, appeared back-to-back in the *International Economic Review* in 1969. Although the particular form of the query differed in the two cases, these two pieces shared a common frustration in that a result that could be obtained when the number of commodities and factors was raised from two to three succumbed to a counter example when *n* equals four.

Kemp and Wegge asked about what came to be known as the *strong* form of the theorem, while Chipman focussed on the *weak* form. The strong form obtains if each sector can be associated with a unique factor of production (the "intensive" factor) such that an increase in any single commodity price raises the return to the associated factor relatively more and lowers the return to all other factors. The weak form is so called because it does not require that all "unintensive" factors lose. These results, of course, could not be expected to hold for any techno-logy—even ones characterized by a lack of joint production, constant returns to scale, and a balance between the number of factors and commodities. Kemp and Wegge assumed that for each factor *i* and commodity *j*, sector *i* used factor *i* intensively in the sense that factor *i*'s distributive share in industry *i* was "large"—relative to any factor's (*k*) share in industry *i*, compared with the analogous ratio of shares of factors *i* and *k* in any other industry. That is, if θ_{ij} denotes the distributive share of factor i in industry j, the Kemp-Wegge assumption is

---

[1] I recall being asked by Kermit Gordon on the occasion of an oral exam at Swarthmore how the Stolper-Samuelson result would fare if the foreign country retaliated with a tariff of its own. My knee-jerk reaction that retaliation always undoes the initial response was caught just in time. Real wages would rise even further.

$$\frac{\theta_{ii}}{\theta_{ki}} > \frac{\theta_{ij}}{\theta_{kj}} \quad \text{for all} \quad i, \ k \neq i, \ j \neq i,$$

(Chipman makes a somewhat weaker assumption, that $\theta_{ii} > \theta_{ij}$). Although a counter-example proved the insufficiency of this condition for n $\geq$ 4, Kemp and Wegge did establish that theirs was a necessary condition.

An example of a production structure that satisfies the Kemp-Wegge conditions and is even strong enough to guarantee the strong form of the Stolper-Samuelson theorem illustrates the close connection between this theorem and the specific factors model of the production (see Jones 1971 and Samuelson 1971). These two models, often portrayed as staunchly different in small-scale versions (2×2 and 3×2), actually have much in common. In the specific factors model when there are many goods, each produced by using a unique factor combined with a mobile factor, the rise in any commodity price unambiguously improves the real return (or rent) to the factor of production only used in that sector, and reduces the real return to all other specific factors. These results accord with strong Stolper-Samuelson. The difference in the income distribution fallout of a price rise is found in the return to the mobile factor—it rises, but not as much, relatively, as the increase in the commodity price. But, as illustrated in Jones and Marjit 1985, 1991, if the mobile factor is itself produced by all the "specific" factors, in any manner that involves them all, the resulting n$\times$n production structure must exhibit strong Stolper-Samuelson properties. Mathematically this corresponds to the result that the inverse of the sum of a positive matrix of rank one and a positive diagonal matrix must exhibit a positive diagonal and negative off-diagonal elements. Each final commodity is produced by mixing some amount of the "produced mobile factor" with some amount of a unique factor which, when counting direct and indirect inputs, is thus seen to be used intensively in producing the commodity.

The strong form of the Stolper-Samuelson Theorem posits three results. First, it establishes that a change in a commodity price causes factor prices to change by relatively *more*, so that *real* factor returns change unambiguously. The asymmetric assumption that productive activities each combine many inputs to produce a single output (non-joint production) is the key to this asymmetry in the spread of factor returns relative to commodity prices. Secondly, the Kemp-Wegge condition pinpoints for each commodity price rise which factor will be the unambiguous winner, the intensively used factor. But a third aspect is involved as well—a symmetry in the fate of the unintensive factors—they all lose. This symmetry in result reflects a symmetry in productive structure. Roughly speaking, such symmetry is provided if the ratios of shares of the unintensive factors cannot differ by very much from industry to industry. As established in Jones, Marjit, and Mitra 1991, a *sufficient* condition for the strong form of the Stolper-Samuelson Theorem to hold is that the difference $\{ \frac{\theta_{ii}}{\theta_{ki}} - \frac{\theta_{ij}}{\theta_{kj}} \}$ not only be positive, but that it exceed the expression $\sum r \neq i, k, j \left| \frac{\theta_{ri}}{\theta_{ki}} - \frac{\theta_{rj}}{\theta_{kj}} \right|$, and this hold for all i, j. In a special case—the so-called Produced-Mobile-Factor structure of Jones and Marjit discussed above, each discrepancy in the ratio of shares of unintensive factors in this sum vanishes, so that the Kemp-Wegge conditions are sufficient. These extra conditions limiting the discrepancy between ratios of unintensive factor shares are vacuous unless the number of factors and commodities equals at least four, helping to explain why Kemp and Wegge's counterexample was reached only at this count.

The strong or weak forms of the Stolper-Samuelson Theorem are not the only candidates which could be considered as the appropriate generalization to higher dimensions. For example, note that the original 2×2 version specified a balance between the numbers of winners and losers consequent to a price rise, whereas the strong version of the $n \times n$ case posits an extreme asymmetry in income distribution: a single price rise awards the intensive factor an increase in its real reward and causes $(n-1)$ factors to lose.[2] An alternative productive structure, the "neighborhood" structure of Jones and Kierzkowski 1986, attempts to highlight a feature which, if at all present, destroys the strong version of the Stolper-Samuelson Theorem in higher dimensions: factors of production have

---

[2] Ken-ichi Inada 1971 described a production structure at the opposite end of the spectrum: any price rise causes a single factor to lose (big) and all other factors to gain, at least in nominal terms.

limited job opportunities.[3] We take this almost to the extreme, avoiding complete specificity, by assuming each industry employs only two of n factor types and each factor has access to only two of the n industries (its "neighbors" in a regional interpretation of the model). A rise in a single commodity price increases the returns to half the factor groups and lowers them from the remaining factors.[4] Of course, if $n = 2$, the 2×2 version of the Stolper-Samuelson model re-emerges. Such a structure perhaps should have equal claim to represent the general version.

My own preference for the appropriate higher-dimensional generalization of the Stolper-Samuelson Theorem is none of the above. Descending from the lofty plain of these highly stylized models one might ask a weaker question: What limitations on productive activity and dimensionality suffice to ensure that any productive factor can unambiguously gain in real terms by the indirect route of a change in relative commodity prices, engineered perhaps by commercial policy or other forms of public taxes or expenditures? The reference to the indirect route confirms that no account is taken of tax or tariff revenues raised by such a policy—just as this direct form of subsidy was ignored in the original Stolper-Samuelson contribution. The answer to this question is that the restrictions on technology are much weaker than provided in Kemp and Wegge. As shown in Jones 1985, the lack of joint production and the existence of at least as many actively produced commodities as factors suffice to guarantee that *any* factor can rely on some simple set of commodity price changes to create an unambiguous improvement in its real earnings. Some other factors might gain also, and it may take more than a rise in a single commodity price, but from a political economy point of view these features seem not to matter. Indeed, any particular factor might well prefer to pursue a policy in which it did not stand out nakedly as the only beneficiary. This is the stuff of politics.

The absence of joint production is important. Suppose n independent activities are undertaken, all of which yield outputs in the

---

[3] The existence of a single zero θ_{ij} disallows the strong version.

[4] If n is odd, a price increase raises the rewards for $(n + 1)/2$ factors.

same proportions. A rise in any commodity price will increase the value of all activities in the same proportion and, as well, the returns to all factors. There would be no change in income distribution. More generally, even with elements of joint production, changes in relative commodity prices cause alterations in relative factor prices and these could be ranked relative to each other. The change in any factor price could be compared with the average, which is the same as the average of changes in all producer prices. If tastes are the same from group to group, statements as to changes in *real* incomes of individual factors could be attempted, depending on whether the terms of trade have been improved or worsened. Of course, one advantage of the original Stolper-Samuelson scenario is precisely that it dispenses with such assertions about tastes.

Questions concerning the effects of government policies on the distribution of income are, if anything, more prominent today than half a century ago. This is the age of suspicion—of awareness that government measures such as commercial policy may be undertaken not because the national interest warrants, but because special interests are involved in rent seeking. The Stolper-Samuelson analysis of the effects of tariffs provides a solid foundation for the pursuit of these vital questions in political economy.

A year before Bertil Ohlin died I had a conversation with him in Stockholm about his contribution to trade theory. He seemed somewhat annoyed at the tendency to think of Heckscher-Ohlin Theory in terms of the simple 2×2 model launched by the Stolper/Samuelson article, inasmuch as his book had so much more. My own attitude, expressed with reservations, was that many grand visions in economics end up rather neglected unless the central ideas can be conveyed in a clean, stripped-down version of a model. With the aid of Stolper/Samuelson and the work subsequently launched, Ohlin's ideas did get conveyed, and his future reward was assured.

References

Chipman, John. 1969. "Factor Price Equalization and the Stolper-Samuelson Theorem," *International Economic Review* 10:399-406.

Inada, Ken-ichi. 1971. "The Production Coefficient Matrix and the Stolper-Samuelson Condition," *Econometrica* 39:219-40.

Jones, Ronald. 1971. "A Three-Factor Model in Theory, Trade, and History," Ch.1 in Bhagwati, Jones, Mundell and Vanek: *Trade, Balance of Payments and Growth*. Amsterdam: North Holland.

Jones, Ronald. 1985. "Relative Prices and Real Factor Rewards: A Reinterpretation," *Economic Letters* 19:47-49.

Jones, Ronald, and Henryk Kierzkowski. 1986. "Neighborhood Production Structures with an Application to the Theory of International Trade," *Oxford Economic Papers* 38:59-26

Jones, Ronald, and Sugata Marjit. 1985. "A Simple Production Model with Stolper-Samuelson Properties," *International Economic Review*, 19:565-67.

Jones, Ronald, and Sugata Marjit. 1991. "The Stolper-Samuelson Theorem, The Leamer Triangle and the Produced Mobile Factor Structure," Ch. 6 in Takayama, Ohyama, and Ohta (eds.), *Trade, Policy and International Adjustments*. New York: Academic Press.

Jones, Ronald, Sugata Marjit, and Tapan Mitra. 1991. "The Stolper-Samuelson Theorem: Links to Dominant Diagonals," unpublished.

Kemp, Murray, and Leon Wegge. 1969. "On the Relation between Commodity Prices and Factor Rewards," *International Economic Review* 10:407-413.

Samuelson, Paul. 1971. "Ohlin was Right," *Swedish Journal of Economics* 73:365-84.

Stolper, Wolfgang, and Paul Samuelson. 1941. "Protection and Real Wages," *Review of Economic Studies* 9:58-73.

CHAPTER 16

THE STOLPER-SAMUELSON THEOREM AND THE PROBLEM OF AGGREGATION

*John S. Chipman**

Introduction

In its elegant and striking conclusion that a tariff on imports would raise real wages and lower the rental on capital if the import-competing industry is more labor-intensive than the export industry, the theorem established by Stolper and Samuelson (1941) demonstrated the power of the neoclassical general-equilibrium approach to international trade. It provided a reason why it was in labor's interest to press for tariff protection and thus the elements needed for an explanation of the existence of tariffs. While this had been basically (but vaguely) understood by the mercantilists and their successors, it was not until Stolper and Samuelson's contribution that the proposition had been put on a sound footing and was thus able to be incorporated into mainstream economic thought.

However, it has come to be recognized[1] that unless severe and rather unrealistic assumptions are made, the proposition does not generalize to models with many products and factors—i.e., one cannot say that there is some one-to-one associaton of commodities and factors such that if the price of commodity i rises, the rental of factor i will rise more than proportionately. The relevance of the proposition to the real world has therefore come to be questioned. Are we then back where we started?

---

* Research supported by NSF grant SES-8607652. I wish to thank Ronald Jones for valuable comments.

[1] Cf. Chipman (1969), Kemp & Wegge (1969), Wegge & Kemp (1969), Uekawa (1971), and Inada (1971).

Some authors[2] have shown that it is possible to salvage at least one aspect of the Stolper-Samuelson theorem in a higher-dimensional setting: from elementary properties of matrix multiplication it follows that, when the number of commodities is equal to the number of factors, and the factor-output coefficients are all positive, a rise in the price of any commodity will entail a fall in the rental of at least some factor and, moreover, a more than proportionate increase in the rental of some factor. On the other hand, while for any factor there is some commodity a rise in whose price will reduce the factor's rental, it is not the case that for every factor there is a commodity a rise in whose price will raise the factor's rental more than proportionately.[3] This is described by Jones & Scheinkman (1977, p. 919) by saying that while "every factor has at least one natural enemy" it is not true that every factor has

---

[2] Ethier (1974), Kemp & Wan (1976), and Jones & Scheinkman (1977).

[3] Using the notation of Section 3 below, if $s_{ij} = w_i b_{ij}/p_j$ is the share of factor i in the cost of production of commodity j, and $S = [s_{ij}]$ is the $n \times n$ matrix of these shares (whose columns sum to 1), from $S^{-1}S = I$ it follows that the product of the ith row of S^{-1} (which is the vector of elasticities of factor rentals with respect to the ith price) with any column of S other than the ith is zero. Assuming that the factor-output coefficients b_{ij} are all positive, this means that a positive linear combination of the elements of the ith row of S^{-1} is equal to zero. Since the elements of the ith row of S^{-1} cannot all be zero (or S^{-1} would not exist), it follows that at least one of them (say the kth) must be negative (i.e., a rise in the ith price leads to a fall in the kth factor rental). Suppose by way of contradiction that all the remaining elements in the ith row of S^{-1} are ≤ 1. Then the inner product of the ith row of S^{-1} with the ith column of S (which sums to 1) is < 1; this is a contradiction. Therefore one of the elements of the ith row of S^{-1}, say the jth, must be > 1; but this is the elasticity of the jth factor rental with respect to the ith price. The converse is not true, however. That is, from $SS^{-1} = I$ one cannot conclude that each column of S^{-1} has an element > 1, since nothing is known about the *row* sums of S.

one natural friend. And in explaining why protectionist measures are introduced, it is clearly the latter kind of proposition that one would like to find.

In the present paper my approach is to look at this question as an aggregation problem. While it is true that different groups of workers push for tariffs and quotas on particular products, it is not clear that any one of these pressure groups would have enough political clout to influence the government—or to succeed in achieving its ends even if it did—if they acted separately rather than in combination. It makes sense, therefore, to ask whether there are conditions under which the separate labor factors might gain in the aggregate (or even separately) if tariffs are imposed simultaneously on an array of import goods.

In his seminal treatment of the theory of linear aggregation, Theil (1965) distinguished two types of conditions that would permit perfect aggregation of a model to a smaller number of dimensions. These may be illustrated by the simple Keynesian consumption function. Suppose that the i th household has a consumption function $c_i = a_i + b_{i y_i}$, where c_i is its consumption and y_i its income. Let aggregate consumption and income be denoted $C = \sum_{i=1}^{n} c_i$ and $Y = \sum_{i=1}^{n} y_i$ respectively. Then clearly there are two alternative conditions that will make it possible to express the aggregate consumption function as $C = a + bY$, where $a = \sum_{i=1}^{n} a_i$: (1) $b_i = b$ for $i = 1, 2, ..., n$; this may be called the case of *structural similarity*. (2) $y_i = \lambda_i Y$ where $\lambda_i > 0$ and $\sum_{i=1}^{n} \lambda_i = 1$ (so that $b = \sum_{i=1}^{n} \lambda_i b_i$); this is the case of *multicollinearity*. Either one of these assumptions (or a combination of the two) will lead to the desired result.

In an elegant article, Neary (1985) has shown how the multicollinearity approach can be used to aggregate a high-dimensional trade model to a 2×2 model, by assuming that import and export prices always move in proportion. In fact, such an approach had already been introduced by Kemp & Wan (1976). Neary obtained close analogues of the Stolper-Samuelson and Rybczynski theorems for the aggregative model.

In the present paper I will follow the structural approach, in which no constraints are placed on the variables under consideration (prices in the Stolper-Samuelson case, endowments in the Rybczynski case). It is evident that this is simply a generalization of the nonlinear aggregation problem as formulated by Solow (1956). Solow posed the question: when can a production function whose arguments include several types of capital be consolidated into a production function in which the capital inputs enter as an index of capital? In the present problem, the generalization is two-fold: first, all factors are simultaneously aggregated into groups; secondly, there are several outputs, and these are simultaneously aggregated into groups as well. The analysis is carried out in terms of the minimum-unit-cost functions dual to the production functions.

The main results are these: If commodity prices and factor rentals are aggregated by Laspeyres price indices, then the conditions for perfect aggregation of the Stolper-Samuelson mapping are that each aggregated industry (e.g., the export industry, or the import-competing industry), must absorb the endowments of each of the different types of labor (resp. capital) in the same proportions. The fact that these conditions are stated in terms of allocative shares of factor endowments, which are the elasticities of factor demand with respect to outputs, shows that they depend on properties of the dual Rybczynski mapping. Likewise, if commodity outputs and factor endowments are aggregated by Laspeyres quantity indices, the conditions for perfect aggregation of the Rybczynski mapping are that each aggregated factor (e.g., total labor, or total capital) should contribute the same fraction of unit costs in each of the component industries of the aggregated industry. The fact that these conditions are stated in terms of shares of factors in unit costs, which are the elasticities of unit costs with respect to factor rentals, shows that they depend on properties of the dual Stolper-Samuelson mapping. Since the Rybczynski mapping is linear (when the country diversifies and prices are given), the above conditions for its perfect aggregation are global; however, except for the case of fixed technical coefficients, the above conditions for perfect aggregation of the Stolper-Samuelson mapping are only local. As shown in Section 3, under a Cobb-Douglas technology global conditions may be obtained for the latter by using geometric rather than arithmetic means for the price and rental indices; but these would have to be combined with arithmetic quantity indices.

Before treating the aggregation problem as such, it is necessary to tackle the question of whether, in the general model to be aggregated, one can allow for unequal numbers of commodities and factors, or whether these should be equal. I shall argue that if world prices are truly exogenous, a country will produce no more commodities than it has factors. It could of course produce fewer; but factor rentals would then depend on endowments as well as prices. I will go through this analysis in the next section; the final section will deal with the aggregation problem.

Equal or Unequal Numbers of Commodities and Factors

Defining our country's production-possibility set by

$$Y(l) = \left\{ y = (y_1, y_2, ..., y_n) \middle| \begin{array}{ll} y_j = f_j(v_{1j}, v_{2j}, ..., v_{mj}) & (j = 1, 2, ..., n) \\ \sum_{j=1}^{n} v_{ij} \leq l_i & (i = 1, 2, ..., n) \end{array} \right\}$$

where y_j is the output of the j th commodity, l_i is the endowment of the i th factor, v_{ij} is the input of the i th factor into the production of the j th commodity, and f_j is the production function for the j th commodity, assumed concave and homogeneous of degree 1.[4] The domestic-product function is defined, for any price vector p, as

$$\Pi(p,l) = \max\{p y | y \in Y(l)\}$$

---

[4] This assumption is readily relaxed if economies of scale are external to individual firms, as shown by Inoue (1981).

If Π is differentiable with respect to p, we know that (cf., e.g., Chipman 1987)

$$\frac{\partial \Pi(p,l)}{\partial p} = \hat{y}(p,l)$$

gives the single-valued Rybczynski function. A necessary condition for this differentiability is $m \geq n$; if $m < n$ the country's production-possibility frontier is a ruled surface as illustrated in Figure 1 for the case $n = 3$ and $m = 2$. Any hyperplane tangential to this surface at an interior point necessarily touches it along a one-dimensional line segment (in the illustration), and in general, along a manifold of dimension $m - n$.

If Π is differentiable with respect to l, we know that

$$\frac{\partial \Pi(p,l)}{\partial l} = \hat{w}(p,l)$$

gives the Stolper-Samuelson mapping. Unlike the case of the Rybczynski function, this is generally single-valued so long as the production functions are differentiable. However, Π, and thus $\hat{w}$, is in general not differentiable with respect to p if $n > m$ (this will be illustrated below). The Stolper-Samuelson function $\hat{w}$ has the important property (at the basis of Samuelson's (1953) factor-price equalization theorem) that, for $n \geq m$, it is locally independent of l for certain values of p and l.

The standard 2×2 case is illustrated in Figure 2 showing cross-sections of the domestic-product function (the second panel also shows the Rybczynski lines). In the cones of diversification the contours of this function have flat segments; as endowments vary, the marginal value productivities of the factors remain constant.

If $m = 2$ and $n = 1$, $\hat{w}$ always depends on l so long as the single production function does not itself have any flat segments. If $m = 3$ and $n = 2$, the boundary (in the three-dimensional space of factor endowments) of the convex hull of the union of the sets $\{l \mid f_j(l_1, l_2, l_3) \geq 1/p_j\}$

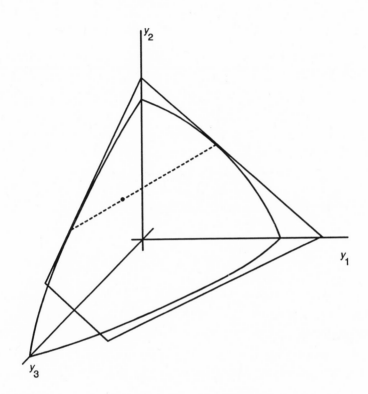

Figure 1: Ruled Production-Possibility Surface

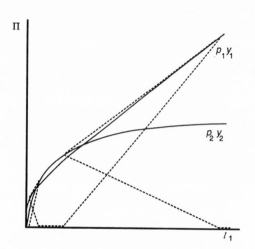

Figure 2B: Vertical Cross-Section of the Domestic -Product Function

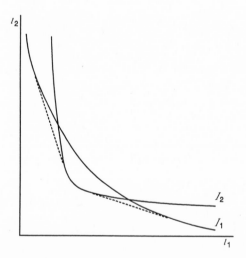

Figure 2A: Horizontal Cross-Section of the Domestic -Product Function

($j = 1,2$) will be a ruled surface. Hence, the vector of endowments may vary along a one-dimensional manifold on this surface without affecting factor rentals. However, such variation would constitute a "freak case" as one used to say, or would be "nongeneric" as one would say today. Essentially (generically), then, for the Stolper-Samuelson function to be locally independent of l we require $n \geq m$.

Now let us consider the case $n > m$. Going back to Figure 1 we see that if there was an initial interior solution, world prices would have to change in a nongeneric way for a new equilibrium to remain an interior solution close to the initial one. An arbitrary small change in one price would drive equilibrium discontinuously to a corner. The situation can be seen more precisely in Figure 3 for $m = 2$ and $n = 3$. Isoquant I_j indicates the input combinations that will produce a dollar's worth of commodity j at the initial price p_j, i.e., the locus of points $\{(l_1, l_2) | f_j(l_1, l_2) = 1/p_j\}$. The arrow indicates the country's assumed endowment vector, enclosed in the large diversification cone shown by the solid rays from the origin. Suppose p_2 falls to p_2', so that the isoquant I_2 shifts upward to I_2'. Then the country will move discontinuously from producing all three goods to producing only commodities 1 and 3, yet factor rentals will remain unchanged. On the other hand if p_2 rises to p_2'', there will be two new cones of diversification in two commodities, one indicated by the dashed rays from the origin enclosing the country's endowment vector, in which commodities 1 and 2 are produced and the country ceases producing commodity 3, and w_2 rises relatively to w_1; if the endowment vector were in the other cone (not shown) w_2 would fall relatively to w_1. In either case, the left and right derivatives of each $\hat{w}_i$ with respect to p_2 are different.

The nondifferentiability of the Stolper-Samuelson function with respect to the other two prices could also easily be deduced from Figure 3. Thus, at the assumed position of the endowment vector, if p_3 falls the country moves discontinuously from producing all three goods to producing only commodities 1 and 2; but if p_3 rises, the country will

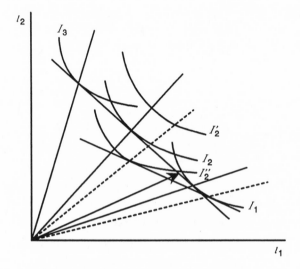

Figure 3: Effects of Price Changes with Three Commodities and Two Factors

cease production of commodity 2 and produce only commodities 1 and 3. In the first case factor rentals remain unchanged, whereas in the second case w_2 rises relatively to w_1. Finally, if p_1 falls, production of commodity 3 will cease, whereas if p_1 rises production of commodity 2 will cease, and while in both cases w_1 moves in the same direction as p_1, the left and right derivatives will be different, since in the first case the model is equivalent to a two-commodity model in which only commodities 1 and 2 are produced, whereas in the second case it is equivalent to one in which only commodities 1 and 3 are produced.

The situation depicted in Figure 1 is clearly one in which our country strongly influences world prices. It is therefore illegitimate in this case to assume that world prices can be treated as exogenous. Denoting by $g_j(w) = g_j(w_1, w_2, ..., w_m)$ the minimum-unit-cost function dual to the production function f_j, the range of the mapping $g(w) = (g_1(w), g_2(w), ..., g_m(w))$ has dimension at most m; if $n \geq m$ it is an m-dimensional manifold (in fact, a cone) in n-dimensional space. If all n commodities are produced, the Stolper-Samuelson mapping $w = \hat{w}(p, l)$ must satisfy $p = g(w)$, i.e., p must be in the range of g. Any variation in an external price must be accompanied by suitable modifications in the remaining prices in order to maintain this restriction. It is not enough simply to "normalize" the prices to a unit simplex $\sum_{j=1}^{n} p_j = 1$, $p_j > 0$ (cf. Kemp & Wan 1976); in the case $n = 3$ and $m = 2$, for example, the price vector p would still have to be confined to a one-dimensional manifold in this simplex, namely the intersection of the simplex with the range of g.[5]

---

[5] As a simple example, suppose the three minimum-unit-cost functions are given by $p_1 = g_1(w_1, w_2) = w_1^{.8} w_2^{.2}$, $p_2 = g_2(w_1, w_2) = w_1^{.2} w_2^{.8}$, $p_3 = g_3(w_1, w_2) = w_1^{.5} w_2^{.5}$. Solving the first two equations for the rentals and substituting them in the third we obtain $p_3 = p_1^{.5} p_2^{.5}$, which defines the range of g. Intersecting it with the unit simplex gives $p_1 + p_2 + p_1^{.5} p_2^{.5} = 1$.

We may conclude that for external prices to be truly exogenous we must assume that $m \geq n$, where n is the number of *produced* commodities in the country. Thus if our country is capable of producing three commodities, and started out specializing in commodities 1 and 2 and was not on the verge of producing commodity 3, we could use the standard two-commodity–two-factor apparatus.

How should we decide the question whether $m > n$ or $m = n$? At first glance it might seem absurd that if there are exactly 1,758,243 commodities, there must also be exactly 1,758,243 factors. However, I suggest that mere counting is not the right way to look at the problem. The fact is that our notions of "commodities" and "factors" are purely conventional. We consider tables and chairs to be two distinct commodities, because our language groups flat objects with four legs and calls them "tables," and similar objects (of appropriate dimensions) with backs and calls them "chairs." But we know that no two tables and no two chairs are exactly alike. Similarly with factors. The proper way to pose the question is: which model best represents reality? For example, if $m > n$ (where n is the number of produced tradable goods) we know that a unilateral transfer to a country with nontradable goods will affect the relative prices of tradables and nontradables, whereas this will not be the case if $m = n$. The null hypothesis $m = n$ can be tested by investigating whether capital inflows or outflows cause significant changes in relative prices.[6] In the simpler model with no nontradable goods, one can still—with any available grouped data on factor rentals, commodity prices, and factor endowments—test the null hypothesis that the Stolper-Samuelson function $\hat{w}(p,l)$ is independent of factor endowments, l.

The Aggregation Problem

We start with a minimum-unit-cost mapping $g : \mathcal{W} \rightarrow \mathcal{P}$ where $\mathcal{W}$ and $\mathcal{P}$ are n-dimensional spaces of vectors of factor rentals w and prices p;

---

[6] Such a test was carried out in Chipman (1985) and the null hypothesis was accepted.

thus, $g(w)=p$. We postulate the existence of grouping mappings $\varphi : \mathcal{W}$ → $\overline{\mathcal{W}}$ and $\psi : \mathcal{P} \to \overline{\mathcal{P}}$, where $\overline{\mathcal{W}}$ and $\overline{\mathcal{P}}$ are $\bar{n}$-dimensional spaces of aggregate factor rentals and aggregate commodity prices, e.g., rental and price indices. These are defined as follows, where w and p are considered to be row vectors: the n factors are partitioned into $\bar{n}$ groups, and may be so numbered that w^μ is the row vector of rentals of the factors in the μth group; likewise for a partition of the n commodities into $\bar{n}$ groups. Thus $w = (w^1, w^2, ..., w^{\bar{n}})$ and $p = (p^1, p^2, ..., p^{\bar{n}})$. The mappings φ and ψ then have the form

$$\bar{w} = \varphi(w) = \left((\varphi_1(w^1), \varphi_2(w^2), ..., \varphi_{\bar{n}}(w^{\bar{n}}))\right) = (\bar{w}_1, \bar{w}_2, ..., \bar{w}_{\bar{n}})$$

$$\bar{p} = \psi(p) = \left((\psi_1(p^1), \psi_2(p^2), ..., \psi_{\bar{n}}(p^{\bar{n}}))\right) = (\bar{p}_1, \bar{p}_2, ..., \bar{p}_{\bar{n}}).$$

The minimum-unit-cost mapping g will be said to satisfy the conditions for *perfect aggregation* (with unrestricted domain) if there exists a minimum-unit-cost mapping $\bar{g} : \overline{\mathcal{W}} \to \overline{\mathcal{P}}$ such that

$$\psi(g(w)) = \bar{g}(\varphi(w)) \text{ for all } w. \tag{1}$$

This is illustrated in Figure 4; perfect aggregation means that the diagram commutes, i.e., $\psi \circ g = \bar{g} \circ \varphi$. Under these conditions, the Stolper-Samuelson mapping may also be consolidated into a mapping between spaces of smaller dimension, i.e., $\varphi(g^{-1}(p)) = \bar{g}^{-1}(\psi(p))$ for all p.

In what follows, for simplicity of exposition and ease of notation I shall present the analysis in terms of an example of six commodities and factors which are to be aggregated to two of each; however, it will be evident that the same reasoning can handle the general case of aggregation from n to $\bar{n} < n$ groups. Let us assume in our illustration that there are three import-competing industries and three export industries (so that $n = 6$), and that commodities are so labelled that the first three are import-competing and the last three are exported; let them

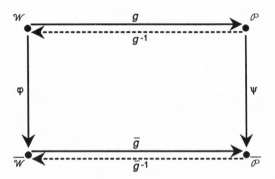

Figure 4: Commutative Diagram for the Stolper-Samuelson Mapping

be aggregated into the corresponding export and import-competing groups (so that $\bar{n} = 2$). Likewise, let us assume that there are two labor factors (say, skilled and unskilled) and four capital factors, and that these are labelled so that the first two factors are kinds of labor and the last four are kinds of capital. The corresponding grouping mappings may then be written

$$
\begin{aligned}
\psi(p_1,p_2,p_3,p_4,p_5,p_6) &= \left(\psi_1(p_1,p_2,p_3),\psi_2(p_4,p_5,p_6)\right) = (\bar{p}_1,\bar{p}_2) \\
\varphi(w_1,w_2,w_3,w_4,w_5,w_6) &= \left(\varphi_1(w_1,w_2),\varphi_2(w_3,w_4,w_5,w_6)\right) = (\bar{w}_1,\bar{w}_2).
\end{aligned}
\tag{2}
$$

From the above definitions,

$$
\begin{aligned}
\psi(g(w)) &= \left(\psi_1(g_1(w),g_2(w),g_3(w)),\psi_2(g_4(w),g_5(w),g_6(w))\right) \\
\bar{g}(\varphi(w)) &= \left(\bar{g}_1(\varphi_1(w_1,w_2),\varphi_2(w_3,w_4,w_5,w_6)),\bar{g}_2(\varphi_1(w_1,w_2),\varphi_2(w_3,w_4,w_5,w_6))\right).
\end{aligned}
\tag{3}
$$

This implies that the composed function $\psi \circ g$ is separable in (w_1,w_2) and (w_3,w_4,w_5,w_6).[7]

---

[7] When the aggregator functions φ and ψ are linear as in (6) below, a sufficient condition for this is that the individual cost functions be themselves separable, i.e., $g_j(w)=c_j(\chi_{j1}(w_1,w_2),\chi_{j2}(w_3,w_4,w_5,w_6))$.
From the formula

$$
\begin{bmatrix} 0 & \partial g_j/\partial w \\[2mm] \dfrac{\partial g_j}{\partial w'} & \dfrac{\partial^2 g_j}{\partial w'\partial w} \end{bmatrix} = \begin{bmatrix} 0 & \partial f_j/\partial v_j \\[2mm] \dfrac{\partial f_j}{\partial v_j'} & \dfrac{\partial^2 f_j}{\partial v_j'\partial v_j} \end{bmatrix}^{-1}
$$

relating the cost function $g_j(w)$ and its dual production function $y_j = f_j(v_j) = f_j(v_{1j},...,v_{nj})$, and by application of Jacobi's theorem and use of Leontief's (1947) conditions, we see that the corresponding separability properties hold for the production functions.

250 The Stolper-Samuelson Theorem

Generalizing Solow's (1956) procedure, we may differentiate the two sets of two equations (3) with respect to the w_i and equate them, to obtain

$$
\begin{bmatrix}
\dfrac{\partial g_1}{\partial w_1} & \dfrac{\partial g_2}{\partial w_1} & \dfrac{\partial g_3}{\partial w_1} & \dfrac{\partial g_4}{\partial w_1} & \dfrac{\partial g_5}{\partial w_1} & \dfrac{\partial g_6}{\partial w_1} \\[2mm]
\dfrac{\partial g_1}{\partial w_2} & \dfrac{\partial g_2}{\partial w_2} & \dfrac{\partial g_3}{\partial w_2} & \dfrac{\partial g_4}{\partial w_2} & \dfrac{\partial g_5}{\partial w_2} & \dfrac{\partial g_6}{\partial w_2} \\[2mm]
\dfrac{\partial g_1}{\partial w_3} & \dfrac{\partial g_2}{\partial w_3} & \dfrac{\partial g_3}{\partial w_3} & \dfrac{\partial g_4}{\partial w_3} & \dfrac{\partial g_5}{\partial w_3} & \dfrac{\partial g_6}{\partial w_3} \\[2mm]
\dfrac{\partial g_1}{\partial w_4} & \dfrac{\partial g_2}{\partial w_4} & \dfrac{\partial g_3}{\partial w_4} & \dfrac{\partial g_4}{\partial w_4} & \dfrac{\partial g_5}{\partial w_4} & \dfrac{\partial g_6}{\partial w_4} \\[2mm]
\dfrac{\partial g_1}{\partial w_5} & \dfrac{\partial g_2}{\partial w_5} & \dfrac{\partial g_3}{\partial w_5} & \dfrac{\partial g_4}{\partial w_5} & \dfrac{\partial g_5}{\partial w_5} & \dfrac{\partial g_6}{\partial w_5} \\[2mm]
\dfrac{\partial g_1}{\partial w_6} & \dfrac{\partial g_2}{\partial w_6} & \dfrac{\partial g_3}{\partial w_6} & \dfrac{\partial g_4}{\partial w_6} & \dfrac{\partial g_5}{\partial w_6} & \dfrac{\partial g_6}{\partial w_6}
\end{bmatrix}
\begin{bmatrix}
\dfrac{\partial \psi_1}{\partial p_1} & 0 \\[2mm]
\dfrac{\partial \psi_1}{\partial p_2} & 0 \\[2mm]
\dfrac{\partial \psi_1}{\partial p_3} & 0 \\[2mm]
0 & \dfrac{\partial \psi_2}{\partial p_4} \\[2mm]
0 & \dfrac{\partial \psi_2}{\partial p_5} \\[2mm]
0 & \dfrac{\partial \psi_2}{\partial p_6}
\end{bmatrix}
=
\begin{bmatrix}
\dfrac{\partial \psi_1}{\partial w_1} & 0 \\[2mm]
\dfrac{\partial \psi_1}{\partial w_2} & 0 \\[2mm]
0 & \dfrac{\partial \psi_2}{\partial w_3} \\[2mm]
0 & \dfrac{\partial \psi_2}{\partial w_4} \\[2mm]
0 & \dfrac{\partial \psi_2}{\partial w_5} \\[2mm]
0 & \dfrac{\partial \psi_2}{\partial w_6}
\end{bmatrix}
\begin{bmatrix}
\dfrac{\partial \bar g_1}{\partial \bar w_1} & \dfrac{\partial \bar g_2}{\partial \bar w_1} \\[2mm]
\dfrac{\partial \bar g_1}{\partial \bar w_2} & \dfrac{\partial \bar g_2}{\partial \bar w_2}
\end{bmatrix}.
\tag{4}
$$

Since by Shephard's duality theorem $\partial g_j/\partial w_i = b_{ij}$ where b_{ij} is the amount of factor i needed per unit of output of commodity j, and similarly $\partial \bar g_v/\partial \bar w_\mu = \bar b_{\mu v}$, this equation may be written compactly as

$$
B\Psi = \Phi \bar B,
\tag{5}
$$

where Ψ and Φ are grouping matrices, i.e., matrices with exactly one nonzero (in fact positive) element in each row. It is clear that condition (5) holds quite generally for the case of aggregating from n to $\bar n$

commodities and factors. From the assumption of constant returns to scale, the cost mapping $g(w)$ and its inverse Stolper-Samuelson mapping $g^{-1}(p)$ may be written as the matrix transformations between the row vectors w and p:

$$wB(w) = p \quad \text{and} \quad pB(g^{-1}(p))^{-1} = w.$$

The commutativity condition (5) is illustrated in Figure 5.

In order to interpret conditions (4) let us consider the usual case in which the aggregator functions are linear-homogeneous, i.e., numerators of Laspeyres price indices:

$$\varphi(w) = (l_1 w_1 + l_2 w_2, l_3 w_3 + l_4 w_4 + l_5 w_5 + l_6 w_6)$$
$$\psi(p) = (y_1 p_1 + y_2 p_2 + y_3 p_3, y_4 p_4 + y_5 p_5 + y_6 p_6) \tag{6}$$

where the l_i and y_j are respectively factor endowments and commodity outputs in some base period, which will be identified with the initial period. Then the above system of equations (4) may be written as

$$
\begin{bmatrix}
\dfrac{b_{11}y_1}{l_1} & \dfrac{b_{12}y_2}{l_1} & \dfrac{b_{13}y_3}{l_1} & \vdots & \dfrac{b_{14}y_1}{l_1} & \dfrac{b_{15}y_2}{l_1} & \dfrac{b_{16}y_3}{l_1} \\[2mm]
\dfrac{b_{21}y_1}{l_2} & \dfrac{b_{22}y_2}{l_2} & \dfrac{b_{23}y_3}{l_2} & \vdots & \dfrac{b_{24}y_1}{l_2} & \dfrac{b_{25}y_2}{l_2} & \dfrac{b_{26}y_3}{l_2} \\[2mm]
\cdots & \cdots & \cdots & \cdots & \cdots & \cdots & \cdots \\[2mm]
\dfrac{b_{31}y_1}{l_3} & \dfrac{b_{32}y_2}{l_3} & \dfrac{b_{33}y_3}{l_3} & \vdots & \dfrac{b_{34}y_1}{l_3} & \dfrac{b_{35}y_2}{l_3} & \dfrac{b_{36}y_3}{l_3} \\[2mm]
\dfrac{b_{41}y_1}{l_4} & \dfrac{b_{42}y_2}{l_4} & \dfrac{b_{43}y_3}{l_4} & \vdots & \dfrac{b_{44}y_1}{l_4} & \dfrac{b_{45}y_2}{l_4} & \dfrac{b_{46}y_3}{l_4} \\[2mm]
\dfrac{b_{51}y_1}{l_5} & \dfrac{b_{52}y_2}{l_5} & \dfrac{b_{53}y_3}{l_5} & \vdots & \dfrac{b_{54}y_1}{l_5} & \dfrac{b_{55}y_2}{l_5} & \dfrac{b_{56}y_3}{l_5} \\[2mm]
\dfrac{b_{61}y_1}{l_6} & \dfrac{b_{62}y_2}{l_6} & \dfrac{b_{63}y_3}{l_6} & \vdots & \dfrac{b_{64}y_1}{l_6} & \dfrac{b_{65}y_2}{l_6} & \dfrac{b_{66}y_3}{l_6}
\end{bmatrix}
\begin{bmatrix}
1 & 0 \\
1 & 0 \\
1 & 0 \\
\cdots & \cdots \\
0 & 1 \\
0 & 1 \\
0 & 1
\end{bmatrix}
=
\begin{bmatrix}
1 & 0 \\
1 & 0 \\
\cdots & \cdots \\
0 & 1 \\
0 & 1 \\
0 & 1 \\
0 & 1
\end{bmatrix}
\begin{bmatrix}
\bar{b}_{11} & \bar{b}_{12} \\
\bar{b}_{21} & \bar{b}_{22}
\end{bmatrix},
\tag{7}
$$

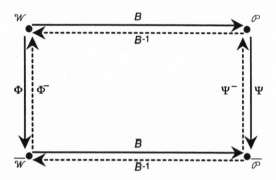

Figure 5: Commutative Diagram for the Stolper-Samuelson Transformation

or, defining the diagonal matrices $Y=diag\{y_j\}$ and $L=diag\{l_i\}$,

$$RH=\overline{GB} \text{ where } R=L^{-1}BY \text{ and } G=L^{-1}\Phi, \quad H=Y^{-1}\Psi.$$

The elements of the matrix R are simply the proportions of the factors allocated to the various industries, i.e., the elasticities of factor demands with respect to commodity outputs; the inverse matrix R^{-1} is the matrix of elasticities of the inverse (Rybczynski) transformation from endowments to outputs. The condition (8) is known in the literature on aggregation in input-output models as the "Hatanaka condition" (cf. Hatanaka 1952). What it states is that in each block of the matrix R, the row sums are equal to one another:[8] That is, the proportion of the total endowment of skilled labor allocated among the three import-competing industries must be the same as the proportion of the total endowment of unskilled labor allocated among these same industries (northwest block of R); and the same for the export industries (northeast block of R), which—in this case of only two aggregated industries—follows from the fact that R has unit row sums. Similarly (southwest block of R), the three import-competing industries must together employ the country's endowments in each of the four types of capital in the same proportion, and similarly for the export industries (southeast block of R).

Another way to interpret these conditions is as follows. Let $\mathcal{I}_\mu$ denote the set of integers i such that factor i is aggregated into the μth group of factors, and let $\mathcal{J}_v$ denote the set of integers j such that commodity j is aggregated into the vth group of commodities. In our illustration, $\mathcal{I}_1 = \{1,2\}$, $\mathcal{I}_2 = \{3,4,5,6\}$, and $\mathcal{J}_1 = \{1,2,3\}$, $\mathcal{J}_2 = \{4,5,6\}$. Then for any aggregated industry $\mathcal{J}_v$ and any aggregated combination of factors $\mathcal{I}_\mu$,

---

[8] This characterization was noted by Ara (1959); for a detailed exposition see Charnes & Cooper (1961, I, Appendix E). See also Chipman (1976, pp. 651-3, 745-8).

$$\frac{\sum_{j \in J_v} b_{ij} y_j}{\sum_{j \in J_v} b_{i'j} y_j} = \frac{l_i}{l_{i'}} \quad \text{for} \quad i, i' \in \mathcal{I}_\mu, \ i \neq i'.$$

That is to say, the ratio of skilled to unskilled labor employed in each aggregated industry (export and import-competing) is the same as the endowment ratio, and similarly for the ratio of any two types of capital. Thus we see that the conditions for perfect aggregation involve a very strong form of degeneracy in the technology, which should not surprise us.

It should be noted that since the units of measurement in the aggregate rental and price indices are a dollar's worth, the matrix $\bar{B}$ is also the matrix of elasticities of factor demands with respect to outputs, hence $\bar{B}$ has unit row sums. This may be seen from the explicit solution of (8),

$$\bar{B} = G^- R H = \Phi^- B \, \Psi$$

where $G^- = (G'G)^{-1} G'$ and $\Phi^- = G^- L^{-1}$—see Figure 5. In our illustration this may be written out as

$$
\begin{bmatrix} \bar{b}_{11} & \bar{b}_{12} \\ \bar{b}_{21} & \bar{b}_{22} \end{bmatrix} =
$$

$$
\begin{bmatrix} \dfrac{1}{2} & \dfrac{1}{2} & \vdots & 0 & 0 & 0 & 0 \\[2mm] 0 & 0 & \vdots & \dfrac{1}{4} & \dfrac{1}{4} & \dfrac{1}{4} & \dfrac{1}{4} \end{bmatrix}
\begin{bmatrix}
\dfrac{b_{11}y_1}{l_1} & \dfrac{b_{12}y_2}{l_1} & \dfrac{b_{13}y_3}{l_1} & \vdots & \dfrac{b_{14}y_1}{l_1} & \dfrac{b_{15}y_2}{l_1} & \dfrac{b_{16}y_3}{l_1} \\[3mm]
\dfrac{b_{21}y_1}{l_2} & \dfrac{b_{22}y_2}{l_2} & \dfrac{b_{23}y_3}{l_2} & \vdots & \dfrac{b_{24}y_1}{l_2} & \dfrac{b_{25}y_2}{l_2} & \dfrac{b_{26}y_3}{l_2} \\[3mm]
\cdots & \cdots & \cdots & \vdots & \cdots & \cdots & \cdots \\[2mm]
\dfrac{b_{31}y_1}{l_3} & \dfrac{b_{32}y_2}{l_3} & \dfrac{b_{33}y_3}{l_3} & \vdots & \dfrac{b_{34}y_1}{l_3} & \dfrac{b_{35}y_2}{l_3} & \dfrac{b_{36}y_3}{l_3} \\[3mm]
\dfrac{b_{41}y_1}{l_4} & \dfrac{b_{42}y_2}{l_4} & \dfrac{b_{43}y_3}{l_4} & \vdots & \dfrac{b_{44}y_1}{l_4} & \dfrac{b_{45}y_2}{l_4} & \dfrac{b_{46}y_3}{l_4} \\[3mm]
\dfrac{b_{51}y_1}{l_5} & \dfrac{b_{52}y_2}{l_5} & \dfrac{b_{53}y_3}{l_5} & \vdots & \dfrac{b_{54}y_1}{l_5} & \dfrac{b_{55}y_2}{l_5} & \dfrac{b_{56}y_3}{l_5} \\[3mm]
\dfrac{b_{61}y_1}{l_6} & \dfrac{b_{62}y_2}{l_6} & \dfrac{b_{63}y_3}{l_6} & \vdots & \dfrac{b_{64}y_1}{l_6} & \dfrac{b_{65}y_2}{l_6} & \dfrac{b_{66}y_3}{l_6}
\end{bmatrix}
\begin{bmatrix}
1 & 0 \\
1 & 0 \\
1 & 0 \\
\cdots & \cdots \\
0 & 1 \\
0 & 1 \\
0 & 1
\end{bmatrix}
$$

$$
= \begin{bmatrix}
\dfrac{1}{2}\displaystyle\sum_{i=1}^{2}\sum_{j=1}^{3}\dfrac{b_{ij}y_j}{l_i} & \dfrac{1}{2}\displaystyle\sum_{i=1}^{2}\sum_{j=4}^{6}\dfrac{b_{ij}y_j}{l_i} \\[5mm]
\dfrac{1}{4}\displaystyle\sum_{i=3}^{6}\sum_{j=1}^{3}\dfrac{b_{ij}y_j}{l_i} & \dfrac{1}{4}\displaystyle\sum_{i=3}^{6}\sum_{j=4}^{6}\dfrac{b_{ij}y_j}{l_i}
\end{bmatrix} \tag{9}
$$

This states that each $\bar{b}_{\mu\nu}$ is equal to the average of the (equal) row sums (and therefore the common value of these row sums) of the elements in block $\mu\nu$ of R. More formally, denoting by ι_n the column vector of n ones, since R, H, and G have unit row sums, and any left inverse G^- of G has unit row sums[9] (since $G\iota_{\bar{n}}=\iota_n$ implies $G^-\iota_n=G^-G\iota_{\bar{n}}=\iota_{\bar{n}}$), it follows from 8) that

$$\bar{B}\iota_{\bar{n}} = G^-G\bar{B}\iota_{\bar{n}} = G^-RH\iota_{\bar{n}} = G^-R\iota_n = G^-\iota_n = \iota_{\bar{n}}.$$

From these developments we see that the conditions for perfect aggregation of the Stolper-Samuelson mapping depend on properties of the Rybczynski mapping. It is evident that a complete analysis requires us to investigate the conditions for perfect aggregation of the dual Rybczynski mapping.

We have denoted by $B(w)$ the transpose of the Jacobian $\partial g(w)/\partial w$ of the system $g(w)$ of minimum-unit cost functions. $B(w)$ itself is the Jacobian of the system of resource-allocation equations

$$B(w)y' = l', \quad \text{or} \quad l = r(y) \equiv yB(w)' \tag{10}$$

where y' and l' are the column vectors of outputs and factor endowments respectively, and $r(y)$ denotes the resource requirements for outputs y at any fixed w (the argument w being suppressed). For each fixed w this defines a mapping from the n-dimensional space $\mathcal{Y}$ of output vectors y to the n-dimensional space $\mathcal{L}$ of endowment vectors l (y and l being considered as row vectors) whose inverse for each fixed p is the Rybczynski mapping $y' = B(g^{-1}(p))^{-1}l'$, where $g^{-1}(p)=w$. We

---

[9] Note that this is simply a generalization of the result that the inverse of a matrix with unit row (resp. column) sums itself has unit row (resp. column) sums; cf. Chipman (1969), p. 402, formula (1.10).

may investigate the conditions under which this system may be aggregated to an $\bar{n} \times \bar{n}$ system

$$\bar{B}(\bar{w})\bar{y}' = \bar{l}', \quad \text{or} \quad \bar{l} = \bar{r}(y) = \bar{y}\bar{B}(\bar{w})' \tag{11}$$

defining for each $\bar{w}$ (already determined from the previous aggregation) a mapping from an $\bar{n}$-dimensional space $\mathcal{Y}$ to an $\bar{n}$-dimensional space $\mathcal{L}$, where $\bar{y} = \psi^*(y)$ and $\bar{l} = \varphi^*(l)$ are grouping mappings from $\mathcal{Y}$ to $\mathcal{Y}$ and $\mathcal{L}$ to $\mathcal{Y}$ conformable to the mappings $\bar{p} = \psi(p)$ and $\bar{w} = \varphi(w)$, i.e.,

$$\begin{aligned}
\psi^*(y_1, y_2, y_3, y_4, y_5, y_6) &= \left(\psi^*(y_1, y_2, y_3), \psi_2^*(y_4, y_5, y_6) \right) = (\bar{y}_1, \bar{y}_2) \\
\varphi^*(l_1, l_2, l_3, l_4, l_5, l_6) &= \left(\varphi_1^*(l_1, l_2), \varphi_2^*(l_3, l_4, l_5, l_6) \right) = (\bar{l}_1, \bar{l}_2).
\end{aligned} \tag{12}$$

Note that for consistency, the aggregate structural matrix $\bar{B}(\bar{w})$ should correspond to the one obtained by aggregating the transformation from factor rentals to commodity prices.

Proceeding as before we arrive at the condition

$$\begin{bmatrix} \dfrac{\partial \varphi_1^*}{\partial l_1} & \dfrac{\partial \varphi_1^*}{\partial l_2} & 0 & 0 & 0 & 0 \\[2ex] 0 & 0 & \dfrac{\partial \varphi_2^*}{\partial l_3} & \dfrac{\partial \varphi_2^*}{\partial l_4} & \dfrac{\partial \varphi_2^*}{\partial l_5} & \dfrac{\partial \varphi_2^*}{\partial l_6} \end{bmatrix} \begin{bmatrix} b_{11} & b_{12} & b_{13} & b_{14} & b_{15} & b_{16} \\ b_{21} & b_{22} & b_{23} & b_{24} & b_{25} & b_{26} \\ b_{31} & b_{32} & b_{33} & b_{34} & b_{35} & b_{36} \\ b_{41} & b_{42} & b_{43} & b_{44} & b_{45} & b_{46} \\ b_{51} & b_{52} & b_{53} & b_{54} & b_{55} & b_{56} \\ b_{61} & b_{62} & b_{63} & b_{64} & b_{65} & b_{66} \end{bmatrix}$$

$$= \begin{bmatrix} \bar{b}_{11} & \bar{b}_{12} \\ \bar{b}_{21} & \bar{b}_{22} \end{bmatrix} \begin{bmatrix} \dfrac{\partial \psi_1^*}{\partial y_1} & \dfrac{\partial \psi_1^*}{\partial y_2} & \dfrac{\partial \psi_1^*}{\partial y_3} & 0 & 0 & 0 \\ 0 & 0 & 0 & \dfrac{\partial \psi_2^*}{\partial y_4} & \dfrac{\partial \psi_2^*}{\partial y_5} & \dfrac{\partial \psi_2^*}{\partial y_6} \end{bmatrix}$$

or, in compact notation,

$$\Phi^* B = \bar{B} \Psi^*. \tag{13}$$

This commutativity condition is illustrated in Figure 6, where, interpreting l and p as row vectors, the Jacobian of the transformation is the transpose matrix $B(w)'$.

As before, we may take the case in which the functions φ^* and ψ^* are linear-homogeneous, e.g., numerators of Laspeyres quantity indices:

$$\begin{aligned} \varphi^*(l) &= (w_1 l_1 + w_2 l_2, w_3 l_3 + w_4 l_4 + w_5 l_5 + w_6 l_6) \\ \psi^*(y) &= (p_1 y_1 + p_2 y_2 + p_3 y_3, p_4 y_4 + p_5 y_5 + p_6 y_6) \end{aligned} \tag{14}$$

where the l_i and y_j are now variable and the w_i and p_j are fixed weights, say corresponding to the rentals and prices in the initial base period. Then we may write the above system in the form

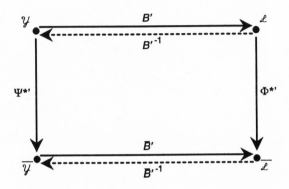

Figure 6: Commutative Diagram for the Rybczynski Transformation

$$\begin{bmatrix} 1 & 1 & : & 0 & 0 & 0 & 0 \\ 0 & 0 & : & 1 & 1 & 1 & 1 \end{bmatrix} \begin{bmatrix} \dfrac{w_1 b_{11}}{p_1} & \dfrac{w_1 b_{12}}{p_2} & \dfrac{w_1 b_{13}}{p_3} & : & \dfrac{w_1 b_{14}}{p_4} & \dfrac{w_1 b_{15}}{p_5} & \dfrac{w_1 b_{16}}{p_6} \\[2ex] \dfrac{w_2 b_{21}}{p_1} & \dfrac{w_2 b_{22}}{p_2} & \dfrac{w_2 b_{23}}{p_3} & : & \dfrac{w_2 b_{24}}{p_4} & \dfrac{w_2 b_{25}}{p_5} & \dfrac{w_2 b_{26}}{p_6} \\[2ex] \dots & \dots & \dots & : & \dots & \dots & \dots \\[1ex] \dfrac{w_3 b_{31}}{p_1} & \dfrac{w_3 b_{32}}{p_2} & \dfrac{w_3 b_{33}}{p_3} & : & \dfrac{w_3 b_{34}}{p_4} & \dfrac{w_3 b_{35}}{p_5} & \dfrac{w_3 b_{36}}{p_6} \\[2ex] \dfrac{w_4 b_{41}}{p_1} & \dfrac{w_4 b_{42}}{p_2} & \dfrac{w_4 b_{43}}{p_3} & : & \dfrac{w_4 b_{44}}{p_4} & \dfrac{w_4 b_{45}}{p_5} & \dfrac{w_4 b_{46}}{p_6} \\[2ex] \dfrac{w_5 b_{51}}{p_1} & \dfrac{w_5 b_{52}}{p_2} & \dfrac{w_5 b_{53}}{p_3} & : & \dfrac{w_5 b_{54}}{p_4} & \dfrac{w_5 b_{55}}{p_5} & \dfrac{w_5 b_{56}}{p_6} \\[2ex] \dfrac{w_6 b_{61}}{p_1} & \dfrac{w_6 b_{62}}{p_2} & \dfrac{w_6 b_{63}}{p_3} & : & \dfrac{w_6 b_{64}}{p_4} & \dfrac{w_6 b_{65}}{p_5} & \dfrac{w_6 b_{66}}{p_6} \end{bmatrix}$$

$$= \begin{bmatrix} \bar{b}_{11} & \bar{b}_{12} \\ \bar{b}_{21} & \bar{b}_{22} \end{bmatrix} \begin{bmatrix} 1 & 1 & 1 & : & 0 & 0 & 0 \\ 0 & 0 & 0 & : & 1 & 1 & 1 \end{bmatrix} \tag{15}$$

or, defining the diagonal matrices $P = diag\{p_j\}$ and $W = diag\{w_i\}$,

$$G^*S = \bar{B}H^* \quad \text{where} \quad S = WBP^{-1}$$
$$\text{and} \quad G^* = \Phi^* W^{-1}, \quad H^* = \Psi^* P^{-1}. \tag{16}$$

(Note that G^* and H^* are the transposes of the respective matrices G and H of (8).) The elements of the matrix S are simply the shares (in the initial period) of the various factors in the costs of production in the several industries, i.e., the elasticities of minimum-unit costs with respect to factor rentals; thus the columns of S sum to unity. The inverse matrix

S^{-1} is the matrix of elasticities of the inverse (Stolper-Samuelson) transformation from commodity prices to factor rentals. What the dual Hatanaka condition (16) states is that in each block of the matrix S, the column sums are equal to one another: that is, the share of labor (skilled and unskilled) in unit costs (northwest block of S), and thus the share in unit costs of the aggregate of the four kinds of capital (southwest block of S), must be the same in each of the three import-competing industries; likewise in the three export industries (northeast and southeast blocks of S). An argument similar to the preceding shows that $\bar{B}$ has unit column sums.

Now let us consider the Stolper-Samuelson transformation, given by the inverse of the system of minimum-unit-cost functions. From (5) we have (see also Figure 5)

$$\Phi = B\Psi\bar{B}^{-1} \quad \text{hence} \quad B^{-1}\Phi = \Psi\bar{B}^{-1}. \tag{17}$$

Written out in the case of our example, with the linear-homogeneous aggregator functions, this is, denoting $B^{-1} = [b^{ij}]$ and $\bar{B}^{-1} = [\bar{b}^{\mu\nu}]$,

$$
\begin{bmatrix}
b^{11} & b^{12} & b^{13} & b^{14} & b^{15} & b^{16} \\
b^{21} & b^{22} & b^{23} & b^{24} & b^{25} & b^{26} \\
b^{31} & b^{32} & b^{33} & b^{34} & b^{35} & b^{36} \\
b^{41} & b^{42} & b^{43} & b^{44} & b^{45} & b^{46} \\
b^{51} & b^{52} & b^{53} & b^{54} & b^{55} & b^{56} \\
b^{61} & b^{62} & b^{63} & b^{64} & b^{65} & b^{66}
\end{bmatrix}
\begin{bmatrix}
l_1 & 0 \\
l_2 & 0 \\
0 & l_3 \\
0 & l_4 \\
0 & l_5 \\
0 & l_6
\end{bmatrix}
=
\begin{bmatrix}
y_1 & 0 \\
y_2 & 0 \\
y_3 & 0 \\
0 & y_3 \\
0 & y_4 \\
0 & y_5
\end{bmatrix}
\begin{bmatrix}
\bar{b}^{11} & \bar{b}^{12} \\
\bar{b}^{21} & \bar{b}^{22}
\end{bmatrix}.
$$

Since the b^{ji} are the Stolper-Samuelson derivatives $\partial\hat{w}_i/\partial p_j$, the above may be summarized by the equations

$$\frac{\partial}{\partial p_j} \sum_{i=1}^{2} l_i \hat{w}_i = y_j \bar{b}^{11} \quad \text{and} \quad \frac{\partial}{\partial p_j} \sum_{i=3}^{6} l_i \hat{w}_i = y_j \bar{b}^{12} \quad \text{for} \quad j = 1,2,3$$

$$\frac{\partial}{\partial p_j} \sum_{i=1}^{2} l_i \hat{w}_i = y_j \bar{b}^{21} \quad \text{and} \quad \frac{\partial}{\partial p_j} \sum_{i=3}^{6} l_i \hat{w}_i = y_j \bar{b}^{22} \quad \text{for} \quad j = 4,5,6.$$

If we now assume (referring to (9) that in each block of B, each row has at least one positive b_{ij}, and that all outputs and factor endowments are positive, then the elements of $\bar{B}$ are all positive. It follows that the matrix $\bar{B}^{-1}$ has either positive diagonal and negative off-diagonal elements or negative diagonal and positive off-diagonal elements. Supposing the former, so that the import-competing industries are labor intensive in the aggregate and the export industries capital intensive in the aggregate, the above equations state that a rise in any one of the import prices will lead to a rise in a Laspeyres index of wages (with the labor endowments as weights) and a fall in a Laspeyres index of rentals of capital (with the capital endowments as weights); likewise, a rise in any one of the export prices will have the opposite effect. Moreover, these changes will be proportionate to the outputs of the respective import-competing or export goods. It follows that a rise in a price index of importables (with any positive weights—e.g., amounts of imports rather than outputs in the base period) will lead to a rise in the wage index and a fall in the rental index, and similarly for a price index of exportables. If the weights in the price indices are outputs, however, and if the conditions (5) for perfect aggregation hold, then—since $\bar{B}^{-1}$ defines precisely the matrix of elasticities of rental indices with respect to price indices—these elasticities are respectively greater than unity and less than zero.

Development of the Rybczynski transformation is entirely similar. From (13) we have

$$\Psi^* = \bar{B}^{-1} \Phi^* B \quad \text{hence} \quad \Psi^* B^{-1} = \bar{B}^{-1} \Phi^*. \tag{18}$$

In the case of our example with aggregator functions (14), this gives

$$\begin{bmatrix} p_1 & p_2 & p_3 & 0 & 0 & 0 \\ 0 & 0 & 0 & p_4 & p_5 & p_6 \end{bmatrix} \begin{bmatrix} b^{11} & b^{12} & b^{13} & b^{14} & b^{15} & b^{16} \\ b^{21} & b^{22} & b^{23} & b^{24} & b^{25} & b^{26} \\ b^{31} & b^{32} & b^{33} & b^{34} & b^{35} & b^{36} \\ b^{41} & b^{42} & b^{43} & b^{44} & b^{45} & b^{46} \\ b^{51} & b^{52} & b^{53} & b^{54} & b^{55} & b^{56} \\ b^{61} & b^{62} & b^{63} & b^{64} & b^{65} & b^{66} \end{bmatrix}$$

$$= \begin{bmatrix} \bar{b}^{11} & \bar{b}^{12} \\ \bar{b}^{21} & \bar{b}^{22} \end{bmatrix} \begin{bmatrix} w_1 & w_2 & 0 & 0 & 0 & 0 \\ 0 & 0 & w_3 & w_4 & w_5 & w_6 \end{bmatrix}.$$

Since the b^{ji} are the Rybczynski derivatives $\partial \hat{y}_j / \partial l_i$, this reduces to

$$\frac{\partial}{\partial l_i} \sum_{j=1}^{3} p_j \hat{y}_j = w_i \bar{b}^{11} \quad \text{and} \quad \frac{\partial}{\partial l_i} \sum_{j=4}^{6} p_j \hat{y}_j = w_i \bar{b}^{21} \quad \text{for} \quad i = 1,2$$

$$\frac{\partial}{\partial l_i} \sum_{j=1}^{3} p_j \hat{y}_j = w_i \bar{b}^{12} \quad \text{and} \quad \frac{\partial}{\partial l_i} \sum_{j=4}^{6} p_j \hat{y}_j = w_i \bar{b}^{22} \quad \text{for} \quad i = 3,4,5,6.$$

From the solution $\bar{B} = G^* S H^{*-}$ (where H^{*-} is a right inverse of H^*) it is clear that as long as in each block of B, each column has at least one positive element, and all prices and rentals are positive, the elements of $\bar{B}$ are all positive. Supposing as before that $\bar{B}^{-1}$ has negative off-diagonal elements, the above equations imply that a rise in the endowment of either skilled or unskilled labor will lead to a rise in a Laspeyres index of output of importables (with prices of importables as weights) and a fall in a Laspeyres index of output of exportables (with prices of exportables as weights), and a rise in any of the capital endowments will have the opposite effect. The remaining conditions analogous to the Stolper-Samuelson case also hold.

Putting all this together we see that in order for both the Stolper-Samuelson and Rybczynski mappings to be perfectly aggregable, the two sets of conditions (5) and (13) must both hold, hence the matrix B of factor-output coefficients must be subject to the double bilinear restriction

$$\Phi^- B \Psi = \bar{B} = \Phi^* B \Psi^{*-} \tag{19}$$

where Φ^- and Ψ^{*-} are left and right inverses of Φ and Ψ^* respectively. This is quite a stringent requirement. However, it is not an unreasonable one provided the matrices are empirically stable. Recall that in (7) the l_i and y_j are fixed weights corresponding to the initial endowments and outputs, and the $b_{ij}(w)$ are evaluated at the factor rentals prevailing in the initial equilibrium. (7) then expresses a local condition for perfect aggregation of the Stolper-Samuelson mapping. Of course, if the technical coefficients b_{ij} are fixed as in Leontief's (1951) model, then it is a global condition. Turning to (15) we recall that the w_i and p_j appearing in the formula are now fixed weights corresponding to the initial rentals and prices, and the $b_{ij}(w)$ are evaluated at these fixed rentals; the share matrix S is therefore fixed, and (15) expresses a global condition for perfect aggregation of the Rybczynski mapping.

It would of course be preferable if we could find some global conditions, expressed in terms of the underlying parameters of the model, for simultaneous perfect aggregation of both the Stolper-Samuelson and Rybczynski mappings. This would require us of course to make some parametric specifications concerning the production functions and thus their dual minimum-unit-cost functions.

If production functions are of the Cobb-Douglas type then we know that the dual minimum-unit-cost functions are also of the Cobb-Douglas type:

$$g_j(w_1, w_2, ..., w_6) = v_j w_1^{\beta_{1j}} w_2^{\beta_{2j}} ... w_6^{\beta_{6j}} \quad (j = 1, 2, ..., 6).$$

In this case it is clearly appropriate to replace the arithmetic means specified by the forms (6) and (14) chosen for the price and quantity indices (2) and (12) by geometric means:

$$
\begin{aligned}
\varphi(w) &= (w_1^{\theta_1} w_2^{\theta_2}, w_3^{\theta_3} w_4^{\theta_4} w_5^{\theta_5} w_6^{\theta_6}) = (\bar{w}_1, \bar{w}_2) \quad (\theta_i > 0) \\
\psi(p) &= (p_1^{\upsilon_1} p_2^{\upsilon_2} p_3^{\upsilon_3}, p_4^{\upsilon_4} p_5^{\upsilon_5} p_6^{\upsilon_6}) = (\bar{p}_1, \bar{p}_2) \quad (\upsilon_j > 0).
\end{aligned}
\tag{20}
$$

We then have

$$
\psi(g(w)) = \left[\prod_{j=1}^{3} v_j^{\upsilon_j} \prod_{i=1}^{6} w_i^{\sum_{j=1}^{3} \beta_{ij}\upsilon_j}, \ \prod_{j=4}^{6} v_j^{\upsilon_j} \prod_{i=1}^{6} w_i^{\sum_{j=4}^{6} \beta_{ij}\upsilon_j} \right]
$$

$$
\bar{g}(\varphi(w)) = \left[\bar{v}_1 \prod_{i=1}^{2} w_i^{\theta_i \bar{\beta}_{11}} \prod_{i=3}^{6} w_i^{\theta_i \bar{\beta}_{21}}, \ \bar{v}_2 \prod_{i=1}^{2} w_i^{\theta_i \bar{\beta}_{12}} \prod_{i=3}^{6} w_i^{\theta_i \bar{\beta}_{22}} \right].
$$

For these to be equal for all w, the following equation must be satisfied:

$$
\begin{bmatrix}
\beta_{11} & \beta_{12} & \beta_{13} & \beta_{14} & \beta_{14} & \beta_{14} \\
\beta_{21} & \beta_{22} & \beta_{23} & \beta_{24} & \beta_{24} & \beta_{24} \\
\beta_{31} & \beta_{32} & \beta_{33} & \beta_{34} & \beta_{34} & \beta_{34} \\
\beta_{41} & \beta_{42} & \beta_{43} & \beta_{44} & \beta_{44} & \beta_{44} \\
\beta_{51} & \beta_{52} & \beta_{53} & \beta_{54} & \beta_{54} & \beta_{54} \\
\beta_{61} & \beta_{62} & \beta_{63} & \beta_{64} & \beta_{64} & \beta_{64}
\end{bmatrix}
\begin{bmatrix}
\upsilon_1 & 0 \\
\upsilon_2 & 0 \\
\upsilon_3 & 0 \\
0 & \upsilon_4 \\
0 & \upsilon_5 \\
0 & \upsilon_5
\end{bmatrix}
=
\begin{bmatrix}
\theta_1 & 0 \\
\theta_2 & 0 \\
0 & \theta_3 \\
0 & \theta_4 \\
0 & \theta_5 \\
0 & \theta_6
\end{bmatrix}
\begin{bmatrix}
\bar{\beta}_{11} & \bar{\beta}_{12} \\
\bar{\beta}_{21} & \bar{\beta}_{22}
\end{bmatrix},
$$

or, since the share matrix S is now the fixed matrix $[\beta_{ij}]$,

$$S\Upsilon = \theta\bar{B} \tag{21}$$

This expresses the conditions for perfect aggregation of the Stolper-Samuelson mapping in terms of weighted averages of the exponents of the Cobb-Douglas production functions.

We could try replacing the arithmetic endowment and output indices (14) by the geometric ones

$$\varphi^*(l) \;=\; (l_1^{\theta_1^*} l_2^{\theta_2^*}, \; l_3^{\theta_3^*} l_4^{\theta_4^*} l_5^{\theta_5^*} l_6^{\theta_6^*}) \;=\; (\bar{l}_1, \bar{l}_2) \qquad (\theta_i^* > 0)$$

$$\psi^*(y) \;=\; (y_1^{\upsilon_1^*} y_2^{\upsilon_2^*} y_3^{\upsilon_3^*}, \; y_4^{\upsilon_4^*} y_5^{\upsilon_5^*} y_6^{\upsilon_6^*}) \;=\; (\bar{y}_1, \bar{y}_2) \quad (\upsilon_j^* > 0) \tag{22}$$

in order to aggregate the factor-demand mapping (10) to (11), to obtain the composed functions

$$\varphi^*(r(y)) \;=\; \left[\prod_{i=1}^{2} \left[\sum_{j=1}^{6} b_{ij} y_j \right]^{\theta_i^*}, \; \prod_{i=3}^{6} \left[\sum_{j=1}^{6} b_{ij} y_j \right]^{\theta_i^*} \right]$$

$$\bar{r}(\psi^*(y)) \;=\; \left[\bar{b}_{11} \prod_{j=1}^{3} y_j^{\upsilon_j^*} + \bar{b}_{12} \prod_{j=4}^{6} y_j^{\upsilon_j^*}, \; \bar{b}_{21} \prod_{j=1}^{3} y_j^{\upsilon_j^*} + \bar{b}_{22} \prod_{j=4}^{6} y_j^{\upsilon_j^*} \right] .$$

However, upon differentiating these two composite functions with respect to the y_j and equating, one finds that the restrictions are in the form of extremely complicated nonlinear equations; hence these conditions could not be expected to be empirically stable. We are therefore compelled to fall back on the linear quantity indices (14) for the aggregation of the Rybczynski relations.

With Cobb-Douglas technology, geometric price and rental indices, and arithmetic output and endowment indices, we now have the following double bilinear restriction on the constant share matrix S,

$$G^* S H^{*-} \;=\; \bar{B} \;=\; \theta^- S \Upsilon, \tag{23}$$

where all the matrices entering the condition are constant. While this restriction has the advantage of being a global one (provided the technology is Cobb-Douglas), it has the distinct disadvantage of asymmetry in the choice of geometric means for price indices and arithmetic means for quantity indices, and it may involve considerable specification error if the technology departs at all significantly from the Cobb-Douglas type.

The condition (19) combined with the assumption of Laspeyres price and quantity indices thus seems to be a sounder criterion in general for simultaneous perfect aggregation of the Stolper-Samuelson and Rybczynski mappings. Of course, nobody believes such a condition to be literally true; its virtue is that it is capable of exact interpretation, and forms a benchmark by which one may assess the goodness of approximation of estimated production coefficients to the conditions for simultaneous perfect aggregation of the Stolper-Samuelson and Rybczynski mappings. Aggregation may be justified provided the distance between the matrices $\Phi^- B \Psi$ and $\Phi^* B \Psi^{*-}$ (a concept which can be made perfectly precise—see Chipman 1976) is sufficiently small. And recent advances in the development of heuristic algorithms for integer programming make it possible to find close-to-optimal modes of aggregation of commodities and factors into groups so as to achieve a suitably low level of aggregation error (cf. Chipman and Winker 1992). In the last analysis, the robustness of the Stolper-Samuelson theorem must be tested by empirical application, and the framework developed here is offered as a means to that end.

References

Ara, Kenjiro. 1959. "The Aggregation Problem in Input-Output Analysis," *Econometrica* 27:257–262.

Charnes, A., and W. W. Cooper. 1961. *Management Models and Industrial Applications of Linear Programming*, 2 vols. New York: John Wiley & Sons, Inc.

Chipman, John S. 1966. "A Survey of the Theory of International Trade. Part 3: The Modern Theory," *Econometrica* 34:18–76.

Chipman, John S. 1969. "Factor-Price Equalization and the Stolper-Samuelson Theorem," *International Economic Review* 10:399-406.

Chipman, John S. 1972. "The Theory of Exploitative Trade and Investment Policies: A Reformulation and Synthesis," in Luis Eugenio Di Marco, ed., *International Economics and Development*. New York: Academic Press, pp. 881-916.

Chipman, John S. 1975. "Optimal Aggregation in Large-Scale Econometric Models," Sankhy Series C, 37:121-159.

Chipman, John S. 1976. "Estimation and Aggregation in Econometrics. An Application of the Theory of Generalized Inverses," in *Generalized Inverses and Applications* (edited by M. Zuhair Nashed). New York: Academic Press, pp. 549-769.

Chipman, John S. 1978. "Towards the Construction of an Optimal Aggregative Model of International Trade: West Germany, 1963-1975," *Annals of Economic and Social Measurement* 6:535-554.

Chipman, John S. 1985. "Relative Prices, Capital Movements, and Sectoral Technical Change: Theory and an Empirical Test," in Karl G. Jungenfelt and Douglas Hague, eds., *Structural Adjustment in Developed Open Economies*. London: The Macmillan Press, pp. 395-454.

Chipman, John S. 1987. "International Trade," in John Eatwell, Murray Milgate, and Peter Newman, eds., *The New Palgrave: A Dictionary of Economics*, Vol. 1. London: The Macmillan Press, and New York: The Stockton Press, pp. 922-955.

Chipman, John S. and Peter Winker. 1992. "Optimal Aggregation by Threshold Accepting: An Application to the German Industrial Classification System." Diskussionsbeitrag Nr. 180, Sonderforschungsbereich 178, Universit at Konstanz (June).

Ethier, Wilfred. 1974. "Some of the Theorems of International Trade with Many Goods and Factors," *Journal of International Economics* 4:199-206.

Ethier, Wilfred. 1984. "Higher Dimensional Issues in Trade Theory," in Ronald W. Jones and Peter B. Kenen, eds., *Handbook of International Economics*, Vol. I. Amsterdam: North-Holland Publishing Co., pp. 131–184.

Fisher, Franklin B. 1982. "On Perfect Aggregation in the National Output Deflator and Generalized Rybczynski Theorems," *International Economic Review* 23:43–60.

Hatanaka, Michio. 1952. "Note on Consolidation within a Leontief System," *Econometrica* 20:301–303.

Inada, Ken-ichi. 1971. "The Production Coefficient Matrix and the Stolper-Samuelson Condition," *Econometrica* 39:219–239.

Inoue, Tadashi. 1981. "A Generalization of the Samuelson Reciprocity Relation, the Stolper-Samuelson Theorem, and the Rybczynski Theorem under Variable Returns to Scale," *Journal of International Economics* 11:79–98.

Jones, Ronald W. 1977. *"Two-ness" in Trade Theory: Costs and Benefits*. Princeton, N.J.: International Finance Section, Department of Economics, Princeton University, Special Papers in International Economics No. 12 (April).

Jones, Ronald W., and Jose A. Scheinkman. 1977. "The Relevance of the Two-Sector Production Model in Trade Theory," *Journal of Political Economy* 85:909–935.

Kemp, Murray C. 1976. *Three Topics in the Theory of International Trade*. Amsterdam: North-Holland Publishing Company.

Kemp, Murray C., and Henry Y. Wan, Jr. 1976. "Relatively Simple Generalizations of the Stolper-Samuelson and Samuelson-Rybczynski Theorems," in Kemp (1976), pp. 49–59.

Kemp, Murray C., and Leon L. F. Wegge. 1969. "On the Relation between Commodity Prices and Factor Rewards," *International Economic Review* 10:407–413. Reprinted in Kemp (1976), pp. 3–24.

Leontief, Wassily. 1947. "A Note on the Interrelation of Subsets of Independent Variables of a Continuous Function with Continuous First Derivatives," *Bulletin of the American Mathematical Society* 53:343–350.

Leontief, Wassily. 1951. *The Structure of American Economy, 1919-1939*, 2nd edition enlarged. New York: Oxford University Press.

Lerner, Abba P. 1952. "Factor Prices and International Trade," *Economica*, N.S., 19:1-15.

McKenzie, Lionel W. 1967. "The Inversion of Cost Functions: A Counterexample," *International Economic Review* 8:271-278. "Theorem and Counterexample," 8:279-285.

Malinvaud, Edmond. 1956. "L'agregation dans les modeles economiques," *Cahiers du S'eminaire d'Econometrie* 4:69-146.

Neary, J. Peter. 1985. "Two-by-Two International Trade Theory with Many Goods and Factors," *Econometrica* 53:1233-1247.

Nikaido, Hukukane. 1968. *Convex Structures and Economic Theory*. New York: Academic Press.

Nikaido, Hukukane. 1972. "Relative Shares and Factor Price Equalization," *Journal of International Economics* 2:257-263.

Rybczynski, T. M. 1955. "Factor Endowment and Relative Commodity Prices," *Economica*, N.S., 22:336-341.

Samuelson, Paul A. 1953. "Prices of Factors and Goods in General Equilibrium," *Review of Economic Studies* 21, 1:1-20.

Shephard, Ronald W. 1953. *Cost and Production Functions*. Princeton, N.J.: Princeton University Press. Reprinted, Berlin-Heidelberg-New York: Springer-Verlag, 1981.

Solow, Robert M. 1956. "The Production Function and the Theory of Capital," *Review of Economic Studies* 23, 2:101-108.

Stolper, Wolfgang, and Paul A. Samuelson. 1941. "Protection and Real Wages," *Review of Economic Studies* 9:58-73.

Theil, Henri. 1954. *Linear Aggregation of Economic Relations*. Amsterdam: North-Holland Publishing Company.

Uekawa, Yasuo. 1971. "Generalization of the Stolper-Samuelson Theorem," *Econometrica* 39:197-217.

Wegge, Leon L. F., and Murray C. Kemp. 1969. "Generalizations of the Stolper-Samuelson and Samuelson-Rybczynski Theorems in Terms of Conditional Input-Output Coefficients," *International Economic Review* 10:414-425. Reprinted in Kemp (1976), pp. 11-24.

CHAPTER 17

SYMPOSIUM REMARKS

Wilfred J. Ethier

Participation in this symposium is both a pleasure and a privilege for me. Devotion of an entire conference (or symposium) to a single published paper is certainly an unusual event. Indeed, the event is doubly unusual in that the paper is even older than I am! Stolper and Samuelson's classic is perhaps the only paper for which such treatment seems eminently appropriate. "Protection and Real Wages" was published by the *Review of Economic Studies* in its issue of November 1941. Shortly thereafter followed the bombing of Pearl Harbor. I don't mean to suggest cause and effect, but one never knows.

It is worth making a distinction between the Stolper–Samuelson paper and the Stolper-Samuelson theorem, inasmuch as the contributions of the two are not identical. Let me briefly review for you several of the contributions of the Stolper-Samuelson paper.

- First, of course, is the celebrated theorem, to which I shall return in a moment.
- At least as importantly, the paper was a decisive step in the crystallization of the ideas of Heckscher and Ohlin into what has become known as the Heckscher-Ohlin-Samuelson model—the favorite plaything of several generations of international trade theorists. Since the application of this structure turned out to be an important step in the evolution of the practice of using formal (general-equilibrium) modelling to analyze economic questions, the Stolper-Samuelson paper also played a central role in determining the way we now do economics.
- The Stolper-Samuelson paper used the term, for the first time in the literature as far as I know, "Heckscher-

271

Ohlin theorem." However, Stolper and Samuelson used this term to refer to the proposition that free trade in commodities tends to equalize factor rewards across countries, and not to the proposition that the pattern of such trade is determined by relative factor endowments.
• The Stolper-Samuelson paper also used the term "paradoxical outcome," again as far as I know for the first time in the collection of articles that has come to be known as the "modern theory of international trade." Unfortunately, much of this literature was polluted during the fifties and sixties by excessive use of just this term, so perhaps this accomplishment should rate as a minus rather than as a plus (still, it's better than Pearl Harbor).

Let me now turn to the Stolper-Samuelson theorem itself. The Symposium organizers asked us for our "reflections" on the Stolper-Samuelson theorem and not (thank God) for still more theorems of our own. But this does oblige us to reflect: better late than never.

My own attitudes toward the Stolper-Samuelson theorem have for some time been dominated by two overriding impressions (or prejudices) that are somewhat at odds with each other. Let my "reflections" take the form of sharing these impressions with you.

The first powerful impression I have is of the Stolper-Samuelson theorem's remarkable irrelevance to actual day-by-day experience. Of course the theorem is very useful for understanding and explaining actual historical experience—we have all used it for this in our classroom lectures (and, some of us, in our textbooks). Perhaps Ohlin had already said it all. But the theorem doesn't help at all in understanding the daily newspaper's account of who wants what from trade policy.

In this regard I think the Stolper-Samuelson theorem comes off rather poorly compared to its cousins, the Heckscher-Ohlin theorem and the factor-price equalization theorem. Such an attitude would have astounded economists several decades ago, when the Heckscher-Ohlin theorem was being buffeted by the Leontief paradox (to use that unfortunate term again), and when the factor-price equalization theorem was widely thought to be irrelevant to the real world and regarded, by more than a few economists, as an acute embarrassment.

This is not necessarily a bad thing. Most of us have concluded that we don't see the Stolper-Samuelson theorem at work on a day-by-day basis because in practice intersectoral immobility causes people's incomes to be more closely tied to the sector with which they are affiliated than to the factors whose earnings generate those incomes. It would be churlish indeed to hold that immobility against a theorem whose purpose, after all, is to describe what complete intersectoral mobility implies for the relation between commodity prices and factor rewards. Nor should we forget that a major accomplishment of the Stolper-Samuelson paper was to expose the fallacy in the former presumption that sufficient intersectoral mobility would allow all sizeable factors to share in the gains from a movement to free trade.

The second powerful impression I have is of the remarkable robustness—as a proposition in theory—of the Stolper-Samuelson theorem's basic message. Higher dimensions, economies of scale, time-phasing, joint production, nontraded goods, traded factors, and produced means of production have had a go at the theorem. Each of them has of course taken its toll, with some drawing more blood than others. I've participated in all this in my own research, so I have a strong sense of how it all comes out. What impresses me most is the degree to which, when all the sound and fury has passed, the basic messages of the Stolper-Samuelson theorem remain significantly relevant. After fifty years the theorem still lives.

CHAPTER 18

STOLPER-SAMUELSON AND THE VICTORY OF FORMAL ECONOMICS

Paul Krugman

I am well aware that in a conference like this one I am in a special position, as an aggressive exponent of what you might call post-modern trade theory. But I do not want to talk about Stolper-Samuelson in the light of the changes that have taken place in economics since 1980. Instead I want to talk about the role that Wolfgang and Paul's remarkable paper played in the changes that swept through economics in the 1940s. For it is only in that context that one can understand just how important their paper was.

One of my pastimes is rummaging around in the history of economic thought. The period of the 1940s is a particularly fascinating one, because it was a time of massive transition. The intellectual environment in which Stolper-Samuelson was published was completely different from what economists have come to consider the norm. And the most important thing about Stolper-Samuelson is the way that it helped to create economics as we know it.

Nowadays we take it for granted that economics is a formal, model-oriented field, with an analytical core based on the concepts of maximization and equilibrium. That kind of economics has a long history; but circa 1940 it was by no means completely dominant. Institutional economics, with its literary style and historical style of research, remained a powerful force. Indeed, one could still find reverential references to the work of John R. Commons, who was still widely regarded as a, perhaps the, leading American economist.

What actually happened, of course, was a complete rout of institutional economists by modelers. Paul Samuelson was, without doubt, the key figure in that rout; and his paper with Stolper was a significant factor in his victory.

At the time of the Stolper-Samuelson paper, many people who considered themselves economists had little interest in or respect for formal theoretical models. The central tenet of institutional economics (as far as I can understand it) was indeed that one could not usefully discuss an economy with simplified abstract models, because not only the behavior but even the objectives of firms and households depended crucially on history.

It is easy to see how someone expressing this point of view could seem wiser and more impressive than an economist who claimed to be deriving broad conclusions from some silly, patently unrealistic little model, especially if the institutionalist backed his assertions with massive historical scholarship. Yet what happened instead was a complete victory of the nerds. Why?

The most important reason was, of course, the success of Keynesian economics. What could institutionalists say about the Great Depression? They naturally asserted that the business cycle was deeply rooted in the institutional structure of capitalism, that one could only understand it through careful and detailed study of those institutions, and that there would be no easy answers. Then along came young economists, brandishing abstract models with no historical or institutional context, who asserted that the whole thing could be fixed by increasing G—and who turned out to be right. Although many economic theorists have since repudiated or ignored Keynes, it is clear from reading the literature of the time that the contrast between the effectiveness of macroeconomic modelers and the ineffectuality of alternative schools was startling, and completely shifted the balance of intellectual power and prestige. One can make the case that the enterprise of economics as we know it rests ultimately on the credibility that modeling gained from the Keynesian Revolution—in much the same way that high-energy physics is still living off the Manhattan Project. (Of course, high-energy physics has produced nothing useful since, whereas economics—actually, never mind).

This was macroeconomics—a field in which Paul Samuelson was a key leader and propagandist. But how did formal modeling also come to dominate microeconomics, aside from some general methodological spillover? Here is where Stolper-Samuelson played a crucial role.

Before the Stolper-Samuelson paper, formal modeling in microeconomics was a somewhat marginal enterprise. Marshall did it, but preferred to do it in private. And general equilibrium theory was viewed more as an intellectual exercise than as a useful tool.

Then came Stolper-Samuelson, which did several revolutionary things, all at once.

First, it presented general equilibrium, not as a broad logical structure for contemplation, but in the form of a specific model aimed at answering a real-world question. That is, Stolper-Samuelson was arguably the first paper that used general equilibrium reasoning actually to do something.

Second, as many of the other people at this conference have noted, Stolper-Samuelson introduced a new set of techniques that made it possible to keep track of a large number of interrelated variables.

Finally, and most important, Stolper-Samuelson used general equilibrium to demonstrate, in an irrefutable way, that informal intuition could be badly misleading.

I am quite sure that if you had asked most pre-Stolper-Samuelson international economists about the effects of protection on low-wage workers, you would have gotten the same seemingly judicious answer that you still get in Wall Street Journal-level discussions: "Well, protecting labor-intensive industries may shift the distribution of income slightly in favor of unskilled workers, but it will lower overall income, and on balance will normally hurt them." What is important is not just that Stolper-Samuelson showed that this seemingly reasonable argument was wrong-flatly, irretrievably wrong—but that they showed it in an essentially general-equilibrium way. That is, there is no way to understand the Stolper-Samuelson proposition without talking about the interrelationship of markets, and indeed without using something like the techniques introduced in the Stolper-Samuelson paper.

In other words, Stolper-Samuelson showed that it was not enough to be a reasonable, well-spoken, thoughtful person to be a competent economist; unless you understood how to make and use formal general equilibrium models, you were going to be in danger of being purely and simply wrong about very basic issues.

It turned out, furthermore, that the two-sector model introduced by Stolper and Samuelson was ideally suited to the task of puncturing the ideas of casual thinkers. In subsequent years the model was to be used to explore such disturbing propositions as factor price equalization, the Rybczynski effect, and, in the field of public finance, the surprisingly tricky business of determining the incidence of taxes. Again and again, economists whose thinking was sloppy because they avoided making models were embarrassed; and after enough such embarrassments, making models came to be part of the essential definition of economics.

Of course the triumph of Stolper-Samuelson had a down side as well. In 1941 the use of careful formal reasoning to cut through the vagueness of literary economics was a radical, liberating idea. Perhaps inevitably this liberation gradually turned into a new kind of strait-jacket, as intellectually insecure economists began to feel that only mathematically difficult papers were worthwhile. And the Heckscher-Ohlin model of trade, which Stolper and Samuelson first formalized, gradually took on a sort of sacred status that was a betrayal of the brash spirit of its creators.

For what Stolper and Samuelson really did was to show how formal models could be used, not to reinforce orthodoxy, but to shatter it. Anyone who uses mathematics to simplify, not to complicate, who uses careful reasoning to refute, not confirm, what everyone thinks, and who challenges the stylistic conventions of his or her era without compromising intellectual rigor, is following in the tradition of that wonderful paper.

CHAPTER 19

ENDOGENOUS PROTECTION AND REAL WAGES

Stephen P. Magee

When I was invited to this symposium, I thought it was probably because of my 1980 paper, "Three Simple Tests of the Stolper-Samuelson Theorem." I was, frankly, a little embarrassed, and I felt obligated to remind the organizers that the Stolper-Samuelson theorem had, in fact, flunked all three of the tests. Well, they assured me that I should come along anyway, probably because I had recanted in a series of subsequent articles and a book on endogenous protection with Brock and Young (1989). The reconciliation is that a specific-factor model explains lobbying over trade policy in the short-run (with time-series data) while the Stolper-Samuelson approach works better in explaining why countries protect their scarce factor in the long run (using cross-national data). An interesting time-series test of Stolper-Samuelson is provided by Choi (1991).

What happens to the Stolper-Samuelson theorem when protection itself is endogenous?

I will demonstrate below that when protection is endogenous, protection and the fortunes of the scarce factor follow the Stolper-Samuelson predictions in response to factor endowment shocks but a modification is needed in response to terms of trade shocks. The details of the argument here are in Magee, Brock and Young (1989).

Some Fond Memories

I have wonderful memories of my graduate student days at MIT in the mid-to-late 1960s. Paul Samuelson taught the second semester microeconomics course and his lectures were inspiring. The most entertaining lectures occurred when he would come straight to class from the airport with no lecture notes. On those occasions, he would tell wild tales about the giants of the profession. I learned the Stolper-Samuelson theorem from Charles Kindleberger in the international economics course. He was as encyclopedic as Samuelson when it came to economic history. Unfortunately, Kindleberger never labelled any of the axes when he put the four-quadrant Meade diagrams on the board.

Samuelson was on my dissertation committee. I remember his asking me a convoluted question about a controversy between Pigou and Haberler. As I recall, the question had a "yes" or "no" answer, and I guessed right.

My dissertation investigated the basic theorems in the pure theory of international trade with factor market distortions present. The Stolper-Samuelson theorem worked with distortions, so long as the factor intensities of production were defined in terms of the factor income shares rather than the physical factor intensities. Ronald Jones also worked on this problem and helped me clarify my understanding of this point soon after I finished by dissertation.

After finishing graduate school, I inflicted the Stolper-Samuelson theorem on graduate students at Berkeley from 1969–1971; at the University of Chicago from 1971–1976; and at Texas thereafter. Chicago was colorful in the early 1970s because of the weekly drama that played in either Stigler's Industrial Organization Workshop or Friedman's Money Workshop. It was important for junior faculty such as myself to plan workshop presentations like a war game, with multiple presentations. The presentation selected would be determined by whether carnivores, herbivores, or herbs showed up at the workshop.

Unfortunately, Robert Mundell had just left the University of Chicago when I arrived in 1971. But, Harry Johnson was there throughout my stay, and he created excitement in the Workshop in International Economics. Harry Johnson was occasionally wrong, but he was never in doubt. He loved to whittle and would carve to occupy his hands during seminars. He got furious at a workshop speaker who asserted that inflation could be better explained by sociology than by economics. To emphasize his displeasure, he opened the sawblade on his knife, set his whittling board up on the seminar table, and proceeded to saw away on a very large board. I do not know what effect this had on the seminar speaker, but I lost all interest in sociology.

I wrote "Three Simple Tests of the Stolper-Samuelson Theorem" at the University of Chicago in 1975. Harry Johnson had been a friend and a mentor to me. I presented this paper at an Oxford Conference in memory of Johnson in 1978, and the paper appeared in the conference volume in 1980, edited by Peter Oppenheimer.

Endogenous Protection

What happens to the Stolper-Samuelson theorem with endogenous protection? I will demonstrate that the tariff can rise and yet labor, the scarce factor, can be worse off. In general this will be the case when the tariff rises because of an increase in the country's terms of trade: see Chapters 10 and 11 of Magee, Brock, and Young (1989).

Consider the simplest 2 x 2 case in which tariffs are exogenous in a small open economy and let labor be the scarce factor. If the usual assumptions hold, a rise in the tariff raises wages. The same result holds with endogenous tariffs, except that factor returns are also impacted by the variables driving the tariff rate and the latter may dominate.

First, some background. Tariffs are endogenous if they can be described by maximizing behavior by all of the players. To answer the question, consider the model of endogenous protection which Brock, Young, and I have developed. It is built squarely on the Heckscher-Ohlin-Samuelson (HOS) model and the Stolper-Samuelson theorem. We have 2 goods, 2 factors, 2 lobbies and 2 political parties, yielding a $2 \times 2 \times 2 \times 2$ game with rationally-ignorant Downesian voters choosing between a protectionist party that supports a tariff, which helps the scarce factor (labor), and a proexport party that sponsors an export subsidy, which helps the abundant factor, capital. Think of this in terms of the U.S. Congress, following Robert Baldwin's work. The labor lobby gives money to the protectionist Democrats while the physical and human capital lobby channels funds to the Republicans. Findlay calls this the "two-by-four model" because of its stark emphasis on self-interest.

In an endogenous policy model, policies play the same role in politics as prices play in an economy: both are equilibrating variables that adjust until opposing forces are balanced. When the demand for wheat is high, the price of wheat is high. Similarly, powerful groups with high demands for protection will obtain higher tariffs than smaller and weaker groups. Just as prices equate demand and supply at the margin, so do redistributive policies equate, at the margin, pressures for and against a given type of redistribution. The textile lobby may obtain a 20 percent tariff while a weaker lobby such as leather may obtain only a 5 percent tariff. If these are equilibrium tariffs, attempts to increase the textile tariff from 20 to 21 percent would encounter greater opposition than support (as would an increase from 5 to 6 percent for the leather tariff).

What are the effects of an endogenous political system on an economy? *A priori*, the political system should benefit labor relative to capital the higher the electoral success rate of the Congressional Democrats, the higher tariff on labor-intensive imports, and the lower the export subsidy on capital-intensive exports. However, all three of these variables are endogenous and are driven by the exogenous economic and political variables in the $2 \times 2 \times 2 \times 2$ model.

A Modified Stolper-Samuelson Theorem With Price Shocks

With Leontief production, an increase in a country's terms of trade causes the equilibrium level of protection to rise and the export subsidy to fall. To illustrate, consider the importation of automobiles into the United States from Japan. The entry of Japan into the world auto market lowered the world price of autos; this lowered the price of imports into the United States; and this stimulated pressures by labor and protectionists to keep the autos out. The lowered price of imports puts downward pressure on wages because the import-competing industries are labor-intensive. Lower wages stimulate labor to substitute out of economic activity and into political activity. The labor lobby expands because lower wages reduce its costs.

Thus, the rise in the terms of trade caused by the decline in U.S. import prices caused the U.S. endogenous political equilibrium to shift to greater protection. And the rise in the tariff is always insufficient to offset the initial move in world prices.

The Stolper-Samuelson theorem, narrowly defined as linking protection with the scarce factor, does not hold with endogenous protection. When the theorem is stated more broadly, it holds, e.g., increases in the world price of labor-intensive good raise wages.

This illustrates a compensation effect. When a special-interest group's return from economic activity declines because of any adverse shock, the group compensates by investing more resources in lobbying and politics. Its political party responds with an increase in the policy variable that benefits it. There has been a decline in the U.S. terms of manufacturing trade in the last decade. Advances by the Japanese and other countries in autos, steel, and textiles have reduced the world prices of U.S. importables and, thus, improved the U.S. terms of trade. Following the compensation principle, U.S. factors of production in importables have increased their lobbying and received more protection, particularly in these senile industries. But the increased protection was not enough to offset the effect on wages of the initial import-price decline.

The compensation effect suggests that endogenous political activity has effects on wages that are progressive. That is, they move to partially offset both capital gains and capital losses. For example, when the price of the labor-intensive good increases on world markets, labor benefits domestically. But labor's induced loss of interest in political activity at the margin causes its political investments to decrease and the tariff to decline as a partial offset. Consider now the effect of endowments.

Stolper-Samuelson Holds with Endowment Shocks

Endogenous policy theory suggests an endowment theory of protection: the equilibrium tariff increases with the ratio of the country's scarce factor to its abundant factor. Equilibrium export subsidies, similarly, decrease with this ratio. In traditional (HOS) trade theory, factor endowments played a key role in determining the pattern of trade but did not influence factor returns. With endogenous policy, relative endowments determine not only a country's trade pattern but also its structure of trade protection. With Leontief production, procapital parties do better in capital abundant countries.

In general, an increase in a factor leads to an increase in the policy favoring that factor and to the returns of that factor. Thus, Stolper-Samuelson holds in its original form with endowment shocks because the policy and the returns to the factor move together.

Figure 1 illustrates increasing returns to politics. For example, the more capital an economy has, the higher will be returns to capital. The mechanism works as follows. When the capital endowment increases, rentals fall initially. The lower opportunity cost of capital causes the procapital lobby to expand its activities. It obtains a more favorable policy than before and the procapital party gets elected more often. Together, these two effects offset the normal diminishing returns to capital.

This runs counter to the usual story that exogenous capital inflows into a small economy (a) would decrease capital returns because of diminishing returns if the economy were closed to international trade or (b) not affect rentals if the economy were open to international trade, *a la* Rybczynski and factor price equalization. These factors plus Stolper-Samuelson effects increase the returns to capital.

The previous results suggest another, namely, geographical polarization of world capital endowments. Countries well endowed with capital will have high capital returns and will attract even more capital while labor abundant countries should have low returns and lose capital. While it is fanciful to think that this might explain the capital gap between the developed and the developing countries, it certainly reinforces the existing geographical pattern.

Special-interest politics will lead to political dominance: capital will be more successful electorally in capital-abundant countries, and labor will dominate in labor-abundant countries.

Countries with higher capital endowments and capital returns will be blessed with the *Brazilian vitality* while those with lower capital returns will be cursed with the *Indian disease*. Brazilian vitality describes a country with higher than world returns to capital so that capital enters and the returns continue to increase. The domestic capital returns may be high initially because the country has a high capital endowment or be-

Return to Capital

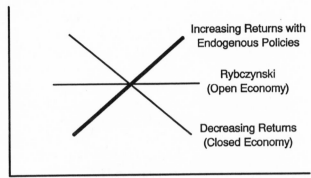

Increasing Returns with
Endogenous Policies

Rybczynski
(Open Economy)

Decreasing Returns
(Closed Economy)

Country Endowment of Capital per Laborer

Figure 1

**Increasing Returns to Factor Endowments
with Endogenous Policies
Contrasted with Two Traditional Cases**

cause capital is potent politically. The reverse case we characterize as the Indian disease; i.e., countries with lower than world returns to capital penalize capital politically so that capital exits and the capital returns continue to decrease. The country becomes increasingly labor dominant. I do not know how the process ends.

The increasing return implication of endogenous policy theory is suggestive but, as yet, untested.

Three Simple Tests of the Stolper-Samuelson Theorem

I conclude with a brief review of one of the three simple tests of the Stolper-Samuelson theorem versus the Ricardo-Viner-Cairnes model of tariff lobby behavior in the United States. If capital and labor from a given industry are always on the opposite side of the free trade-protection issue (irrespective of their industry location), then Stolper-Samuelson would hold. However, the data show the reverse: both capital and labor in import competing industries favored protection while capital and labor in the export industries favor freer trade. The results might suggest that fixed factor models are the best approach to explain lobbying over tariffs. But in actuality: "It depends."

Figure 2 shows the data. Stolper-Samuelson would predict that the industry observations should be in off-diagonal boxes while the Ricardo-Viner-Cairnes model would predict that the observations should be along the diagonal. Notice that 19 of 21 industries fall along the diagonal. The data come from the positions of capital (both physical and human) and labor on hearings for the Trade Act of 1974.

These results are driven by an institutional feature of U.S. trade legislation which has been around since 1934: namely, the tendency for U.S. trade legislation to require renewal every four years or so. Thus, lobbying behavior tested here applies to lobbies who are discounting future benefits for only four years into the future. Because of this short time horizon, the results are biased against the Stolper-Samuelson theorem and toward the Ricardo-Viner-Cairnes model.

The Ricardo-Viner-Cairnes model is a better description of lobbying for short-lived trade legislation and for industry-specific

Position of the Industry's Labor

	1 Protectionist	2 Free Trade
1 Protectionist **Position of Industry Capital**	11 distilling textiles apparel chemicals plastics rubber shoes leather shoes stone products iron & steel cutlery hardware bearings watches	12 tobacco
2 Free Trade	21 petroleum	22 paper machinery tractors trucks aviation

Figure 2

The Empirical Results for Lobbying
on the 1974 Trade Act

explanations of trade policy. However, when it comes to explaining the level of a country's tariffs, a politicized version of the Heckscher-Ohlin-Samuelson model of international trade is more insightful than the Ricardo-Viner-Cairnes model for predicting long-term behavior on trade policy. Empirical support for this view is the alignment of blue-collar workers, a scarce factor in the United States, with the protectionist Democrats in the U.S. Congress and an alignment of many management trade associations with freer trade and with the (proexport) Congressional Republicans. Similarly, tariff rates across countries are correlated with the country's endowment of capital per laborer.

References

Choi, Nakgyoon. 1991. *Essays in International Trade: Endogenous Tariff Theory*. Ph.D. Dissertation in Economics, University of Texas at Austin.

Magee, Stephen P. 1980. "Three Simple Tests of the Stolper-Samuelson Theorem," in Peter Oppenheimer (ed.), *Issues in International Economics: Essays in Honor of Harry G. Johnson*. London: Oriel.

Magee, Stephen P., William A. Brock, and Leslie Young. 1989. *Black Hole Tariffs and Endogenous Policy Theory*. New York: Cambridge University Press.

CHAPTER 20

COMMEMORATING THE FIFTIETH BIRTHDAY OF THE STOLPER-SAMUELSON THEOREM

Edward E. Leamer

Ideas are like sea turtles. Multitudes are hatched, but most perish moments later as they flop frantically from the beach to the relative safety of the sea. Many that make it that far are gobbled up by predators within another week or two. But the few that survive through adolescence live long, fruitful, seemingly endless lives. The Stolper-Samuelson Theorem is one of these.

An idea that survives fifty years is closer to its birth than to its death. A fiftieth birthday for an idea is not a time to look back, to eulogize or to memorialize. It is a time to look forward, to rejoice over the future.

But I cannot get in the mood. I am worried about the future. I am afraid this old sea turtle we are examining today has no viable progeny. Maybe it is the nuclear testing. Maybe it is the depletion of the ozone layer. I know we are hatching more eggs than ever before. But most of these ideas are flopping aimlessly on the beach. Some have enormous bodies, others only one leg, and others are born without heads. Those few that manage to flop into the ocean seem like weaklings in comparison with the Stolper-Samuelson theorem. I cannot imagine they will last for more than a decade.

To survive an idea must have an *issue*, a question: that's the head. It also needs a healthy body: a conceptual framework, a *theory*. And it will not get far without a set of strong legs to connect it firmly to reality: it needs *data* and evidence. Ideas with a small head, or a weak body or hardly any legs will not survive for long, certainly not in competition with healthy, robust ideas. What I see out there now are lots of deformed ideas flopping on the beach. Most of us are theorists who give birth to ideas with enormous theory bodies, but hardly any data legs and often no issue heads at all. Some of us call ourselves econometri-

289

cians and have offspring with gigantic, powerful flippers instead of legs, which would be alright if these ideas could reach the ocean, but they have no heads, and they end up flopping in circles until they perish in the hot sun.

Wait a minute! Do you hear what I hear? Take a look over there behind the Economics building. That old sea turtle is shamelessly mating with a Banach space and a Riemann-Stieltjes integral. It seemed OK when he dated the simplex algorithm, but this is too much. Just listen to it. It's disgusting! Those mathematical ideas are brutes, all dressed up in leather. They are mocking that old turtle, claiming he is trivial, not really a theorem at all. But the sea turtle doesn't mind; he seems to get turned on by the abuse. How pathetic! If his parents, the Le Chatelier Principle and the Second Law of Thermodynamics, could see this, they would be so disappointed. No, they would be incensed. As should we! It's not the nuclear testing, or the hole in the ozone. The problem is the turtle's reckless behavior. That old turtle is having a hell of a good time without giving one iota of concern to his descendants.

You know, now that I take a closer look at it, I don't see any legs on that turtle after all. The Stolper-Samuelson theorem does have an attractive head, and a beautiful and simple body. But I wonder how he got to the sea without any legs.

TWO-NESS AND THE STOLPER-SAMUELSON THEOREM

The political implications of the familiar two-good, two-factor model of international trade are a simple and well known consequence of the Stolper-Samuelson Theorem: the abundant factor prefers access to international markets as a way to increase the demand for its services, and the scarce factor prefers to avoid direct competition with low paid foreign counterparts. Thus the scarce factor favors and the abundant factor opposes protection. This simple result has a ring of truth to it that seems likely to extend to higher dimensional settings. Rogowski (1987), for example, has made use of the three-good, three factor model to explain the historical formation of political groups on the assumption that the scarce factors favor trade restrictions and the abundant factors oppose restrictions.

But is it theoretically valid to claim that the scarcest factor favors protection, when there are more than two goods? Probably not, you may be thinking, since the difficulties of linking commodities and factors in higher dimensional general equilibrium models are serious and well known. But the attempts of which I am aware to link commodities and factors in higher dimensional settings refer to technologies, not to the direction of trade. For example, here is a theorem applicable to the two-good two-factor model: an increase in the price of a commodity gives rise to an increase in the (real) return of the factor used relatively intensively in that industry. This technologically based linkage between commodities and factors will not generalize in a linguistically felicitous way to higher dimensional problems because there is no high-dimensional counterpart to the phrase "used relatively intensively in that industry." Leamer (1987) does provide a diagrammatic treatment of the 3×3 case and gives the following sufficient conditions: "If commodity A is more intensive in factor L relative to both of the other factors, then an increase in the price of commodity A leads to an increase in the real return to factor L."

Although the search for technologically based linkages of commodities and factors has proven unsuccessful, I am unaware of an attempt to link commodities and factors using the direction of trade. The kind of proposition that might apply in higher dimensional settings is: (1) the scarcest factor favors tariffs on any good. A weaker proposition is: (2) the scarcest factor favors equal tariffs on all imports. A still weaker proposition is: (3) the scarcest factor favors tariffs on at least one of the imported goods. The weakest proposition is: (4) the scarcest factor favors some combination of tariffs. This last result seems probable in light of Jones' (1987) observation that there is some combination of price increases that will increase the real return of a factor. But *none* of these propositions is true, which I will make clear in two counterexamples.

The first counterexample has been suggested by Alan Deardorff. Make a 3×3 model out of a standard 2×2 model by splitting the abundant factor L arbitrarily into two inputs, L_1 and L_2, that are perfect substitutes, say right- and left-handed workers, and by splitting one of the goods, say good A, into A_1, and A_2, which are also perfect substitutes. Clearly you can make left-handed workers as scarce as you want, yet this scarcest factor is hurt by protection (since in the underlying 2×2 case it is abundant).

If this logic is uncomfortable, another version of the same idea may be helpful. Suppose that there are three commodities: one agricultural good and two manufactures. The agricultural good is produced with land, lots of labor and a little capital. The two manufactured goods are produced with labor and capital, but no land. Suppose that capital is the scarcest factor where scarcity is defined in the physical sense that the share of the world's capital stock located in this country is less than the share of the world's land or labor. Since capital is the scarcest factor, one would suppose that capital would favor protection. But this need not be the case. The equilibrium in this model can be solved in two steps. Because land is used only in agriculture, we must allocate all land to agriculture and combine it with a suitable portion of the capital and labor. (The input coefficients are fixed because of factor price equalization.) After extracting a little capital and a lot of labor for the agricultural sector, the ordering of the factors can be reversed: For manufacturing, capital is abundant and labor is scarce. Now the 2×2 Stolper-Samuelson theory applies to the manufacturing sector. Thus this economy exports the agricultural commodity and the capital intensive manufacture; it imports the labor-intensive manufacture. Thus capital opposes protection and labor favors it.

This seems to render the Stolper-Samuelson Theorem pretty useless since the content of the result does not extend even one small step to the 3×3 model. Although I have known this since the original version of this paper was written in 1987, I have not really been willing to end on such a destructive note and I have left this paper sitting in my files. I thought perhaps a price-definition of factor abundance would help, but I have generally been reluctant to refer in theorems to unobservables like autarky prices.

The occasion of the 50th birthday party of the Stolper-Samuelson in November was enough incentive for me to dust off this paper. Fortunately and fortuitously, an off-hand remark by Paul Samuelson at the birthday party provided the key. I am not sure that he will recall or own up to it, but it doesn't matter since a message requires a sender and a receiver. I "heard" him say:

Theorem: If a factor is "scarce enough," it will favor protection of some form.

This theorem is true for many definitions of "scarce enough," but it is uninteresting for most. One definition that allows a very easy proof and that seems interesting as well refers to the reduction of the supply of the factor in question until complete specialization occurs:

Definition: A factor is "scarce enough" if any reduction in its supply would take the factor supply vector completely out of the cone of incomplete specialization.

The proof of the theorem uses the duality between the Stolper-Samuelson derivatives and the Rybczynski derivatives. Suppose that labor is the resource in question. As we extract labor from the economy, the high-dimensional version of the Rybczynski Theorem implies that at least one sector expands and at least one contracts. The one sector which disappears when complete specialization occurs obviously must have contracted. Thus the Rybczynski derivative of output with respect to this factor supply, $\ddot{u} Q_i / \ddot{u} L$, is positive for this sector i. By the Samuelson duality result, the derivative of the wage rate with respect to the price of product i is equal to the Rybczynski derivative and thus is positive as well. Finally, since, with this supply of labor, none of commodity i is produced, it must be an imported good, provided that another produced item is not a perfect substitute.[1] Thus a tariff on this good raises the wage rate on labor, the scarcest factor.

With this as the pessimistic beginning, I now propose to plow ahead, and to say as much as I can about the three-by-three model.

---

[1] This condition is violated by the first counterexample.

The Stolper-Samuelson Theorem

The usual statement of the Stolper-Samuelson theorem in the two-good
two-factor case links commodities and factors in a way that depends on
the input intensities. Here is Ethier's (1984 p. 146) version:

> A small change in relative prices will increase, in terms
> of both goods, the reward of the factor used intensively
> in the production of that good whose price has risen and
> will reduce, in terms of both goods, the reward of the
> other factor, provided that both goods are produced.

Here is Ethier's (1984 p. 153) proposed generalization to higher
dimensions:

> To extend fully this result to the higher dimensional
> context we would wish any change in relative commo-
> dity prices to cause each factor price to either rise or fall
> in terms of all goods.

These propositions contrast with the conjecture that I explore here:

> Some combination of price increases on the imported
> goods would increase the return of the scarcest factor
> relative to the price of some good.

The most important difference between these propositions is that mine
links the scarce factor with the imported goods, whereas Ethier's links
a factor with the good that uses it intensively. Another difference is that
I weaken the proposition to allow the real return to the factor to either
increase or decrease depending on its consumption basket. As it turns
out, my conjecture is false.

The Stolper-Samuelson Derivatives in the Three-by-Three Model

The graphical method of Leamer (1987) can be used to determine the effects that price changes have on the returns to factors in the context of the three-good three-factor model. Figure 1 is an endowment triangle that is formed by intersecting the three dimensional factor space with a plane. The corners of the endowment triangle correspond to the axes in the three dimensional space and are labelled K (capital), L (labor) and T (land). A vector in the three dimensional space, representing all endowment vectors with the same ratios of capital, labor and land, becomes a point in the endowment triangle. The essential feature of this endowment triangle is that an increase in one factor, say labor, holding fixed the other two factors, moves the endowment point on a straight line toward the labor vertex. Along this line, the ratio of the other two factors is accordingly constant. This property allows us to compare the relative supplies of factors at points in the endowment triangle.

The expansion vectors of three commodities are also depicted by points in this diagram. Two manufactured commodities (M_1 and M_2) use as inputs capital and labor, but no land. The manufacture M_1 is relatively labor intensive (closer to the labor vertex). A third commodity A is an agricultural commodity that uses all three inputs. The point representing this commodity is located to the left of a line connecting the land vertex with the M_1 commodity point, which means that the capital per man in agriculture is assumed to be less than the capital per man in either manufactured commodity.

The Stolper-Samuelson linkage of commodities and factors can be determined as described in Leamer (1987). The argument first identifies the signs of the derivatives of outputs with respect to endowments (the Rybczynski derivatives) and then appeals to the Samuelson duality relations which equate the Rybczynski derivatives to the derivatives of factor returns with respect to product prices (the Stolper-Samuelson derivatives). The signs of the Rybczynski derivatives are found as follows. A vector of derivatives of outputs dq with respect to changes in factor supplies dV satisfies the equation system $\mathbf{B}dq = d\mathbf{V}$, where B is the matrix of input intensities, each column containing the input mix in an industry. In words, the change in factor supplies is ex-

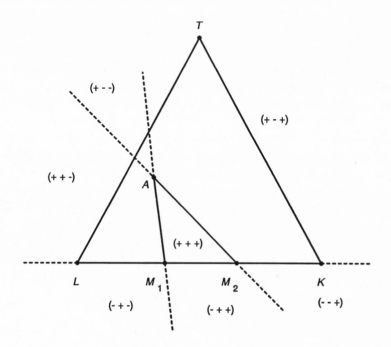

Figure 1: Endowment Triangle

pressed as a linear combination of the input vectors. If, for example, the change in factor supplies $d\mathbf{V}$ is proportional to one of the input vectors, then output of only that industry changes. If the change in factor supplies $d\mathbf{V}$ is expressible as a combination of only two of the input vectors, then outputs of only those two industries change and the third output is unchanged. Input changes that are expressible as linear combinations of two of the input vectors fall on lines connecting the points representing the three commodities in Figure 1. As one moves from one side of such a line to the other, the Rybczynski derivative corresponding to the other vertex changes sign. This logic divides the endowment triangle into the seven "visible orthants" that are labelled by their sign patterns in Figure 1, with commodity ordering: A, M_1, M_2. The signs of the Stolper-Samuelson derivatives (changes of factor prices with respect to changes in commodity prices) are then determined according to the orthants in which the corners of the endowment triangle lie since these corners represent endowment change vectors $d\mathbf{V}$ equal to one of the coordinate vectors.. For example, the land vertex lies in the $(+,-,+)$ orthant, which implies that the return to land is positively associated with the price of the agricultural commodity and the capital intensive manufacture, and negatively associated with the price of the labor intensive manufacture. These Stolper-Samuelson derivatives applicable to the technologies displayed in Figure 1 are collected together in Table 1.

Table 1
Stolper Samuelson Linkages:
Derivatives of Returns to the Factor
With Respect to a Change in the Price of a Commodity

	A	M_1	M_2
K	0	-	+
L	0	+	-
T	+	-	+

This table has been constructed on the assumption that agriculture has the lowest capital per man. The implications of a more capital intensive agricultural good can be found by swinging the agricultural point (A) in the figure toward the capital vertex (K). This changes the orthant in which the land vertex (T) lies from $(+,-,+)$ to $(+,-,-)$ and finally to $(+,+,-)$. Thus if agriculture is intermediate in capital per man, the return on land is negatively associated with the price of both manufactures, and if agriculture has the highest capital per man, then the return on land is positively associated with the price of the labor intensive manufacture. This could be summarized as follows: the return on land is positively associated with only the most distant manufactured commodity.

Table 1 indicates the effects that price changes have on the returns to factors, but not on the utility of factor owners which would also be affected by changes of the prices of goods that are consumed. Price increases that lower the return to factors further lower the utility of the factors through the consumption effect. The minuses in Table 1 apply also to utility, and the zeroes should be interpreted as minuses because of the consumption affects. The pluses in the table may actually be minuses if consumption concentrates on the commodities whose price has changed. See Ethier (1984 pp. 152–53) for a discussion.

Trade Patterns

These Stolper-Samuelson derivatives are not enough to determine preferences for trade protection since that would depend also on the commodities that are imported. The conditions under which a commodity is exported or imported are also discussed in Leamer (1987).[2] The

---

[2] The Heckscher-Ohlin-Vanek (HOV) model implies a set of relationships between the trade vector, T, the endowment vector V, the world endowment vector V^w, the consumption share s and the matrix of input requirements B:

$$BT = V - s\,V^w.$$

triangle with the commodity vectors as vertices is depicted in Figure 2. This triangle is divided into a region of endowment supplies in which the agricultural good is necessarily exported and a region in which the agricultural good is necessarily imported. The point V_W represents the factor endowments of the world as a whole, and Figure 2 is formed by drawing a line through W parallel to the line connecting M_1 and M_2. Roughly speaking, if the endowment supplies are similar (dissimilar) in mix to the input requirements in agriculture, then the agricultural commodity is exported (imported).

Figure 3 then identifies six different regions with the corresponding trade patterns in Table 2. The center of this figure represents the endowment vector of the world as a whole. The lines emanating from this point are parallel with the sides of the triangle.

The consumption share can be written as $s = (1-b)w'V/w'V^w$ where b is the ratio of the trade surplus to GNP, w is the vector of factor prices and w'V is GNP. Substituting for s, the HOV equations become $BT/GNP = (V/GNP) - (V^w/GNP^w) + bV^w/GNP^w$. Using lower case to represent variables scaled by GNP this becomes

$$Bt = v - v^w + bv^w.$$

The difference in trade of two countries with endowment differences δv is the solution to $B\delta t = \delta v$. These two countries would have the same level of trade/GNP of one commodity if δv is in the space generated by the other two columns of B. In figure 2, endowment vectors that lie on the line segment connecting M^1 to M^2 necessarily have the same level of imports/GNP of the agricultural product since none is produced. Lines of constant trade in agriculture are parallel with this line segment. The dotted line in the figure corresponds to zero trade in agriculture if trade is balanced, since then an endowment proportional to the world endowment would imply no trade in any product. The region of agricultural exports would be larger if there were a trade surplus, but its border would still be parallel to the line segment connecting M^1 to M^2, since these are contours of constant agricultural trade. Incidentally this implies that trade imbalances (capital exports) alter the preferences of the factors for trade restrictions.

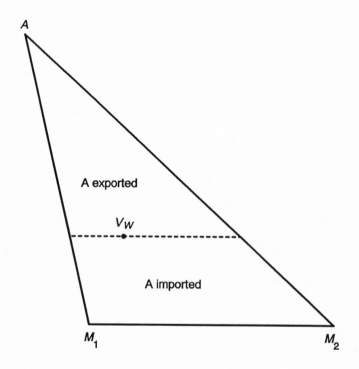

Figure 2: Agricultural Trade

Table 2
Trade Patterns
(+ = Export, - = Import)

Region	1	2	3	4	5	6
A	+	+	+	-	-	-
M_1	+	-	-	-	+	+
M_2	-	-	+	+	+	-

The Stolper Samuelson Theorem

We now have the apparatus necessary to explore possible generalizations of the Stolper-Samuelson Theorem in the three-by-three model:

Proposition 1:   The scarcest factor favors tariffs on any good.

Proposition 2:   The scarcest factor favors equal tariffs on all imports.

Proposition 3:   The scarcest factor favors tariffs on at least one of the import goods.

Proposition 4:   The scarcest factor favors some form of tariff protection.

These are all false!

The critical point is that these propositions inappropriately refer to factor abundance when the regions in Figure 3 are formed from the relationships between endowments and the input mixes of the commodities. This is a major difference between the two-by-two model and the higher dimensional model, since for the two-by-two model, the two types of regions would conform.

The regions corresponding to different ratios of factors are depicted in Figure 4. These regions are formed by connecting the world

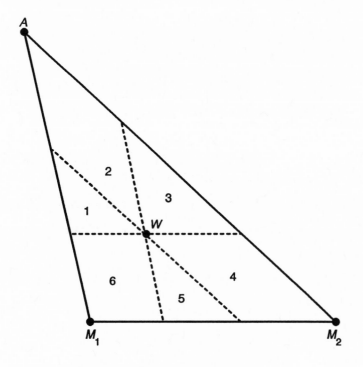

Figure 3: Regions of Trade Patterns

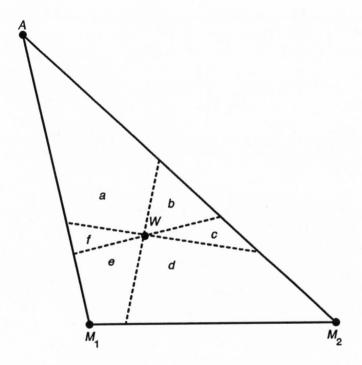

Figure 4: Regions of Factor Abundance

endowment point W to the vertices of the endowment triangle (not shown). For example, in Figure 4, starting from the world endowment point W, an increase in land moves the endowment point upward on the line segment separating region **a** from region **b**. An increase also in capital moves the point toward the capital vertex and thus into region **b**. Within region **b**, labor is the scarce factor and land is the abundant factor in the sense that $L/L_w < K/K_w < T/T_w$.

Now look back at region 3 in figure 3. In this region, the labor intensive manufacture is imported and the other two commodities are exported. A rise in the price of the import good increases the return to labor, and reduces that return to the other two factors. Thus labor favors trade restrictions, and capital and land oppose restrictions. Can it be said that the scarce factor favors protection and the abundant factor opposes protection? If this is correct, then labor would have to be the scarce factor and either capital or land the abundant factor. But region 3 in figure 3 overlaps with regions a, b and c in figure 4, with the three different orderings of factor abundance: $K/K_w < L/L_w < T/T_w$, $L/L_w < K/K_w < T/T_w$, $L/L_w < T/T_w < K/K_w$. Though labor is unambiguously scarce compared with land, capital can be anywhere in the ordering. Even when capital is the scarcest factor, it opposes protection!

In retrospect it is not difficult to understand why this anomaly (region 3a) arises. In this region, capital is the scarcest factor, yet is harmed by protection. The reason for this is that the abundance of land gives rise to a substantial output of the agricultural commodity, which is very labor intensive. After extracting the capital and labor used in agriculture, capital is the relatively abundant factor, not the relatively scarce factor.

The imported goods, preferences for protection and factor abundance orderings are all reported in table 3. The preferences for protection are indeterminate when more than one good is imported and the prices of the two goods have opposite effects on the return to the factor. Cases that contradict the Stolper-Samuelson conjectures are reported in table 3 in bold face type. As discussed above, in region 3, capital is pro-trade but may be the scarcest factor. Similarly, land in region 1 is anti-trade, but may be the most abundant factor. The other anomalies all occur when there is more than one import good. The weaker version of the Stolper-Samuelson theorem continues to apply for these cases: the scarcest factor prefers protection for at least one of the imports.

Conclusion

Turtles of every type are welcome in my house.

Table 3
Trade Preferences and Factor Orderings

Region	Imports			Trade Preferences			Factor Orderings		Coalitions
	A	M₁	M₂	K	L	T			
1		*		-	+	-	a:	K<L<T	(K,T) anti-trade
1		*		-	+	-	f:	K<T<L	(K,T) anti-trade
2		*	*				a:	**K<L<T**	(K,T) anti/pro
3		*		+	-	+	a:	**K<L<T**	(K,T) pro-trade
3		*		+	-	+	b:	**L<K<T**	(K,T) pro-trade
3		*		+	-	+	c:	L<T<K	(K,T) pro-trade
4	*	*		+			c:	**L<T<K**	(K,L), (K,T) pro
4	*	*		+			d:	**T<L<K**	(K,L), (K<T) pro
5	*			+	+	-	d:	T<L<K	(K,L) pro-trade
6	*		*		+		e:	**T<K<L**	(K,T) anti (K,L) pro
6	*		*		+		f:	**K<T<L**	(K,T) anti (K,L) pro

+ = pro-trade, opposes any combination of tariffs
- = anti-trade, favors any combination of tariffs
(Anomalies appear in **bold**)

References

Deardorff, Alan V. 1980. "The General Validity of the Law of Comparative Advantage," *Journal of Political Economy* 88:941–57.

Deardorff, Alan V. 1982. "The General Validity of the Heckscher-Ohlin Theorem," *American Economic Review* 72:683–694.

Deardorff, Alan V. and Staiger, Robert W. 1988. "An Interpretation of the Factor Content of Trade," *Journal of International Economics* 24:93–108.

Dixit, Avinash and Norman, Victor. 1980. *Theory of International Trade*. Cambridge: Cambridge University Press.

Ethier, Wilfred J. 1984. "Higher Dimensional Issues in Trade Theory," in Volume I, Ronald W. Jones and Peter B. Kenen (eds.), *Handbook of International Economics*. Amsterdam: North-Holland Publishing Company.

Jones, Ronald. 1987. "Relative Prices and Real Factor Rewards: A Reinterpretation," *Economics Letters* 19:47–49.

Leamer, Edward E. 1987. "Paths of Development in the Three-Factor N-Good General Equilibrium Model," *Journal of Political Economy* 95:961–99.

Rogowski, Ronald. 1987. "Political Cleavages and Changing Exposure to Trade," *American Political Science Review* 81:1121–37.

Samuelson, Paul. 1947. *Foundations of Economic Analysis*, Cambridge: Harvard University Press.

CHAPTER 21

COMMENTS ON THE STOLPER-SAMUELSON THEOREM

Robert E. Baldwin

The most significant impact of the 1941 article by Stolper and Samuelson, in my view, was that it completed the development of the two-good, two-factor, two-country model that has profoundly influenced international trade analysis over the last fifty years. Edgeworth 1925 and Marshall 1924 had popularized the notions of depicting the production set available to a country with a given technology and factor endowment in terms of a two-commodity, increasing-cost production-possibilities curve and the country's willingness to trade in terms of a reciprocal demand or offer curve. Edgeworth 1925, pp. 323–324 and Pareto 1919 had also pointed out how the utility received by an individual from two commodities could be depicted in terms of indifference curves. Using the concept of nonintersecting community indifference curves, Leontief 1933 then demonstrated how the equilibrium trading terms, as well as production and consumption, could be determined graphically in a two-country, two-commodity model by deriving each country's offer curve from its production-possibility curve and indifference curves.

By assuming that the two commodities were produced with two productive factors using constant-returns-to-scale production technology, Stolper and Samuelson were able to link changes in commodity prices to changes in factor prices, thus completing a simple general equilibrium model of international trade. Samuelson 1948, 1949 pointed out that free trade in such a model could achieve complete factor-price equalization, while in 1955 Rybczynski demonstrated the link between changes in the endowments of the two factors and changes in the outputs of the two goods under constant returns and identical technology in both countries.

With Rybczynski's contribution, it also became easy to demonstrate the Heckscher-Ohlin relationship between relative factor endowments in two countries, relative factor intensities involved in producing the two goods, and the pattern of trade between the two countries.

Samuelson 1953–54 had earlier pointed out the duality relationship between the change in the supply of a factor and changes in the outputs of the goods (with commodity prices held constant) and the change in the price of a product and changes in the prices of the factors (with factor endowments held fixed).

In my comments I wish to make two general points about the two-good, two-factor, two-country model. First, the model has been enormously successfully not only in gaining insights into the effects of international trade and the factors influencing this trade but in better understanding domestic economic activity. Secondly, however, until relatively recent years, there has been an undue reluctance by trade economists to provide further structure to the model by introducing additional assumptions when analyzing various issues of concern to scholars and policymakers alike. Because of this reluctance, trade theory has come to be regarded by many policy officials (and even by economists in other fields) as irrelevant for dealing with many policy issues. The trade field also has lagged behind other fields of economics in terms of using modern empirical methods in testing various hypotheses. I should hasten to add, as is apparent from their subsequent work, that Stolper and Samuelson had nothing to do with this hesitancy to provide further structure to the model. The responsibility rests with those of us who followed after their pioneering analysis.

The great benefits that have flowed from the 2x2x2 model are apparent when one considers what was being said about the consequences of trade on factor prices or the effects of factor accumulations on outputs prior to the development of the model. As Stolper and Samuelson point out in their paper, most economists thought that all factors of production would gain in real welfare terms through the move from (say) autarky to free trade, although the more careful analyzers admitted the possibility that some large factor could lose absolutely. Similarly, while I have not seen a survey of economic thinking prior to Rybczynski's paper concerning output changes in response to an increase on the supply of some non-specific major productive factor, I think that most economists believed that outputs of all goods would generally increase. Demonstrating in the simple model that price and factor increases raise one of the factor's real returns or output of one of the goods by a magnified amount and lower the return of the other factor or output of the other good has had an important effect in making economists more cautious in discussing the benefits of trade.

We trade economists have, however, been too hesitant in adding assumptions to the model. A good example is the way we have treated the trade policy implications of the Stolper-Samuelson theorem. Even though the authors pointed out that the theorem still holds if there are many products and two-factors, they were only prepared to conclude that "there is a grain of truth in the pauper labor type argument for protection." Their reason is that no clear conclusions can be drawn when there are three or more productive factors, and they are reluctant to lump all factors into two broad groups.

As Magee 1980 has pointed out, one strong piece of evidence against the implications of the Stolper-Samuelson theorem is that labor and capital in a particular industry almost always either both support or oppose protectionist policies. Since groups tend to behave according to their economic self-interests, one would expect labor and capital to take opposite trade policy positions according to the Stolper-Samuelson theorem. It is now generally agreed that the specific-factors model, whose modern formulation is due to Jones 1971 and Samuelson 1971 (who felt the need to escape from "the straight-jacket of the box diagram" (p. 366)), is more appropriate than the 2x2x2 Heckscher-Ohlin model for explaining short-run trade-policy behavior. In the version of this model that can be regarded as a short-term form of the Hecksher-Ohlin model, labor is mobile but capital is sector-specific in the short-run. In the sector in which the price of the product has fallen, perhaps because of increased import competition, the real return to capital in the industry declines, while the real return to labor rises in terms of the industry's output but declines in terms of all other goods. A knowledge of taste patterns is needed to predict the actual change in labor's real income position.

I (1984) developed a simple model that eliminates this ambiguity by including another feature of the short-run, namely, sector-specific skills and thus labor rents. If workers move to another industry, they must accept lower wages until they acquire the special skills gained over time by working in the industry. Consequently, there is a range in which wages will fall by the same percentage as the price of the product, and labor will not move because its earnings in other industries would be even lower. Since real wages in the sector with the price decline remain unchanged in terms of this product and fall in terms of all other products, both labor and capital in this industry unambiguously lose. The opposite holds in the other industries.

The specific-factors model is currently very popular because it seems much better suited for understanding the short-run effects of changes in product prices as well as in factor supplies than the traditional model. But it took twenty years before trade economists were willing to modify the Heckscher-Ohlin model in this manner and focus on short-run policy and empirical issues.

The manner in which higher dimensional issues have been handled for the Stolper-Samuelson and Rybczynski theorems also illustrates the reluctance of trade economists to add further structure to their models in order to come up with more definite results. There have been imaginative efforts to extend these two theorems beyond the two-good, two-factor case by such writers as Chipman 1969, Kemp and Wegge 1969, Jones and Scheinkman 1977, and Ethier 1984, but with little success. In teaching students about these propositions in a multi-good, multi-factor framework, we generally give the results that Ethier (1984) presents in his *Handbook* chapter on higher dimensionality, namely, that a rise in any single commodity price (factor supplies being held constant) will cause the real reward of some factor to increase and the real reward of some other factor to fall. Similarly, an increase in the endowment of a nonspecific factor (product prices being held constant) causes a more than proportional increase in some output and fall in the output of some other good.

It is little wonder that there has been so little empirical research on the Stolper-Samuelson and Rybczynski theorems when our propositions on these theorems are so weak when we go beyond the 2x2 case. Yet important public policy issues are related to these propositions. For example, it is maintained by some that the price pressures due to more intense import competition have been the main reason why the real wages of unskilled and semi-skilled workers have risen so little in the past decade or so. However, labor economists rather than trade economists have done most of the empirical analysis of this issue. Similarly, there is considerable interest in many countries concerning the output effects of significant increases in the number of immigrant workers.

It would seem from casual observation that changes in product prices and factor endowments are not as indeterminate as the standard model implies. One reason is that productive factors and sector outputs adjust at different rates. As the specific-factors model postulates, it is reasonable to assume that labor adjusts faster than the capital stock. If this notion is applied, for example, to a two-factor, three-good model in which there is an increase in the supply of one of the factor and in which prices are held constant, the pattern of output changes for the three goods is not indeterminate in the move to a new equilibrium, as the standard model with perfect mobility for both factors implies. It seems to me that there are many other realistic assumptions we could introduce to reduce significantly the indeterminacy in our current models at higher levels of dimensionality. We trade economists have been so insistent on keeping our assumptions to a bare minimum that our models are not very useful in providing guidance on many research topics of interest and on major public policy issues.

Still another example of this practice is the manner in which we present and test the Heckscher-Ohlin model. We typically assume identical, constant returns-to-scale technology in all countries, identical homothetic tastes among all consumers in the world, equalization of all factor prices in all countries, the immobility of productive factors internationally but perfect mobility within countries, and perfect competition in product and factor markets. Since direct observation indicates the invalidity of most of these assumptions, it should hardly be surprising that the results are poor when we test a strict version of this model. In contrast, when a weaker version that emphasizes the relationship between factor endowments and patterns of trade is tested, the results are very good.

While it was important to isolate theoretically the implications of relative factor endowments by assuming away other possible influences on trade, we should now, in my view, devote more attention to building models more consistent with economic realities. Ignoring transportation costs and thus concluding that trade can lead to factor-price equalization is a particularly bad modelling approach, in my view. Technology is also clearly not identical across countries. Seeking for systematic ways it differs among countries and modelling these may help narrow the gap between our theory and empirical results. While some work is being done on the effects of increasing returns on trade, more research along these lines is needed. Recognizing and modelling the important role played by direct foreign investment in shaping trading patterns is another promising approach. The objective should be to improve our understanding of the relative importance of the various factors that can influence trading patterns for different countries at different times.

I should note that most of the so-called new trade theorists are much more willing to loosen the various assumptions that limit the relevancy of traditional trade theorists. Of course, the main assumption they have dropped is perfect competition. But in doing so, they have also prepared, for example, to drop the general equilibrium approach of traditional trade theorists and to make strong assumptions about technology at the firm level. While one may not agree with the appropriateness of some of these assumptions, they do illustrate the greater theoretical flexibility of these economists, a flexibility that has, I think, led to important contributions to our understanding of international trade. Traditional trade economists should be more willing to demonstrate similar flexibility in their modelling.

References

Baldwin, Robert E. 1984. "Rent-Seeking and Trade Policy: An Industry Approach," *Weltwirtschaftliches Archiv* 120:662–677.

Chipman, John S. 1969. "Factor Price Equalization and the Stolper-Samuelson Theorem," *International Economic Review* 10:399–406.

Edgeworth, P.T. 1925. *Papers Relating to Political Economy, II.* London: Macmillan.

Ethier, Wilfred J. 1984. "Higher Dimensional Issues in Trade Theory," in Ronald W. Jones and Peter B. Kenen (eds.), *Handbook of International Economics*, Vol. I. Amsterdam: North Holland.

Jones, Ronald W. 1971. "A Three Factor Model in Theory, Trade and History," in Jagdish Bhagwati et al. (eds.), *Trade, Balance of Payments, and Growth: Essays in Honor of Charles P. Kindleberger.* Amsterdam: North Holland.

Jones, Ronald W. and Jose Scheinkman. 1977. "The Relevance of the Two-Sector Production Model in Trade Theory," *Journal of Political Economy* 85:909–935.

Kemp, Murray C. and Leon F. Wegge. 1969. "On the Relation Between Commodity Prices and Factor Rewards," *International Economic Review* 10:407–413.

Leontief, Wassily W. 1933. "The Use of Indifference Curves in the Analysis of Foreign Trade," *Quarterly Journal of Economics* 47:493–503.

Magee, Stephen P. 1980. "Three Simple Tests of the Stolper-Samuelson Theorem," in Peter Oppenheimer (ed.), *Issues in International Economics.* London: Oriel Press.

Marshall, Alfred. 1924. *Money, Credit and Commerce.* New York: Macmillan.

Pareto, V. 1971. *Manuel of Political Economy.* Translated by Ann S. Schwier, edited by Ann S. Schwier and Alfred Page. New York: A.M. Kelley.

Pareto, V. 1919. *Manuale di Economia Politica.* Milan: Piccola Biblioteca.

Rybczynski, P.T. 1955. "Factor Endowment and Relative Commodity Prices," *Economica* 22:336–341.

Samuelson, Paul A. 1948. "International Trade and the Equalization of Factor Prices," *Economic Journal* 58:163–184.

Samuelson, Paul A. 1949. "International Factor Price Equalization Once Again," *Economic Journal* 59:181–197.

Samuelson, Paul A. 1953. "Prices of Factors and Goods in General Equilibrium," *Review of Economic Studies* 21:1–20.

Samuelson, Paul A. 1971. "Ohlin Was Right." *Swedish Journal of Economics* 73:365–384.

CHAPTER 22

STOLPER-SAMUELSON AND THE STRUCTURE OF PRODUCTION

Ulrich Kohli

The Stolper-Samuelson Theorem, and its dual, the Rybczynski Theorem, are among the neatest results of economic theory. There are not many examples in all of the fields of economics of such elegant and powerful propositions. The Stolper-Samuelson Theorem is now fifty years old, and it is a time for celebration for trade economists, production theorists and general equilibrium analysts alike.

The Stolper-Samuelson Theorem was already thirty years old when I first heard about it; this was in 1971 when, as a student at Queen's University, I took my first course in international trade theory from Steven Kaliski. Although I was a late comer, the Theorem has greatly influenced my thinking and has had a lasting effect on my research.

In what follows, I would like to develop briefly three themes. First, the Theorem has stimulated my attempts to estimate well defined production structures with aggregate data and to quantify important theoretical concepts. From my training at the University of British Columbia, I inherited the urge to conduct empirical work within a tight theoretical framework: here was a golden opportunity to narrow somewhat the gap between theory and applied work that is so patent in much of international economics. Second, I have attempted to address some of the questions raised by Stolper and Samuelson in the context of larger and less restrictive models. Third, I have studied new production structures which yield similar results.

The Heckscher-Ohlin-Samuelson (HOS) Production Structure

A difficulty one encounters when trying to estimate a 2x2 HOS production model with aggregate data is that information on the allocation of
resources between industries is not readily available. Although data on
the quantities of factor services used by any major industry in the
traditional sense do exist, the concept of industries—or sectors—used in
the HOS model is much broader than the conventional definition since
it encompasses direct as well as indirect factor requirements.

Fortunately, this difficulty can be side-stepped if one uses a joint
cost function to describe the aggregate technology. Hall 1973 has shown
that under nonjointness (in input quantities) the aggregate cost function
becomes additive. By appropriately choosing the functional form, this
restriction can be imposed and/or tested. Using a Generalized-Linear
Generalized-Leontief (GLGL) function, and allowing for two outputs
(investment goods and consumption goods) and two inputs (labor and
capital), I have estimated such a model for the United States (Kohli
1981). Although the constraints implied by nonjointness were rejected,
it was nonetheless interesting to compute the elasticities implied by the
model since no such estimates were available in the literature. Table 1
reports an updated set of Stolper-Samuelson and Rybczynski elasticities.
One notices the familiar sign pattern suggested by the Stolper-Samuelson
and Rybczynski Theorems. Moreover, it is apparent that the investment
good industry is relatively labor intensive and that the consumption good
industry is relatively capital intensive.

The GNP Function Model

While the Stolper-Samuelson and Rybczynski Theorems are truly
remarkable, it is clear that they crucially depend on the form of the
technology, and particularly the assumption that both outputs are
produced by separate production functions. Neither theorem holds under
joint production. I would argue that, in the aggregate, nonjointness is
unlikely to be satisfied. Moreover, in applied analysis, it is mostly a hin-

Table 1. Heckscher-Ohlin-Samuelson Model, Generalized-Leontief Generalized-Linear Functional Form: Stolper-Samuelson and Rybczynski Elasticity Estimates for Selected Years

	1948	1960	1970	1980	1987

Price elasticities of inverse factor demands (Stolper-Samuelson elasticities):

$$e_{ji} \equiv \partial \ln[w_j(p_I, p_C)]/\partial \ln(p_i)$$

	1948	1960	1970	1980	1987
εLI	2.055	1.925	1.861	1.841	1.864
εLC	-1.055	-0.925	-0.861	-0.841	-0.864
εKI	-1.711	-1.896	-2.021	-2.066	-2.015
εKC	2.711	2.896	3.021	3.066	3.015

Quantity elasticities of output supplies (Rybczynski elasticities):

$$e_{ij} \equiv \partial \ln[y_i(p_I, p_C, x_L, x_K)]/\partial \ln(x_j)$$

	1948	1960	1970	1980	1987
εIL	4.538	4.291	4.332	4.522	4.830
εIK	-3.538	-3.291	-3.332	-3.522	-3.830
εCL	-0.711	-0.696	-0.674	-0.654	-0.641
εCK	1.711	1.696	1.674	1.654	1.641

The subscripts are defined as follows: I: investment goods; C: consumption goods; L: labor; K: capital

Source: Kohli 1991a, p. 148.

drance; I have therefore abandoned this assumption in much of my empirical work.

Allowing for joint production makes it easy to move on to higher dimensions, without being constrained by the necessity for the number of inputs to be equal to the number of outputs. Moreover, duality theory makes it possible to build models that are well suited to one's specific needs. Thus, one has total freedom in chosing which quantities and which prices are to be exogenous, and which ones are to be determined by the model. A particularly useful way to describe the aggregate technology is with the help of a GNP function that treats good prices and factor endowments as given (see Samuelson 1953–54, Diewert 1974, Kohli 1978, and Woodland 1982).

I report in Table 2 recent estimates of Stolper-Samuelson and Rybczynski effects based on a GNP function model where output is disaggregated between consumption, investment, exports and imports, and where two domestic factors are considered: labor and capital. Naturally this production structure departs significantly from the HOS model in some key respects, and the Stolper-Samuelson and Rybczynski Theorems do not hold under these conditions. Nevertheless, many of the same concerns do arise. It is apparent from these estimates that an improvement in the terms of trade predominantly benefits labor, and that the return to capital is mostly tributary to the price of consumption goods. It is also noteworthy that, although negative elasticities are not necessary in this model, there are several instances of negative price and quantity effects.

Stolper-Samuelson- and Rybczynski-like Results in Two by Two Production Models

Even though it might be most appropriate to view the aggregate technology as joint, it is of undeniable interest to investigate, and to test, particular production structures. Specific assumptions, such as separability and nonjointness, yield some very powerful results. Moreover, if they do hold, the corresponding restrictions ought to be taken into account in econometric work in order to get statistically more efficient estimates.

Table 2. 2x4 GNP Function Translog Functional Form Stolper-
Samuelson and Rybczynski Elasticity Estimates for Selected Years

	1948	1960	1970	1980	1987

Price elasticities of inverse factor demands (Stolper-Samuelson elasticities): $e_{ji} \equiv \partial \ln [w_j (p_M, p_X, p_I, p_c, x_L, x_K)] / \partial \ln (p_i)$

	1948	1960	1970	1980	1987
εLM	-0.142	-0.153	-0.170	-0.210	-0.220
εLX	0.139	0.122	0.134	0.175	0.149
εLI	0.615	0.594	0.572	0.569	0.563
εLC	0.388	0.437	0.464	0.466	0.508
εKM	0.075	0.067	0.051	0.012	0.000
εKX	-0.017	-0.036	-0.025	0.015	-0.010
εKI	-0.143	-0.174	-0.201	-0.205	-0.207
εKC	1.085	1.144	1.175	1.178	1.217

Quantity elasticities of output supplies (Rybczynski elasticities):
$e_{ij} \equiv \partial \ln [y_i (p_M, p_X, p_I, p_c, x_L, x_K)] / \partial \ln (x_j)$

	1948	1960	1970	1980	1987
εML	1.848	1.507	1.280	1.043	1.000
εMK	-0.848	-0.507	-0.280	-0.043	-0.000
εXL	1.118	1.296	1.159	0.941	1.054
εXK	-0.118	-0.296	-0.159	0.059	-0.054
εIL	1.255	1.291	1.345	1.355	1.380
εIK	-0.255	-0.291	-0.345	-0.355	-0.380
εCL	0.291	0.333	0.351	0.353	0.358
εCK	0.709	0.667	0.649	0.647	0.642

The subscripts are defined as follows: M: imports; X: exports; I: investment goods; C:
consumption goods; L: labor; K: capital

Source: Kohli 1991a, p.

The Stolper-Samuelson and Rybczynski Theorems reflect the structure of production underlying the HOS model. Since restricting the way inputs are combined into outputs can lead to such spectacular results, one wonders if other constraints on the form of the technology can yield similar sets of propositions. The Stolper-Samuelson Theorem has fueled my interest in alternative production structures, starting with some work I did on nonjoint production (Kohli 1983). I present here some results that can be viewed as the mirror image of the Stolper-Samuelson and Rybczynski Theorems, though viewed from different angles; this discussion is based on Kohli 1991b.

Throughout this section, I consider two outputs and two inputs, and I assume that the production possibilities set is a convex cone. It may be that both goods are produced jointly by both factors in which case little more can be said about the structure of production. Or perhaps one can be more precise about what takes place inside the black box of technology, about the exact way inputs are combined into outputs.

One example of a simple production structure is imbedded in the HOS model where there are two production functions, one for each output, where inputs are mobile between the two industries, and where the total supply of factors must be allocated between them. This form of production is said to be *nonjoint in input quantities*. As we all know, of course, Stolper and Samuelson 1941 demonstrated half a century ago that an increase in the price of one good, for given factor endowments, raises the rental price of the factor used relatively intensively in the production of that good, and lowers the rental price of the other good. Furthermore, as shown by Rybczynski 1955, an increase in the endowment of one factor, for given output prices, leads to an increase in the production of the good that uses that factor relatively intensively, and lowers the output of the other good. These results are summarized in the first part of Table 3 where I assume that industry 1 is relatively factor-1 intensive. It is noteworthy that the output price change does impact on the output mix, but that the change in factor endowments has no effect on factor rental prices (see Samuelson 1949). This reveals a basic asymmetry between the two Theorems.

Next, I consider the case where the two goods are again produced by separate production functions, but where the two inputs can

**Table 3. Stolper-Samuelson- and Rybczynski-like Results
in 2x2 Production Models**

i) nonjointness in input quantities (HOS model)

$$y_i = f^i(x_{1i}, x_{2i}) \ , \qquad i = 1, 2$$
$$x_j = \Sigma x_{ji} \ , \qquad j = 1, 2$$
$$p_i = c^i(w_1, w_2) \ , \qquad i = 1, 2$$

$\hat{p}_1 > 0 \ \rightarrow \qquad \hat{w}_1 > 0, \ \hat{w}_2 < 0 \ ; \qquad \hat{y}_1 > 0, \ \hat{y}_2 < 0$

$\hat{x}_1 > 0 \ \rightarrow \qquad \hat{y}_1 > 0, \ \hat{y}_2 < 0 \ ; \qquad \hat{w}_1 = 0, \ \hat{w}_2 = 0$

ii) nonjointness in input prices (public inputs model)

$$p_i = c^i(w_{1i}, w_{2i}) \ , \qquad i = 1, 2$$
$$w_j = \Sigma w_{ji} \ , \qquad j = 1, 2$$
$$y_i = f^i(x_1, x_2) \ , \qquad i = 1, 2$$

$\hat{y}_1 > 0 \ \rightarrow \qquad \hat{x}_1 > 0, \ \hat{x}_2 < 0 \ ; \qquad \hat{p}_1 > 0, \ \hat{p}_2 < 0$

$\hat{w}_1 > 0 \ \rightarrow \qquad \hat{p}_1 > 0, \ \hat{p}_2 < 0 \ ; \qquad \hat{x}_1 = 0, \ \hat{x}_2 = 0$

iii) nonjointness in output prices (production stations model)

$$w_j = r^j(p_{1j}, p_{2j}) \ , \qquad j = 1, 2$$
$$p_i = \Sigma p_{ij} \ , \qquad i = 1, 2$$
$$x_j = h^j(y_1, y_2) \ , \qquad j = 1, 2$$

$\hat{x}_1 > 0 \ \rightarrow \qquad \hat{y}_1 > 0, \ \hat{y}_2 < 0 \ ; \qquad \hat{w}_1 < 0, \ \hat{w}_2 > 0$

$\hat{p}_1 > 0 \ \rightarrow \qquad \hat{w}_1 > 0, \ \hat{w}_2 < 0 \ ; \qquad \hat{y}_1 = 0, \ \hat{y}_2 = 0$

Table 3 cont.,

iv) nonjointness in output quantities

$$x_j = h^j(j_{1j}, y_{2j}) \ , \qquad j = 1, 2$$
$$y_i = \Sigma y_{ij} \ , \qquad\qquad i = 1, 2$$
$$w_j = r^j(p_1, p_2) \ , \qquad j = 1, 2$$

$$\hat{w}_1 > 0 \ \rightarrow \qquad \hat{p}_1 > 0, \ \hat{p}_2 < 0 \ ; \qquad \hat{x}_1 < 0, \ \hat{x}_2 > 0$$
$$\hat{y}_1 > 0 \ \rightarrow \qquad \hat{x}_1 > 0, \ \hat{x}_2 < 0 \ ; \qquad \hat{p}_1 = 0, \ \hat{p}_2 = 0$$

A "hat" ($\hat{\ }$) denotes a relative change; the p's are output prices, the y's are output quantities, the x's are input quantities, and the w's are input prices. See the text for the assumptions concerning relative factor and output intensities.

be used by both industries at the same time. Thus, the inputs have public properties. However, they need not be public goods in the conventional sense of the word: it simply might be that the inputs can perform different tasks, or work for different employers, during the same time period. In such a situation, the total payment to each factor is equal to the sum of the revenues drawn from the two industries. This type of production structure is said to be *nonjoint in input prices*, and it yields the following results (Kohli 1985). First, an increase in the production of one good, for given factor rental prices, increases the requirements of the input in which the good is relatively price intensive, and it lowers the requirements of the other input. Second, an increase in the rental price of one factor, for given output quantities, raises the cost of the good that is relatively price intensive in this factor, and it reduces the price of the other good. These results are summarized in the second part of Table 3 (I assume that industry 1 is relatively factor-1 price intensive), and they can be viewed as the mirror image of the Stolper-Samuelson and Rybczynski Theorems. It is noteworthy that an increase in the production of one good, for given factor rental prices, raises its price and lowers the price of the other good; an increase in the price of one input, on the other hand, has no effect on input requirements.

Consider now an economy where production of each output requires it to be treated by each factor separately. Each factor, in turn, is involved in processing both types of outputs. More specifically, each output must go through two production stations. Each station is manned by a single factor with its own transformation (or factor requirements) function. Since each output must transit through each station, both inputs must handle identical quantities of outputs. This form of production structure is called *nonjoint in output prices*. The price of each output can be written as the sum of the value added at each phase of production, i.e., at each production station. Under these conditions, the following results hold (Kohli 1991b). First, an increase in the endowment of one factor, for given output prices, leads to an increase in the production of the output in which the factor is relatively price intensive, and to a fall in the production of the other output. Second, an increase in the price of an output, for given factor endowments, raises the rental price of the factor that is relatively price intensive in that output, and it decreases the rental price of the other factor. These results are summarized in the third part of Table 3; I have assumed that factor 1 is relatively output-1 price intensive. Again observe the symmetry with the Stolper-Samuelson and Rybczynski Theorems. It is noteworthy that the change in factor endowments does affect factor rental prices, but that the change in output prices has no impact on the output mix.

Consider finally an economy where each factor again has its own production possibilities frontier, but assume now that each factor is fully capable on its own of producing both outputs. The total supply of each output is obtained by summing up the quantities produced by the individual production units. The output mix of each factor depends on relative output prices. This production structure is said to be *nonjoint in output quantities*. The following two propositions can easily be demonstrated (Kohli 1991b). First, an increase in the rental price of one factor, for given output levels, raises the price of the good that is produced relatively intensively by that factor, and it lowers the price of the other good. Second, an increase in the output of one good, for given factor rental prices, leads to an increase in the requirements of the factor that produces that good relatively intensively, and it lowers the requirements of the other factor. These results, which once again are merely reflections of the Stolper-Samuelson and Rybczynski Theorems, are summarized in the last part of Table 3 where I assume that factor-1 produces good-1 relatively intensively. Once again one can note the asymmetry between the two theorems in that a change in rental prices does affect factor requirements, while a change in the output mix has no impact on output prices.

Concluding Comments

The Stolper-Samuelson and Rybczynski Theorems can be viewed as the outcome of the inversion of the Hessian of a joint cost function, a Hessian that contains a null block on its diagonal as a consequence of the nonjoint production assumption. It is this null block that is ultimately responsible for the fact that the effects of a change in output prices on the distribution of income are fully captured by the inverse of a two-by-two positive matrix. This is, of course, precisely what produces the familiar sign pattern. The purpose of this paper was not only to show that similar results hold for alternative production structures that contain zero restrictions of their own, but also to draw attention to the mere existence of these other structures.

Some readers might find that several of the production structures described in this paper are somewhat far-fetched. Yet, the fact that we are all used to think in terms of HOS-like production models should not hide the fact that this production structure too is rather unlikely. Indeed, it is difficult to imagine an industry that produces a single output, and where all factors are used for one job exclusively. In just about every industry, outputs are many, and all factors, labor most prominently, are assigned to a variety of tasks. Moreover, outputs must often transit through several production stations, and identical outputs may be produced by quite different production units. Thus, the aggregate technology probably contains elements of all the production structures discussed here. Which one, if any, comes closest to describing the aggregate technology is mostly an empirical question. It may be that each form of nonjointness is an important ingredient in a much more complex production structure. In particular, one may note that one form of nonjointness at one level does not preclude another form of nonjointness at a different level. Thus, in the HOS model, the national technologies are nonjoint in input quantities, but the world technology is nonjoint in output quantities.

References

Diewert, W. Erwin. 1974. "Applications of Duality Theory," in M.D. Intriligator and D.A. Kendrick (eds.) *Frontiers of Quantitative Economics*, Vol. 2. Amsterdam: North-Holland.

Hall, Robert E. 1973. "The Specification of Technology with Several Kinds of Output," *Journal of Political Economy* 81:878–892.

Kohli, Ulrich. 1978. "A Gross National Product Function and the Derived Demand for Imports and Supply of Exports," *Canadian Journal of Economics* 11:167–182.

Kohli, Ulrich. 1981. "Nonjointness and Factor Intensity in U.S. Production," *International Economic Review* 22:3–18.

Kohli, Ulrich. 1983. "Nonjoint Technologies," *Review of Economic Studies* 50:209–219.

Kohli, Ulrich. 1985. "Technology and Public Goods," *Journal of Public Economics* 26:379–400.

Kohli, Ulrich. 1991a. *Technology, Duality, and Foreign Trade: The GNP Function Approach to Modeling Imports and Exports*. Ann Arbor: University of Michigan Press.

Kohli, Ulrich. 1991b. "Stolper-Samuelson- and Rybczynski-like Results in Two by Two Production Models," unpublished manuscript, University of Colorado, Boulder.

Rybczynski, T.M. 1955. "Factor Endowments and Relative Commodity Prices," *Economica* 22:336–341.

Samuelson, Paul A. 1949. "International Factor Price Equalisation Once Again," *Economic Journal* 59:181–197.

Samuelson, Paul A. 1953-54. "Prices of Factors and Goods in General Equilibrium," *Review of Economic Studies* 21:1–20.

Stolper, Wolfgang F. and Paul A. Samuelson. 1941. "Protection and Real Wages," *Review of Economic Studies* 9:58–73.

Woodland, Alan D. 1982. *International Trade and Resource Allocation*. Amsterdam: North-Holland.

CHAPTER 23

COMMERCE AND COALITIONS: AN EXTENSION OF THE STOLPER-SAMUELSON THEOREM TO POLITICAL CONFLICTS SINCE 1850

Ronald Rogowski

From at least 1966, when Barrington Moore, Jr., published *Social Origins of Dictatorship and Democracy*, students of comparative politics and history have returned repeatedly to a central puzzle raised by that work: why, in nineteenth-century Europe and America, did labor, capital, and land ally in almost every possible permutation, with such different long-term implications for social and institutional development?

In Britain, to simplify drastically, labor and capital joined increasingly after 1832 in support of free trade and an expanded franchise. In the renewed protectionist agitation of the 1870s, and yet more clearly in the struggle over budgetary power and the House of Lords in 1910–11, British landowners were decisively defeated.

In Germany, the pattern was startlingly different: from 1878 until at least 1912, industrialists and landowners had remained locked in the protectionist and profoundly anti-democratic "marriage of iron and rye." (Rosenberg 1943, Gerschenkron 1943) Workers increasingly supported Europe's largest Socialist party, which were also free trade's only ardent supporters. (Similar protectionist coalitions of land and capital emerged in Spain, Italy, Sweden, and much of Eastern Europe.)

The United States presented an inverted image of Britain: labor and capital united to support the highly protectionist Republicans, who ruled almost uninterruptedly from 1861 to 1932. Agriculture, which alone supported free trade, was the mainstay of radical Populism. (Sundquist 1983) (Similarly dominant protectionist coalitions of labor and capital appeared elsewhere, notably in Canada, Australia, and New Zealand. In much of Latin America, labor and capital supported protection but were defeated by free-trading landowners.)

In pre-1914 Russia, workers and landowners alike supported free trade and resented equally the extreme "infant industries" protectionism of the post-1887 Czarist regime (Robinson 1932); those resentments contributed in no small part to a visceral anti-capitalism that rapidly pervaded both urban workers and rural society generally.

The longer-term effects of these alternative coalitions seemed plain: where labor and capital coalesced, whether in support of free trade or of protectionism, liberal democracy thrived. Fascism, by contrast, appeared subsequently only (but by no means always) where land and capital had united in this period to exclude labor; Socialism, chiefly where farmers and urban workers had allied historically in opposition to capital.[1]

Far less clear were the causes of these various coalitions. Moore 1967 had advanced a rich but confusing model, which contained more variables than cases. Subsequent work in the Moore tradition, notably by Gourevitch 1977, 1986, was historically rich but narrative rather than explanatory.

Completely untrained as an economist, I happened to read the Stolper-Samuelson paper as part of a weekly study group on trade issues in which I was involved. At the same time, and for independent reasons, my mind was focused on the problem of nineteenth-century social coalitions. A week or two later, two curious and (it appears) previously unnoticed aspects of the problem occurred to me. (1) In each of the nineteenth-century cases, owners of locally abundant factors appeared to have coalesced against owners of locally scarce factors. (2) In each case, conflicts over trade fundamentally, perhaps chiefly, determined the lines of political cleavage and coalition: owners of scarce factors advocated protection; owners of abundant factors embraced free trade.

Britain in the 1870s was the world's most advanced economy: plainly, capital was abundant. It was also among the most densely populated regions on the planet: labor abundant, land scarce. Labor and capital had coalesced to support free trade against protectionist landowners. Germany in the same period had scarcely begun its economic

---

[1] "Red-Green" coalitions analogous to the Russian one, but far more benign, appeared subsequently in Sweden and Norway.

development, but it too was very densely populated by world standards: capital and land scarce, labor abundant. Protectionist capital and land had united against free-trading labor. The United States was abundant in land and scarce in labor; and, despite rapid development, it remained (as revealed by its exports) scarce also in capital. Free-trading land had opposed protectionist labor and capital. (Nineteenth-century Canada, Australia, New Zealand, and Latin America duplicated the U.S. pattern, both of endowments and of political conflict.)

In Russia, land was undoubtedly abundant, capital scarce.[2] Paradoxically, however, labor was also abundant. Lewis 1954 and Myint 1958, 1980 have elaborated how, in general, the vestiges of slavery, serfdom, or the primitive village can foster such pervasive underemployment that labor may be moved into manufacturing or export-production at virtually zero marginal cost to other forms of output and thus may appear (in Lewis's memorable phrase) as "unlimited" in supply.[3] Russia's own modernizing leaders of the period (Vishnegradksy, Witte, Stolypin) complained repeatedly about the vast rural underemployment that they saw as a legacy of serfdom (abolished only in 1861)[4]; and the very rapidity of Russia's economic growth, both between 1890 and 1914 and again after 1930, suggested the existence of great reserves of underemployed labor. Again the abundant factors, in this case land and

---

[2] As late as 1896, according to Mulhall 1896, pp. 22 and 381, Russia's labor-land ratio remained 44 persons per square kilometer of land in crops or pasture, in the same neighborhood as that of the United States (49/km.2) or Canada (36) and far below the contemporary figures for England (277) or France (105).

[3] Hopkins 1973, pp. 128 and 321 seq. has provided a concrete illustration of the phenomenon: exports from (thinly populated) West Africa, including chiefly palm oil, peanuts, and cocoa, roughly tripled between 1850 and 1900 and quadrupled again by 1914, with minimal investment of external capital and no evident loss of productivity in other branches.

[4] "The masses of the people remain in enforced idleness. A considerable part of our peasant population does not know to what to put its hand in winter." Witte, quoted in Kochan 1966 p. 11.

labor, supported free trade and opposed the protectionism of scarce capital.

A second important uniformity seemed to emerge. Everywhere, the free-trading owners of abundant factors were strengthened politically in the nineteenth century. Labor and capital in England, labor in Germany, farmers in the United States, landowners and workers in Russia, challenged the existing political order and advocated fundamental change. Often, their agitation was turned back (notably in Germany and the United States); but everywhere, it seemed, owners of abundant factors gained ground, while owners of scarce factors were thrown onto the defensive.

Stolper and Samuelson seemed to me to shed considerable light on these patterns. When tariffs decline, they argued, owners of abundant factors gain; absent any redistribution of the gains of trade, owners of scarce factors lose. Yet it is elementary that transportation costs work as an exogenously imposed tariff; and, if we know anything about the economic history of the nineteenth century, it is that transportation costs declined precipitously. According to Woytinsky and Woytinsky 1955, p. 310, railroads lowered the costs of overland transport by between 85 and 95 percent. Steam, improved ship design, and new canals lowered the average rates for seaborne carriage by more than 50 per cent between 1850 and 1890. Moreover, as Kindleberger 1951 first argued, the *Pax Brittanica* substantially lowered the risks of international shipping between 1815 and 1914. Despite some tariff increases after 1870, every nation experienced during the later nineteenth century the equivalent of a drastic *decrease* of tariffs.

It follows (*if* we can generalize the Stolper-Samuelson result to a world of more than two factors and two products) that, in each country, owners of abundant factors will have gained in this period and owners of scarce factors will have lost—or, at the very least, will have felt a profound threat of loss. It can hardly surprise us if the latter group mobilized in support of offsetting tariff protection, or that the former attempted to expand trade and to translate their trade-induced windfall into increased political power.[5] (See Rosenberg 1967, pp. 47-51, and also Gerschenkron 1943, pp. 33-36.) While victory in such struggles seems to have depended on local structure or accident, the fronts are accurately predicted by local scarcity or abundance of factors.

Once this point is seen, it can be extended to situations that Moore did not consider. The collapse of world trade in the Depression of the 1930s, although occasioned by political rather than technological factors,[6] had the same effect as a massive rise in tariffs: locally scarce factors gained to some degree, locally abundant ones suffered. In politics, owners of scarce factors claimed back some share of power and owners of abundant factors were thrown onto the defensive.

In Latin America, the long-suppressed protectionist coalition of scarce labor and scarce capital came to power in many countries, pushing aside the long-dominant landowners. In central, southern, and eastern Europe and in Asia, Fascist, highly protectionist coalitions of owners of scarce land and scarce capital crushed formerly assertive (and, usually, free-trading) working-class movements.[7] America's perennially scarce factor, labor, broke with owners of capital (long since grown abundant) and benefited under the New Deal as never before or since. In the Soviet Union, Stalin's state capitalist regime crushed both land and labor.

---

[5] One must avoid the delusion that all movements of the "oppressed" reflected increasing immiseration. As Rosenberg has emphasized, German Socialism grew precisely with the increasing wealth and leisure, rather than the poverty, of German workers; and, rightly linking their prosperity to cheap food and growing manufactures of labor-intensive exports, they almost unanimously endorsed free trade.

[6] From the standpoint of most countries, the decline in external markets was exogenous: i.e., neither caused by, nor remediable through, domestic policy.

[7] Italian, Spanish, and Japanese Fascism fit this mold; so does the "white terror" of Chiang Kai-Shek in China and of the French colonial regime in Vietnam; also the more traditional authoritarianisms of Bulgaria, Greece, Hungary, Lithuania, Poland, Portugal, Rumania, and Yugoslavia. German Fascism is clearly of a different order.

I advanced some suggestions along these lines in 1987 in a paper read at the annual meeting of the American Political Science Association and in an article in the *American Political Science Review*; in 1989, they appeared more fully in a book called *Commerce and Coalitions* (Rogowski 1981, 1989). With surprising rapidity, they have gained acceptance as the most plausible account to date (in, admittedly, weak competition) of the patterns that Moore and others had identified. Three main lines of criticism, however, deserve mention as bearing not only on my argument but on the original Stolper-Samuelson theorem and some of its subsequent elaboration in economics.

Hall and Nelson 1991 argue forcefully that the theorem can have no validity beyond the case of two factors and two products: hence "Rogowski's...interesting historical discussions [are] without theoretical foundation." Reaching in precisely the opposite direction, Midford 1991 contends that at least a ten-factor model (as employed by Leamer) would have been needed to reach sustainable results.

Taking a third and perhaps more significant tack, Robert Keohane and Helen Milner, along with some others, have questioned my adoption of the Stolper-Samuelson assumption of unlimited domestic mobility of factors. Citing Magee's 1980 classic study, they suggest that over the short to medium run a specific-factors model of the kind advanced by Mussa 1974 offers greater empirical accuracy: workers and owners divide along sectoral, not factoral, lines, according to whether the human and physical capital employed in their particular line is specific or not.

I suppose that my answer to all of these objections, however philistine it may be, is chiefly empirical. (I trust that, in obedience to comparative advantage, economists will offer more elegantly theoretical responses.) I claim, so far without refutation, to have observed an extremely surprising and regularity: that, for roughly a century after 1860 (and indeed more widely, as I argue in my book), locally abundant factors have virtually without exception opposed locally scarce ones and have done so with particular intensity during periods of rapid expansion or contraction of international trade. Indeed, much of the warrant for that claim antedates anything I wrote; hence I can hardly have jiggered the evidence to support it. Those who find fault with the trade-based (and, ultimately, Stolper-Samuelson-based) effort to explain the empirical regularity owe us some equally plausible alternative account—which, needless to say, I eagerly await.

In the meantime, I feel obliged to state my self-evident debt to the pioneering paper that this occasion celebrates. Economists are only too aware that, like Japan, they show a persistent and sometimes annoying trade surplus with neighboring domains. Still, it must be rare that a product manufactured a half-century earlier can enjoy so substantial and appreciative a reception abroad.

References

Gerschenkron, Alexander. 1943. *Bread and Democracy in Germany*. Berkeley and Los Angeles: University of California Press.

Gourevitch, Peter. 1977. "International Trade, Domestic Coalitions, and Liberty: Comparative Responses to the Crisis of 1873–1896," *Journal of Interdisciplinary History* 8:281–313.

Gourevitch, Peter. 1986. *Politics in Hard Times: Comparative Reponses to International Economic Crises*. Ithaca, NY: Cornell University Press.

Hall, Keith, and Douglas Nelson. 1991. "The Structure of Simple Political-Economy Models: The Endogenous Policy Approach," unpublished manuscript.

Hopkins, Anthony. 1973. *An Economic History of West Africa*. New York: Columbia University Press.

Kindleberger, Charles. 1951. "Group Behavior and International Trade," *Journal Political Economy* 59:30–46.

Kochan, Lionel. 1966. *Russia in Revolution, 1890–1918*. London: Weidenfeld and Nicolson.

Lewis, Arthur. 1954. "Economic Development with Unlimited Supplies of Labour," *Manchester School of Economic and Social Studies* 22:139–91.

Magee, Stephen. 1980. "Three Simple Tests of the Stolper-Samuelson Theorem," in Peter Oppenheimer (ed.) *Issues in International Economics*. London: Oriel Press.

Midford, Paul. 1991. "International Trade Theory and Rogowski's Model of Domestic Political Cleavages," unpublished manuscript.

Moore, Barrington, Jr. 1966. *Social Origins of Dictatorship and Democracy*. Boston: Beacon Press.

Mulhall, Michael. 1896. *Industries and Wealth of Nations*. New York and London: Longmans, Green, and Co.

Mussa, Michael. 1974. "Tariffs and the Distribution of Income: The Importance of Factor Specificity, Substitutability, and Intensity in the Short and Long Run," *Journal of Political Economy* 82:1191–1203.

Myint, Hla. 1958. "The 'Classical Theory' of International Trade and the Underdeveloped Countries," *Economic Journal* 68:317–37, and *The Economics of the Developing Countries*, 5th ed. London: Hutchinson, 1980.

Robinson, Geroid. 1932. *Rural Russia under the Old Regime*. Berkeley and Los Angeles: University of California Press.

Rogowski, Ronald. 1981. "Political Cleavages and Changing Exposure to Trade," *American Political Science Review* 81:1121–37.

Rogowski, Ronald. 1989. *Commerce and Coalitions: How Trade Affects Domestic Political Alignments*. Princeton: Princeton University Press.

Rosenberg, Hans. 1943. "Political and Social Consequences of the Great Depression in Europe, 1873–1896," *Economic History Review* 13:58–73.

Rosenberg, Hans. 1967. *Grosse Depression und Bismarckzeit*. Berlin: Walter de Gruyter.

Sundquist, James L. 1983. *Dynamics of the Party System: Alignment and Realignment of Political Parties in the United States*, rev. ed. Washington, D.C.: The Brookings Institution.

Woytinsky, W. S. and E. S. Woytinsky. 1955. *World Commerce and Governments: Trends and Outlook*. New York: Twentieth Century Fund, p. 310.

Part V

Further Reflections

CHAPTER 24

AFTERTHOUGHTS ON "PROTECTION AND REAL WAGES"

Wolfgang F. Stolper

The idea for this symposium came as a complete surprise to me. It touched me greatly, and I am grateful for this thoughtfulness of my colleagues who are also my friends. Indeed, I consider myself fortunate. Having such teachers and friends as Schumpeter, Haberler, and Samuelson, being at Harvard at a time of lively turmoil in economics, then being sheltered at Swarthmore with students like Ronald Jones, Janet Goodrich Chapman and her husband, John, and Beth Ringo who is now Jim Tobin's wife, finally to be welcomed at Michigan: who could ask for more?

I have been from the first quite aware that the durability of "Protection and Real Wages" owes immensely to the collaboration of Paul. In Paul's article which he wrote on the occasion of my 75th birthday—surely the best birthday present anyone could wish—he seriously underplayed his contribution to our joint effort. To start with, he recognized before me what it was I had stumbled upon. The application of the Edgeworth box was entirely his idea. It was also he who suggested the literature search; though, if memory serves we shared this task. And if memory serves, we literally dictated alternate sentences of the final version to patient Marion, a version incidentally which the *American Economic Review* rejected as brilliant but irrelevant and suggested we rewrite it from page 2 on!

The, in economics unusual, longevity of the contribution is, I believe, due to the fact that it really has nothing to do with protection or real wages, but that it is possibly the first clean analysis of the relation of the prices of goods and of factors. I simply took over the idea, previously developed by Paul in his "Gains from Trade," that as the result of protection, the relative prices of goods would change. It was Lloyd Metzler who then worked out the specific effects of protection. To me it is also an important finding that, under the assumptions made, an infinity of factor proportions in individual industries is compatible with fixed factor proportions in the economy as a whole. In other words, the interesting and important problems were on the micro, not the macro level.

The longevity of the theorem seems to me due to the fact that it allowed further development with varying assumptions, yet still fundamentally the same technique and insights, that it was possible to arrive at definite conclusions essentially by the same reasoning as that employed in the original article.

My own work continued for a while along location theoretical lines, while Paul proceeded with his important work on factor price equalization and the generalization of the relation of factor and goods prices. In location problems, it turned out that factor price equalization was possible only in a subjective sense, and only with specialization, and that it was not really possible to maintain the assumption of linear homogeneous production functions. But I left these problems because they got to be too difficult for me. Ethier has worked along these lines.

Rybczynski has extended the work to growth, and I believe that it is not too difficult to extend it to changes in production functions, at least as long as you stick to simple changes and comparative statics.

I cannot possibly mention all the significant extensions of the model. They prove to me, however, that the original model had greater generality than I, for one, saw at the time.

The awareness of these results helped me enormously in my work in Nigeria—which on a practical level was, of course, quite useless. It was not only that my African friends respected me because they knew it. It helped in dealing with such essentially useless propositions as that less developed countries should go in for labor intensive industrialization, or its opposite to decide in favor of large scale techniques because they would produce larger savings, a proposition assumed rather than proved, all attempts to get around using profitability.

The question has naturally posed itself: has the Stolper-Samuelson theorem exhausted the possibilities for further development? Perhaps it has, because it really is a strict equilibrium analysis, its dynamics are confined to comparative statics, and the future is likely to belong to evolutionary problems. But even evolutionary considerations do not throw results of equilibrium theory away but integrate them into a wider framework. So there may be some hope yet.

So I find myself quite happy at the thought that at least once in my life I have been allowed to make a fundamental contribution to theory, a contribution which possibly insures me a footnote in a chapter on Paul in a history of economic thought. But having tasted blood once, I now also know what a truly fundamental contribution is, of which Paul has made so many that there cannot be one Samuelson theorem.

I used to say to myself that I would give my left eye if I could succeed in making another lucky throw. Well, I have lost the use of my left eye, but to no avail. So there is an admixture of sadness in the recognition of my serious limitations as a theorist—which in my system of values has the highest rank, provided, of course, that it deals with real life problems—which has induced me to change first to the study of growth problems under a communist sign, and then to the analysis of less developed countries growth problems to see, if possible, with my own eyes how a modern economy arises, and now to the history of thought and the enormous pleasure which the collaboration with Paul Samuelson has given me.

And this has quite gently been reconciled to being just a footnote.

References

Samuelson, Paul A. 1939. "The Gains from International Trade," *Canadian Journal of Economics and Political Science* 5:195-205.

CHAPTER 25

TRIBUTE TO WOLFGANG STOLPER ON THE FIFTIETH ANNIVERSARY OF THE STOLPER-SAMUELSON THEOREM

Paul A. Samuelson

The British mathematician G.H. Hardy summed it all up: "Well, I've lived a good life. I have collaborated with Littlewood and Ramanujan." Indeed the Trinity mathematician reported that the one romance in his career had been his discovery of Ramanujan's genius in a letter that came over the transom, his success in bringing Ramanujan to England before his early death, and their historic collaborations.

Well, I have had a good life. I've collaborated with Stolper—and Solow and Modigliani. None was more fun than our exciting progress after Wolfgang brought to me his seminal insight. "How can Haberler and Taussig be right about the necessary harm to a versatile factor like labor from America's tariff, when the Ohlin theory entails that free trade must hurt the factor of production that is scarce relative to land?"

The rest is history. So fundamental a point is obvious in retrospect but the earth moves when first you hear it. "You have something here. Work it out, Wolfie," I said. He worked it out. But suddenly, like all breakthroughs, the analysis opened up a new continent. The newly married Stolpers and Samuelsons lived on the same Ware Street in earshot of Harvard Yard's bells. We talked about new puzzles when we met, and each week a surprising lemma knocked on our brains' door. Was it really possible and mandatory that free trade raise the American land/labor ratio in both food and clothing!

I have always insisted I was the midwife, helping to deliver Wolfie's brain child. Eventually Stolper turned stubborn, saying he could not conscientiously take sole credit for what had involved a fruitful collaboration. I yielded gracefully, understanding that I was the junior partner but that the senior partner might never feel completely comfortable under any other arrangement.

Never was there a more harmonious conception. Gilbert & Sullivan were never like that: always, Sullivan felt as if he were slumming in the lucrative partnership with the vulgar Gilbert. Even the great physics pair of Yang and Lee ceased to be friends in consequence of priority disputes over the Violation of Parity Conservation. I shall digress to speak of an equally famous *contretemps*. When James Watson's *Double Helix* was first written, the Harvard University Press turned it down under its original title of *Lucky Jim*. Harvard feared a law suit from Sir William Bragg, the head of Cambridge's lab. I was one of many who read the MS. "Publish it," I advised the Head of the Press. "Publish it as it is. If a man will write such an account of cutthroat competition in science, let it get embalmed in the record." Harvard was chicken and missed publishing this single greatest chronicle of a fundamental science breakthrough. But it was not Bragg who was offended. Actually Bragg wrote a Foreword for the book. And most people have thought that it was the dead Rosalind Franklin whose accomplishment was most slighted by the account of how Crick and Watson one-sidedly benefited from her crystallography x-rays of helix structures. But at the time I mentioned to Watson the view that it was Crick who might take major offence. "I don't know whether the discovery was a 50-50 affair, but to me the account conveys a suggestion of Watson 55 and Crick 45." And for years Crick and Watson were not on their old intimate terms.

Stolper-Samuelson has always been quite a different matter. Naturally, therefore, I was puzzled some 25 years ago when Katherine Ruggles Gerrish, Assistant Editor of the *Quarterly Journal of Economics* and an old friend, called me on the telephone to ask where "my polemic with Stolper" had been published. "I know of no quarrel with Wolfgang. How does your *QJE* author describe it?" I laughed when she read out to me the words: "According to the Stolper-Samuelson argument...." Our English language has its delicious ambiguities. If anything, the junior partner has been accorded too much credit. This is in accordance with Robert K. Merton's "Matthew Effect" in the history of science: *To him who hath shall be given.*

In Europe there is a custom of celebrating 50th anniversaries of a scholar's Ph.D. thesis. Preserved in the record is what Niels Bohr said to Wolfgang Pauli and to Paul Ehrenfest on his way to attend the 50th Birthday Party for Hendrik Lorentz's doctoral dissertation. By coincidence 1991 is the birthday of my own 1941 Harvard thesis, *Foundations of Economic Analysis*. How nice to be given two birthdays in one year. It reminds me of what my mother-in-law said after 18 people visited her in the nursing home on her ninetieth birthday, "That is the way it should be every day!"

As yet, I have not seen the texts of any of today's lectures. I can guess that some will speak of Stolper-Samuelson theorems, Rybczynski's Lemmas, duals to the S-S theorem, and such like things. And that is as it should be. But now that I focus anew on our 1941 opus, I perceive that what it represents is something that quite transcends mere international trade. Our 1941 child registers the quantum jump from Marshallian *partial* equilibrium in economic theory to *general* equilibrium. The whole post-1941 literature is different in a way that can be appreciated only by those of us who were brought up in the *Ancien Régime*.

But, you will say, Léon Walras discovered general equilibrium in 1874–78; and Vilfredo Pareto perfected it in 1894–98. Yes, yes. And I will add, Bertil Ohlin's 1933 trade classic has a general equilibrium appendix that goes beyond Walras, Cassel, Schlesinger, and Wald. (Bertil Ohlin's 1924 Swedish thesis has just been translated by Harry Flam and June Flanders for the MIT Press—along with an unabridged version of Eli Heckscher's classic 1919 article. Already by age 25 Ohlin had done all that brought him a deserved Nobel Prize in 1978.)

What put general equilibrium, so to speak, on the undergraduate classroom map after 1941, was bringing it out of the realm of $n+m$ equations and $n+m$ unknowns to the beautifully simple diagrams of land and labor, cloth and corn. Finally a *manageable* general equilibrium system—one with texture and content—was at hand. Never again could an Ohlin not understand his own system, as when he denied the logical possibility of perfect factor-price equalization!

Stolper-Samuelson was an overture to a symphony that has never stopped playing. But always there are overtures to overtures. On this occasion I must call attention to an unconscious influence that was operating on us back in 1940—operating at least on Paul if not on Wolfgang.

Wolfgang has recalled that my late wife Marion Crawford did on occasion serve as ammanuensis for our joint draftings. Indeed there must exist somewhere in Marion's clear handwriting drafts of my *Foundations* and early mathematical articles, some of them dictated while driving at cruising speed between Cambridge and Berlin, Wisconsin. As readers of the 1941 paper will remember, we were conscientious in seeking earlier anticipations of our analytical relationships between the production-possibility frontier and the Stolper-Samuelson production box diagram. The pickings were very slim indeed. We could find many imprecise statements about the optimality of free trade, but only in one unrelated Benham item were we able to find crisp remarks about relative factor intensities of corn and cloth and mandatory induced shifts in their terms of trade under relative-output shifts.

Today I could add a 1941 classic by Joan Robinson on rising supply prices. But at the time of gestation of Stolper-Samuelson that had not yet appeared. Nor had Viner's 1950 similar supplement to his classic 1931 piece on cost curves and supply curves by then appeared, even though he tells us that by 1938 he had glimpsed the essential point. (In 1991 I have retrieved a 1930 Harrod reference that would be relevant and which for three decades I had lost track of. And of course no one before Lionel Robbin's 1950 rediscovery in his files of Abba Lerner's lost 1933 term paper on factor price equalization even had any notion of that classic's existence.)

But we did twice refer conscientiously to Marion Crawford's celebrated term paper on the Australian case for a tariff on labor intensive imports, calculated to raise that land-rich country's population and real wage rate. I can refer interested readers to my 1989 post mortem on that Crawford Australian breakthrough. I ought to add now what I failed to stress earlier, that my unconscious mind must certainly have benefited enormously in 1940–41 from knowledge of Marion's 1939 *QJE* findings.

This is the occasion to do justice to that influence. The point goes beyond Stolper-Samuelson and international trade theory. Indeed, as I shall explain, I have come to realize that the whole antiquarians' literature on the essence of classical economics à la Smith, Ricardo, and Mill is long overdue for a drastic revision of interpretation.

Let me explain what Marion Crawford Samuelson made explicit. Ricardo did not contemplate a labor-only model such as he and we use in simplest comparative-advantage paradigms. At a minimum, the classicals and the 1925 Australian economists had to deal with a labor and land model, in which an agricultural good used both inputs while by contrast a second good required only labor. I am going to skip over the complication of time-phasing, which Ricardo in some moods admitted did require qualifying his labor-theory-of-value. His grudging admissions in this regard, despite Stigler's defenses of Ricardo as having a "93% labor theory of value" are grossly inadequate: but that is another story and not one treated in the Australian or Stolper-Samuelson literature.

Without the Stolper-Samuelson box diagram, Marion Crawford could handle the p-p frontier of the 2 good case where one of them utilized only labor. That could have provided Joan Robinson, Jacob Viner, Roy Harrod, Stolper-Samuelson, and indeed Heckscher-Ohlin with a manageable analysis for unambiguous classroom explication. (Remark: The Haberler-Jones-Samuelson 1974 model of labor as the only transferable input intersects with the S-S box-diagram in this singular Crawford instance.)

I doubt not that my midwifery benefited from this unconscious source. What surprises me was my dullness in not benefiting more explicitly from this same source. Commentators on Smith-Ricardo-Mill—such as Mark Blaug, Samuel Hollander, and scores of lesser lights—will at the end of the day realize that their Sraffian expositions of natural prices set by horizontal classical *ss* curves can never validly characterize the classical system as it was actually debated in discussion of the Corn Laws. Malthus and Ricardo were far better in their applied economics than they were in their articulated notions about value and distribution theory. Their gap behind Mill and Jevons and Walras was less than they would have been proud to insist upon. Alas, David Ricardo never really understood "his" own system.

The hour is late. Enough of dry substance. Let me conclude with some fond remembrances of Wolfgang Stolper.

When I came to Harvard, he exuded unconscious charm. European charm. Stolper was Cambridge's link with Schumpeter's days at Bonn. I can recall Wolfgang's indignation when his complaint about the warmth of the Mosel wine served him was met by a waiter who returned with an ice cube plunked down into the wine glass. If Wolfgang had asked that same waiter to cut his Cuban cigar, no doubt he would have returned with two equal pieces.

In 1938 Wolfgang returned from summer vacation with his beautiful Swiss bride. To European eyes America presented many strange features worth commenting on. In his gentle way, Wolfgang suggested: "Vögi, ride with the punches. It's really not polite to comment on each perceived difference." Therefore, when the terrible Hurricane of 1938 hit us, Vögi observed urbanely: "Your usual autumnal disturbance, I presume?" Once Vögi Stolper complained to me that Wolfgang had bought a cigarette rolling machine. "What's so terrible about that?" I asked. She had to explain: "But Wolfie doesn't smoke cigarettes."

Wolfgang knew Hitler's evil and was an interventionist in the pre-war debate with isolationists. The late Dick Slitor, who was to have an important career at the U.S. Treasury, shared a tutorial suite in Leverett House with Stolper. I was friend to both of them and they argued incessantly. To patch things up, I took Stolper aside and said: "Look, don't argue every point with Dick. Let's face it. He's a character, a strange guy." "What do you mean he's a strange guy?" "Well, just as an example, Dick Slitor shampoos his hair every day." "What's the matter with that?" Wolfie asked. "I shampoo my hair every day."

I am sure Wolfgang thought me a crude American. For one thing I never knew the proper temperature at which a Riesling should be served. For another I once revealed an unbelievable gaucherie. In those days we had short-lasting 78 classical records. You were always having to get up to change the record. Then semi-automatic record changers arrived on the market. You had to get up only half as often. I made the mistake of revealing to Wolfgang that I saved effort by listening to Beethoven's Sixth Symphony in the following order: First, the first movement. Then the third movement. Then the fourth movement. And then the second movement. He was incredulous. Just as incredulous as Bob Bishop used to be when I did not lay down the bridge hand seven steps ahead of its inevitable ending. I realized that Wolfgang Amadeus and Wolfgang Friedrich must use a different half of the brain than I did when listening to music.

Wolfie also had a better grasp on theology than I did. Yes, my calculus was better than his but on the exact meaning of Grace his was the more expert opinion. One thing we did have in common was our affection and respect for Schumpeter. Mine was great, his was unbounded.

That was a magic pre-war world in the Harvard Yard. And no one is preserved more perfectly in the amber of my affectionate memory than Wolfie Stolper—friend and collaborator.

Part VI

Annotated Bibliography

CHAPTER 26

SELECTED ANNOTATED BIBLIOGRAPHY ON THE STOLPER-SAMUELSON THEOREM

Sundari R. Baru
Alan V. Deardorff
Robert M. Stern

Acheson, K. 1970. "The Aggregation of Heterogeneous Capital Goods and Various Trade Theorems," *Journal of Political Economy* 78:565–71. — Finds that the Stolper-Samuelson conclusions hold when more than one input is classified as 'capital'.

Anderson, K. 1980. "The Political Market for Government Assistance to Australian Manufacturing Industries," *Economic Record* 56:132–44. — Applies the emerging neo-classical economic theory of politics to the question of why some industries receive more government assistance than others.

Baldwin, R. E. 1984. "Rent-Seeking and Trade Policy—An Industry Approach," *Weltwirtschaftliches Archiv* 120, 4:662–77. — Points out that the long-run Heckscher-Ohlin model is not appropriate for analyzing the protectionism that characterizes recent trade policy, and hence the Stolper-Samuelson theorem is not very useful in understanding the nature of today's protectionist pressures.

Balkhy, H. O. and G. C. Hufbauer. 1974. "Cost of Redistributing Income through Trade Policy," *Weltwirtschaftliches Archiv* 110:38–54. — Studies the linkage between potential real-income loss and distributional changes due to tariff protection.

Batra, R. N. and F. R. Casas. 1974. "Traded and Non-Traded Intermediate Inputs, Real Wages, and Resource Allocation," *Canadian Journal of Economics* 7:225–39. — Examines the conditions under which the Stolper-Samuelson Theorem remains valid when protection is granted by a combination of output and input tariffs.

Batra, R. N. and F. R. Casas. 1976. "Synthesis of Heckscher-Ohlin and Neoclassical Models of International Trade," *Journal of International Economics* 6:21–38. — Synthesizes the neo-classical and Heckscher-Ohlin models into a 2-sector, 3-factor model and shows that a modified version of the Stolper-Samuelson Theorem applies to this model.

Bechler, E. 1977. "International Trade and Capital Movements—Reexamination," *Hitotsubashi Journal of Economics* 18:25–30. — Employs the Stolper-Samuelson theorem in a modified Mundell (1957) and Kojima (1975) model.

Benham, F. 1935. "Taxation and the Relative Prices of Factors of Production," *Economica* N.S. 2:198–203. — Examines the 2x2 model for the effects of taxes on factor prices. Comes quite close to the Stolper Samuelson Theorem without actually getting it.

Berglas, E. and A. Razin. 1974. "Protection and Real Profits," *Canadian Journal of Economics* 7:655–64. — Introduces profits into the Stolper-Samuelson analysis in cases with one and more than one mobile factor.

Bhagwati, J. 1959. "Protection, Real Wages, and Real Incomes," *Economic Journal* 69:733–48. — Identifies and elaborates three versions of the Stolper-Samuelson Theorem, ranging from a restrictive version comparing autarky and free trade, to a general version involving changes in protection, and delineates the assumptions needed for each. (Reprinted above).

Bhagwati, J. 1964. "The Pure Theory of International Trade—A Survey," *Economic Journal* 74:1–84. — Includes the Stolper-Samuelson analysis in a survey of the pure theory of international trade.

Bhagwati, J. N. and R. A. Brecher. 1980. "National Welfare in an Open Economy in the Presence of Foreign-Owned Factors of Production," *Journal of International Economics* 10:103–15. — Applies the Stolper-Samuelson Theorem in analyzing the effect of trade policy changes on national welfare with foreign-owned factors.

Bhagwati, J. and H. G. Johnson. 1961. "A Generalized Theory of the Effects of Tariffs on the Terms of Trade," *Oxford Economic Papers* 13:167–95. — Generalizes and extends the results of Lerner and Metzler for effects of tariffs on the terms of trade, and also includes effects on domestic prices that are needed for the Stolper-Samuelson result.

Borsook, I. 1987. "Earnings, Ability and International Trade," *Journal of International Economics* 22:281–95. — Incorporates Stolper-Samuelson results in a 2-factor, 2-good model of human capital and international trade with a continuum of abilities.

Brecher, R. A. 1974. "Minimum Wage Rates and Pure Theory of International Trade," *Quarterly Journal of Economics* 88:98–116. — Uses the Stolper-Samuelson and other theorems to extend the standard Heckscher-Ohlin analysis of an open economy to a case in which there is unemployed labor with and without a minimum wage constraint.

Brecher, R. A. and J. N. Bhagwati. 1981. "Foreign Ownership and the Theory of Trade and Welfare," *Journal of Political Economy* 89:497–511. — Uses the Stolper-Samuelson Theorem in considering national and aggregate welfare differences in a model with fixed supplies of foreign inputs in the home country.

Brock, W. A. and S. P. Magee. 1978. "Economics of Special Interest Politics—Case of Tariff," *American Economic Review* 68:246–50. — Mentions the Stolper-Samuelson Theorem as one of 2 polar models in international trade theory predicting the redistributive effects of tariffs, the other model being the specific factors model.

Burgess, D. F. 1976a. "Income Distributional Effects of Processing Incentives—General Equilibrium Analysis," *Canadian Journal of Economics* 9:595–612. — Tests the Stolper-Samuelson Theorem in a situation with 2 goods and 2 intermediate inputs (primary products) by analyzing the effect of various processing incentives on real wages.

Burgess, D. F. 1976b. "Tariffs and Income Distribution—Some Empirical Evidence for U.S," *Journal of Political Economy* 84:17–45. — Tests the income distributional effects of tariffs in post-war U.S. with and without factor substitutability between the services and goods sectors in the context of the Stolper-Samuelson Theorem.

Burgess, D. F. 1980a. "Protection, Real Wages, and the NeoClassical Ambiguity with Interindustry Flows," *Journal of Political Economy* 88:783–802. — Mentions (in a footnote) that the introduction of inter-industry flows into the Heckscher-Ohlin model leaves intact the basic distributive effects obtained by the Stolper-Samuelson Theorem.

Burgess, D. F. 1980b. "Protection, Real Wages, Real Incomes, and Foreign Ownership," *Canadian Journal of Economics* 13:594–614. — Analyzes the effect of tariff protection of secondary industries in a small open economy on real wages.

Burney, N. A. 1988. "The Rybczynski and Stolper-Samuelson Theorems in the Presence of External Economies of Scale," *Australian Economic Papers* 27:111–27. — Shows that the Stolper-

Samuelson theorem holds at the Marshallian-stable equilibrium in an economy with external economies of scale.

Butlin, M. W. 1983. "Protection, Real Wages, Real Incomes, and Foreign Ownership—A Comment," (Note) *Canadian Journal of Economics* 16:350–56. — Critiques Burgess (CJE, 1980) and shows that a form of the Stolper-Samuelson Theorem must hold once there is more than one non-traded primary input that is used in the production of both commodities.

Cassing, J. 1977. "International Trade in Presence of Pure Monopoly in the Non Traded Good Sector," *Economic Journal* 87:523–32. — Shows that the existence of product market imperfections (e.g., monopoly in the Non-Traded Goods sector) can modify the Stolper-Samuelson result especially in terms of the Non-Traded Good.

Cassing, J. 1978. "Transport Costs in International Trade Theory—Comparison with the Analysis of Non-Traded Goods," *Quarterly Journal of Economics* 92:535–50. — Shows that the Stolper-Samuelson result is not straightforward in a Heckscher-Ohlin-Samuelson model with transportation costs.

Cassing, J. 1981. "On the Relationship between Commodity Price Changes and Factor Owners' Real Positions," *Journal of Political Economy* 89:593–95. — Extends the friends-enemies version of the Stolper-Samuelson Theorem by showing that, while a factor need not have a natural friend (whose price raises its factor price more than proportionately), every factor can nonetheless improve its real position with some price increase, taking into account its expenditure pattern.

Cassing, J., T. J. Mckeown, and J. Ochs. 1986. "The Political Economy of the Tariff Cycle," *American Political Science Review* 80:843–62. — Shows that differences in regional interests create protectionist coalitions that are formed during business cycle troughs and broken in business cycle peaks, contrasting with the labor vs. capital tariff politics suggested by the Stolper-Samuelson Theorem.

Cassing, J. H. and P. G. Warr. 1985. "The Distributional Impact of a Resource Boom," *Journal of International Economics* 18:301-19. — Applies the Stolper-Samuelson Theorem in a simple general equilibrium trade model aimed at exposing the effects of a resource 'boom' on factor owners' real incomes.

Chacholiades, M. 1985. "Circulating Capital in the Theory of International Trade," *Southern Economic Journal* 52:1-22. — Shows that the Stolper-Samuelson theorem is not always valid in a modified Leontief-Sraffa general equilibrium model.

Chang, W. W. 1979. "Some Theorems of Trade and General Equilibrium with Many Goods and Factors," *Econometrica* 47:709-26. — Derives explicit expressions for the Stolper-Samuelson matrix and uses the properties of the matrix to obtain further results.

Chang, W. W. 1981. "Production Externalities, Variable Returns to Scale, and the Theory of Trade," *International Economic Review* 22:511-25. — Shows that if returns to scale are non-decreasing in each industry and inter-industrial externalities are non-positive, then the Stolper-Samuelson theorem can be restored at a stable equilibrium.

Chang, W., W. Ethier, and M. C. Kemp. 1980. "The Theorems of International Trade with Joint Production," *Journal of International Economics* 10:377-94. — Analyzes the properties of the Stolper-Samuelson (and other) Theorems with composite goods.

Chipman, J. S. 1966. "A Survey of the Theory of International Trade," *Econometrica* 34:18–76. — Includes the Stolper-Samuelson Theorem in a survey of the modern theory of international trade.

Chipman, J. S. 1969. "Factor Price Equalization and the Stolper-Samuelson Theorem," *International Economic Review* 10:399–406. — Develops criteria for the strong and weak forms and global and local versions of the Stolper-Samuelson Theorem to hold for (equal) numbers of n goods and factors. It turns out to be difficult to prove any version of the Theorem with n > 3. (Reprinted above).

Chipman, J. S. 1978. "Towards the Construction of an Optimal Aggregate Model of International Trade: West Germany, 1963–1975," *Annals of Economic and Social Measurement*, 6:535–54. — Maps international prices to domestic prices using German data, and produces a "generalized Stolper-Samuelson mapping."

Chung, J. W. 1980. "Trade Liberalization and Factor Prices—Application to the United States Manufacturing Sector," *Journal of Policy Modeling* 2:101–20. — Examines the empirical evidence relating to the Stolper-Samuelson Theorem for 16 major U.S. manufacturing industries and confirms the weak version of the Stolper-Samuelson theorem.

Clark, D. P. 1980. "The Protection of Unskilled Labor in the United States Manufacturing Industries—Further Evidence," *Journal of Political Economy* 88:1249–54. — Points to the Stolper-Samuelson Theorem (in a footnote) as demonstrating that free trade will reduce the real income of the scarce factor of production.

Danielsen, A. L. 1974. "Positive Theory of Trade and Compensation," *Southern Economic Journal* 40:571-78. — Examines conditions under which trade and compensation policies will be adopted by a nation, given that the Stolper-Samuelson Theorem holds.

Deardorff, A. V. 1984. "An Exposition and Exploration of Krueger's Trade Model," *Canadian Journal of Economics* 17:731-46. — Examines the effect of a non-prohibitive tariff in a three-factor model of a small developing country with and without capital mobility. Includes implications for the Stolper-Samuelson Theorem.

Deardorff, A. V. 1986. "FIRless FIRwoes—How Preferences can Interfere with the Theorems of International Trade," *Journal of International Economics* 20:131-42. — Presents a 2-factor, 2-country, 4-good trade model that produces results equivalent to a 2-good model with Factor Intensity Reversals and discusses the implications for the Stolper-Samuelson and other theorems of trade.

Dixit, A. K. and V. Norman. 1980. *Theory of International Trade.* Welwyn, Hertford: Nisbet, and Cambridge, U.K.: Cambridge University Press. — Derives the Stolper-Samuelson Theorem in the form of Stolper-Samuelson "derivatives" using a dual approach to the Heckscher-Ohlin model. Focuses more on nominal than on real factor prices.

Egawa, I. 1978. "Some Remarks on the Stolper-Samuelson and Rybczynski Theorems," *Journal of International Economics* 8:525-36. — Develops criteria that provide a necessary and sufficient condition for a weak form of the Stolper-Samuelson Theorem to hold even where the number of primary factors is greater than the number of products.

Ethier, W. J. 1972. "Nontraded Goods and the Heckscher-Ohlin Model," *International Economic Review* 13:132–47. — Develops versions of the Stolper-Samuelson Theorem and other trade theorems when there are non-traded goods.

Ethier, W. J. 1974. "Some of the Theorems of International Trade with Many Goods and Factors," *Journal of International Economics* 4:199–206. — Derives weak but general versions of the Stolper-Samuelson and Rybczynski Theorems for the case of equal numbers of goods and factors. (Reprinted above).

Ethier, W. J. 1979. "The Theorems of International Trade in Time-Phased Economies," *Journal of International Economics* 9:225–38. — Develops versions of the Stolper-Samuelson Theorem and other trade theorems that apply when capital is treated explicitly.

Ethier, W. J. 1981. "A Reply to Professors Metcalfe and Steedman," *Journal of International Economics* 11:273–77. — This reply to Metcalfe and Steedman (*JIE*, 1981 2:267–72) also contains an additional version of the Stolper-Samuelson Theorem relevant to time-phased models.

Ethier, W. J. 1982a. "The General Role of Factor Intensity in the Theorems of International Trade," *Economic Letters* 10:337–42. — Derives general versions of the Stolper-Samuelson and Rybczynski Theorems with any numbers of goods and factors, in the form of correlation-like results. (Reprinted above).

Ethier, W. J. 1982b. "National and International Returns to Scale in the Modern Theory of International Trade," *American Economic Review* 72:389–405. — Develops versions of the Stolper-Samuelson Theorem and other trade theorems that apply when there are scale economies, monopolistic competition and differentiated producer goods.

Ethier, W. J. 1984a. "Higher Dimensional Issues in Trade Theory," in R. W. Jones and P. B. Kenen (eds.), *Handbook of International Economics*, Vol. 1. Amsterdam: North-Holland. — Examines the sensitivity to higher dimensions of the basic propositions of the modern theory of international trade and concludes that Stolper-Samuelson results apply to some factors or goods, but not necessarily to all.

Ethier, W. J. 1984b. "Protection and Real Incomes Once Again," *Quarterly Journal of Economics* 99:193–200. — Investigates the implications of tariff protection on real incomes under a policy of neutral distribution of tariff revenues.

Ethier, W. J. and M. C. Kemp. 1976. "A Note on Joint Production and the Theory of International Trade," in M. C. Kemp, *Three Topics in the Theory of International Trade*. Amsterdam: North-Holland, pp. 81–84. — Considers duality between Stolper-Samuelson-like and Rybczynski-like results valid even if the technology exhibits joint production.

Ethier, W. J. and L.E.O. Svensson. 1986. "The Theorems of International Trade with Factor Mobility," *Journal of International Economics* 20:21–42. — Develops versions of the Stolper-Samuelson Theorem and other trade theorems that apply when some factors are internationally mobile.

Findlay, R. 1959. "Economic Growth and the Distributive Shares," *Review of Economic Studies* 27:167–78. — Constructs a model based on Kaldor (1955–56) and Hicks (1932 & 1936) and discusses the determination of the secular change in distributive shares. Obtains the Stolper-Samuelson result in a diagrammatic representation of the model.

Findlay, R. 1974. "Relative Prices, Growth and Trade in a Simple Ricardian System," *Economica* 41:1–13. — Analyzes a Ricardo-Pasinetti model and finds that the Stolper-Samuelson results hold.

Findlay, R. and H. Kierzkowski. 1983. "International Trade and Human Capital—A Simple General Equilibrium Model," *Journal of Political Economy* 91:957–78. — Finds that the Stolper-Samuelson results hold in a 2-sector general equilibrium model of international trade that incorporates the formation of human capital.

Grossman, G. M. 1983. "Partially Mobile Capital—A General Approach to 2-sector Trade Theory," *Journal of International Economics* 15:1–17. — Develops the concept of partial factor mobility and discusses the implications for the theorems of international trade.

Grossman, G. M. and J. Levinsohn. 1989. "Import Competition and the Stock Market Return to Capital," *American Economic Review* 79:1065–87. — Develops a method for testing the responsiveness of returns to capital to variations in prices of import competing goods and other exogenous shocks and finds that the specific factors model captures reality more closely than the Stolper Samuelson Theorem for many U.S. industries.

Harris, R. 1981. "Trade and Depletable Resources: The Small Open Economy," *Canadian Journal of Economics* 14:649–64. — Investigates the implications for the Stolper-Samuelson Theorem (and the Rybczynski Theorem) when the 2-product/ 2-factor static trade model is extended to a dynamic context allowing for depletable resources.

Heckscher, E. 1919. "The Effect of Foreign Trade on the Distribution of Income," *Economic Tidskrift* 21:497–512. Translated into English by Professor and Mrs. Svend Laursen and reprinted in H. S. Ellis and L. A. Metzler (eds.), *Readings in the Theory of International Trade*. Homewood, IL: Richard D. Irwin, Inc. — Lays down what has come to be known as the Heckscher-Ohlin Theorem, and also makes loose statements of several of the model's main theorems. Makes statements that imply a relative version of the Stolper-Samuelson Theorem, but does not discuss real factor prices.

Helpman, E. and P. Krugman. 1985. "Welfare," in *Market Structure and Foreign Trade.* Cambridge: MIT Press, pp. 179–195. — Employs the Stolper-Samuelson analysis to determine the gains from trade in a 2x2x2 Increasing Returns to Scale model with sector-specific factors. (Based on Krugman 1981, *JPE* 89:959–73.)

Herberg, H., M. C. Kemp, and M. Tawada. 1982. "Further Implications of Variable Returns to Scale," *Journal of International Economics* 13:65–84. — Provides a more general description of the production side of the economy, also accounting for inter-industrial externalities, and reviews the effects on the Stolper-Samuelson results.

Hill, J. K. and J. A. Mendez. 1983. "Factor Mobility and the General Equilibrium Model of Production," *Journal of International Economics* 15:19–25. — Generalizes the 2-sector production model to accommodate any degree of factor mobility and shows that many elements of the Stolper-Samuelson Theorem generalize.

Inada, K. 1971. "The Production Coefficient Matrix and the Stolper-Samuelson Condition," *Econometrica* 39:219–40. — Studies necessary and/or sufficient conditions for the Stolper-Samuelson Theorem to hold in a generalized n-commodity, n-factor case.

Inkster, I. 1990. "Henry George Protectionism and the Welfare of the Working Class," *American Journal of Economics and Sociology* 49:375–84. — Discusses the impact of Henry George's views regarding protectionism on the present-day debates on protectionism, and argues that Henry George's belief in the market mechanism is not applicable in the contemporary world. Mentions the Stolper-Samuelson Theorem as a contribution to the arguments against protectionism as long as the losing factor is compensated.

Inoue, T. 1981. "A Generalization of the Samuelson Reciprocity Relation, the Stolper-Samuelson Theorem and the Rybczynski Theorem under Variable Returns to Scale," *Journal of International Economics* 11:79–98. — Demonstrates a generalization of the Stolper-Samuelson Theorem (and other theorems) under Variable Returns to Scale when n commodities and n productive factors exist.

Ishizawa, S. 1991. "Increasing Returns, Public Inputs and Transformation Curves," *Canadian Journal of Economics* 24:144–60. — Shows that when a public input is a 'friend' to both labor and capital, Marshallian stability holds if and only if the relative price version of the Stolper-Samuelson Theorem holds.

Johnson, H. G. 1969. "Standard Theory of Tariffs," *Canadian Journal of Economics* 2:333–52. — Discusses the effects of the introduction of tariffs in circumstances in which free trade would be Pareto-optimal from the world point of view.

Jones, R. W. 1965a. "Duality in International Trade: A Geometrical Note," *Canadian Journal of Economics and Political Science* 31:390–93. — Illustrates geometrically the duality between the Stolper-Samuelson and Rybczynski Theorems.

Jones, R. W. 1965b. "The Structure of Simple General Equilibrium Models," *Journal of Political Economy* 73:557–72. — Discusses the dual nature of the Stolper-Samuelson and Rybczynski Theorems. (Reprinted above).

Jones, R. W. 1968. "Variable Returns to Scale in General Equilibrium Theory," *International Economic Review* 9:261–72. — Discusses the fate of the Stolper-Samuelson Theorem when there exist external increasing returns to scale. The theorem fails if the commodity that is labor-intensive in the average (usual) sense is capital-intensive for marginal changes.

Jones, R. W. 1971. "A Three Factor Model in Theory, Trade, and History," in J. Bhagwati et al. (eds.), *Trade, Balance of Payments and Growth*. Amsterdam: North-Holland, pp. 3–21. — Analyzes a 2-good, 3-factor model where only two factors enter the production of any one commodity and shows that the magnification effect (the real return to the factor used intensively in a tariff-protected industry) is preserved for the specific factors, but not for the mobile factor.

Jones, R. W. 1972. "Activity Analysis and Real Incomes—Analogies with Production Models," *Journal of International Economics* 2:277–302. — Relates diverse topics in trade theory such as the transfer problem, Stolper-Samuelson Theorem and the Rybczynski Theorem.

Jones, R. W. 1983. "International Trade Theory," in E. C. Brown and R. M. Solow (eds.), *Paul Samuelson and Modern Economic Theory*. New York: McGraw-Hill, pp. 69–103. — Includes a discussion of the Stolper-Samuelson article and how it fits in with other Samuelson contributions to Heckscher-Ohlin theory.

Jones, R. W. 1985. "Relative Prices and Real Factor Rewards: A Reinterpretation," *Economic Letters* 19:47–49. — Re-interprets the Stolper-Samuelson result so as to generate a robust theorem in the n x n non-joint production context. (Reprinted above).

Jones, R. W. 1987. "Heckscher-Ohlin Trade Theory," In John Eatwell, M. Milgate and P. Newman (eds.), *The New Palgrave—A Dictionary of Economics*. New York: Stockton Press, pp. 619–27. — Discusses the four core propositions of Heckscher-Ohlin Theory.

Jones. R. W. 1993. "Reflections on the Stolper-Samuelson Theorem," in H. Herberg and N. V. Long (eds.), *Trade Welfare and Economic Policies: Essays in Honor of Murray C. Kemp.* Ann Arbor: University of Michigan Press, pp. 21-36. — Explores the robustness of the Stolper-Samuelson theorem in higher dimensions and in conditions of joint productions of outputs and inputs.

Jones, R. W. and H. Kierzkowski. 1986. "Neighborhood Production Structures with an Application to the Theory of International Trade," *Oxford Economic Papers* 38:59-76. — Develops an n x n model in which factors have limited access to produce commodities and each commodity only employs two different kinds of factors. The 2 x 2 version yields Stolper-Samuelson results.

Jones, R. W. and S. Marjit. 1985. "A Simple Production Model with Stolper-Samuelson Properties," *International Economic Review* 26:565-67. — Generalizes the Stolper-Samuelson results in the strong form in a model and reveals the close similarity between Stolper-Samuelson properties in an n x n setting and the behavior of factor returns in an (n+1) x n specific factors model.

Jones, R. W. and S. Marjit. 1991. "The Stolper-Samuelson Theorem, The Leamer Triangle, and the Produced Mobile Factor Structure," in Takayama, Ohyama, and Ohta (eds.), *Trade, Policy and International Adjustments.* New York: Academic Press, 95-107. — Illustrates a geometric device that shows when the Stolper-Samuelson Theorem will be satisfied.

Jones, R. W. and J. Scheinkman. 1977. "The Relevance of the Two-Sector Production Model in Trade Theory," *Journal of Political Economy* 85:909-35. — Generalizes the 2x2 model of a competitive economy and shows that the Stolper-Samuelson Theorem holds regardless of the number of factors and commodities, as long as there is no joint production. Also proves that if the number of factors equals the number of commodities, every factor has at least one natural enemy, and modifies the Stolper-Samuelson result so that not every factor can rely upon some commodity price rise to improve its real position. (Reprinted above).

Kemp, M. C. 1969. *The Pure Theory of International Trade and Investment*. Englewood Cliffs, N.J.: Prentice Hall. — Examines two ideal cases in the absence of constant returns to scale and develops conditions under which the Stolper-Samuelson conclusions hold in each of these cases.

Kemp, M. C. 1973. "Heterogeneous Capital Goods and Long-Run Stolper-Samuelson Theorems," *Australian Economic Papers* 12:253–60, and in *Three Topics in the Theory of International Trade: Distribution, Welfare, and Uncertainty*. North-Holland:Amsterdam, 1976. — Obtains the Stolper-Samuelson conclusions in a model which accommodates produced inputs of any finite durability and any time pattern of productivity.

Kemp, M. C. and R. W. Jones. 1962. "Variable Labor Supply and the Theory of International Trade," *Journal of Political Economy* 70:30–36. — Discusses the Stolper-Samuelson Theorem when the labor endowment can vary with wages and prices because of the demand for leisure.

Kemp, M. C., Y. Uekawa, and L. Wegge. 1973. "P and PN Matrices, Minkowski and Metzler Matrices, and Generalizations of the Stolper-Samuelson and Samuelson-Rybczynski Theorems," *International Economic Review* 14:53–76. — Establishes several generalizations of the Stolper-Samuelson Theorem using a parallel between P and PN matrices and between Minkowski and Metzler matrices.

Kemp, M. C. and H. Y. Wan. 1976. "Relatively Simple Generalizations of the Stolper-Samuelson and Samuelson-Rybczynski Theorems," in M. C. Kemp, *Three Topics in the Theory of International Trade: Distribution, Welfare and Uncertainty*, North-Holland: Amsterdam. — With some restrictions on the Input-Output matrix, it is shown that a small autonomous increase in any commodity price, with factor endowments and other commodity prices held constant, gives rise to an unambiguous improvement in the real reward of at least one factor and an unambiguous deterioration of the real reward to at least one factor.

Kemp, M. C. and L. Wegge. 1969. "On the Relation Between Commodity Prices and Factor Rewards," *International Economic Review* 10:407-13. — Extends the Stolper-Samuelson theorem to the n-good, n-factor case and finds that the Stolper-Samuelson conclusions carry over in full strength if $n=3$ and in weakened form if $n=4$. (Reprinted above).

Kenen, P. B. 1957. "On the Geometry of Welfare Economics—A Suggested Diagrammatic Treatment of Some Basic Propositions," *Quarterly Journal of Economics* 71:426-47. — Represents the Stolper-Samuelson Theorem in the Bowley-Edgeworth box.

Kenen, P. B. 1959. "International Trade—A Diagrammatic Analysis," *Kyklos* 12:629-38. — Diagrammatically represents an equilibrium which takes account of variations in the distribution of income and traces their impact upon the pattern of international trade.

Knight, J. B. 1976. "Devaluation and Income Distribution in Less Developed Economies," *Oxford Economic Papers* 28:208-27. — Uses the Stolper-Samuelson Theorem and its assumptions in developing the relationships between the exchange rate and income distribution in less developed countries.

Kohli, U. 1984. "Terms of Trade and Welfare—Estimates," *Kyklos* 37:577–97. — Empirically estimates the welfare effects of changes in a country's terms of trade and its import tariffs for Australia, Canada, Switzerland and the United States.

Kohli, U. 1991. *Technology, Duality, and Foreign Trade*. Ann Arbor: University of Michigan Press. — Uses the GNP function approach as the basis for empirical estimation of a trade model for the U.S., including estimates of Stolper-Samuelson elasticities.

Kuhn, H. W. 1968. "Lectures on Mathematical Economics," in G. B. Dantzig and A. F. Veinott, Jr. (eds.), *Mathematics of the Decision Sciences*, Part 2. Providence, R.I.: American Mathematical Society, pp. 49–84. — Reviews Chipman's extension of the Stolper-Samuelson Theorem to include 3 goods and 3 factors and also establishes some general properties for the Stolper-Samuelson Theorem to hold.

Lal, D. 1986. "Stolper-Samuelson-Rybczynski in the Pacific: Real Wages and Real Exchange Rates in the Philippines, 1956–78," *Journal of Development Economics* 21:181–204. — Develops a simple regression model and explains movements of real wages in the Philippines in terms of the trade-theoretic Stolper-Samuelson-Rybczynski model.

Lancaster, K. 1957. "Protection and Real Wages—A Restatement," *Economic Journal* 67:199–210. — Reformulates the Stolper-Samuelson Theorem in order to obtain a universally valid general statement about the effect of protection on real wages.

Leamer, E. E. 1987. "Paths of Development in the Three-Factor, n-Good General Equilibrium Model," *Journal of Political Economy* 95:961–99. — Geometrically illustrates the extension of the Stolper-Samuelson Theorem to the 3 x 3 model and also illustrates the determination of the signs of the Stolper-Samuelson effects.

Linde, R. 1977. "Note on Influence of Product Prices on Distribution of Real Income," *Jahrbucher fur Nationalokonomie und Statistik* 192:276–81. — Analyzes the relationship between product prices and the ratio of real incomes of 2 social groups and shows that the re-distributional effect of a product price change not only depends on sectoral factor intensity differences (Stolper-Samuelson Theorem), but also on differences in the structures of consumption of both social groups and in their contributions to total factor supplies.

Lloyd, P. J. 1987. "Protection Policy and the Assignment Rule," in H. Kierzkowski (ed.), *Protection and Competition in International Trade: Essays in Honor of W. M. Corden.* London: Basil Blackwell, 4–21. — Extends the friends-enemies version of the Stolper-Samuelson Theorem to an n-good model with intermediate inputs.

Magee, S. P. 1972. "Welfare Effects of Restrictions on U.S. Trade," *Brookings Papers on Economic Activity* 3:645–707. — Provides an estimate of the welfare effects in the United States of both existing protection and greater protection, and in particular the possible effects of the Burke-Hartke proposal. Includes the Stolper-Samuelson Theorem in a discussion of free trade and the appropriateness of trade restrictions as a policy tool.

Magee, S. P. 1980. "Three Simple Tests of the Stolper-Samuelson Theorem," in Peter Oppenheimer (ed.), *Issues in International Economics*, London: Oriel Press, 138–153. — Uses data on lobbying positions of capital and labor to test the Stolper-Samuelson Theorem against the implications of the specific factors model. Results favor the latter. (Reprinted above).

Martin, J. P. 1976. "Variable Factor Supplies and Heckscher-Ohlin-Samuelson Model," *Economic Journal* 86:820–31. — Examines the Heckscher-Ohlin-Samuelson Theorem and shows that with positive factor supply elasticities and incomplete specialization, the Stolper-Samuelson Theorem breaks down. Also shows that tariffs could cause the standard Stolper-Samuelson results to fail.

Martin, T. L. 1989. "Protection or Free Trade: An Analysis of the Ideas of Henry George on International Commerce and Wages," *American Journal of Economics and Sociology* 48:489–501. — Demonstrates that the Stolper-Samuelson theory was anticipated by Henry George in his arguments against protectionism.

Matusz, S. J. 1985. "The Heckscher-Ohlin-Samuelson Model with Implicit Contracts," *Quarterly Journal of Economics* 100:1313–29. — Demonstrates that in a world of multiplicative production uncertainty and implicit labor contracts, the Stolper-Samuelson Theorem may not hold.

Mayer, W. 1971. "Effective Tariff Protection in a Simple General Equilibrium Model," *Economica* 38:253–68. — Derives a modified Stolper-Samuelson Theorem explaining how tariffs on intermediate goods can affect the relative prices of primary factors.

Mayer, W. 1976. "The Rybczynski, Stolper-Samuelson, and Factor Price Equalization Theorems under Price Uncertainty," *American Economic Review* 66:797–808. — Finds that the Stolper-Samuelson and other theorems are valid under price uncertainty if the phrase "change in price" in the certainty model is replaced with "change in expected price, with higher central moments constant."

McGuire, M. C. 1982. "Regulation, Factor Rewards, and International Trade," *Journal of Public Economics* 17:335–54. — Uses the Stolper-Samuelson Theorem to show that regulation can lead to specific unambiguous income redistribution.

Meade, J.E. 1968. "Memorandum," Cited reprinted by Kemp and Wan (1976) as having been written in early 1968. — A very short memorandum that states and proves the Friends and Enemies version of the Stolper-Samuelson Theorem.

Metcalfe, J. S. and I. Steedman. 1981. "On the Transformation of Theorems," *Journal of International Economics* 11:267–72. — A comment on Ethier (*JIE* 1979).

Metzler, Lloyd A. 1949a. "Tariffs, International Demand, and Domestic Prices," *Journal of Political Economy* 57:345–51. — Describes the extent of the shifts in international demand that occur when tariffs are imposed and analyses the conditions that leave the domestic ratio of import to export prices unaltered in the tariff-imposing country.

Metzler, L. A. 1949b. "Tariffs, the Terms of Trade, and the Distribution of National Income," *Journal of Political Economy* 57:1–29. — Shows that under certain conditions of international demand, a tariff that changes the terms of trade does not benefit the scarce factor, and that under these conditions free trade is more beneficial to the scarce factor than protection. (Reprinted above).

Minabe, N. 1966. "Stolper-Samuelson Theorem under Condition of Variable Returns to Scale," *Oxford Economic Papers* 18, 2:204–12. — Extends the Stolper-Samuelson theorem to the case of variable returns to scale assuming neutral external economies, and finds that if the PPF is a straight line or is convex to the origin, the Stolper-Samuelson theorem does not hold, and that the theorem holds if the PPF is concave to the origin.

Minabe, N. 1967. "The Stolper-Samuelson Theorem, the Rybczynski Effect, and the Heckscher-Ohlin Theory of Trade Pattern and Factor Price Equalization: The Case of a Many-Commodity, Many-Factor Country," *Canadian Journal of Economics and Political Science* 33:401–19. — Discusses n x n extensions of the Stolper-Samuelson Theorem.

Minabe, N. 1974. "Stolper-Samuelson Theorem and Metzler Paradox," *Oxford Economic Papers* 26:328–33. — Reinterprets the Metzler paradox using average elasticity and average propensity to import and concludes that the likelihood of the Metzler paradox depends on the height of the tariff rate.

Mundell, R. A. 1957. "International Trade and Factor Mobility," *American Economic Review* 47:321–35. — Shows that an increase in restrictions to factor movements stimulates trade and that an increase in trade impediments stimulates factor movements.

Mussa, M. 1974. "Tariffs and Distribution of Income—Importance of Factor Specificity, Substitutability, and Intensity in the Short and Long Run," *Journal of Political Economy* 82:1191–1203. — Uses the properties of the Stolper-Samuelson and specific factors models to show that the short-run and long-run determinants of the behavior of factor incomes are very different, and that these differences necessarily imply a conflict between factor owners' short-run and long-run interests.

Mussa, M. 1979. "The Two Sector Model in terms of Its Dual: A Geometric Exposition," *Journal of International Economics* 9:513–526. — Derives the Stolper-Samuelson Theorem from the dual to the Lerner-Pearce diagram.

Neary, J. P. 1978. "Capital Subsidies and Employment in an Open Economy," *Oxford Economic Papers* 30:334–56. — Shows that the Stolper-Samuelson conclusions can be derived in a 2x2 model if the rankings of the two sectors differ by physical and value factor-intensity.

Neary, J. P. 1985. "Two-by-Two International Trade Theory with Many Goods and Factors," *Econometrica* 53:1233–47. — The Stolper-Samuelson and other Heckscher-Ohlin properties are generalized by appropriate aggregations.

Nikaido, H. 1968. *Convex Structures and Economic Theory*. New York: Academic Press. — Touches on the implication of an n-good, n-factor version of the Stolper-Samuelson Theorem for factor price equalization.

Ohlin, B. 1933. *Interregional and International Trade*. Cambridge: Harvard University Press. Revised edition, 1967. — Develops in detail the structure and implications of what has come to be called the Heckscher-Ohlin model of international trade, including that trade will lower the wage of the scarce factor relative to that of the abundant factor.

Panagariya, A. 1980. "Variable Returns to Scale in General Equilibrium Theory Once Again," *Journal of International Economics* 10:499–526. — Demonstrates that given fixed factor supplies and variable returns to scale in production, it is possible for a rise in the price of a commodity to raise the real returns to both factors in terms of one commodity and to lower them in terms of the other. Also shows that, in general, the validity of the Stolper-Samuelson or Rybczynski Theorems is neither necessary nor sufficient for the Production Possibility Frontier to be strictly concave to the origin.

Pope, C. 1972. "Impact of Ante-Bellum Tariff on Income Distribution," *Explorations in Economic History* 9:375–421. — Uses the Stolper-Samuelson theorem in analyzing the impact of a tariff on the South.

Rao, V. S. 1971. "Tariffs and Welfare of Factor Owners—Normative Extension of Stolper-Samuelson Theorem," *Journal of International Economics* 1:401–15. — Analyzes the effect of tariffs on the welfare of factor owners in a 2x2 model and develops necessary and sufficient conditions for compensating the losing factor.

Rogowski, R. 1990. "Why Changing Exposure to Trade Should Affect Political Cleavages," *Commerce and Coalitions: How Trade Affects Domestic Political Alignments*. Princeton: Princeton University Press, pp. 3–20. — Presents a 3-factor model and shows that the Stolper-Samuelson Theorem implies an urban-rural conflict in certain types of economies and implies class conflict in others.

Rousslang, D. J. 1991. "Domestic Trade and Transportation Costs in International Trade Theory," *International Economic Journal* 5:49–61. — Adds domestic costs of trade and transportation inside the countries of the Heckscher-Ohlin model and finds that a number of results change, including the Stolper-Samuelson Theorem.

Ruffin, R. J. and R. W. Jones. 1977. "Protection and Real Wages: the Neo-Classical Ambiguity," *Journal of Economic Theory* 14:337–48. — Analyses the link between protection and real wages without the Stolper-Samuelson assumptions, using the Ricardo-Viner model where labor is the only mobile factor. Presents a definition of an unbiased commodity and shows that if labor consumes like the rest of the population, then labor benefits in real terms from a rise in the price of a commodity if and only if that commodity is exported.

Sakai, Y. 1978. "Simple General Equilibrium Model of Production—Comparative Statics with Price Uncertainty," *Journal of Economic Theory* 19:287–306. — Shows that in a 2x2 model with constant returns to scale and price uncertainty, the Stolper-Samuelson theorem may fail to hold in certain cases.

Samuelson, P. A. 1953. "Prices of Factors and Goods in General Equilibrium," *Review of Economic Studies* 21:1–20. — Discusses the effects of free trade in goods on factor prices in the general case of any numbers of goods and factors.

Samuelson, P. A. 1971. "Ohlin Was Right," *Swedish Journal of Economics* 73:365–84. — Examines the conditions under which full and partial factor price equalization takes place in the context of Ricardo-Viner technology.

Samuelson, P. A. 1987. "Joint Authorship in Science—Serendipity with Wolfgang Stolper," *Journal of Institutional and Theoretical Economics* 143:235–43. — Writes of the partnership between Stolper and himself in producing the Stolper-Samuelson paper.

Sodersten, B. and K. Vind. 1968. "Tariffs and Trade in General Equilibrium," *American Economic Review* 58:394–408. — Analyzes the effect of tariffs on prices and national income in a 2x2 model and shows that the Stolper-Samuelson theorem holds without qualifications.

Steedman, I. and J. S. Metcalfe. 1977. "Reswitching, Primary Inputs and the Heckscher-Ohlin-Samuelson Theory of Trade," *Journal of International Economics* 7:201–08. In I. Steedman, *Fundamental Issues in Trade Theory*, Macmillan: London. — Shows that the Stolper-Samuelson theorems are unaffected by assuming a positive interest rate in a 2x2x2 Heckscher-Ohlin-Samuelson model of trade.

Stern, R. M. 1973. "Tariffs and Other Measures of Trade Control—Survey of Recent Developments," *Journal of Economic Literature* 11:857–88. — Includes the Stolper-Samuelson analysis

in a survey of the theory and techniques of international trade
policy.

Thompson, H. 1989. "Do Tariffs Protect Specific Factors?" *Canadian
Journal of Economics* 22:406–12. — Shows that a tariff can
lower the payment to a specific factor in the protected industry
if there are more than one non-specific factors.

Travis, W. P. 1964. *The Theory of Trade and Protection.* Cambridge,
Mass.: Harvard University Press. — Reviews the Stolper-
Samuelson Theorem in his chapter on "Protection and Trade."

Uekawa, Y. 1971. "Generalization of the Stolper-Samuelson Theorem,"
Econometrica 39:197–213. — Establishes the validity of the
Stolper-Samuelson theorem and the Factor Price Equalization
theorem for the n x n case.

Uekawa, Y. 1979. "Theory of Effective Protection, Resource Allocation
and the Stolper-Samuelson Theorem—Many Industry Case,"
Journal of International Economics 9:151–71. — Presents
necessary and sufficient conditions for the strong Stolper-
Samuelson theorem to hold and also special conditions when the
weak Stolper-Samuelson theorem holds in a general equilibrium
model with many industries.

Uekawa, Y. 1984. "Some Theorems of Trade with Joint Production,"
Journal of International Economics 16:319–33. — Presents the
necessary and sufficient conditions for the validity of the Stolper-
Samuelson theorem assuming an equal number of industries,
commodities, and factors. Also clarifies the sufficient conditions
for the Stolper-Samuelson theorem.

Uekawa, Y., M.C. Kemp, and L.L. Wegge. 1973. "P and PN Matrices,
Minkowski and Metzler Matrices, and Generalizations of the
Stolper-Samuelson and Samuelson-Rybczynski Theorems,"
Journal of International Economics 3: 53–76. — Explores

several generalizations of the Stolper-Samuelson and Rybczynski Theorems with equal numbers of goods and factors, exploiting various technical properties of the factor requirements matrix.

Wegge, L. and M. C. Kemp. 1969. "Generalizations of the Stolper-Samuelson and Samuelson-Rybczynski Theorems in Terms of Conditional Input-Output Coefficients," *International Economic Review* 10:414-425. — Shows that the Stolper-Samuelson and Samuelson-Rybczynski Theorems are valid for arbitrary 'n' if, in the pair-wise comparison of factor intensities, the input-output coefficients are of the conditional variety.

Willis, R. J. 1991. "Theory of Fertility Behavior," in T. W. Schultz (ed.), *Economics of the Family*. Chicago: University of Chicago Press, 25-75. — Applies the Stolper-Samuelson Theorem to determine the linkage between the wife's shadow price of time and the shadow price of children in a model of child quality and fertility behavior.

Wilson, J. D. 1990. "Trade and the Distribution of Economic Well-Being in an Economy with Local Public Goods," *Journal of International Economics* 29:199-215. — Develops a modified version of the Stolper-Samuelson theorem in a model of a small open economy with many identical communities, 2 types of workers, competitive firms producing 2 tradable public goods and local governments providing a single public good.

Woodland, A. D. 1977a. "Dual Approach to Equilibrium in Production Sector in International Trade Theory," *Canadian Journal of Economics* 10:50-68. — Formulates a minimization problem in factor price space in order to obtain the equilibrium in the production sector of the economy and shows this formulation to be useful in obtaining and illustrating standard results in international trade theory.

Woodland, A. D. 1977b. "Joint Outputs, Intermediate Inputs and International Trade Theory," *International Economic Review* 18:517–33. — Finds that the Stolper-Samuelson theorem does not survive under the assumption of joint production, while it does survive the presence of intermediate inputs.

Ylonen, S. 1987. "The Stolper-Samuelson Theorem under Decreasing Returns to Scale," *Economics Letters* 24:83–87. — Derives the necessary and sufficient condition for the Stolper-Samuelson theorem under decreasing returns to scale.

SUBJECT INDEX

NOTE: The following is an index to subjects relating to the Stolper-Samuelson Theorem as represented in the above Bibliography. In each case, the full subject entry would also include "and the Stolper-Samuelson Theorem," "of the Stolper-Samuelson Theorem," or a similar extension.

Contributors

Robert E. Baldwin
University of Wisconsin

Sundari R. Baru
University of Michigan

Jagdish N. Bhagwati
Columbia University

John S. Chipman
University of Minnesota

Alan V. Deardorff
University of Michigan

Wilfred J. Ethier
University of Pennsylvania

Ronald W. Jones
University of Rochester

Murray C. Kemp
University of New South Wales

Ulrich Kohli
University of Geneva

Paul R. Krugman
Massachusetts Institute of Technology

Edward E. Leamer
University of California, Los Angeles

Stephen P. Magee
University of Texas

Lloyd A. Metzler
University of Chicago

Ronald Rogowski
University of California, Los Angeles

Paul A. Samuelson
Massachusetts Institute of Techonolgy

Jose A. Scheinkman
University of Chicago

Robert M. Stern
University of Michigan

Wolfgang F. Stolper
University of Michigan

Leon Wegge
University of California, Davis

Reprint Permissions

Chapter 3: *Review of Economic Studies*, November 1941, pp. 58–73. Reprinted with permission of the editor.

Chapter 4: *Journal of Political Economy*, 57:1, February 1949, pp. 24–57. Reprinted with permission of University of Chicago Press.

Chapter 5: *Economic Journal*, 69:276, pp. 733–748. Reprinted with permission of Blackwell Publishers.

Chapter 6: *Journal of Political Economy*, 73:6, December 1965, pp. 557–572. Reprinted with permission of University of Chicago Press.

Chapter 7: *International Economic Review*, October 1969, pp. 399–406. Reprinted with permission of Managing Editor.

Chapter 8: *International Economic Review*, October 1969, pp. 407–413. Reprinted with permission of Managing Editor.

Chapter 9: *Journal of International Economics*, 4:2, May 1974, pp. 199–206. Reprinted with permission of Elsevier Science Publishers, B. V.

Chapter 10: *Journal of Political Economy*, 85:5, October 1977, pp. 906–935. Reprinted with permission of University of Chicago Press.

Chapter 11: Peter Oppenheimer (ed.), *Issues in International Economics*, Routledge and Kegan Paul, 1980. Reprinted with permission of International Thomson Publishing Services, Ltd.

Chapter 12: *Economics Letters*, 10:3–4, 1982, pp. 337–342. Reprinted with permission of Elsevier Science Publishers, B. V.

Chapter 13: *Economic Letters*, 19:1, 1985, pp. 47–49. Reprinted with permission of Elsevier Science Publishers, B. V.